Caring for the Chronic Mentally Ill

Donald Brieland, Advisory Editor
Jane Addams College of Social Work
University of Illinois, Chicago

Caring for the Chronic Mentally Ill

URSULA C. GERHART

RUTGERS–THE STATE UNIVERSITY OF NEW JERSEY
NEW BRUNSWICK

F. E. PEACOCK PUBLISHERS, INC.
ITASCA, ILLINOIS

To
ALEX *and*
PATTY, JUDY, JENNIE, *and* ALEXIS

BRIEF CONTENTS

CONTENTS

FOREWORD

THE CHRONIC MENTALLY ILL are among the most highly disadvantaged groups in our society. They suffer from profound medical and social problems compounded by stigma and neglect. The services they need are typically underfinanced, fragmented, and chaotic. Current systems of care are oriented more to acute disorders and problems of living than to the difficult challenges of diminishing despair, promoting function, and improving the quality of life among these chronic patients, who suffer from many difficulties.

In most areas of medical care, health professionals concentrate on those who are most seriously ill and who most need care to contain illness and disability and reduce suffering. The treatment of mental illness has been a disconcerting exception to this general rule. Prior to 1955 many of the seriously mentally ill received care in long-stay mental hospitals. Most returned home after a few months, but those who stayed beyond a year often spent much of their lives receiving custodial care in such institutions. With the deinstitutionalization of the mentally ill, there was a tragic failure to develop the promised community-care structures essential to protecting the victims of mental illness during periods of high vulnerability and need. Professionals representing all the major mental health disciplines—psychiatry, psychology, social work, and psychiatric nursing—focused their skills and attention on clients who were typically less seriously ill and disabled.

Many factors contributed to abdication of responsibility: ideologies, economics, and prestige. In the years following the Second World War, mental illness was erroneously seen as a single continuum—justifying the view that early recognition and intervention could prevent more serious and profound disorder. This intriguing idea, however, had little basis in fact. As psychoanalysis and psychodynamics became more popular and influential, the idea took root in and later dominated educational programs of mental health professionals, which encouraged an exaggerated emphasis on developmental intrapsychic issues and psychotherapy. In its unrealistic search for "cures," psychodynamics displaced and sometimes denigrated more practical orientations and roles that sought to help clients achieve a better adjustment to their disabilities and life circumstances. Social work education, which had a long and distinguished tradition in community problem solving through casework and group processes, was carried along in the wake of psychodynamic ideology and practice.

The psychotherapeutic imperative was reinforced by economic factors and had other unfortunate effects. Most of those who could pay for psychotherapy were either affluent or had good insurance coverage that shared the costs of treatment. Few chronic patients fell in these groups and thus were not attractive candidates for attention. Nor was it clear how the esoteric psychodynamic theories that prevailed could be much use to patients with such obvious disabilities, which made them difficult and often unattractive clients for psychotherapeutically oriented professionals who preferred articulate and functioning patients. Unlike other areas of health care, a bizzare system of recognition evolved that accorded prestige to those who treated the least sick and least needy clients. In all mental health professions, students, following their mentors and the imperatives of their training, aspired toward careers doing individual psychotherapy, preferably with affluent, attractive, and appreciative patients.

The care of chronic mental illness offers enormous challenges, but most professional schools are ill prepared to provide the necessary training based on well-established practice models for the management of mental disability and needed rehabilitation and on mentors experienced in working with the most seriously mentally ill. The privatized orientation of many faculty and students, with the continuing focus on psychodynamic psychotherapy, and the care of "neurotic patients," diminishes the social work tradition and distorts social priorities.

The fact is that there are impressive technologies available for managing the chronic mentally ill that control symptoms, reduce disabilities, sustain abilities to function, and enhance the quality of life. These technologies used by sensible and sensitive mental health professionals have the capacity not only to diminish the enormous pain of patients and their families but to reduce the burdens and risks that mental illness imposes on the community as a whole. But applying these models requires an entirely different orientation than that which characterizes the private psychotherapist.

In *Caring for the Chronic Mentally Ill,* Ursula Gerhart defines the dimensions of the challenge for the social worker and the opportunities to contribute in important ways. As she notes, the appropriate treatment analogy is not the short-term acute condition but such chronic diseases as diabetes, which may require recurrent and perhaps lifetime management. She describes the cultural environments within which the social worker must work, and their special models of assessment and evaluation as they relate to the expertise of psychiatrists and other mental health professionals. She lays out how social workers function in the health-care delivery system, and how they carry out their roles in crises and emergencies in both the community and in inpatient settings. She reviews the wide range of treatment modalities in which social workers become involved as therapists and team members, elucidating social work responsibilities at varying stages of the mental illness process. Consistent with the traditions of the profession of social work, she defines the involvement of the social worker in every phase of management, including such critical issues as housing and the obligation for responsible advocacy.

This book—the first social work practice book I know of that addresses the needs of chronic mental patients—represents an important turning point in social work education. By focusing on this highly dependent population and their special profound needs, it begins to redress the extraordinary imbalance that presently exists. As other educators and practitioners join Dr. Gerhart in calling for a new commitment and teaching new models and new skills appropriate to the challenge of severe mental illness, social work education can be enhanced and better aligned with community needs. But if social work is to be truly effective, its renewed commitment to the disadvantaged must be accomplished by public services that allow the professional to exercise skills in a caring and efficient way. A well-trained professional, supported by effectively organized and financed service structures, can help transform the current shameful state of affairs.

David Mechanic, Ph.D.
University Professor and
René Dubos Professor of Behavioral Sciences
Rutgers University, New Brunswick, N.J.

PREFACE

THE DRAMATIC deinstitutionalization of the chronic mentally ill that has taken place within the past two decades has confronted our society with profound dilemmas. Libertarians, idealists, and cost-conscious legislators, many with different agendas, have severely criticized mental hospitals and have encouraged the large-scale discharge of the mentally ill into the "community" in the name of liberty and improved care and treatment. On the other hand, critics of deinstitutionalization have characterized it as a *de facto* "dumping" of fragile and helpless mentally ill persons on uncaring and inhospitable communities. Many of these critics urge rehospitalization. Cities, states, and the federal government, confronted with massive and difficult problems, had tended in the past to abdicate responsibility, permitting the condition of many mentally ill persons to deteriorate drastically.

Within the last several years, however, significant initiatives on behalf of the mentally ill have been undertaken by states, communities, private foundations, and by such voluntary organizations as the National Association for the Mentally Ill, or NAMI. Increased resources are now being devoted to research and programs aimed at stabilizing and improving the health and living conditions of the chronic mentally ill. Thousands of professionals and paraprofessionals are being drawn to this new area of practice. This new level of care consists of a humane, individualized, and carefully designed provision of a wide spectrum of social supports and psychosocial therapies that are aimed at developing the coping capacities of the mentally ill as well as making their environment more responsive to their needs.

This book is devoted to a presentation and analysis of the theories and practice principles underlying work with chronic mentally ill persons and their families. It presents a broad range of material, much of it quite new, that is needed for students and clinicians who hope to practice with competence in this field.

The book consists of four parts. Part I provides core background knowledge for practice. Chapter 1 presents a brief history of the care of mentally ill persons in the United States and deals with current problems and treatment of this population by the mental health system and society in general. Chapter 2 treats the theories and nature of major mental illnesses, emphasizing schizophrenia, and analyzes how these disorders affect specific groups, such as older and younger persons, females and males, and members of at-risk and minority groups. Chapter 3 familiarizes social work practitioners with the credentials and work of colleagues from other professions—such as psychiatry, nursing, psychology, and paraprofessionals—who will be working with them on treatment teams. The nature of interdisciplinary teams and teamwork is thoroughly discussed.

Part II introduces fundamental practice theories and principles. Chapter 4 presents practice principles, such as involving clients and their families in treatment planning, and discusses significant service delivery policies, such as continuity of care services. Chapters 5, 6, and 7 deal with practical aspects of accurate clinical diagnoses and social functioning assessments, all essential underpinnings to subsequent treatment and care approaches.

Part III emphasizes practice in the hospital. Chapter 8 discusses psychiatric crises that call for emergency services, where the usual result is admission to a hospital. Principles dealing with admission standards and treatment planning are examined in chapter 9. Chapter 10 deals with issues pertaining to somatic therapies, such as psychotropic medication and electroconvulsive therapy, focusing not only on their benefits but also on their adverse side effects. Chapter 11 examines some of the treatment modalities that are most commonly, but not exclusively, used in hospitals. These include milieu therapies, the token economy, and social skill training. A discussion of discharge planning and implementation is presented in chapter 12.

Part IV deals with a variety of practice approaches that are used extensively, though again not exclusively, in community settings. Here we deal with case management (chapter 13); matching clients to housing options (chapter 14); working with families (chapter 15); the nature of and practice with social and support networks (chapter 16); and advocacy on behalf of the mentally ill (chapter 17).

ACKNOWLEDGMENTS

I CONSIDER MYSELF very fortunate in having had the help I was given in the writing of this book and am deeply grateful to those who gave it. First and foremost I want to express my greatest appreciation to Alex Brooks, who gave me enormous, unstinting support and encouragement during the entire time it took to conceive and write this book. His advice in the conceptualization and drafting of the many issues discussed here and his superb editorial skills were of unsurpassed value. I owe thanks to Linda Aiken for setting an example and for giving me moral and tangible support. I owe much to David Mechanic, not only for writing the Foreword to this book, but also for his personal support and for the intellectual stimulation provided by the seminars and colleagueship of the Rutgers Institute of Health, Health Care Policy, and Aging Research, of which he is director.

Donald Brieland provided invaluable editorial assistance and advice as I completed the final version of this book. I am also grateful to Ovid Lewis, then dean of the Nova Law School, who provided me with an office and access to the Law School's resources at a critical time when the first draft of the book took shape. Also, special thanks to Bea Saunders whose sound advice and encouragement provided the impetus to bring this book to completion.

Many thanks go to the directors and staff of social work departments of psychiatric hospitals and community organizations serving the chronic mentally ill in New Jersey, New York, Florida, and Fulton, Missouri, who kept me abreast of developments in the field and who cheered me on. Special thanks go to Aileen Ackerman, Judy Banes, Doris Young, Jane Bierdeman-Fike, Nancy Johnson, Elaine Laughlin, Marshal Rubin, Eppie Stackhouse, Molly Tatlock, Bill Ullrich, Doris Young, and Janice Victor. I owe much of my understanding about mental health advocacy to Rose Suelto, an outstanding patient advocate. My special thanks to her.

I want to express by gratitude to my social work students, many of whom brought me new perspectives on the current state of the art in helping chronic mentally ill persons and who shared with me their practice problems, experiences, and successes.

Finally, my sincere thanks to Ted Peacock, the publisher, whose personal interest and high standards made a substantial contribution to the quality of this book.

PART I   The
         Mental Health
         System
         and Its
         Clients

CHAPTER 1

CARING FOR PERSONS
WHO HAVE A CHRONIC
MENTAL ILLNESS:
A HISTORICAL OVERVIEW

As the 1980s come to a close and we confront the 1990s, mental health professionals who work with persons who have a chronic mental illness face challenges that will make great demands on their professionalism.

Today's mental health scene differs radically from that which prevailed in previous decades. For many years emphasis had been on placing and "treating" chronic mentally ill persons in mental hospitals, where many remained for most of their lives without adequate treatment, stimulation, or care. But that began to change in the late 1960s and early 1970s. Since that time, the process of deinstitutionalization—fueled by developments in treatment by medication, by legal reforms, by new legislation, and by changing policies— has made a major turnabout in the mental health system. Today, a large number of the chronic mentally ill are, for better or worse, in the community. Hospitalization, no longer the norm, is reserved for emergencies. Hospital stays are shorter than before and continue to become shorter. The new objec-

3

tive of hospitalization is not retention, but the rapid restoration and stabilization of patients, who are returned to the community as quickly as possible.

Community-based care of the chronic mentally ill is the prevailing approach, although there are vigorously expressed claims that deinstitutionalization is not "working." We are all familiar with the well-publicized mentally ill bag ladies and the homeless on the streets of large cities like New York. But the successes of deinstitutionalization have been as well publicized as the failures. In spite of the massive difficulties, great efforts continue to be exerted to make community-based treatment accepted as efficient and cost effective.

Maintenance of the chronic mentally ill in community settings calls for social workers to employ an entirely new battery of practice techniques and skills, which are currently being developed and refined. Today's practice approaches reflect totally new insights into the care of the mentally ill. After all, chronic mentally ill persons have been in the community for a relatively short time. We are in the early stages of learning how to handle their problems effectively.

ORIGINS OF THE CARE OF MENTALLY ILL PERSONS

How did such a radical shift from hospital to community care come about? To answer this question we must review the historical origins of the treatment of the mentally ill in the United States.

In the early colonial period, persons who had a mental illness were not deemed to be a social problem. The families and individuals who settled this country had to be entirely self-sufficient. Families were expected to completely look after their own and shoulder all responsibility for their sick, aged, and disabled members. The behavior of the mentally ill may have presented problems to their families, but not to neighbors, who tended to live at some distance. Furthermore, mental illness was not recognized as such. Those who displayed the erratic and bizarre behavior that we recognize today as expressive of mental illness were considered to be "lunatics," or individuals whose behavior was governed by the phases of the moon. They were also considered to be "idiots" and "distracted persons."

However, as the population expanded—and with the development of villages, towns, and cities—mentally ill persons became more visible and their often unpredictable behavior increasingly irksome to their neighbors. Families, especially those who did not have large, self-sustaining farmsteads, grew less able to provide for all the needs of their ill and frail members and looked to their communities for help. Therefore self-governing local communities in colonies such as Massachusetts, Connecticut, and New Jersey began to assume responsibilities for the problems presented by their most vulnerable members, including those who were mentally ill. For example, a 1641 legal code enacted by the colony of Massachusetts provided for material support and guardianship of "idiots and distracted persons" whose behavior was tractable enough to allow them to live in the community. But other arrange-

4

ments had to be made for those considered to be too "chargeable and troublesome" to remain at large (Grob 1973, p. 9). The colonies tended to address their problems by confining them in really established and locally administered alms- and poorhouses.

The lot of almshouse inmates was notoriously hard. Because most of them were unable to work, they were regarded as worthless by a society whose highest values were hard work, piety, and independence. Almshouse operators were punitive and exploitative. They provided little food and barely any heat during the harsh winter months. Those inmates who were able to work were forced to slave as "able bodied paupers" for the profit of the almshouse operators. Inmates who were disliked or difficult to control were chained, beaten, or jailed in dungeons. Many of the seriously mentally ill were kept in cages or were driven out of the poorhouse and their communities without food, money, or clothing (Mechanic 1968, p. 371). Many surely must have died of hunger, disease, and exposure.

In 1751 the city of Philadelphia established Pennsylvania Hospital, the first institution designed to care for the sick and the mentally ill. "Lunaticks, Persons Distemper'd in mind, and (persons) deprived of their rational Faculties" were subjected to the worst treatment. They were confined in cold and damp cells and immobilized in "straight waistcoats" and specially designed restraining chairs. Their treatment consisted of blood letting, blistering, emetics, and warm and cold baths. Many mentally ill patients saw escape as their only release from their intolerable "treatment" and, according to the hospital's records, a great many succeeded in their attempts (Grob 1973).

During the eighteenth century, while care for the indigent mentally ill deteriorated, treatment and care of prosperous persons was remarkably good. Under the influence of the English Quaker merchant William Tuke, a therapy known as **moral treatment** was introduced in Philadelphia during the first decade of the nineteenth century.

The theory of moral treatment was that mentally ill persons could be substantially cured when exposed to an accepting, healthful, and "moral" environment where they would be treated firmly but kindly. The moral environment constituted the crux of treatment—as it was designed to counteract the "moral" causes of mental illness, which included infidelity, overwork, envy, gluttony, drinking, sexual excesses, and the like. Tuke first put his theory in action in 1792 when he founded the York Retreat, a peaceful and pleasant asylum located at some distance from the nearest city. Treatment at the Retreat required that the mentally ill be completely removed from the everyday stress of their home environments. Patients at the retreat were provided with rest, light food, tonics, healthful exercise, religion, fresh air, and amusements and games. They were closely attended to and cared for by staff who treated them with respect and deference. Patients were encouraged to give free vent to their innermost thoughts and feelings. There was no pressure and no time limit to their treatment. It was expected that most patients would recover spontaneously, in good time.

5

The success of the Retreat prompted American Quakers to establish the Friend's Asylum in Pennsylvania in 1813 and to introduce moral treatment to nonsectarian mental hospitals (Grob 1973).

Whether "moral treatment" was actually a success is unclear. First-year recovery estimates ranged from an overly enthusiastic and undoubtedly exaggerated 90 percent of all patients to the conservative figure of only 20 percent (Ozarin 1973). According to research undertaken by the oldest American state hospital, Worcester State Hospital in Massachusetts, the recovery rate without subsequent relapse was 58 percent for all discharged patients. At the time, Worcester State Hospital provided moral therapy for all its patients. In evaluating success rates reported more than 150 years ago we have no way of assessing the accuracy of the diagnoses of patients. We don't know how many patients suffered from chronic and severe schizophrenic illness and from other, less severe conditions. Because comparative diagnostic data are not available to us, we also don't know who was and who was not helped by moral treatment. Also, we know very little about the nature of the environment and care that discharged patients received when they returned to their communities.

Whatever the statistics tell us, we can assume that the humane aspects of moral therapy did no harm and probably enhanced some patients' potential for spontaneous remission. This was the approach to patient care that was advocated by Dorothea Dix for the public mental hospitals she helped to establish. Moral treatment also foreshadowed contemporary milieu therapy, which became popular during the early part of the twentieth century.

By the nineteenth century the wretched conditions of the almshouses and the indigent mentally ill finally aroused the concern of the public and of social activists. Dorothea Lynde Dix, known in her own time as the "The Gentle Reformer," is the best known of these activists. She worked untiringly and vigorously to replace almshouses with spacious, clean, safe, and curative asylums. Dix accomplished her aims through advocacy techniques that were ingenious and highly effective. As a first step, she made it a point to learn all she could about the care and conditions of mentally ill person in a given state. Dix's second step was to call on the governor and legislators of that state personally and to describe vividly to them the deplorable conditions she had found. Her final move was to propose to the lawmakers a remedy for these conditions. Most often her remedy consisted of asking for large tracts of state-owned land on which asylums for mentally ill persons could be established. Dorothea Dix is credited with having been the moving force behind the founding of 32 American mental hospitals as well as others in Canada, Scotland, and Japan (Greenstone 1979).

At the time they were established, state mental hospitals provided high quality, individualized care that resulted in a high rate of patient recovery, as shown by the success rate of Worcester State Hospital. Physical restraints were used only rarely and then only for the most violent residents. Agitated patients were given such "chemical restraints" as mild opiates. Given such

6

humane treatment, state mental hospitals developed a reputation of being places where persons could be cured of their mental illness. These conditions, however, did not prevail for long.

At the beginning of the twentieth century powerful economic and political forces elbowed out restorative and humane concerns. The country continued to grow—in large part due to immigration. With the increase of population, the existing mental hospitals were compelled to accept many more patients than they had been designed for. Moreover, they were forced to accept patients who had no potential for rehabilitation. These were the aged, persons who suffered from irreversible organic brain damage, and those who were in the tertiary and fatal stage of syphilis (Grob 1983). For example, the admission rate of persons aged 65 years and over increased threefold by 1939 from what it had been in 1885. From small treatment facilities housing from 500 to 1000 patients where staff knew most of the patients, state hospitals became huge, unwieldy, and alienating institutions. In 1939 the average state hospital housed between 1500 and 3000 patients (Kiesler and Sibulkin 1987).

Moral therapy could no longer be practiced in these large and over-crowded institutions. Also, its practice did not provide remissions or even relief for incurable and fatal conditions. The professionals who were assigned to care for and "cure" the patients became discouraged and dispirited. Instead of providing therapy to those who could benefit from it, they were forced to become custodians of the incurables. The low salaries paid to mental health professionals made matters worse. The best-trained and most highly skilled left public mental hospitals, accelerating the declining quality of care.

Thus, during the first half of the twentieth century patients in public mental hospitals were once again neglected and abused. They received neither psychiatric treatment nor rehabilitative care. The outside world forgot them. The once pleasant furnishings and hospital grounds fell into disrepair. The food became barely edible or nutritious. Many mental health professionals gave up on hospitalized patients, despairing that anything could be done for them in such surroundings.

THE DEINSTITUTIONALIZATION MOVEMENT: FORCES AND IDEALS

The 1950s and 1960s witnessed a confluence of forces that resulted in the movement that has come to be known as deinstitutionalization. Deinstitutionalization has been defined not only as the policy of discharging a large number of patients from mental hospitals but also as the policy of settling and maintaining the discharged persons outside of institutions, in the least restrictive community settings. (See chapter 4 for a discussion of the "least restrictive" concept.) According to the U.S. General Accounting Office, the aim of deinstitutionalization policy is threefold. The first is to prevent unnecessary admissions and retention in institutions. The second is to find suitable treatment and social resources in a community setting for those persons who otherwise would need to be cared for in an institution. The third is to improve the conditions, care, and treatment in institutions, such as mental hospitals, for those persons who cannot manage outside of an institution (U.S. General Accounting Office 1977).

Four forces fueled the deinstitutionalization movement: (1) economic considerations, (2) idealism, (3) legal developments, and (4) the development of antipsychotic medications.

ECONOMIC FORCES

Economic pressures were in large part responsible for setting off the process of deinstitutionalization. These pressures emanated from two sources: first, from the state and local legislatures, who wanted to save money, and second from private interests, who wanted to make money.

State legislators were particularly concerned over the large operating costs of mental hospitals and the projected expenses involved in restoring them. They knew that many old hospital facilities were so deteriorated as to be beyond repair. But the politicians were exposed to a public outcry that something had to be done about the scandalous conditions of most public mental hospitals. This outcry stemmed from newspaper stories, books, and movies—such as *One Flew over the Cuckoo's Nest, The Snake Pit,* and *Titticut Follies*—which exposed the abominable patient care and even abuse that existed in many mental hospitals. Politicians knew that it would have been prohibitively expensive to modernize them. The most expedient solution was to close entire hospitals, or at least certain wards and wings. Only the wholesale discharge of patients would speed the closing of the old "snake pits."

Other financial benefits were envisioned. State legislatures and policymakers believed that it would cost less to care for persons with mental illnesses in communities than in hospitals. This notion was first advanced in 1961 by the Joint Commission on Mental Illness and Mental Health that had been established by Congress to study the effectiveness and cost of care of mentally ill persons. The Joint Commission noted that

> Experience with certain community outpatient clinics and rehabilitation centers would seem to indicate that many mental patients could be better treated on an outpatient basis at much lower cost than by a hospital (Joint Commission on Mental Illness and Health 1961, p. 7).

The idea that community care was less costly to the states than mental hospitals was reinforced by 1962 Social Security regulations that provided for categorical assistance for the chronic mentally ill and other disabled persons (U.S. Congress 1962). These were the so-called APTD categories, or Aid to the Permanently and Totally Disabled. Prior to APTD categorical welfare, mentally ill persons who were unable to sustain themselves through employment or other sources could count on only short-term general assistance grants.

The establishment of community mental health centers in 1963 gave additional hope to state legislators that the federal government would relieve them of the financial burden of operating mental hospitals and providing other services to mentally ill persons. Community mental health centers were created primarily in order to provide care and a wide variety of services for the newly discharged patients (U.S. Congress 1963). Thus, state legislators became increasingly convinced that they could save money while, at the same time, helping their mentally ill citizens.

As politicians aimed for savings, the private sector aimed for profit. Because many patients were shifted from public mental hospitals to privately run nursing homes and boarding homes, the owners of these institutions had to expand their facilities to make room for the new wave of residents. They welcomed and supported the profitable influx of discharged mental patients. For example, California board and care home owners vigorously lobbied their legislators to support the discharge of hospitalized mental patients.

IDEALISM

Not everyone had selfish or economic motives, of course. Many psychiatrists, social workers, sociologists, and lawyers were motivated by idealism. They regarded mental hospitals as destructive of human values. Prestigious sociologists claimed that hospitals were responsible for actually creating and reinforcing chronic mental illness rather than alleviating it (Goffman 1961). They argued that mental illness was not only exacerbated but also became incurable as a consequence of such abusive treatment as padded cells, isolation rooms, straitjackets, water therapies,[1] and electric and insulin shock therapies.

Moreover, since most hospitals were not easily accessible by public transportation, hospitalized patients were virtually isolated from contact with friends and relatives. Patients were totally at the mercy of staff. The idealists reasoned that life in these institutions was so atrocious that life in the community by definition had to be better for the mentally ill. This belief was reinforced by planners and policymakers who believed that communities would welcome the newly discharged patients and provide housing and other services for them (Bachrach 1978).

Further, argued the idealists, hospitalization ultimately made matters worse for those who could be discharged. It was believed that the stigma of

---

1. Violent and agitated patients were immersed in special long bathtubs that were filled with cold or warm water, or with alternating hot and cold water. Patients had to remain in these tubs for hours at a time. A covering canvas cloth allowed only patients' heads to protrude, while preventing them from leaving.

mental hospitalization prevented many from getting their driver's licenses, finding employment, getting married, and living normal lives even when they were able to do so. Friends and family would no longer relate to the ex-mental patient as they had prior to the patient's hospitalization. Instead, the patient would be treated as an ill or inferior person. The idealists proposed that everything possible should be done to keep persons with mental illnesses from being admitted to mental hospitals (Flomenhaft *et al.* 1969). Some even suggested that mentally ill persons would be much better off if mental hospitals were altogether abolished (Chamberlin 1978).

LEGAL DEVELOPMENTS

Legal developments also influenced deinstitutionalization. The earliest of a new breed of statutes that dealt with assuring the rights of mental patients was the California Lanterman-Petris-Short Act of 1968, which was aimed at protecting mentally ill persons from inappropriate involuntary civil commitment. This innovative statute established new standards and procedures—emphasizing dangerousness and using the state's police power as a preeminent basis for involuntary confinement, rather than parens-patriae considerations (which emphasized the obligation of the state to care for the helpless). The new statute guaranteed hearings with procedural protections that had been previously ignored. This statute was followed by similar enactments in other states and by judicial decisions in Wisconsin and elsewhere that extended legal protections to the mentally ill.

THE DEVELOPMENT OF ANTIPSYCHOTIC MEDICATIONS

The discovery of antipsychotic medication in the early 1950s electrified the mental health system, especially its public sector. These quick acting and seemingly easily administered drugs not only promised restoration from mental illness but also provided a solution to many of the problems of mental hospitals. Most physicians and other mental health professionals embraced the drugs unquestioningly and enthusiastically, providing the first large push toward deinstitutionalization. Many patients were hastily discharged to the community, where, it was anticipated, they would remain fully functional by continuing to use antipsychotic drugs. In a 1984 interview with a *New York Times* reporter, Dr. Robert Felix, director of the National Institute of Mental Health during the late 1950s, retrospectively regretted the wholesale and rapid discharge of hospitalized patients:

> Many of those patients who left the state hospitals never should have done so. We psychiatrists saw too much of the old snake pit, saw too many people who shouldn't have been there and we overreacted. The result is not what we intended, and perhaps we didn't ask the questions that should have been asked

when developing a new concept, but psychiatrists are human, too, and we tried our damnedest (Lyons 1984, p. C1).

DEINSTITUTIONALIZATION: THE REALITY

We now acknowledge that many of the goals of the deinstitutionalization movement have not been realized. The savings that were expected to materialize from the closing of mental hospitals were never achieved. Special interest groups—such as unionized mental hospital staff and businesses in communities dependent on hospitals as a major source of income—successfully lobbied to prevent the closure of hospitals.

UNREALIZED GOALS

Most communities into which chronic mentally ill persons had been discharged did not welcome them. They opposed their presence and continue to do so to this day. The issue of housing illustrates this opposition. One of the reasons for the current pervasive homelessness is that state and local governments have not met the housing needs of the mentally ill. Many localities have made it clear that the mentally ill are unwelcome. The media feature many accounts of prosperous neighborhoods that petition against, picket, and even vandalize group homes for the mentally ill. As a result, many discharged mental patients are ghettoized in deteriorating and dangerous neighborhoods. Instead of becoming reintegrated in neighborhood life, many of the deinstitutionalized are treated like outcasts, harassed and arrested for the most trivial of offenses (Kirk and Therrien 1975). Often neighborhood businesses demand that the police clear out the mentally ill from their areas, thus adding to their harassment.

The type of comprehensive service network that is needed to sustain mentally ill persons outside of institutions has been established in relatively few communities. Some communities, of which New York City is characteristic, openly acknowledge lack of coordination in providing services. Other communities, such as Austin, Texas, and Columbus, Toledo, and Cincinnati, Ohio, have made great progress in establishing a significant network of coordinated services. In most cities, the service delivery system consists of numerous public and private organizations each going its own way. In some communities identical services are provided by two or more organizations, each with a vested interest in its role, while other needed services are nonexistent—because no agency wants to provide them or has insufficient funds to do so. Case management illustrates the fragmentation and confusion in service delivery. As discussed in chapter 13, persons with mental illnesses can greatly benefit from case managers with whom they have formed a good working relationship and whose responsibilities include the coordination and linking of clients to needed services. But most mentally ill persons do not have such case managers, and those who do often have a succession of case managers within a short period of time. Some may have several case managers from different agencies at the same time, each one performing different or overlapping functions (Deitchman 1980). Moreover, the organizations that comprise the mental health system have not yet agreed on what the role, function, and status of the case managers should be, let alone on which organization should provide what type of case management service to which persons within their community (Dill 1987).

Most community mental health centers also have not lived up to their original expectations. Although established for the express purpose of serving the deinstitutionalized chronic mentally ill, it has been shown that the centers have instead devoted most of their resources to serving more articulate, attractive, intelligent, affluent "walking worrieds" who are more prestigious and less costly to serve (Goldman *et al.* 1983). The chronic mentally ill require more care, such as administration of antipsychotic medications, emergency services, daycare services, outreach services, transportation, and the like. Also, they are a perceived as a riskier clientele whose potential to harm themselves or others can create legal liability.

A new problem, not expected by the planners of deinstitutionalization, has been raised by a small but highly visible group, the so-called "young adult chronic patients." These are mentally ill persons who have come to maturity without any long-term hospitalization (McCreath 1984; Bender 1986). Because of their vulnerability, many of them became drug addicts, alcoholics, and drifters. Unmarried parenthood in this group is on the rise. Many resist the help offered by their families and mental health professionals, refusing medications and social interventions. It is arguable that those who have become addicted to drugs and alcohol, who are preyed upon by muggers, and who do not avail themselves of medical, psychiatric, and social services are in worse shape than they would be had they been confined in an institution.

Finally, the most regressed patients were really not deinstitutionalized. They were, in reality, "trans-institutionalized," or shifted from the confinement of a hospital to the frequently more restricted confinement and less regulated and more lax care of a nursing home. Nursing home care costs are often, though not always, as high as or higher than those of hospitals where the care of patients is, in most instances, worse (Kiesler and Sibulkin 1987). Nevertheless, we should realistically acknowledge that there are some persons who can be maintained only in some form of caretaking institution. Among these are the severely incapacitated and the uncontrollably violent or self-destructive persons (Ames 1983).

In view of the difficult problems presented by some mentally ill persons, stirrings of deinstitutionalization are beginning to be felt. For example, in some states, such as Washington, new legislation has been enacted that significantly loosens the requirements for involuntary hospitalization, as a result of which a substantial number of mentally ill persons have already been removed from the community and rehospitalized. One consequence of this move to

12

rehospitalize has been excessive congestion in mental hospitals, resulting in a poorer and deteriorating quality of care (Durham and La Fond 1985 and 1988; Stone 1987).

REALIZED GOALS

On the positive side, important goals of the deinstitutionalization movement have indeed been realized. Foremost among these is the satisfaction that discharged patients express when they no longer have to be confined in mental hospitals. In interviews, the majority of discharged patients typically indicate unqualified preference for life in the community over that of the hospital. They much prefer their freedom and independence to the regimented life of an institution, even in instances when community living does not meet their basic needs for adequate food, shelter, and medical care (Dickey *et al.* 1981).

Once they are in the community, the mentally ill cannot remain forgotten. The most articulate of them have organized themselves into self-help and advocacy groups just as their families did. The National Alliance for the Mentally Ill is the largest and fastest-growing organization of this kind. These groups keep the problems and needs of the mentally ill in the eyes of the public and of politicians. As a result, there are continuing new legislation and judicial decisions aimed at helping the mentally ill in the community. For example, the U.S. Supreme Court has declared unconstitutional certain zoning laws that have discriminated against the mentally disabled by setting up restrictive standards limiting the establishment of group homes (City of Cleburne *v.* Cleburne Living Center 1985).

New and imaginative interventions are being developed that are designed to improve the quality of the lives of the chronic mentally ill and to keep the symptoms of mental illness under control. These new approaches focus on the environment of the mentally ill and their interactions with family, friends, employers, and professionals. Among the newly developed practice approaches are psychoeducational family interventions, social network therapy, and social skill training, all of which will be discussed and analyzed within.

Inpatient care has improved markedly, as evidenced by shorter hospital stays. The average period of an inpatient stay in 1969 was 421 days. By 1981 such stays had decreased to 147 days. The shorter stay has stabilized the cost of inpatient care in spite of the fact that daily cost has risen steeply, from $14.00 in 1969 to $40.00 in 1981—a dollar amount that has been corrected for inflation (Kiesler and Sibulkin 1987).

Finally, there are a number of public and privately funded research endeavors involved in exploring such aspects of mental illness as the organic and environmental causes of schizophrenia, the forms that schizophrenia and other illnesses take, the socially and biologically determined courses of mental illness, in psychopharmacology and the like. One day we may have the knowledge and the tools to prevent mental illness from occurring. In the near future, however, research efforts should pay off in steadily improved care and treatment of the mentally ill.

SUMMARY

After more than a decade of deinstitutionalization, a major ideological battle continues to rage over the question of whether large-scale discharge of mental patients into the community was a massive mistake or merely the first traumatic stage in a long-term process that will eventually provide meaningful care for a large number of chronic mentally ill persons who can survive, and even prosper, in the community when their basic needs are met.

On one hand, some influential opinion shapers (Applebaum 1987) argue that taking most mentally ill persons off the streets and returning them to mental hospitals is the only way in which they can be properly cared for. They point to the obvious failures of community care and insist that these deficiencies are intractable and cannot be remedied.

On the other hand, there are mental health professional leaders who continue to believe that the process of caring for mentally ill persons in the community has not yet been given a real trial. They urge that greater effort must be made to provide such services as housing, continuity of care, case management, and the like in the community. If this is done, deinstitutionalization will "work." For example, the Robert Wood Johnson Foundation of Princeton, N.J., has undertaken a multimillion-dollar program to fund larger communities that have presented effective, coordinated programs for the care of chronic mentally ill persons. Nine such communities are currently using Foundation and federal funds to provide more effective care. Many states, such as New York and Ohio, are also making significant efforts to provide such services. Slowly but surely, many states and communities are beginning to recognize and meet their responsibilities toward the chronic mentally ill and to acknowledge that care in the community is both feasible and effective.

As we approach the 1990s, the struggle over the best way to care for persons with chronic mental illness continues. Although it is not entirely clear what the final outcome will be, it is difficult to envision wholesale rehospitalization as the "wave of the future," especially as major mental hospitals continue to close their doors.

In this new stage, the social worker can and should be a major player. Mastery of newly developed skills and approaches to care will enable social workers to play an increasingly important role in the development and delivery of community care. The problems presented by chronic mentally ill persons are difficult, but not insuperable. This book is dedicated to the proposition that these problems can be mastered by showing the way toward effective care.

CHAPTER 2

MENTAL ILLNESS AND CHRONIC MENTALLY ILL PERSONS

Several years ago Frank Molnar,[1] an excellent social work student at the school where I teach, suddenly started to hallucinate actively while seeing clients at his field agency. He was taken to a nearby general hospital where his condition was diagnosed as a form of schizophrenia. Frank was placed in the psychiatric ward of that hospital. After a few days I visited Frank at the hospital, where I met his parents, a middle-class, intelligent, and friendly couple in their early fifties. Frank's parents expressed concern about their son, but insisted he had not been diagnosed correctly. They told me with confidence that it was impossible for Frank to be mentally ill. Quite out of the question. According to the parents, Frank had been under too much strain from his studies, and suffered only from a temporary "nervous breakdown" caused by

---

1. Although all the case histories provided in this book are based on fact, all the names of persons and agencies have been thoroughly disguised.

the stress of his studies. The parents were about to have their son discharged from the hospital so that they could take him to other, more competent doctors.

The notion that Frank could indeed be mentally ill was totally unacceptable to Frank's parents. Their denial was complete. Were Frank's parents very different from others whose children are stricken with a chronic mental illness?

The reactions of Frank's parents are not atypical. Mental health professionals know that mental illness is one of the least acceptable of all illnesses and disabling conditions. Why? The answer, in part, is that mental illness threatens the very core of our identity.

Our identities, our sense of self and purpose, are largely anchored in our ability to perceive accurately ourselves and our environments, as well as our ability to contemplate our past, present, and future. We can think about our future and plan for it. Most of us place enormous value on our ability to think, and we tend to value intelligence more than sheer physical strength and agility. We dread any unwanted tampering with our thought processes, such as the "brainwashing" to which some prisoners of war have been subjected or the forced administration of intoxicants. Thought tampering is equated with a loss of self. As such it is regarded as dehumanizing.

There are times when some of the typical symptoms of mental illness—such as delusions, hallucinations, and agitations—flare up, playing havoc with thinking, memory, and perception, rendering the person substantially unable to function. We refer to these flare-ups as the **florid** phase and active symptoms of mental illness. At such times a person loses most of the conscious control over thought processes and over much of behavior. Even when the active symptoms of mental illness are brought under control and abate, personality changes and lower levels of social functioning become evident. These are known as the negative symptoms of mental illness. Without proper treatment, many mentally ill persons are no longer their original selves after the first few flare-ups of their illness. They become strangers to their families, friends, and neighbors.

Throughout history the most disturbed mentally ill have been cast out by their clans and communities. Often they have been treated as objects of derision or curiosity, even in mental institutions—a case in point is London's infamous Bethlehem Hospital, whose nickname "Bedlam" generated a new word in the English language, descriptive of the atmosphere in mental hospitals years ago. In the not-too-distant past, mentally ill persons were confined and isolated for most of their lives in prisonlike institutions. More recently they have gained notoriety as bag ladies, drifters, and recalcitrant, strange persons who would rather sleep on the street over heating grates than accept an offer of shelter.

I am sure that Frank Molnar's parents equated the mentally ill with unkempt and homeless street persons or with vacant-eyed, immobilized catatonics. There are such persons, but they are far from typical. Although Frank suffered from one severe episode of mental illness, his contact with reality

16

was readily restored with the help of medications and psychotherapy. In due time he resumed his studies, graduated, and is currently able to work, part-time, as a counselor for others who have mental illnesses.

Not all who are stricken with active symptoms of mental illness have the chronic, or long-lasting, form of the illness in which many functional capacities deteriorate over time. Persons such as Frank who experience only one or two acute episodes of the illness are not considered to be chronically ill. What then is chronic mental illness? Who are the chronic mentally ill? How do they get along and where do they live?

WHAT IS CHRONIC MENTAL ILLNESS?

A chronic illness, whether physical or mental, persists for an indefinite period of time, often for a lifetime. We should not expect "cures" of these conditions in the sense in which we "cure" a cold or "cure" malaria. But with proper care many chronically ill persons can look forward to long-term remissions and relief from symptoms. As an analogy, consider diabetes, which, though never "cured," can be kept well controlled by diet, insulin, or other medications. The more severe symptoms of certain chronic mental illnesses can be kept in check through the use of antipsychotic medications and psychosocial interventions.

We differentiate between mental illness and mental retardation. In the case of mental illness there is the potential for restoration, recovery, stabilization, or remission of symptoms through the use of appropriate treatments, and sometimes spontaneously. At some rare times the "remission" may last for the remainder of a person's life for reasons that are not yet clear to us. But in the case of retardation, none of these can occur. The retarded person can be taught to perform certain functions and enabled to do as much as possible unaided. Even severely retarded persons can be taught to dress, to write their names, to clean their rooms, and the like. Moderately retarded persons can do much more, including work in a number of occupations. But unlike the mentally ill person, a retarded person's basic mental condition cannot be changed.

Are personality or character disorders, including sociopathy, a form of mental illness? This remains a controversial question. Many psychiatrists refuse to characterize these disorders as illnesses, claiming that sociopaths, for example, are not mad but bad. Although personality disorders are listed in *DSM-III-R* as mental disorders to be treated by the psychiatric profession, there is wide agreement that medications, psychotherapy, and other typical psychiatric interventions have so far not been shown to be helpful in treating the problems of personality disorders. In fact, many legislative statutes and judicial decisions do not recognize personality disorders as a form of mental illness that justifies involuntary commitment to a mental hospital. For our purposes, personality disorders will not be treated as mental illness, but conditions such as schizophrenia, mood disorders, and other psychoses will be.

17

Characteristically, mental illness, particularly when left untreated, progressively erodes functional capacities, such as the capacity to get along with others, to learn, to work in competitive environments, to take care of basic personal and hygienic needs, and to conform to legal and moral community standards. The degree of erosion varies with the severity of the illness along a continuum, where at one end we find persons who are able to function relatively "normally" whereas at the other we find those whose coping capacities have deteriorated to such an extent that they cannot do anything for themselves.

CAUSES OF MENTAL ILLNESS

The long-standing debate about the factors that give rise to mental illness remains unsettled. On one hand there are the proponents of the "sociogenic" approach, which holds that environmental factors, such as an individual's interaction with his or her family, cause mental illnesses as schizophrenia. On the other side are the biogeneticists, who argue that mental illness is hereditary and biologically based.

THE NATURE VERSUS NURTURE CONTROVERSY

If the environment is indeed the cause of mental illness, then it should logically follow that mental illness can also be prevented or cured through appropriate changes in the environment. One can't quarrel with the environmental changes recommended by partisans of sociogenic theories. These include the establishment of benign environments such as relatively stress-free workplaces, the provision of basic resources for all members of society, and relationships that are based on patience, love, understanding, structure, forthrightness, and wise guidance.

The biogeneticists do not discount the role of environmental stress in the way mental illness is played out in the life of an individual. Rather than seeing stress as the root cause of mental illness, however, they regard it as contributing factor to the severity of illness in an individual who is predisposed to or has already become ill. Further, the biogeneticists do not see how, given our current technology, mental illness could be prevented by altering the environment of persons who, like diabetics, are genetically or biologically vulnerable. Today's evidence from the biological, chemical, physical, and medical sciences now strongly supports this view.

Biogeneticists have tried to prove their propositions empirically. In the absence of biological markers predictive of future development of mental illness, such as genes that can be identified as the "carriers" of depressive disorders, the biogeneticists have had to disentangle the influences of environment from those of heredity. In many instances this is almost impossible. For example, no one has yet been able to factor out exactly how the countless interactions among our parents, other relatives, and friends shape

18

our inherited characteristics. But attempts are being made to find rough indicators than can differentiate the effects of upbringing from those of heredity. Researchers such as Kety (1976) have studied children who, at birth, had been placed in adoptive homes. They have also studied identical twins who were placed in adoptive or foster homes shortly after birth and thereafter had no contact whatsoever with their biological parents. The adoptive parents did not know of the characteristics of the natural parents and therefore did not modify their behavior toward their adoptive children accordingly. The natural children of schizophrenic parents who were placed with non–mentally ill adoptive parents developed schizophrenia at a higher rate than would be expected of children of non–mentally ill parents, and at the rate that children who are brought up by mentally ill parents do. These findings strongly suggest that the children's mental illness was genetically determined rather than brought about by the environment.

Researchers also studied monozygotic twins, those from the same egg and therefore identical. The identical twins in these studies had been separated at birth and then placed in different adoptive homes in Scandinavian and other countries that permit researchers access to the records of biological parents of adopted children (Kety 1976). Even though the twins had no contact with each other, many developed the same illnesses, including mental illness, at almost the same times and at the same rates. Even in their professional, occupational, and leisure interests, the twins were more like each other than like their adoptive families.

Newer, rigorously designed studies have continued to confirm the hereditability of mental illness. For example, one study matched 723 first-degree relatives of schizophrenic patients with a comparison group of over one thousand first-degree relatives of surgical patients (Kendler *et al.* 1985). Schizophrenia occurred eighteen times as frequently in families of schizophrenic patients as in the comparison group. These findings from the so-called hard sciences are persuasive in suggesting that our genetic inheritance exerts a more powerful influence in shaping us than had previously been believed.

BIOLOGICAL CAUSES

Although we have ample and persuasive evidence that such illnesses as schizophrenia and depression run in families, this tells us little if anything about causation. For example, it is generally agreed that schizophrenic conditions are accompanied by genetic, biochemical, and structural changes in the brain (Andreasen 1986; Barnes 1987; Pakkenberg 1987). Schizophrenia is associated with an overproduction of the chemical compound dopamine, which the brain needs to perform its functions. The neural receptors that process dopamine are unable to handle the influx of the chemical, resulting in schizophrenia's positive symptoms, such as delusions and hallucinations (Mackay and Crow 1986). The effectiveness of antipsychotic medications lies in their ability to block the dopamine receptors and thus mute positive symptoms.

19

But we still don't know what causes the overproduction of dopamine and its faulty transmission within the brain, nor do we know whether changes in the brain are the result or the cause of schizophrenia.

Searches for the causes of schizophrenia are following intriguing leads. The illness appears among those who have experienced birth injuries, who were born during cold winter months, and whose parents had an infectious disease within one year of their birth. Scientists are speculating whether these factors, singly or in combination, so weaken the immune system of a new-born as to permit entry of a virus that will later in life give rise to mental illness (Crow 1986).

The most promising finding has been the identification of specific genes responsible for carrying the genetic codes that give rise to major depression. Some promising research, conducted among families in which depressive illness was clearly transmitted from generation to generation, has found associations between certain genetic markers and the affected families. The genetic markers, however, are not found in each depressed person; and markers may also be present in some who may never experience major depression (Egeland and Hostetler 1983).

All these at times contradictory, at times ambiguous findings lead to further questions. Are there many distinct illnesses we now call by a handful of names (schizophrenia, depression, and mood disorders)? If there are, how will we identify them? How many types will we find? Who is most likely to develop what illness? What treatment will be most effective for which disorder?

CHARACTERISTICS OF CHRONIC MENTALLY ILL PERSONS

What are the general characteristics of the chronic mentally ill?

1. Because of their illness, they are particularly vulnerable to stress. Schizophrenic persons will often respond disproportionately and pathologically to a degree of stress that would not unduly disturb the "normal" person. For example, persons with a schizophrenic illness have been known to experience a flare-up of their symptoms, or to **decompensate**[2] for such seemingly trivial reasons as being turned down for a date, or not being able to find an item of clothing in the closet.

2. Many chronic mentally ill tend to be excessively dependent on others, perceiving themselves as vulnerable, helpless, and in need of enormous material and emotional support from families, friends, agencies, and others.

3. The third characteristic is related to the second. About two-thirds of chronic mentally ill persons display a significant deficit in coping skills that are needed in everyday living: grooming, shopping, budgeting,

---

2. See the Glossary for definitions of relevant terms.

cooking meals, using public transportation, making and keeping appointments, and the like (Grinker and Harrow 1987).

4. A fourth characteristic is a substantial inability to form and maintain close, reciprocal personal relationships. It is difficult for many chronic mentally ill persons to make and keep friends or even to maintain trusting, reciprocal, and stable relationships with parents, friends, and others.

5. Many chronic mentally ill persons find it difficult to maintain steady, competitive employment. Persons who suffer from the most severe forms of the illness or those whose illness first became manifest early in their lives, who decompensate frequently and exhibit severe problems in social functioning, may either not work at all or work sporadically, holding jobs for short periods of time and changing them frequently. Their work performance tends to be poor, unless the work is relatively free of stress and expectations regarding performance are deliberately kept low. On the other hand, persons with less severe forms of the illness and whose illness has been successfully kept in remission for long periods of time are able to hold competitive employment and work productively and creatively.

It should be kept in mind that antipsychotic medications that tend to mute delusions, hallucinations, and agitations do not significantly cause an improvement in important social skill areas. Ironically, medications often have an adverse impact on social skills.

DISTRIBUTION

There are about two million chronic mentally ill persons in the United States. Most of them have been diagnosed as having schizophrenic or mood disorders. Surveys show that over half of this large population are able to live at home, whether with their families, in group living arrangements, or on their own. Contrary to popular misconceptions, a large proportion of the chronic mentally ill are able to lead satisfactory lives outside institutions.

- 40.4% live with their families
- 10.1% live on their own
- 15.1% live in nursing homes
- 15.1% stay in foster homes, group homes, or other supervised settings
- 10.1% are in mental hospitals
- 1.3% are in jails or prisons
- 7.5% are in public shelters or are homeless

(U.S. Office of Special Education and Rehabilitation Services 1984)

The data also reveal the disabling consequences of mental illness. More than 25 percent of chronic mentally ill persons live in closed, structured institutions such as nursing homes and mental hospitals. Approximately 15 per-

21

cent need the semistructured and supervised living arrangements of group homes.

One in ten do not live in institutions but are poorly equipped to manage and look after themselves. This is a highly visible and troublesome group for the communities in which they live. Among them are the homeless, persons who loiter in public places such as train stations, drug users, and lawbreakers who have aroused enormous concern among the public and mental health professionals. The mental health system is currently struggling to come up with effective means to help them.

IN THE COMMUNITY

A 1980 nationwide survey of 248 case managers who provided data concerning 1471 randomly selected chronic mentally ill clients living in the community has produced a wealth of information about their life-styles (Tessler *et al.* 1982). But since these data do not include those mentally ill persons who do not use or need case management services, the survey does not tell us anything about either the least or the most disabled persons. The findings of this study replicate those of other, smaller, and more modest studies (*e.g.*, Caton 1981; Cohen and Berks 1985; Lewis and Hugi 1981; Pepper *et al.* 1981; Spivack *et al.* 1982). The data indicate that

1. Composition:
   89% were white.
   47% were males and 53% were females.
2. Marriage:
   56% were never married.
   26% were divorced or separated.
3. Education:
   19.3% had attended college or received a college degree.
   35% had a high school diploma.
4. Life-style:
   55% lived alone or in settings that provide little or no supervision.
   More than 25% do not pursue recreational activities outside their own homes; recreation inside the home consists largely of watching television.
   17% had no regularly scheduled activities.
5. Employment:
   26% were employed.
   42% of the employed (10.9% of the total) work in "open-market" jobs—but mostly in part-time, unskilled jobs.
   58% of the employed (15.1% of the total) work in sheltered workshops or transitional employment programs.
6. Income:
   48% received Supplementary Security income (SSI).
   35% received Social Security disability payments.

22% received state or county welfare benefits.

Their median income, including government payments, was $325 a month.

(Tessler *et al.* 1982)

Most are young adults, about 24 years of age at the time of their first contact with the mental health system. The average mentally ill person has experienced over three admissions to a psychiatric or general hospital and spends almost six weeks as a psychiatric inpatient in any given year. Many persons with mental illnesses also have other health problems, among which the most commonly observed are obesity, undernourishment, medication side effects, and impaired motor control.

Most chronic mentally ill persons have fewer friends and smaller social networks than do either neurotic or relatively normal persons. The vast majority are unable to form or maintain their own families or to engage in full-time, competitive employment. Many deny that they are mentally ill, explaining that unfair and unfortunate circumstances have caused them to be unemployed and have contributed to their current condition (Tessler *et al.* 1982). Even when confined to a mental hospital, there are patients who insist that they had been admitted in order to get rest from a demanding job, or because of minor, transient problems with "nerves" (Spivack *et al.* 1982). These rationalizations and denials help to explain why patients in hospitals and day treatment centers tend to avoid therapy and actively seek out and participate in recreational activities (Lewis and Hugi 1981).

IN THE HOSPITAL

Decompensations are ordinarily treated in hospitals. More than three times as many episodes of decompensation are treated in general hospitals as in mental hospitals. Surprisingly, most of the general hospital treatment takes place in hospitals without psychiatric units (Kiesler and Sibulkin 1987). To illustrate: in 1983 1,759,000 decompensation episodes were treated in general hospitals as compared with only 499,000 in state mental hospitals and 198,000 in Veterans Administration hospitals. 61 percent of the general hospitals that treated these episodes in 1983 did not have psychiatric units or wards.

Patients treated in general hospitals tend to have shorter stays than those admitted to state and Veterans Administration hospitals. This can be explained in several ways. First, general hospitals and their emergency units are more accessible and make admission less difficult than do mental hospitals. Second, less stigma is attached to treatment in a general hospital, which makes such treatment more palatable both for mentally ill persons and for their families. Third, general hospitals tend to treat patients with the least severe illnesses while mental hospitals care for those whose illnesses are more severe and chronic. This also accounts for longer stays in mental hospitals.

DANGEROUSNESS

There is a common misconception that the mentally ill are more dangerous than others and that they commit more crimes. This misconception stems in part from the unpredictability of their behavior. Certain psychotic conditions are characterized by rapid mood swings and by sudden and unexpected outbursts of anger that can be directed at unsuspecting targets. Even though a mentally ill person may never actually assault anyone, his or her inexplicable and rapid mood shifts frighten others and present a threatening appearance of potential violence. Case managers of mentally ill clients in community support programs acknowledge that the behavior of a substantial number of their clients does indeed generate complaints. For example, 34 percent of all the case managers' clients had neighbors lodge complaints with police or mental professionals about of the bizarreness of the clients' behavior, including temper tantrums and deviant behavior such as undressing in public (Goldstrom and Manderscheid 1982). Putting aside the issue of motives behind such complaints, it does appear that about one-third of chronic mentally ill persons may behave in ways sufficiently contrary to the acceptable so that apprehension is generated in others.

But does such behavior result in higher crime rates? The media tend to reinforce this notion by emphasizing as newsworthy mentally ill offenders. Headlines such as "Ex-Mental Patient Sets Office Building Ablaze" or "Ferry Passengers Stabbed by Mental Patient" disproportionately link the mentally ill with crime and perpetuate the spurious notion of disproportionate dangerousness.

For legal purposes, dangerous behavior is defined as that which poses a physical danger to oneself, to others, or to property. Danger to self includes the potential of suicide and self-mutilation and an inability to provide food, shelter, clothing, and medical care for oneself. Danger to others and to property includes assaultiveness, fire setting, window breaking, furniture throwing, and other destruction of property. Given these concerns and notoriety, are the chronically mentally ill, in fact, more dangerous than their neighbors?

Research shows that mentally ill persons in the community, given proper care and treatment that keeps their agitation, hallucinations, and delusions under control, are no more dangerous than anyone else (Caton 1981). Like others, the chronic mentally ill tend to adapt to the norms of their communities. When they live in safe, law-abiding neighborhoods, they tend to be law-abiding. If, on the other hand, they live in areas where theft and drug dealing are common, they may do what their neighbors do and engage in criminal activity. Nine out of ten chronic mentally ill community residents are, in fact, model citizens. They are not only law-abiding but also do not engage in nuisance or potentially dangerous behavior. They don't steal, damage property, loiter, or carelessly use matches or stoves (Tessler et al. 1982).

Past patterns are our best predictors of future behavior. Mentally ill persons who have a track record of arrests will, in all probability, tend to engage in activities for which they will be arrested again. On the other hand, mentally ill persons who have not been arrested in the past will probably not be arrested in the future. The criminality of the latter group does not exceed that of the general population (Kiesler and Sibulkin 1987).

When the symptoms of their illness are not under control, a small proportion of mentally ill persons obey their "command voices" or act on their persecutory, paranoid ideas. A hallucinatory command voice may clearly, compellingly, and insistently order the mentally ill person to "free the world" or to protect himself or herself from imagined enemies. Paranoid persons profoundly believe that they have been unjustly persecuted. His or her objective may be to punish tormentors. Delusions and "command voices" may create real danger and should always be taken seriously.

Generally, the dangerousness of these persons eventually becomes evident, as a result of which they are involuntarily committed to mental hospitals. In many states involuntary commitment to a mental hospital requires that the person be both mentally ill and dangerous. Since nine out of ten persons currently admitted to psychiatric hospitals are involuntary, we can deduce that these hospitals now house a high proportion of patients who are regarded as dangerous in the community. Moreover, the number of assaultive and homicidal persons who submit a plea of insanity to the court and are diverted from the criminal justice system to the mental health system adds to the dangerousness of patients in psychiatric hospitals. It has been estimated that the proportion of assaultive patients in public hospitals is as high as one-third of the total population (DeRisi and Vega 1983), as compared to 10 percent in private mental hospitals (Tardiff 1984).

The patients' physical and verbal assaultiveness is directed primarily against those who work most closely with them, such as nursing staff and ward aides. The severity of most physical assaults is relatively minor, and severe injuries are a rare occurrence (Haller and Deluty 1988). Younger males are prominent among those who engage in physical violence, both as inpatients and as outpatients (Tardiff and Koenigsberg 1985). Why are these younger patients more violent than the older ones? Strikingly different socialization processes have shaped their behavior and life-styles.

LIFE-STYLES

Life-style differences may be observed among chronic mentally ill persons, some of which are indirect results of age—which is to say generation rather than the aging process itself.

OLDER PERSONS

Until the beginning of the current deinstitutionalization movement in the 1960s, lifelong confinement to a mental hospital was common for many chronic mentally ill persons, who were often hospitalized early in life when their illness first became evident, usually in their teens or early twenties. These early-committed patients grew up in the mental hospital, which became their world, supplying all their basic needs and shaping their thinking and behavior. Patients soon learned that in order to survive as comfortably and painlessly as possible, they had to submit to institutional rules and to the expectations of staff. They learned to obey rules, not to make trouble, to seek out the best the hospital had to offer, and to avoid unpleasantness. Patients also learned the helplessness role. Their meekness and seeming inability to shift for themselves came to be known as the institutionalization syndrome. Unfortunately, the institutionalization syndrome coupled with their illness caused many to deteriorate to the point where they became helpless, "backward" patients.

When new law required the discharge of nondangerous patients who suffered from the institutionalization syndrome, they were quite unprepared for life on the outside. They could not easily learn the numerous taken-for-granted tasks performed by those who live in the community, such as shopping for groceries, paying rent, or buying and preparing food. Many of the most helpless of these backward persons became "backstreet" persons, the homeless who were neglected by one and all (Talbott 1978). A substantial number of persons who had lost their functional capacities were trans-institutionalized to nursing and boarding homes (Kiesler and Sibulkin 1987). The best functioning of these ex-patients returned to their families or learned to live in group homes or in single-room-occupancy hotels. Even under the best of circumstances only a few of the older group have become restored to the point where they are able to hold remunerative jobs (Harding *et al.* 1987).

YOUNG ADULTS

The presence of young, chronic mentally ill persons in the community is a post-deinstitutionalization phenomenon. The life-style of these younger persons is strikingly different from that of their older predecessors. They did not grow up in mental hospitals, and they are hospitalized only when they decompensate. Most have grown up in their own homes; many still live with their families. Among the 18- to 34-year-old group, 68 to 91 percent live with families, and up to 90 percent have never been married. They are better educated than the older chronic patients. Fifty-five percent of them have completed high school, 20 percent have some college education, and 16 percent have received college degrees (Bachrach 1982; Kiesler and Sibulkin 1987; Pepper and Ryglewicz 1984; Spivack *et al.* 1982).

Growing up in the community has both benefits and costs. Benefits include the maintenance of ties with family and friends, and the opportunity to study, to learn a trade, to work, and to live a self-directed life.

Unfortunately, these young adults also are free to use street drugs, to drink excessively, and to avoid general medical, psychiatric, and other care.

For some, this freedom has catastrophic consequences that may be worse than the "institutionalization syndrome" developed by the older generation. Alcohol and street drugs interact harmfully with antipsychotic medication. When a person has the dual diagnosis of alcoholism and mental illness it is often difficult to know which is the predominant disorder and to separate the effects of one from those of the other. The avoidance of psychiatric care and rebelliousness against family and other helpers results in severe deterioration of functional capacities that puts many of this group in dangerous and life-threatening situations (McCreath 1984). The most troublesome of these young adults show few signs of remorse or shame for their antisocial actions and do not accept responsibility for their behavior. This seeming lack of shame or feelings of guilt is typical of sociopathic individuals. Those who have been diagnosed as having a chronic form of schizophrenia together with symptoms of sociopathy have been characterized in the literature as "schizopaths" (Ely 1985). The provision of effective and humane care for this group of mentally ill persons presents a special challenge for social workers and other mental health professionals.

Of course, not all young adults use drugs and alcohol. Not all lead a precarious existence. The pioneering studies of Sheets have identified the following three subgroups among the young:

Percent of All Young Mentally Ill	Functional Capacity
1. 32	Low-energy, low-demand
2. 41	High-energy, high-demand
3. 27	High-functioning, high-aspiration

(Sheets *et al.* 1982)

Low-energy, low-demand persons tend to be passive. They lack interest in life's activities, are docile, and are willing to follow directions. They readily accept the role of a compliant patient who needs others to care and do for them. From the point of view of many doctors and nurses, they are the ideal patients. When they have to be admitted to a hospital, they do not resist or object. They follow their medication regimens and seldom complain. They keep their activity and therapy appointments and stay out of trouble when provided with specific instructions and directions.

But such persons are often too tired to perform even mundane tasks. Many resist getting out of their beds or rooms. Left to their own devices, they neglect personal and hygienic needs. Their passivity is often vexing to their families, teachers, and counselors, who believe that they should be motivated to do more with their lives.

The high-energy, high-demand persons, on the other hand, are more troublesome. They are driven by spurts of energy that keep them moving and restless. They cannot sit still for long, nor can they stay in any one place for long. Often their thoughts seem to race, day and night. Unless they are on medication, these persons have trouble sleeping. When they do fall asleep, they suffer from nightmares. Some move out of their homes, drifting from residence to residence, from one community to another. They may fail to pay their rent, become evicted, or move to another neighborhood, to another town, or to another state. Substance abuse appears widespread in this group. Many may take any street drug that comes their way and—when desperate enough—all the drugs in the medicine cabinet.

Some high-energy, high-demand persons tend to think of themselves as victims of an "unfair system" and consider their families as uncaring and insensitive. Their relationships with parents is usually emotionally charged and ambivalent. They boast that they can get into the best college or obtain a good job any time they want. It is only "the system" that has blocked their progress. The "schizopaths" in this group often get into trouble with the law and have relatively long arrest records. Others who have unrealistically high expectations of themselves and others that cannot be realized eventually become severely depressed. This subgroup is a high suicide risk (Pepper and Ryglewicz 1984).

When members of this subgroup don't think of themselves as impaired it becomes difficult, but not impossible, to involve them in treatment. Some of the treatment resisters may shop around for medical care and social resources but are soon dissatisfied with whatever help they get. Community mental health centers are familiar with those who stridently demand material things "right away" such as money, wristwatches, or portable radios. When these demands are resisted, they may become angry and make all kinds of threats, such as malpractice lawsuits or lodging complaints with public officials. Such actions tend to generate resentment, frustration, and even fear in the best-natured and most well-intentioned mental health professionals who will, as a result, provide inadequate service or even find a reason to withhold it entirely.

Unless a long-term, therapeutic alliance can be formed with the energetic, demanding mentally ill person, mental health professionals have found few effective ways of helping. The most promising treatment approaches are those that include vigorous outreach activities, group activities, an open-door policy for all who just want to drop in and talk, and an array of activities to keep such clients interested and occupied (Ely 1985; Kanter 1985; Pepper and Ryglewicz 1984).

Members of the high-functioning, high-aspiration subgroup appear to be better cared for, better educated, more affluent, and less ill than persons in the two other groups.

Many show enough insight into their mental illness to take every precaution to remain symptom-free and well. They follow the advice of their therapists and take their antipsychotic medications as prescribed, stay on a healthful diet, and exercise. These persons do not want to play a sick-patient role (Thompson 1988). When they have to be hospitalized, their major objective becomes to get well and out of the hospital as soon as possible. In the community, members of the high-functioning group may readily admit to having a mental illness but resist becoming consumers of such services as therapy groups or applying for disability benefits (Maddigan et al. 1976).

In spite of their composure and seeming self-sufficiency, however, these relatively well-functioning clients may need an entire range of social services in order to keep their decompensations to a minimum and lead satisfying lives. They may need help with their family and other personal relations, with work-related problems, with housing and the like. A long-lasting therapeutic alliance is invaluable for these ambitious persons so that they can be supported and enabled to live up to their own aspirations.

THE HOMELESS

Because of their rootlessness, the homeless mentally ill are elusive and difficult to study. We must be cautious and skeptical about statistics and other findings concerning them.

The number of homeless persons, now including many women (15–25 percent) and people under 30 years of age, has been steadily increasing during the past 20 years (Bachrach 1984a). According to census estimates, their number ranges between 192,000 and 350,000 on any given day. Almost half of all homeless have a chronic mental illness such as schizophrenia and/or a mood disorder, with estimates ranging from 40 to 60 percent (Bachrach 1984a; Kiesler and Sibulkin 1987). Forty percent have major alcohol and drug abuse problems.

The following factors have contributed to this growing problem.

1. The release of mentally ill patients from hospitals into communities that failed to provide housing and other supports to sustain them
2. Skyrocketing rents, real estate costs, and real estate taxes. Many low-income persons, who may or may not be mentally ill, find themselves unable to afford the price of shelter and face eviction from their homes. They cannot readily find apartments in public housing, where there are long waiting lists—some as long as three years. This new group of homeless persons has little recourse but to live in the streets and shelters (Baxter and Hopper 1982).
3. The growing number of mentally ill as part of the general population growth. Today's younger mentally ill persons, as for example the previously discussed high-energy, high-demand group, are particularly at risk. In contrast to older persons, they have more problems in getting along with others and greater distrust and rebelliousness toward authority including landlords and resident caretakers. Current data indicate that young mentally ill adults are a fast-growing group among the homeless (Kiesler and Sibulkin 1987).

Among the mentally ill, three distinct types of homelessness have been identified. These are **situational, episodic,** and **chronic** homelessness (Arce and Vergare 1984).

The situationally homeless are only temporarily out of shelter because of a situational crisis, such as the breakup of a marriage, fire, or unexpected financial problems. After one or two weeks most individuals in the situationally homeless group find other housing, even if only makeshift arrangements with friends or relatives.

The episodic homeless tend to be drifters who, when evicted for nonpayment of rent, spend some time roaming about, then either get welfare or a temporary job and settle down, but only temporarily. Episodic homelessness lasts considerably longer and is more severe than situational homelessness, but it is by no means chronic.

Those who are said to be chronically homeless tend to resist being housed. They enter public shelters only when compelled and usually leave as soon as possible. These are highly visible people who spend most of their time in public places. They sleep over heating grates, in doorways, and in train and bus stations, and they usually wash up in public washrooms. Because of their visibility, the number of chronic homeless persons is usually overestimated.

Life on the streets is hard and dangerous. It results in poor physical health, dental problems, deteriorating mental conditions, and deplorable hygiene, including lice, matted hair, and offensive body odors. Homeless mentally ill persons are more likely to present serious medical problems, not avail themselves of outpatient mental health services, and subsist on food from garbage cans than others who have similar mental illnesses (Gelber and Linn 1988).

GENDER DIFFERENCES, MINORITIES, AND SOCIAL CLASS

Membership in a social group may coincide with frequency, severity, or type of mental illness. Stressors associated with group membership may be a contributing factor, but even here biological factors may also play a role. Below we consider the current state of research into the topic.

GENDER DIFFERENCES

Studies concerned with differences in mental illness between men and women are relatively new. This is because until the past decade most studies focused primarily on male subjects, such as patients in VA hospitals, who seemed to the predominantly male researchers more accessible than female subjects. It has been suggested that men tend to develop "classic" schizophrenic conditions at a slightly higher rate than women, while the latter are more prone to develop schizophreniform conditions. Stressors that cause males to relapse seem to have some connection with their role performance as a man, such as criticism of their physical strength or lack of a job, being turned down for a date, and the like. On the other hand, women seem more sensitive to events in their interpersonal relationships. Mentally ill women who perceive problems in their relationships with boyfriends, lovers, or parents may decompensate as a result.

30

There is evidence that women are significantly more prone to depressive disorders than men (Dohrenwend and Dohrenwend 1976; Newman 1987). Regardless of their social class, age, ethnicity, and marital status, women are significantly more likely than men to have a poor self-concept and to feel guilty and blameworthy, sad, and lonely. These feelings are played out in lack of energy, sleep, eating, digestive disturbances, and problems in concentration. All these are symptoms of major, or clinical, depression.

Whether these differences stem from the physiological and hormonal differences between the sexes or from other social factors is not entirely clear. When investigators did find a relationship between women's depression and such single-dimensional factors as marital status, number of children, or employment, they began to look into more complex constructs, such as the social roles women perform, including those of housewife and mother, and types of employment (Radloff 1975). Subsequent investigations concluded that it was not women's roles that caused their depression, but rather the uneven distribution of power between husbands and wives (Rosenfield 1980). Power in the context of family and the workplace is control over income and other material resources, the ability to exercise influence and to make major decisions on the job, in the home, or in business. When women have as much power as men, the incidence and severity of their depression is about the same as that of men. But in situations where they have less power they tend to develop mild to severe depression. On the other hand, when men have less power than women, whether in the home or workplace, they develop depression at the same rate as women. In fact, in marriages where husbands earn less than their wives, husbands tend to develop clinical depressions whereas their wives remain symptom-free (Rosenfield 1980).

Minorities

In spite of their hardships, members of such minority groups as Blacks, Jews, or Hispanics do not develop major mental illnesses at higher or more severe rates than others.

Because of the greater extent of discrimination and exploitation to which Blacks have been subjected, they have been the focus of many psychiatric and sociological studies. At one time it was thought that if indeed the environment caused mental illness, then such illnesses would most likely surface in groups that had been subjected to the greatest deprivation and oppression. But most well-designed studies have not detected any difference in the appearance of schizophrenic and major mood disorders among Blacks and Whites. Well-designed studies used standardized diagnostic protocols and controlled study groups by their income and social status (Neighbors 1984).

Hispanic groups in the United States have not been studied as extensively as have Blacks, but current research indicates that, when controlled for social class, major mental illness is also as evenly distributed among Hispanics as among other groups (Griffith 1984).

The way a mental illness displays itself is, however, related to the racial and ethnic background of a person. For example, Blacks and Hispanics who suffer from major mood disorders tend to exhibit more hallucinations, delusions, or hostility than Whites, whereas the latter show a higher degree of mania, depression, or guilt. There are also some differences among ethnic groups in the way they tolerate antipsychotic medications. For example, Asian-Americans are more sensitive to the effects of medications than other groups. When given dosages of antipsychotic medications similar to those given Whites, Blacks, or Hispanics, they tend to develop severe side effects at a faster rate than the others. Also, Hispanic and Black mentally ill persons appear to need smaller dosages of antidepressant medications than do Anglos in order to achieve similar effects (Lawson 1986). But all the research dealing with ethnic and racial differences in the appearance and treatment of mental illness is still in its infancy. Although there is much that we still don't know about this area, the ongoing research reminds us once again of the importance of being sensitive to and knowledgeable about our clients' racial, ethnic, and cultural backgrounds.

SOCIAL CLASS

The observation that mental illness appears more frequently among members of lower social classes is not new. In 1855 the prominent psychiatrist Edward Jarvis reported to the Massachusetts Commission on Lunacy that pauper classes contributed 64 times as many cases of insanity as the economically independent. Jarvis noted

> Men of unbalanced mind and uncertain judgement do not see the true nature and relation of things, and they manifest this in mismanagement of their common affairs. . . . Hence they are unsuccessful in life; their plans of obtaining subsistence for themselves, or their families, or of accumulating property would fail and they are consequently poor. . . the cause of their mental derangement lies behind, and is anterior to, their outward poverty (Jarvis 1971, p. 55).

Jarvis's reasoning that mental illness is the cause, and not the consequence, of poverty was an early form of the **social drift** theory, which holds that persons who develop a chronic mental illness will, sooner or later, lose their ability to earn a living and ultimately lose their possessions. The debilitating effects of the illness cause the mentally ill to steadily "drift" into greater poverty and lower social class (Clausen and Konn 1954; Eaton 1980; Harkey *et al.* 1976).

The drift theory is discouraging and pessimistic. It posits that one can predict downward social mobility from the emergence of mental illness. Such pessimistic theories are unpopular. Even the most prestigious researchers prefer to refute them. Such was the case with the now classic Hollingshead and Redlich study (1958) that examined the relationship of social class to mental illness. These researchers reported that parents of schizophrenic adult children were in the same social class as their offspring. Since the children did not "drift" into a lower social class the researchers concluded that the drift theory was invalid. Moreover, since there were significantly more seriously mentally ill in the poorer classes, Hollingshead and Redlich surmised that poverty was the cause of mental illness.

The Hollingshead and Redlich study was replicated a decade later by sociologists who found the same inverse relationship between mental illness and social class—the higher the social class, the less likely mental illness will be found (Meyers and Bean 1968). However, they were not as ready to reject the drift theory as were Hollingshead and Redlich. They reported that parents in the lowest social class tended to reject their mentally ill children more than did parents in the upper classes. These parents refused to take their children back home once the latter were released from the hospital and kept in touch with them less frequently. Such a loss of family connections and social support resulted in the children having fewer material and emotional resources than their parents.

Bland and Orn, who conducted an ambitious 14-year longitudinal study of all schizophrenic patients who were first admitted in 1963 to Alberta Hospital in Edmonton, Canada, found that the social status of these persons was predominantly lower class. Moreover, their social status was significantly lower than that of their fathers (Bland and Orn 1981). This suggests that severe mental illness hinders those afflicted from maintaining the social and economic status of their parents, one that they had most likely known when they were children.

SUMMARY

After many centuries of confusion and ignorance about mental illness, we seem today to be making meaningful progress in our understanding of the many forms in which mental illness presents itself. While we will have a long way to go, nevertheless recent researchers are helping us to confront more rationally the problems and situations presented by mental illness. We talk much less about "curing" and much more about maintaining chronic mentally ill persons in ways that reduce suffering and optimize autonomy and functional capacities.

We no longer blame families for the mental illnesses of their children and recognize that genetic factors may be determinative. Little by little we learn more about the characteristics of chronic mentally ill persons and how we can work more effectively with them for their benefit.

Good social work practice depends on an understanding of chronic mental illness that is not based on ideology but on knowledge generated by scientific research. The more we learn about mental illness, the more realistic, effective, and humane our caring strategies will be.

CHAPTER 3

===

MENTAL HEALTH
STAFF
AND TEAMWORK

THE MENTAL HEALTH system is characterized by a set of interdisciplinary relationships that involve psychiatrists, psychologists, nurses, drug and alcoholism counselors, rehabilitation therapists, case aides, and others—each of whom provides different aspects of the broad spectrum of treatment and care needed by the chronic mentally ill. The mental health professional cooperates closely with professionals from other disciplines as well as with nonprofessional staff who bring to their jobs diverse educational backgrounds, socialization, values, and approaches to client care.

Such interdisciplinary work can be very rewarding. Different perspectives and experience tend to enlarge our own focus and understanding of mental illness, its related problems, and the nature of good client care. At their best, interdisciplinary relationships enhance our own expertise and our work satisfaction. Nevertheless, situations do arise that adversely affect cooperative colleagueship. Some professionals may feel threatened by professionals from other disciplines whom they see as encroaching on their "turf," undervaluing their expertise, making seemingly arbitrary decisions, and the like. For example, social workers can regard nurses who help to find housing and other social resources for their patients as stepping on our own expertise. On the other hand, nurses may believe that social workers are invading their turf when they monitor medication side effects of their clients.

When such tensions are allowed to escalate, interdisciplinary relationships can deteriorate, detracting from rather than contributing to client care. The first and most important factor in working harmoniously and effectively with others is to understand where they are coming from. What are the educational backgrounds and values of your fellow professionals? How do they contribute to the care of clients? What roles do they play on interdisciplinary teams? What are the costs and benefits of working in interdisciplinary settings? This chapter will examine these issues.

JOB SATISFACTION ON A TEAM

Job satisfaction of professionals is a central component of good service delivery. Satisfied mental health professionals are less likely to leave their jobs and are more likely to carry out their tasks with care and devotion than those who are dissatisfied (Strauss 1974). Although the problems presented by chronic mental illness may seem to be more vexing and intractable than those of other groups, research has shown that mental health professionals who predominantly practice with chronic mentally ill clients in community settings are just as satisfied with their work as those who work with non–mentally ill clients. In fact, work in the mental health system is generally satisfying (Cherniss and Egnatios 1978).

Nevertheless, two problem areas can be identified. The first is professionals' role diffusion and ambiguity. The second pertains to the rigid hierarchical staff structure.

ROLE DIFFUSION AND AMBIGUITY

Role diffusion and **role ambiguity** are closely related terms. Both refer to the lack of clarity in understanding and carrying out a **role set,** or the functions that go into everyday job performance that distinguish one profession from another. To be more specific, when we speak of the role diffusion of social workers in mental health settings we refer to how their job performances actually overlap and become indistinguishable from those of other mental health professionals. On the other hand, role ambiguity refers primarily to the lack of clarity in a job description or the expectations of one's employers. For example, physicians are expected to "heal" by diagnosing a patient's condition and prescribing appropriate treatment. Nurses are expected to carry out a physician's orders and to provide hands-on patient care. Psychologists are expected to test intelligence and vocational preferences and provide counseling. Social workers are expected to help populations at risk by using their knowledge of their clients' fit with the social environment to identify gaps in service delivery, help to modify their environments, and link them to needed resources.

In interdisciplinary settings, staff members tend to submerge their own professional distinctiveness in favor of a common identity, which finds expression in almost indistinguishable roles (Folkins *et al.* 1981). Except for certain technical functions, such as the administration of medication by physicians and psychological testing by psychologists, there are few discernible differences in professional roles in mental health settings. A good illustration is the fact that psychiatrists, psychologists, nurses, and social workers all practice individual and group psychotherapy (Blum and Redlich 1980; House *et al.* 1978; Mizrahi and Abramson 1985; Olsen and Olsen 1967).

The blending of professional identity is especially difficult for social workers and other professionals whose status is not as secure as that of the older and more established professions such as medicine, law, and nursing. Many social workers who practice psychotherapy prefer to be known as "family therapists," "counselors," or "therapists" rather than as social workers.

This may be because in the mental health system the practice of psychotherapy is regarded by most professionals as the most desirable, challenging, and interesting work whereas case management and other jobs that emphasize the provision of resources and making the environment more responsive to the needs of clients are considered to be at the bottom of the status totempole (Johnson and Rubin 1983). When social workers feel uncomfortable in carrying out the job functions for which their professional education prepared them, and when they strive to engage primarily in psychotherapy—an area in which psychiatrists and clinical psychologists have received more extensive and intensive training—then their entire job performance is bound to suffer.

HIERARCHIES

Although the various professionals in mental health settings often perform similar tasks, they nevertheless operate within a well-established hierarchical system. Psychiatrists, who are at the top of the hierarchy, and who enjoy the greatest status and power, exercise enormous influence over treatment planning, implementation, and administrative aspects of the organizations in which they work. They expect other professionals to subordinate themselves to their decisionmaking.

On the lowest run of the hierarchical structure are untrained workers and paraprofessionals, such as case and activity aides. The ranking of other professional groups such as social workers, psychologists, nurses, and rehabilitation counselors is not as clear-cut. Their ranking depends not only on educational credentials, which may vary widely among individuals of a given professional group, but also on how well they demonstrate their individual expertise in the numerous facets of their job.

The clearest and least ambiguous indicators of status are salaries and other material perquisites, such as the size, furnishings, and location of an office. Professionals with higher status also have more access to clerical help and technical supports such as computer information systems. Finally, status is evidenced in how staff relate to one another. Staff members with lower status defer to higher status professionals in team decisionmaking processes and personal relationships.

CREDENTIALS AND ROLES

Mental health professionals are primarily credentialized through formal education, which not only varies in length and content between professions, but also within any given profession. For example, not all psychiatrists are alike. The education of board-certified psychiatrists is commonly more extensive and rigorous than that of noncertified psychiatrists. Board-certified psychiatrists are given positions and status that noncertified doctors usually don't achieve.

PSYCHIATRISTS

Psychiatrists are usually the highest-paid and most-educated members of any mental health staff. Only a physician is qualified by training and certified by law to prescribe such medical regimens as psychotropic medication and electroconvulsive therapy. As members or leaders of diagnostic and treatment teams they also tend to have the final word about nonmedical psychosocial treatment plans. Finally, the psychiatrist usually deals directly with the most disturbed and violent patients when they are seen in emergency rooms or during other crises that require medical expertise.

The other side of the picture is that psychiatrists have the least amount of sustained contact with patients in public mental hospitals and in community treatment settings. Their primary role is to examine patients and to prescribe medical treatments. Rarely do psychiatrists in public mental health facilities provide the once-a-week, fifty-minute therapy sessions that are more common in the private sector. After an initial workup, their usual pattern is to see patients for brief periods, such as ten to thirty minutes once a month, mainly to check on medications. Many psychiatrists in the public sector have a private practice in addition to their public job. Although the rest of the staff envies the psychiatrists' income and status, psychiatrists consider themselves underpaid and overworked in comparison to other physicians, whose income and status are higher. In addition to exercising their clinical skills, psychiatrists in community mental health centers spend their time in educating, supervising, and consulting with other staff members, as well as holding administrative and management positions (Faulkner *et al.* 1987; Miller 1988).

Not all psychiatrists are equally qualified for their responsibilities. While all psychiatrists must have an M.D. or D.O. degree (doctor of osteopathy), many so-called psychiatrists in the public sector have not had much training nor a residency in psychiatry. An M.D. or D.O. degree is awarded after four years of medical school study. Physicians who hold an M.D. or D.O. degree can call themselves psychiatrists, even though they have had relatively little training in psychiatry.

It takes at least three years of residency training following the award of an M.D. or D.O. degree to prepare a physician for the psychiatric boards, an examination by the State Board of Medical Examiners to obtain certification for a psychiatric specialty. A physician who wants to pursue a specialty within psychiatry, such as child psychiatry, must pursue an additional two years of residency training. The examinations consist of at least two full days of written and oral examinations that test the candidate in many areas of knowledge, ranging from neurology and psychopharmacology to theories of personality and applications of such treatments as psychoanalysis and behavior modification. Passing these examinations results in **board certification,** which is the clearest qualification to treat the mentally ill.

As might be expected, board-certified psychiatrists do not clamor for jobs in the public sector of the mental health system, preferring more lucrative work in the private sector treating the affluent and articulate "worried well." Public mental hospitals and community mental health centers that are required by law to have psychiatrists on their staffs must hire whomever they can get, often foreign-trained physicians who may not be board-certified and who tend to have inadequate psychiatric training. Many of these doctors also have a poor command of English, especially of idiomatic and slang expressions. Furthermore, many have little understanding of the life-styles of American cultural and ethnic subgroups. This can result in grave misunderstandings between doctor and patient and less effective treatment, as exemplified by the following.

> *At the Eastern Seaboard Psychiatric Hospital, an Asian physician, who had been in the United States for only a few years, insisted at a meeting of the treatment team that Mark Binaca, a working-class patient of Italian background, could not be discharged because he was still hallucinating and was unreasonably violent. This puzzled other members of the team, who had found Mark restored and tractable. Later, the team's social worker found out— through discussions with the patient, other staff, and the physician—that in interviews with the doctor Mark had referred to a ward aide as a "meathead," punctuating his discourses with the expression "dig me?" When the physician misunderstood what the patient meant, Mark became furious, thinking that the physician was mocking him because of his cultural background and mental illness.*

Social Workers

Social work offers two accredited degrees toward professional practice. The Bachelor of Social Work (B.S.W.) is the entry degree of the social work profession. This degree identifies those who have majored in social work in college. The more advanced degree is the Master of Social Work (M.S.W.), which requires two years of graduate study. Those who hold the B.S.W. may later obtain the M.S.W. in less than two years. Social workers who have the master's degree are prepared to function more independently and flexibly than those with the bachelor's degree. For example, a direct-practice M.S.W. professional is expected to be able to diagnose, assess, and apply an intervention of choice more accurately and autonomously than a B.S.W. social worker.

Two years after receiving an M.S.W., and after having practiced under qualified supervision, a social worker is eligible to join the Academy of Certified Social Workers (A.C.S.W.). In addition to required supervised work experience, the social worker must pass a qualifying examination to join the A.C.S.W.

Joining the A.C.S.W. takes on added importance because of the many people who, without any formal social work education, are hired in social work positions and who call themselves social workers or caseworkers. The many untrained workers in the social work field is a partial explanation of why professional social workers tend to refer to themselves as "counselors," "psychotherapists," and "family therapists," and not as social workers.

Nurses

Nurses, even those with the highest and most specialized training, always call themselves nurses, using titles such as "nurse practitioner," "registered nurse," "clinical nurse specialist," "nurse therapist," and the like.

Women dominate the nursing as well as the social work profession. Since the nursing profession antedates social work, nursing has had more time to develop rules and licensing procedures that stipulate formal educational requirements for entry into each level of professional practice. Without the required education (which may, however, vary among the states), entry into the nursing profession at any job level is impossible.

In most states a practical nurse, or a nurse's aide, must have an associate of arts degree, which can be obtained in a community college. Registered nurses, or R.N.'s, generally must have a four-year college degree and experience in hospital practice. Nurses who specialize in working with chronic mentally ill persons may be known as **psychiatric nurses, nurse-clinicians,** or **nurse therapists** (S. Lamb 1979). For this work a master's degree in psychiatric nursing and two years' supervised experience in working with mentally ill patients are required. Psychiatric nurses must learn managerial, educational, and consultational skills so that they can also take on administrative and teaching responsibilities (Mian *et al.* 1981). Continuing education is a high priority for psychiatric nurses. In many settings they are required to pursue formal continuing-education programs in order to upgrade their knowledge and skills.

In the hospital the bulk of a nurse's time is devoted to planning and overseeing outpatient and ward activities, staff development and educational activities. Some nurses are in charge of special therapeutic programs, such as milieu therapy, token economy, and group activities (Cason and Beck 1982; McDonagh et al. 1980). Psychiatric nurses tend to spend less time in direct patient contact than in such relatively impersonal activities as the dispensation of medications and recordkeeping.

In community mental health centers the functions of the psychiatric nurse often overlap with the therapeutic activities of psychologists and social workers (Mullaney et al. 1974). Nurses may provide family therapy, group therapy, and individual and couple counseling. The salaries of such psychiatric nurses are higher than those of their social work counterparts, whether at starting or maximum rates. Nurses tend to receive about $3000 more per year than do social workers with similar training in similar institutions (1981 National Survey of Hospital and Medical School Salaries).

PSYCHOLOGISTS

Currently, most practicing psychologists hold a doctorate in any of a variety of specializations such as educational psychology, social psychology, or clinical psychology.

Psychologists with doctorates in social psychology are primarily interested in the interaction of individuals with their environment from both theoretical and practice perspectives. Some social psychologists have had little training in direct practice. Others may focus primarily on researchable problems that can be tested in a laboratory and in other controlled environments.

Most clinical psychologists are highly qualified for direct practice. A rigorous four-year graduate program includes many aspects of clinical practice with an emphasis on such approaches as family therapy, behavior modification, or psychodynamic therapy. The clinical psychology doctoral curriculum emphasizes practice skills, research, middle management, and educational skills. Because there are fewer graduate schools offering a doctorate in clinical psychology than there are medical schools, it is, ironically, sometimes more difficult to be admitted to a clinical psychology program than to a medical school!

The education of practicing psychologists includes the administration and interpretation of a variety of tests, such as those that measure intelligence quotients, of which the Stanford-Binet test is one example. Tests that can identify psychological problems, such as the Rorschach Test, are another illustration. There are a wide variety of vocational-preference tests that can help persons arrive at sound career choices. But most psychologists in community mental health centers prefer to provide psychotherapy, just as do psychiatrists, social workers, and nurses.

Rehabilitation Therapists

Most psychiatric hospital and community mental health settings include rehabilitation therapists on their staff. In working with chronic mentally ill persons, the goal of this therapist's job is to enable clients to develop competencies in everyday living through the acquisition of a variety of social skills, including better speech patterns, coordination of bodily movements, basic interpersonal relationship skills, learning how to use money, budget, and the like. Educational backgrounds of rehabilitation therapists, such as speech or movement and dance therapists, may range from a bachelor's to a doctoral degree, and they include nurses, social workers, teachers, and others who specialized in some aspect of a rehabilitation therapy. Because of their prolonged, intimate contact with clients, rehabilitation therapists should be skilled, as other direct-practice mental health professionals, in establishing supportive, warm, and generally helping relationships (Goering and Stylianos 1988).

Paraprofessionals

A **paraprofessional** is a staff member who does not hold a professional degree. Case aides, ward aides, and human service technicians are all paraprofessionals. Many of them have only a high school diploma (Moffic *et al.* 1984).

These workers are the lowest-paid yet most indispensable service providers in the mental health system. They spend most of their time working directly with people. In hospitals they help patients to bathe, to eat, and generally monitor them during their sleeping and waking hours. In community mental health centers they escort clients to welfare and Social Security offices and to other agencies and appointments. They spend time with clients in the day room, help in meal preparation, and act in a variety of service roles. Because the paraprofessionals' job can be tedious and unpleasant, and because of the low pay, it is difficult to find and retain the better ones.

In public organizations, where civil service tests are employment prerequisites, the qualification for such a job is obtaining an acceptable score on the test. In many mental health organizations there are neither obligatory personal interviews, work experience requirements, nor checks on prior work or criminal records. Paraprofessionals may have been fired from previous jobs for misconduct, or may have had exemplary work histories. They may have a college degree or be barely literate, with a poor command of the English language.

On-the-job training for paraprofessionals may be as superficial as is the hiring process. Job preparation and training of hospital ward aides usually ranges from two to four weeks at most. Training focuses on hospital rules and regulations governing conditions of employment and conduct, such as what to do at mealtime, at bedtime, and the like. There are few, if any, preservice training programs for hospital paraprofessionals that focus on the nature of mental illness, on the behavior of the mentally ill, or on how to communicate with and effectively relate to patients. Yet paraprofessionals who have the most intimate contact with people are the ones who most need this kind of training as well as ongoing education and support from staff professionals.

Community mental health center paraprofessionals usually receive no job-preparation training. It is argued that such training is not needed to accompany patients or to run errands. Nor do paraprofessionals receive much, if any, on-the-job training. It is ironic that while professional staff is away from their jobs attending continuing education programs, the undereducated and undertrained members of the mental health system are left behind, caring for the patients (Moffic *et al.* 1984).

INTERDISCIPLINARY TEAMWORK

An interdisciplinary team has been defined as "a functioning unit composed of individuals with varied and specialized training who coordinate their activities to provide services to a client or a group of clients" (Lowe and Herranen 1981, p. 1). Professional teams in the mental health system originated with the public health model developed in the 1940s that stresses not only the treatment of physical illness and disabilities but also their prevention. To accomplish these two ambitious goals, it was believed that only professionals from various disciplines, working together as a team, could tackle both. In fact, interdisciplinary teams were deemed to be so important that their establishment was mandated by the 1963 Community Mental Health Center Act, as well as by subsequent state legislation.

MEMBERSHIP

The 1963 act and almost all state laws require only that a physician must be a member of an interdisciplinary team. Other team members can presumably be recruited on an "as needed" basis. Today, most teams in psychiatric settings include a psychiatrist, a social worker, a psychologist, a nurse, rehabilitation counselors, and relevant paraprofessionals.

Many psychiatric hospitals use two types of teams. The **intake** team works in the admissions unit. Its primary responsibility is to develop initial diagnostic and treatment plans. The **treatment** team is responsible for ongoing treatment and discharge planning. The treatment team includes staff who are responsible for the care of a patient.

Team leaders are either chosen by team members or designated by administrative staff. The leader reports to the clinical director, who provides both clinical and administrative supervision (Paradis 1987). The responsibilities of

42

the team leader include setting meetings, making agendas focused on treatment plans, and conducting the meetings.

Social workers are playing increasingly important roles in providing leadership and direction in psychiatric teams. According to Toseland *et al.*:

> As team members, social workers appeared to be particularly important for effective team functioning. Although they were rated as the second most influential team members after psychiatrists, they played more roles as team members than did psychiatrists or team members from other disciplines (1986, p. 51).

Social workers can become indispensable in providing information about a person's social resources, in paving the way for a hospitalized patient's return to the community, and in maintaining the patient in the community through the location and coordination of services. Thus the information provided by social workers significantly helps team members in shaping and directing treatment plans.

BENEFITS OF TEAMWORK

Face-to-face meetings of professionals from various disciplines should result in a better quality of patient care than that which is provided by individual professionals. The following benefits that directly affect the client's treatment have been identified (Mechanic 1982; Paradis 1987):

1. *Assessment/diagnosis.* Better assessment of problems of individual patients stemming from the pooling of knowledge from various disciplines
2. *Treatment/provision of care and resources.* Recognizing a wider spectrum of client needs should lead to the use of a broad range of treatment modalities, such as medication, social skill training, family therapy, and the provision of material resources.
3. *Coordinated services.* The provision of coordinated services based on a division of labor among team members
4. *Help for difficult patients.* An increased likelihood of resolving problems presented by patients who have not responded well to treatment in the past
5. *Communication.* Better and faster communication among staff members. Joint deliberations can minimize distortions. Decisions can be made on the spot, saving everyone's time in the long run.

A well-functioning team is characterized by its cohesiveness and ability to get its work done promptly. Its members do not compete with one other over turf issues, but respect the contributions made by everyone. Good multidisciplinary teamwork can benefit its members in the following ways:

1. *Knowledge sharing.* In the course of their work, team members share their professional expertise. Members learn from one another, broadening their professional and administrative knowledge.

2. *Morale boosting.* Members give recognition to others for work well done.
3. *Work improvement.* Members educate one another on how to avoid mistakes. They discuss ways of improving their work and working conditions.
4. *Isolation reduction.* Members share and understand the problems of others on the team. They can provide others "with an opportunity to share joy and the disappointments involved in working with clients. Being able to share work-related difficulties can help to reduce tension and frustration, to avoid worker burnout, and to confirm that individual workers are not alone in experiencing difficulties in performing their designated roles" (Toseland *et al.* 1986, p. 46).
5. *Protection against malpractice litigation.* Mental health professionals are often concerned that a poor outcome of treatment may result in a malpractice lawsuit. The existence of a treatment team tends to eliminate the risk of a malpractice litigation in which the plaintiff could win. Professional negligence often arises when a professional who works alone has failed to consult others when the need arises (Gerhart and Brooks 1985). Any professional may be charged with malpractice, but rarely are mental health professionals who arrive at a treatment decision through team consultation charged with negligence.

Dynamics of Small-Group Teams

What is the dynamic that underlies the functioning of an interdisciplinary team? Most teams consist of four to nine members. They tend to exhibit many of the characteristics that are generally found in small work groups. At the outset, there is an explicit and implicit formulation of rules known as "group norms" that will govern the behavior of its members (Moffic *et al.* 1984). Implicit norms define what is good and bad and what is acceptable or unacceptable behavior. Norms also guide the resolution of conflicts, communication patterns, and members' relationship to their workplace and the community. Explicit rules set forth the scope of the team's responsibility, its functions and purpose, sanctions for rule breaking, the manner in which decisions are to be made, the election of officers, and the like. Rules should be designed to be flexible. One example of inflexible rule making: a team leader, in the interest of efficiency and getting work done, ruled that only nine minutes of discussion would be allotted to each case. Even when complex and difficult cases were brought to the team the leader was adamant in keeping to his time limit.

Inflexibility in teamwork is also illustrated by the substance abuse counselor who could only discuss each problem in terms of a client's substance abuse and who opposed all other approaches except those favored by her orientation to treatment.

The role diffusion so common in mental health facilities is bound to affect team members. Some are presented with a dilemma of loyalties. Should their primary loyalty lie with their team or with their profession? Sometimes the former is favored for the sake of efficiency:

> in the interest of service, it is preferable for the major loyalty of the team member to lie with the team, rather than the profession. An excessive attachment to a professional reference group could render the team member inflexible and unresponsive in his work situation (Kane 1975, p. 22).

On the other hand, too much blurring of professional identification can result in inadequate care. For example, all members of a treatment team at the Midtown Psychiatric Hospital focused primarily on the psychological and emotional pathology of patients under their care. The team's treatment plans consisted in large part of psychodynamic and behavioral therapies. Team members, including the social worker, tended to ignore the patients' social environments and neglected needed interventions in those systems.

PROBLEMS

As noted, interdisciplinary teams are not problem free. Team members will sometimes not get along. At times the personality problems of a member may make the work of others more difficult. And even when personality problems are absent, inherent problems in teamwork may emerge. The following problems tend to contribute to the dilution of care:

1. *"Group-think."* The term **group-think** is used to refer to the almost unanimous agreement that is easily reached in small and cohesive groups whose members get along very well with each other. The longer the members of such teams work together, the greater the possibility that each member will conform to the norms of the group and the more all members will tend to think alike (Toseland *et al.* 1986). This trend toward consensus can dull each member's views and analyses and put a damper on individualized recommendations. As a result, oversights and errors in assessment and treatment may occur.

2. *The disproportionate power of psychiatrists and other physicians.* Although in theory all team members have an equal say in decisionmaking, the physician in fact tends to wield a "disproportionate share of responsibility for both the team's decisions and their outcome" (Schulberg and Baker 1975, p. 207). This unequal distribution of power in a setting where all members are said to be equal typically exists even if the physician has not been formally named as the team leader. Insecure team members who are not physicians may be too timid to oppose or challenge the psychiatrist.

3. *Passing the buck.* When nonphysician team members defer to the physician on the team, they also tend to covertly reinforce the physician's

position of power so that they can avoid many of the risks inherent in patient care (Schulberg and Baker 1975). The risks may include the acceptance of open hostility or complaints from clients and other community members as well as exposure to malpractice litigation. The buck, so to speak, can always be passed on to other team members, or to the team as a whole.

4. *Overvaluing the team over the individual team member.* Sometimes important and valid contributions of an individual team member, especially one who has a relatively low professional status, are not recognized or sufficiently appreciated. Since the team ethos holds that the whole is better than its parts, it may be easy to not hear or to suppress the lone voice of a dissenting member in favor of the consensus of the whole team.

5. *Resistance to team meetings.* Since it is not unusual for professionals to devote from seven to fifteen hours each week to team deliberations, it is reasonable to ask whether these professionals are making the best use of their time in so many time-consuming team meetings. Team members often think that much of the time spent this way is an egregious waste of time, especially since this time is taken away from direct patient contact. Team members may prefer spending more time with their patients to complying with what many consider to be an excessive number or the formality of team meetings.

When a small group of people are placed in a position where they have to relate to one another for any length of time in order to accomplish specific tasks, tension is bound to develop. There will be struggles for leadership positions. Individuals have to give up some of their autonomy in favor of the good of the group. Consciously or subconsciously they must agree on some issues, such as the divisions of tasks, conflict resolution, and decisionmaking. The team relationships will be harmonious when each team member can respect the expertise and the opinions of others without submerging his or her own professional identity. When such relationships are fostered, then the benefits of interdisciplinary team work will indeed far outweigh the costs.

SUMMARY

Team decisionmaking in the mental health system seems to be here to stay. The combined bodies of knowledge, experience, and differing perspectives provided by a variety of mental health professionals tends to ensure more balanced and well-considered judgments on important issues. Studies of team decisions in various areas suggest that they often differ significantly from decisions made by members of one profession, who may have developed a myopic view of mental health problems (Zito *et al.* 1986).

But joint decisionmaking requires keen awareness of potential risks. The social worker can protect the integrity of the process by learning as much as possible about the professional background and values of colleagues. In many cases it is the social worker who assumes the leadership role in the treatment team.

FOR DISCUSSION AND THOUGHT

1. Have you noted role ambiguity and diffusion among the social workers in your agency?

2. If your answer to the above question was yes, discuss why you believe this exists with individual social workers.

3. Provide an example from your actual practice where role diffusion (where it exists) has either helped or hindered service delivery to a client.

4. Do the social workers in your agency make *unique* contributions to the deliberations of a diagnostic or treatment team? If so, what are they? If they do not make unique contributions, why is this so?

5. From your observations of the working of teams in your agency, discuss the advantages and disadvantages of teamwork, giving actual illustrations.

PART II Practice Principles and Diagnostic Processes

CHAPTER 4

PRINCIPLES
AND POLICIES
OF SERVICE
DELIVERY

Direct services to the mentally ill are generally delivered by practitioners who work for organizations like mental hospitals, general hospitals, community mental health centers, family service agencies, and the like, each of which offers specialized services to the chronic mentally ill. While each client presents problems that are special to his or her circumstances, there are nevertheless common problems that result from characteristics of chronic mental illness, such as memory deficits, defective thought processes, vulnerability to stress, and periodic **decompensation.** Decompensation, or the flaring up of the signs and symptoms of mental illness, renders the client helpless to care for the most basic needs and may also cause behaviors that are dangerous to self and to others. Because decompensation is a common and expectable phenomenon in the lives of the chronic mentally ill, organizations that serve them usually include crisis or emergency services as an integral part of their delivery system. An organization's mission should be clearly reflected through its service policies. Putting service policies into practice reflects an organization's approach to community or institutional care. The service policies of an organization whose mission is to help persons with severe mental illnesses could include, for example, interventions with families, social skill training, outreach services, case management approaches, and provision of material resources. Policies that result in the best service provision must be thoughtfully developed and responsive to the cultural values and needs of the clients as well as to today's rapidly generated knowledge in the field of mental illness. Such policies should be "based on careful comparisons of alternative models of managing psychosocial disorder and on consideration of the roles of a variety of professions that work with the mentally ill" (Mechanic 1989, p. *x*).

The effectiveness of service to chronic mentally ill persons is necessarily based on a familiarity with their collective problems. This body of knowledge, derived from empirical research, theoretical formulations, and practice experience, is constantly being expanded and reformulated as we learn more about what works best in the delivery of services. The expansion of our knowledge influences the manner in which practitioners and agencies serve their clients.

This chapter will examine practice principles and policies that address problems of the chronic mentally ill in a variety of settings. We will deal here with two practice principles and four service delivery policies. The two practice principles are (a) the **least restrictive alternative** approach and (b) the **involvement of the client and his or her family in treatment planning.** The four service delivery policies are (a) **continuity of care,** (b) **outreach services,** (c) **crisis intervention services,** and (d) **involving clients and their families in the planning of service delivery.**

PRACTICE PRINCIPLES

Practice principles are the basic rules—derived from values, theoretical assumptions, and practice experience—that provide the individual practitioner with guidance in addressing client problems. The principles are sets of beliefs that inform our practice and that can be put into operation in whatever agency we may work. They are independent of the material resources that agencies have at their disposal and of agencywide service delivery policies that govern such matters as office hours, staff assignments, and the character of interventions offered to clients.

The principle of the least restrictive alternative and of involving clients and their families in treatment planning are derived from societal and legal values and the values of the mental health professions. In some cases these values have become codified into legal rules that govern the conduct of professionals, as is the case with the least restrictive alternative. On the other hand, the principles of involving clients and families in treatment planning and developing attainable, realistic treatment goals are the result of accumulated professional practice experience, empirical research, and professional ethics.

The Least Restrictive Alternative

The least restrictive alternative as a principle of serving the mentally ill has received a great deal of attention in the last twenty years and each year is growing in significance for practitioners. Yet it is an approach that is not well understood either by mental health practitioners or by lawyers and judges. Although the concept originated as a legal rule, it has evolved into a major working principle for mental health professionals. Moreover, applying the least restrictive alternative is legally required in many states.[1]

Essentially, the doctrine (also known as the "least intrusive" or "least drastic" alternative) requires that in serving a client the practitioner should balance the restrictiveness of interventions against the "liberty interests" of the client and make individualized treatment or service decisions that will encroach as little as possible on the client's liberty interests (Brooks 1974, pp. 727–734).

These liberty interests are defined as the client's right to freedom of movement, autonomy with respect to decisionmaking, personal dignity, freedom from harmful treatment effects, and the like. Since interventions on behalf of chronic mentally ill persons are often accompanied by invasions of the client's liberty interests, we must keep them in mind as firmly as treatment concerns. Hospitalization, for example, deprives the client of freedom, dignity, and autonomy. It might also impose on the client the adverse side effects of medication. These are significant deprivations that, in the past, we have often taken for granted as necessary. In some cases they are, but often they are not.

The least restrictive alternative approach recognizes that some encroachments on liberty, such as involuntary hospitalization and the involuntary administration of medication, may in some cases be necessary. When they become necessary, the unwanted or adverse intrusions should be kept to a minimum.

The approach of the least restrictive alternative first arose in a legal case, *Lake* v. *Cameron* (1966), which involved the issue of physical freedom. Mrs. Lake, an elderly woman who suffered from a chronic brain syndrome, was involuntarily committed to St. Elizabeths Hospital in Washington, D.C. She had a propensity for aimless wandering, and often she got lost and did not know where she was. Because of this propensity, it was thought that she was dangerous to herself. The issue presented to the court was whether Mrs.

---

1. The least restrictive alternative is explicitly, legally required in commitment statutes in the following states: California, Colorado, Connecticut, Delaware, Indiana, Minnesota, Mississippi, Montana, Nebraska, Nevada, New Hampshire, New Jersey, North Carolina, Rhode Island, South Dakota, Tennessee, Utah, Virginia, Washington, West Virginia, and Wisconsin. In many other states the least restrictive alternative is implicitly mandated by law, having been referred to as the "suitable alternative treatment," "reasonable alternative treatment," or merely as "alternatives." These states include Arizona, the District of Columbia, Florida, Illinois, Iowa, Kansas, Maine, Michigan, New Mexico, New York, North Dakota, Ohio, and Pennsylvania.

Lake actually required hospitalization for treatment or care or whether she could receive adequate care while living in the community. The court ruled that the "least restrictive" alternative for Mrs. Lake might be a nursing home, halfway house, or the like, rather than a hospital, and ordered a hearing to determine whether there was such a less restrictive alternative. Ironically, because Mrs. Lake "wandered," there was not. No community agency had the resources to adequately care for her. Mrs. Lake remained in St. Elizabeths Hospital for the rest of her life. Yet the principle established in her case lived after her.

The principle is that mental health decisions should not be automatically oriented to care and treatment considerations but should take the liberty interests of the client into account as well. Today this idea may seem obvious, but it was far from obvious a little more than twenty years ago when Mrs. Lake's case was decided. At that time, virtually all care and treatment decisions were made with little concern for a mentally ill person's freedom, autonomy, dignity, and physical well-being. Hospitalization was routine and often automatic, without consideration of viable alternatives. Antipsychotic medications and other medical treatment were administered coercively, without concern for alternatives.

As the notion that patients had certain rights began to emerge, it was recognized that reasonable alternatives to hospitalization and other forms of care were, in fact, available. At the outset the least restrictive alternative principle was applied only to involuntary hospitalization. Judges and mental health professionals began to realize that many mentally ill persons who were being routinely hospitalized did not need to be in a hospital. Effective community treatment was available and was "less restrictive" because it did not deprive the patient of physical freedom. Similarly, as the right to refuse antipsychotic medications emerged, it was acknowledged that there were less intrusive ways of administering medications and that in many cases medications were not needed at all.

Potential Misunderstandings

Two aspects of the least restrictive alternative principle are often misunderstood (Brooks 1974). First, the principle represents a balancing of treatment and care effectiveness against liberty interests. It does not follow that the least restrictive form of care or treatment is always the best. A more restrictive intervention may sometimes be necessary because it is far more efficacious. For example, a client's need for treatment may in some instances absolutely require hospitalization if community care cannot deliver the needed care and treatment. Certain medical procedures, such as the titration of medications under controlled conditions, are best performed in a hospital.

In other cases, however, community care in such settings as an inpatient department of a community mental health center or even the client's own home may be just as effective as hospitalization. In such cases community care becomes the intervention of choice because it is usually less restrictive.

Care should be taken not to promote labels over reality. For example, many mental health professionals and lawyers assume that "community" care is always less restrictive than institutional care. Such a proposition stems from ideology and needs to be carefully examined in every case. To illustrate: some nursing homes "in the community" are far more restrictive of a patient's liberty interests than some hospitals are. Many nursing homes are, in fact, not "homes" but small institutions that provide no "community living" at all. There are also boarding home managers and families who place greater restrictions on a client's freedom than do some institutions.

It is not always easy to determine what is "least restrictive." For example, if a patient becomes agitated, which of the following approaches would be the least restrictive? (a) the administration of a short-acting antipsychotic medication, (b) the administration of a long-acting antipsychotic medication, (c) seclusion, or (d) restraints. Such questions have generated much debate among practitioners. Some argue that seclusion is the least restrictive and long-acting medication the most. Others argue for restraints and short-acting medications. One way of approaching the problem is to determine, in advance if possible, what the client regards as least restrictive for himself or herself. For example, a pregnant woman may prefer to be restrained if she becomes agitated rather than be medicated. Those who respond poorly to medications may prefer seclusion. But in cases where seclusion doesn't "work" it should no longer be regarded as the least restrictive alternative treatment of choice. Another treatment decision should be made.

This leads into the second aspect of least restrictive alternatives that is often misunderstood. The principle does not require that the mental health professional make a "correct" decision. Nor will the professional be punished or held liable for making a "wrong" decision or when others disagree with his or her judgment. The least restrictive alternative doctrine calls only for a good-faith effort to evaluate available alternatives realistically and choose what appears to be the least restrictive. The doctrine does require that the professional be aware of the client's liberty interests in every care and treatment situation and to implement them where they are feasible. Although the least restrictive alternative principle is not a panacea, it will frequently result, in the long run, in better care for the client.

Involving Clients and Families in Treatment Planning

Client Self-Determination and the Limitations of Autonomy

Our second major practice principle is that of involving clients and their families in planning for their own treatment. This is the most meaningful way in which we can show respect for a client's right to **self-determination.** The message conveyed is that persons, despite their mental illness, are often capable of making meaningful decisions relating to their care and the way in which they conduct their lives. Encouraging clients to decide what their own goals are and how best to achieve them is one of the most basic and venerated of social work's practice principles.

Client self-determination was first articulated in 1922 by Mary Richmond, who regarded its application as a practice cornerstone for promoting the client's emotional and intellectual development. She postulated that clinical processes that assisted clients in thinking through their own needs in relation to their own personality would release the clients' "latent possibilities" (Richmond 1922). This principle applies to all clients, even the mentally ill.

But a client's right to self-determination is necessarily limited and must be balanced against the rights of others. More than thirty years ago social workers accepted the proposition that "The client's right to self-determination . . . is limited by the client's capacity for positive and constructive decision making, by the framework of civil and moral law, and by the function of the agency" (Biestek 1957, p. 103).

But what is the fullest participation of which a client is capable and that society will permit? How much of this right can be extended to patients who have been involuntarily committed because they are mentally ill and dangerous? How much of this right can be given to those who, because of their illness, lack the capacity to judge what is in their best interest?

The determination of the areas in which clients have the capacity to make "positive and constructive" decisions can be difficult and time consuming. The mental health professional is constantly tempted to bypass the process and just do for the client what he or she believes is best. Too often, and frequently with the encouragement of their agencies, professionals do not adequately involve their clients in crucial determinations about their care and treatment. But clients and their families whose participatory role is ignored or neglected tend to feel manipulated by professionals who they think do not understand them. Failing to involve clients in planning is manipulation. As noted by Salzberger:

> What is especially odious about manipulation is that it is stealthy. A manipulated person is usually not even aware of his or her options. . . . Thus, two aspects of influence are objectionable: (1) directing persons in ways contrary to their desires and (2) directing persons in such ways that their desires cannot be considered (1979, p. 400).

Limitations on autonomy generate problems for clients, workers, and agencies. It is well known that clients who may be able to exercise sound judgment in one area, such as deciding how best to stretch a limited income, may be unable to do so in other areas. This is illustrated by the case of Ms. Greene, who is competent in many areas but not in making her will.

Roberta Greene is a 65-year-old member of Southland House, a psychiatric rehabilitation center. Her paranoid schizophrenic illness is controlled by the use of medications. She lives in a small house that she inherited from her parents and is able to live within her income. She manages her Social Security disability income payments with the help of her social worker. Ms. Greene's only living relatives are two nieces who live in the same town and see her about once every two months.

One day Ms. Greene's social worker receives a visit from one of the nieces, who wants to enlist the worker's help in persuading Ms. Greene to change her will. Ms. Greene acknowledges that she has written a will in which she has left her house and all her property to the angel Gabriel and Saint Peter, her "dearest and only friends." She says that she does not dislike her nieces, but she does not want them to get her house. Ms. Greene is stubbornly adamant about her decision and no one is able to persuade her to draft a different will.

We know that some mentally ill persons—like many "normal" people—will not give up behaviors that are harmful to themselves, even when they are restored through medications and in contact with reality. For example, there are those who insist on drinking alcohol in spite of the fact that alcohol has a harmful effect in combination with psychotropic medications (Bergman and Harris 1985). Should clients have the right to do this? Some writers argue that they should, claiming that clients have a "right to fail," and that they can learn from their mistakes (McDermott 1975). Others believe that society has a responsibility to protect its impaired citizens, even if against their will, from harming themselves (Weick and Pope 1988).

It is often difficult to make a decision about when hospitalized patients are ready to participate in treatment planning and to what extent they have the capacity to make informed decisions. The degree of impairment affects the capacity to make rational decisions. There is evidence, for example, that the most seriously impaired hospitalized mentally ill persons also tend to refuse medication that would benefit them, whereas those whose illness is less severe and who are better functioning tend to be more compliant with their medication regimens (Marder *et al.* 1983).

Most chronic mentally ill persons suffer from impaired areas of judgment at one time or another, but the person who cannot exercise any judgment in any area at any time is a fairly rare case. When the client understands the harmful consequences that would result from a certain behavior, such as cigarette smoking or excessive drinking, yet persists in such behavior, that person may well have made an informed decision, even if an unsound one.

Guardians: The "Best Interest" and "Substituted Consent" Approaches

If a mental health professional believes that a mentally ill client is unable to make sound decisions in certain areas where decisions are necessary, then the client should be presented to a court for a determination of competency. When a judicial ruling of incompetency is made, then a guardian can be appointed to act on that person's behalf and make those decisions. There are two ways of defining the role of the guardian. The first and more traditional is the so-called **best interest** approach, which reflects a paternalistic philosophy. The guardian decides what is in the best interest of the ward, even if it is necessary to disregard the ward's own wishes or desires. This is illustrated in the following vignette.

> *Martha Williams is the guardian for her 40-year-old niece, Wilma, who is schizophrenic and mentally retarded. Wilma lives alone in a one-room housekeeping apartment. Mrs. Williams manages Wilma's finances and gives her an allowance for clothing and spending money. One day Wilma tells her aunt that she desperately wants cable television to supplement the channels she already receives. Taking the "best interest" approach to this situation, the aunt refuses to allocate a monthly amount for cable television rental. She explains that this would cut too deeply into Wilma's clothing and spending allowance and that she is only doing what is best for her niece.*

The second and more recently developed approach to the guardianship role is generally referred to as the **substituted consent** position. In this role, the guardian does not act exclusively on the basis of what he or she believes to be in the best interest of the ward. Rather, the guardian attempts, as much as possible, to implement the ward's own desires, even if these desires seem unwise or are different from what the guardian would do.

Thus, in our cable television illustration, Mrs. Williams might well allot her niece the cable television rental payments, even if she thinks it unwise. She does so because Wilma wants it so much and would in all likelihood spend her money that way were she not impaired. If, in the future, Wilma complains that she does not have enough money for clothing or for such amenities as an occasional restaurant meal, Mrs. Williams can remind her niece that the choice was hers and that it can always be reconsidered.

On the other hand, if the ward wants to spend money in a manner harmful to self or others, the guardian should not permit it, however strongly the ward wishes it. For example, if the guardian, because of familiarity with the ward's driving record, believes that the ward is an irresponsible driver who is likely to get into a serious accident, the guardian should refuse to buy a car for the ward, even if there is enough money to do so.

The substituted consent approach places greater emphasis on the ward's wishes and maximizes the ward's autonomy wherever possible. But the approach does not require total acquiescence. Otherwise, a guardian would hardly be necessary.

The Treatment Contract

Assessing those areas where the client is capable of exercising judgment, even if that judgment results in choices and behavior at odds with the values of the mental health professional, is the first step in involving the client in treatment planning. The second step is to involve the client and the family or guardian in planning for care and treatment. This is best accomplished by having the client, and the family where possible, participate in the development of a treatment contract. At times the wishes and goals of the family may be at odds with those of the client. Even though such differences make the contracting process more difficult than otherwise can be the case, the long-term benefits of involving families outweigh the short-term costs. Families who believe themselves slighted by mental health professionals, and who disagree with the client's treatment, may consciously or subconsciously tend to undercut the best-laid treatment plans.

A **treatment contract** is an agreement following negotiations with the client and the family or guardian about the nature of treatment goals, how these goals are to be achieved, and in what length of time. This agreement with the client represents a philosophy of caring that recognizes, emphasizes, and supports a client's strengths and autonomy. It is important that the client understand the participatory nature of this agreement. The contract has been described as an explicit understanding between social worker and client whose major value is to give

> . . . both the worker and the client a sense of involvement and participation, and it signifies mutual commitment and responsibility. It provides a common frame of reference for the participants so that each one is clear about what is expected of himself and others. It provides a foundation for periodic reviews of progress and next steps (Northern 1982, p. 196).

When, during subsequent interviews, client and worker decide on the next steps, they engage in revising parts or all of the treatment contract.

When we arrive even at a brief informal agreement, we have made a contract. For example, when after a first interview the worker proposes an additional interview in order to determine whether the client could profitably use the agency's services, and when the client agrees to return for that appointment, a contract has, in effect, been negotiated.

The two critical concepts in treatment contracts are **negotiation** and **agreement.** Negotiation signifies that both parties are to play a role in determining the terms of the agreement. This does not mean, of course, that both parties have an equal say. Power is seldom distributed in equal amounts between contracting parties. Sometimes it is the worker who has more input because of specialized knowledge about available care and treatment options. At other times the balance of power may rest with the client and the family. Regardless of the power distribution, however, treatment contracts should be negotiated in good faith on the part of the worker to bring about change that is beneficial for the client. In the helping professions, the client's best interests are foremost, unlike business contracts that tend to favor the party with the greater power.

The second concept, agreement, is sometimes fraught with difficulty when applied in practice. A violent client may have to be restrained for the client's own sake and against his or her wishes. A hospitalized patient who prefers to remain undisturbed in her bed may have to be prodded to participate in activities. A young client who expects his parents to do everything for him may have to be strongly urged to do more for himself, especially when his family is no longer willing to do for him.

Treatment Goals

The process of contract negotiations begins with the setting of short- and long-term goals. Short-term treatment goals for hospitalized patients include alcohol and drug detoxification and controlling the positive symptoms of mental illness. Their long-term goals focus on discharge and often involve an improvement of their social skills.

Goals relating to improved relationships, such as getting along better with family and friends, have to be set as much as possible by clients. Only their motivation to change can bring about desired involvement in this area. Sometimes the worker has to help the client to set clear and attainable goals. For example, one client's expressed goal seemed more like an unrealistic wish, "To have everyone love and respect me." This was boiled down to "To take leadership in the Y Center's women's group by learning to plan and organize one activity for every two weeks, said activity to be jointly determined by me and other group members."

In setting treatment goals, a client's strengths have to be identified. It is easier to achieve goals when we build on a client's strengths than when we try to eliminate weakness or pathology.

Above all, treatment goals must be realistic and fitted to each client's functional capacity. Setting overambitious goals and having excessively high expectations of chronic mentally ill clients will not only end in frustration for the client and the worker but may also contribute to decompensation.

Goals must be **partialized,** or broken down into their component parts. For example, the goal of "achieving good grooming" can be partialized from basic personal hygiene practices to being well dressed and coiffed. Even these goals can be further partialized: "learning to comb and set my hair in curlers," "learning to take a shower each day," and "learning to buy my own clothes." Some clients can work on a number of subgoals at the same time, others only on one.

With the mentally ill, brief and clearly stated agreements fulfill an additional function by serving as reminders of the numerous details relating to their treatment. The following points should be discussed and agreed on.

1. *The nature of proposed interventions.* This may include a specification of medical and psychiatric treatment, rehabilitation therapy, work with the client's family, skill training, drug and alcohol detoxification, and the provision of material resources such as money, clothing, food stamps, and the like.
2. *The place of proposed interventions.* Here the client is told where interventions will take place, such as the hospital, a drop-in center, a welfare office, or the client's home.

3. *The times of proposed interventions.*
4. *The service providers.* Although it is desirable to provide the names of individual service providers, this is not always feasible for large facilities such as hospitals or welfare offices. In such instances the *functions* of the service provider are specified, as "physical therapist," "dietician," "X-ray technician," and so forth.
5. *The length and frequency of interventions.* These might be the length of time that the client is expected to remain in the hospital; the proposed number of family sessions and the length of each session; how often medications are to be taken, and during what times of the day; or how often and when the client should report to the psychiatrist.
6. *Rules the client is expected to follow.* These may be rules pertaining to not using alcohol while on antipsychotic medications, rules applying to weekend passes, house rules, and the like.

On p. 62 is an example of a written treatment contract used at the Midland Psychiatric Hospital for Mrs. Morton, whose case is discussed on p. 66.

One of the worker's most important functions in negotiating treatment aspects is to obtain the client's trust and willing cooperation in what is known as a therapeutic alliance. This can be done by providing information about available service options and helping the client to make choices among them. Often there are alternative medical courses of treatment that are appropriate for a client's condition. Usually several relatively stress-free jobs are available, such as gardening or low-keyed office work, and the client may prefer one over the other. In other situations there may be few options for the client. There may be only one rehabilitation organization in the area, or only one family agency. Nevertheless, even tight situations present some choices. Where there is only one counseling agency, options about hours or times of the week for a client's attendance can be worked out.

When the client and the family have questions that the worker can't answer, the client should be encouraged to go to those who can provide a satisfactory response before choosing a treatment option. For example, psychiatrists should provide explanations about the consequences of antipsychotic medications, including expected benefits, when improvement will be noted, and long- and short-term side effects. They should also discuss with the client the foreseeable consequences of not following a medication regimen or not undergoing electroconvulsive therapy.

Some clients, when confronted with no choice but to accept certain treatment options, may pretend to "go along" in order to achieve a goal of their own, such as discharge from the mental hospital, getting mother to stop nagging, or providing false reassurances to an anxious worker. Some patients who have been involuntarily committed to a psychiatric hospital "get along by going along." They passively accept whatever treatment is imposed on them, biding their time until they can resume their lives where they left off. Some pretend to accept treatment but do not. For example, some patients may

Name: Elizabeth Morton   Date of Admission: 1-6-88

Reasons leading to admission:
   1. Suicide attempt: slashing wrist with broken glass
   2. Depression: thinks life is empty, cannot cope, is unworthy. Cannot get out of bed, refuses to eat, to get dressed
   3. Family problems. Husband denies there is a serious problem. Mother takes care of children, is an alcoholic. Children do not want to talk with mother, feel conflicted about her suicide attempts.

Strengths:
Family: husband seems genuinely caring. There are financial resources. Family lives in comfortable house in good neighborhood. Active members of church and two civic organizations. Children attend school regularly and perform above average.
   Good medical and psychiatric care outside of hospital.
   Mrs. M. is in good physical health, attractive, college-educated, articulate, charming, and energetic when not depressed.
   There is a large network of relatives and friends.

A. Long-term goals leading to discharge:
   1. Patient no longer suicidal, will eat and sleep normally, take care of her personal needs, show an interest in family and life.

B. Long-term, postdischarge goals:
   1. Maintenance medications
   2. Referral for family therapy

C. Short-term goals (to be implemented until 1-17-88 (next 10 days):
   1. Prevent from suicide attempts: one-to-one watch for next two weeks
   2. Get out of bed by 7:30 am, dressed, breakfast by 9 am
   3. Attend women's group daily. Sit throughout length of group meetings
   4. Individual meetings with clinician, every other day, to focus on immediate concerns, family, strengths
   5. Clinician to meet with husband once a week, focus on the impact of patient's illness on him, the children, rest of family
   6. Encourage husband and his mother to attend psychoeducational meetings, next one scheduled to start 1-15

"cheek" unwanted medications by keeping them in their cheeks when pills are distributed, spitting them out at a later time.
   It is important for clients and their families to understand that whatever has been specified in a treatment contract can be renegotiated and changed. Treatment contracts are not engraved in marble. Their specifications are flexible and subject to change under many conditions, such as the client's changing capacity to work toward goals, the effect of agency policies, a change in workers, and the like.

SERVICE DELIVERY POLICIES

Service delivery policies are explicit statements that guide and justify an agency's planned course of action in relation to its goals and directly affect the manner in which services are delivered. The policies discussed in this chapter bear directly on the welfare of chronic mentally ill clients.

CONTINUITY OF CARE

Services aimed to alleviate a problem should be provided as the problem presents itself and as these services are needed. In the case of chronic mental illness, the lengthy nature of the illness requires that services be provided for an indeterminate length of time, for as long as the client needs them, which is likely to be for the rest of his or her life (Hansell 1978). Continuity of care, or the provision of uninterrupted, long-term services, should be a fundamental policy for agencies serving the chronic mentally ill. To do otherwise is a waste of time. It is unrealistic to think that persons who suffer from a chronic and severe mental illness can be restored to normal functioning or "normalized" or "mainstreamed." Clients whose services have been discontinued solely because of agency policies that stipulate short-term or time-limited services will invariably relapse and reapply for services, probably in worse shape than when their cases were closed.

Frequency of Client Contacts

How often clients should be seen by their workers depends on the nature of services and the changing needs of each client. Most clients who participate in daycare programs come to their agencies every weekday. They may be seen daily by their individual worker, or by a succession of group and activity workers. In a crisis, clients may be seen by members of an emergency team on a daily basis, sometimes for several hours at a time. Clients who are managing well and not experiencing problems can be seen for briefer periods over longer periods of time, as is illustrated in the following vignette.

> *Michael Boggs is a 65-year-old, never-married client of the Inland Community Mental Health Center. He developed a schizoaffective disorder relatively late in life, when he was 40 years old. His illness is currently controlled with medications. Boggs supplements his Social Security disability benefits with occasional errands he runs for neighborhood store owners. He has a good relationship with his case manager at the center, but does not care to participate in the center's social and rehabilitational activities. He is an active member of his church and has a number of friends with whom he prefers to spend time. Boggs sees his case manager once a month just to touch base. Sometimes he cancels his appointments. At other times he stops by without an appointment just "to say hello." While his symptoms are under control, the case manager spends relatively little time on Boggs's case, not more than two hours per month including all paperwork. This changes, however, when Boggs decompensates.*

In spite of taking his medications, Boggs experiences decompensations approximately every fifteen months. The onset of his decompensations is heralded by increasing agitation and irritability that culminates in fights with friends and strangers alike. During these times the case manager helps to arrange Boggs's admission to the hospital, mediates between him and those with whom he has picked fights, sees to it that his rent and other bills are paid. The case manager estimates that during these crises she may spend a minimum of 10 hours a week on Boggs's case.

Continuity of Care by One or More Workers

Mentally ill persons who cannot meet the cost of a private therapist are likely to be seen by a number of different therapists over a period of time, while those who can afford it may remain with the same therapist for twenty or more years. Werner Mendel, in his classic book on the treatment of schizophrenia, reports on a chronic schizophrenic patient whom he saw for over sixteen years in his private psychiatric practice. Over this time he followed his patient in and out of the hospital. Acting in the role of case manager, Dr. Mendel helped his patient find an apartment, attend a vocational school, and participate in recreational activities. When the patient was well enough, the psychiatrist helped him find and retain a suitable job (Mendel 1976).

Clients who use public services for an indefinite length of time may be cared for by many different helpers. At its best, continuity of care is represented by such agencies as Fountain House in New York City or Fellowship House in Miami. These are psychiatric rehabilitation centers that are operated on the clubhouse model, where service users are known as members. Although members develop relationships with other members and staff, their primary loyalty is to the organization itself, in which they have a sense of ownership.

OUTREACH SERVICES

Some mentally ill persons, if left alone, isolate themselves from others. This is their way of protecting themselves from life's stresses and preventing decompensation. When a mentally ill person spends hours on end doing nothing, receiving very little stimulation from the environment, it can be said that the person is living in a condition of **social poverty.** As noted by John Wing in his study of hospitalized chronic schizophrenic patients, such social poverty exacerbates schizophrenia's negative symptoms, whereas a "rich social environment tends to minimize the development of negative symptoms in schizophrenia" (Wing 1977, p. 452). This relationship between social functioning and social isolation has also been noted in mentally ill patients who live in the community (Hogarty *et al.* 1973). Hogarty conducted a longitudinal study to isolate the effects of medication with and without social therapies on schizophrenic patients in the community. He noted that patients who received outreach services that reestablished links to others tended to function better than isolates who did not participate in activities but who were taking their medications. These studies underscore the critical importance of outreach, especially for those who cannot make their needs known but who are desperately in need of help. Outreach is an indispensable and integral part of service delivery. But some mental health care providers neglect their outreach responsibilities.

Outreach services are costly because they are labor-intensive. A worker who makes home visits may be able to see only half the number of clients who can be serviced in the office. In addition, agencies providing outreach must add travel expenses, increased insurance, and other out-of-pocket expenses to their budgets. Nevertheless, the additional costs are far outweighed by the benefits in sustaining and rehabilitating chronic mentally ill clients.

Outreach is primarily carried out through home visits, phone calls, and transportation from homes to appointments and activities. Transportation service and scheduled home visits are typical **scheduled outreach** activities. **Unscheduled outreach** comes into play when clients fail to show up for appointments or don't return phone calls. In the case of clients who have given every indication that they want to continue their relationship with the agency, this could present two possibilities. The first is that the symptoms of the client's illness are flaring up and the client may need emergency care. The second is that negative symptoms may be causing withdrawal and isolation. A little encouragement is often enough to help such clients resume their usual activities. The Training in Community Living program (TCL) in Madison, Wisconsin, one of the more successful rehabilitation programs for chronic mentally ill persons, has demonstrated that a little prodding by the outreach worker can make the difference between dependence and autonomy for a client. TCL workers routinely go to the homes of clients a few hours after they have not shown up for work or activities. They remind their clients that they are late. Without recrimination or a show of undue concern, they tell clients to get ready because they will take them to wherever they are supposed to be. Evidently clients do not object and take well to this approach (Test and Stein 1976).

CRISIS INTERVENTION SERVICES

One of the hallmarks of chronic mental illness is the often unexpected decompensation. Decompensation is a crisis for the client, for the family, and for others close to the client. As discussed in chapter 8, these incidents are not only devastating for the client but also potentially dangerous for the client and others.

Agencies must provide services to deal with crises as they arise, including the provision of 24-hour emergency crisis services. Most hospitals and community mental health centers are equipped to provide such services. Other agencies, as for example psychosocial rehabilitation centers, have staff members who are available on 24-hour call. Organizations that provide crisis services should make this widely known in their communities.

INVOLVING CLIENTS AND FAMILIES IN PLANNING AND POLICYMAKING

When agencies involve mentally ill persons and their families on their boards and committees, both agencies and clients stand to gain. Their experience and perceptions are invaluable for fitting services to the needs of agency clients in particular and the mentally ill in general. The contributions of consumers can set the direction for new service delivery policies and enrich existing services.

NIMH strongly supports consumer participation on agency boards. Following are the benefits envisioned by NIMH (Kopolow 1981):

1. The development of innovative programs serving the chronic mentally ill and their families, such as outreach programs staffed and run by clients whose aim would be to attract new clients who either not had heard of the services or were reluctant to ask for help
2. The development of advocacy programs whose aim would be to improve existing services and lobby for new ones
3. Creating an improved image of the mentally ill. Clients who become visible in their communities by actively promoting the welfare of other mentally ill persons gain respect for themselves and their cause.

Usually agencies select their best-functioning clients to participate on boards, committees, fund-raising activities, and the like. There are many stresses involved in leadership and modeling roles and no one wants clients to decompensate as a result of these activities. But there are benefits for those who can "take it." There is raised self-esteem and status for those who can assume leadership and participatory roles. They demonstrate to others, and most importantly to themselves, that they can be instrumental in solving their own problems. They are productive. They are creative. The clinician may not have to look beyond the agency to involve the client in meaningful work and activities that are not only of therapeutic value to the client but also of benefit to others.

FOR DISCUSSION AND THOUGHT

Elizabeth Morton, 30 years old, is married to a fairly prosperous businessman. The couple have two children aged ten and eight. For the past several years Mrs. Morton has been experiencing periods of severe depression. At those times she loses interest in everything, including in her husband and children. Mrs. Morton has made several serious suicide attempts through wrist slashing and medication overdosing. She has had five hospitalizations. Electroconvulsive therapy has restored her each time, but the effectiveness of her treatments has been decreasing.

Mrs. Morton has once again been admitted to the West Coast Psychiatric Hospital. This time she remains depressed, even after a course of electroconvulsive therapy and the administration of antidepressant medication. She is making suicidal gestures such as attempting to strangle herself with her bathrobe belt and jumping off a table head first. The treatment team discusses the following treatment options: the use of restraints, the use of a secluded, "padded" room where Mrs. Morton cannot hurt herself, family therapy, and drastically increasing her medication.

1. In applying the *least restrictive alternative*, discuss the course of treatment—choosing one or more of the above alternatives—that you would suggest for Mrs. Morton.

2. Is there another course of treatment—still bearing in mind the least restrictive alternative—that you would suggest for Mrs. Morton and her family?

Please refer to the case of Roberta Greene (p. 56). As her therapist, you find that you cannot help her change her mind about her will.

3. Discuss the advantages and disadvantages of not doing anything about the situation now, expecting that the will can be contested after Mrs. Greene's death.

4. Discuss the advantages and disadvantages of having a guardian appointed who would see to it that the will is changed during Mrs. Greene's life.

5. Assume a guardian has been appointed. Would you prefer a "best interest" or "substituted consent" approach in selecting her guardian? Give the reasons for your decision.

Recently a number of organizations dealing with the mentally and physically handicapped have been using such terms as *normalization* and *mainstreaming*.

6. How would you define these terms?

7. Are these terms used in the organization where you work or perform your internship or fieldwork? If so, how does your organization define them?

8. Discuss whether these concepts apply to your clients who are chronically mentally ill.

9. If your organization serves the chronic mentally ill, discuss in what manner such services are implemented.

10. If your organization does not serve the chronic mentally ill, discuss why such services are not provided. Are there organizational or other obstacles to providing this service? Could they be overcome?

CHAPTER 5

CLINICAL
DIAGNOSES

A SOUND COURSE of treatment is invariably based on a thorough assessment that is constructed around judiciously collected data. An assessment should include information about the nature and extent of the client's illness, personal strengths and weaknesses, the areas in which the patient can or cannot function, the environment's effect on the patient and the patient's effect on his or her environment—such as family, neighbors, teachers, and others. The process of data collection begins from the time we first learn of the client and continues throughout our contacts with the client, the family, and others who influence the client's life. The biggest push for data collection is during our first contact. For the chronic mentally ill the first contact usually takes place in a hospital's emergency room while the client is in a state of decompensation. In order to start a course of treatment that will help and not harm the client, data collection must proceed rapidly and efficiently. We do so according to a plan lest we overlook important information or waste time probing for irrelevant data.

Assessments should be parsimonious, pared down to essential data. We focus on selected aspects of the client, the illness, and the client's environment. An assessment that emphasizes the client and the client's illness is known as a clinical diagnosis. Those that focus on the client in the context of the social environment are referred to as psychosocial, or social functioning, assessments.

This chapter will discuss the formulation of the clinical diagnosis. Although social workers and other members of diagnostic teams participate in the formulation of a clinical diagnosis, that diagnosis is ultimately the responsibility of the general physician or psychiatrist. Here a client's disability is categorized in conformity with a medical and psychiatric schema. When discussing clinical diagnoses, we tend to use medical metaphors. For example, clients are referred to as "patients" for whom a course of "therapy" is aimed at alleviating "illness" or "pathology." On the other hand, the development of a social functioning assessment is largely the responsibility of the social worker. In such assessments we refer to "clients" for whom we plan "interventions" in order to improve "psychosocial functioning." The latter type of assessment focuses on and emphasizes the client's strengths, while clinical diagnoses usually aim to identify pathology and disability.

ASSESSMENT PRINCIPLES

We follow two practice principles in formulating an assessment. The first is **documentation of facts;** the second is the principle of **identifying clients' strengths.**

DOCUMENTATION OF FACTS

The value of the contributions of various members of a diagnostic team lies in their reporting of their own observations of the patient's condition, the circumstances of the family, and other facts. Sound assessments are based on "hard" facts, those that have been observed and experienced. We should avoid inferences as much as possible, especially when there are few available facts. For example, when a new client falls asleep during the interview, we know only that the client fell asleep. We may *speculate* or infer that the client fell asleep because of substance abuse, lack of sleep, a neurological disorder, or a heavy dose of antipsychotic medications. We may even wonder whether something is wrong with our interviewing techniques! Each such inference is a tentative hypothesis that must be tested before we can draw a meaningful conclusion about the reason for the client's behavior.

We should document hard facts and avoid the use of statements that involve unwarranted or unsupported conclusions. An example is the notation in the case record that a client's home is "filthy" and that does not provide any facts that document the assertion, such as the presence of bad odors, spilled garbage, overflowing toilets, and the like. Without supportive data, the conclusion is uninformative and may represent a worker's biases rather than an actual condition.

Hard fact documentation provides details of what we have seen, touched, and smelled, what the client has told us and what others have communicated

69

to us. Sound documentation is the underpinning for an accurate diagnosis. It is also the keystone of a credible testimony in judicial and official hearings that mental health professionals are often asked to provide, for example in involuntary admissions, requests for Social Security disability insurance (SSDI) payments, placement of children or the termination of parental rights, and the like.

IDENTIFICATION OF CLIENT STRENGTHS

Because the diagnostic process focuses on the discovery and classification of pathology, it contains within it the danger of paying too much attention to signs and symptoms of illness at the cost of overlooking areas of a client's health and strengths. In the helping process we bring about change by mobilizing and enhancing a client's strengths and resources rather than by aiming to eliminate or overcome deficits or weaknesses.

Resources can be identified in a client's environment, in himself or herself, and in his or her interaction with the environment. Environmental resources can be the following:

1. An adequate income
2. A concerned, caring family
3. A pleasant home
4. A good friend
5. A garden
6. A safe neighborhood
7. Good neighbors
8. A neighborhood that is convenient to shopping, churches, recreational activities, and medical and psychiatric care

The following are examples of personal strengths:

1. Aspects of physical health
2. A sense of humor
3. An ability to care for others
4. Religious beliefs
5. An ability to learn
6. Being able to take responsibility for one's actions
7. Being able to form a good relationship with the mental health professional
8. An ability to exercise sound judgment under various circumstances
9. An ability to live adequately within one's income, however limited

An example of the therapeutic use of a client's resources are strategies aimed to help alcoholic clients to stop drinking. Caring and interested family members (environmental resources) are usually enlisted in the helping process. Family, and also friends, are urged to stop making excuses for the alcoholic's drinking behavior and its consequences and to support attendance at

Alcoholics Anonymous and other therapies. The client's personal resources are enlisted, such as love for family, pride in work, and trust in the therapist.

Strengths should be documented just as carefully as deficits and pathology. Otherwise an assessment would be essentially worthless.

THE PURPOSE OF CLINICAL DIAGNOSES

A major purpose of a clinical diagnosis is to develop an impression of a client's physical, emotional, and mental problems and to categorize them in conformity with a medical or psychiatric model. The categorization is derived from a standard reference book such as the International Classifications of Diseases that provides short descriptions of physical illnesses, their diagnostic nomenclature, and numbered identification codes.

The revised *Diagnostic and Statistical Manual of Mental Disorders*, familiarly known as the *DSM-III-R*, is the reference book used for formulating psychiatric diagnoses. *DSM-III-R* provides psychiatric descriptions, labels, and numerical codes for all currently known mental disorders. But a label is only a shorthand description of a client's mental illness. It does not and cannot describe the many facets and nuances of a client's personality, social situation, or unique illness. In fact, as we will see in the next chapter, the use of a diagnostic label can actually confuse the real person with an artifact of categorization. Why then does the mental health system rely so heavily on diagnostic labels?

USES OF DIAGNOSTIC LABELS

There are three reasons diagnostic labels are needed. The first is to legitimate a client's entry into the mental health system and to guide mental health professionals in their choice of intervention. For example, a client cannot be admitted to a psychiatric hospital or partake of community mental health services without being diagnosed and appropriately labeled as "schizophrenic," "mood-disorder, bi-polar affective," and the like. The labeled diagnosis will further guide the treatment team in the development of a treatment plan that may include prescribed medication and other somatic treatment, long- or short-term psychotherapy, hospital or outpatient treatment, rehabilitation services, and the like.

The second reason for assigning diagnostic labels is to help clients to obtain financial and other material help from government and private insurance companies. Labels and diagnostic codes, such as "Schizophrenia, undifferentiated type, 295.9x," are required by governmental agencies and insurance companies to process benefit claims for clients.

Third, military services require mental status evaluations when deciding whether to accept someone for military service. The presence of major mental illness, encoded in a diagnostic label, is likely to excuse a person from military service.

DEVELOPING A CLINICAL DIAGNOSIS

The development of a clinical diagnosis usually includes a mental status examination covering the client's (1) appearance and behavior, (2) level of consciousness, (3) capacity for attention, (4) memory, (5) mood and affect, (6) language, and (7) form and content of thought. Observations within each area give rise to questions, speculations, or hypotheses about the client that call for further investigation. Our initial hypotheses about the client are, by their very nature, highly tentative. They need to be checked and rechecked in order to become grounded in facts.

THE CLIENT'S APPEARANCE

The systematic assessment process begins as we first set eyes on the client. We note appearance as manifested in the way the client dresses, grooms, and manages personal hygiene.

Clothing

Among the first things we notice is the **condition** of the client's clothing. We note whether the clothes are clean and well tended or dirty and torn. Dirty and torn clothing raises questions about a client's access to laundry facilities, the possibility of homelessness, or the client's inability to care for himself or herself in spite of the availability of amenities.

The **appropriateness** of the clothing is important. Is the client wearing several wool sweaters on a hot summer day? Bedroom slippers when going out on a rainy day? Inappropriate clothing alerts us to the possibility that the client does not care about clothing because of depression, distraction, or an inability to exercise good judgment in clothing selection. On the other hand, it is also possible that the client is poor and simply wearing all that he or she owns.

The **quality** of clothing may provide further clues to a client's taste or social class. For example, clients who wear expensive sneakers and accessories may have obtained them in a second-hand shop or from the Salvation Army. But some clients may come from well-to-do families who are able to provide for them.

Grooming and Personal Hygiene

Grooming and cleanliness provide clues about a client's life-style and state of mind. Several tentative hypotheses come to mind when we meet someone who is dirty, unkempt, and malodorous. The client may be a homeless drifter, or else so disabled by illness as to be unable to care for personal needs, such as changing clothes, bathing, and combing.

We observe the condition of the client's hair, complexion, and fingernails. Unusual odors should be noted, such as a strong smell of perspiration, alcohol, or perfume. We begin to speculate on how a client's poor personal hygiene can affect others. Do others recoil from the client's bad body odors? Do they avoid the client? make fun of the client? We keep in mind that persons who present an overall neglected appearance that is compounded by the aura of poor personal hygiene are more likely than others to be picked up by the police and asked to leave shops and restaurants. They also tend to get short shrift from mental health professionals!

LEVEL OF CONSCIOUSNESS

Level of consciousness refers to whether the client is alert, in a stupor, or comatose. We observe how the client reacts to any pain he or she may experience and to what is going on around. We should suspect greater pathology when a client appears to be indifferent to real pain (such as that made by second- or third-degree burns) than when the client complains of pain when no injury is apparent.

ATTENTION

Attention includes two areas: first, the client's ability to concentrate, and second, the client's ability to notice stimuli in all sensory areas, such as smell, vision, and touch.

MEMORY

Testing a client's memory includes the testing of his or her orientation to the here and now and recall of events that happened in the immediate past as well as more remote events. In probing for "here and now" memory we want to know whether a client knows his or her name and age, where he or she is, the time of day, the day of the week, and what year it is. The client's recall of events from the immediate past is tested by asking for a repetition of something said by the examiner and for recalling what happened ten minutes ago.

MOOD AND AFFECT

Describing and Categorizing Mood

In clinical diagnoses we differentiate between mood and affect. A mood is an emotion of long standing that influences how a person perceives the world and, in turn, is perceived by others. We describe people as characterized by their moods when we say "Mary is always cheerful, no matter what," "He is an angry young man," or "That Priscilla is a sourpuss." On the other hand, affect is a fleeting and changeable display of feelings—a more variable manifestation of one's inner states. For example, Mary, who is characterized as generally cheerful (mood) will, at one time or another, be sad, angry, or unhappy (affect).

73

In referring to mood, affect, and the various classes of mental illness we use the nomenclature provided by the *DSM-III-R*, which identifies six moods.

1. The **euthymic** mood is considered to be within normal range. When we describe clients as euthymic we mean that they are not overly depressed, angry, exuberant, or embittered.
2. The **elevated** mood is a more cheerful mood than is usual, but is not necessarily indicative of pathology.
3. The **euphoric** mood consists of extreme and exaggerated feelings of well-being. Euphoric persons are much more than cheerful—they are most of the time exuberant. They appear to exist in a blissful "never-never" land on a long-lasting emotional "high." One of the marks of euphoric persons is that they generally don't let their feelings control their actions as persons with an expansive mood do.
4. Clients characterized by an **expansive** mood act out their exuberant feelings, usually to their own detriment. For example, they may lavishly treat everyone in the house, whether they know them or not, without regard to the expense and their ability to pay. Expansive persons have difficulties in maintaining friendships because they are constantly bragging about themselves and telling tales about the wonderful things they have done and can do. Their insistent self-praise undermines their credibility and tends to turn off an audience.
5. The **dysphoric** mood is a long-lasting "downer" or a persistently depressed state of being. Dysphoric clients are often anxious and worried. They tend to collect grievances, brood on the many injustices that exist in the world and that are done to them, and tend to see a dark side to even the happiest occasion.
6. The **irritable** mood consists of all-encompassing feelings of tension and anger. Irritable persons go through life carrying a chip on their shoulders. They are known for "having a short fuse" or a "low boiling point" and are quick to take offense or pick fights for the most inconsequential matters.

Describing and Categorizing Affect

In evaluating a client's affect we note its appropriateness to a given situation. For example, a client who smiles happily as she discusses the recent death of her young child is displaying an inappropriate affect. An inappropriateness of affect is an important indicator of pathology.

There are five kinds of affect.

1. The **broad affect** is considered to be normal. When we refer to a client as displaying a broad affect we mean that the client will laugh at a funny joke, be serious when important matters are discussed, show concern when a family member is ill, and the like.

2. **Restricted affect** refers to clients who tend to display only a limited repertoire of emotions. They seem unable to laugh heartily, cry bitterly, or shout with joy. But a restricted affect is not necessarily an indication of mental or emotional disturbance. It may merely reflect a client's upbringing, as for example that of upper-class English persons who have learned not to display intense feelings except in the presence of their immediate families or friends.

3. A **blunted affect** is one where the display of emotions is more circumscribed and more difficult to interpret than in persons with a restricted affect. Persons with a blunted affect seem to have a damper on their feelings. Even when they try, they cannot display deep and intensely felt emotions.

4. Many mentally ill are characterized by a **flat affect** that is even more inexpressive than the blunted or restricted affect. There seems to be no variation in their facial expressions, which on the whole appear to be those of a robot that does not respond differently to different situations. Again, a blunted or flat affect may not necessarily be a symptom of mental illness. Either can be the result of antipsychotic medication that produces side effects of zombielike expressions and movements.

5. Finally, there is the **labile affect,** which is characterized by rapid changes in displayed emotions. These are often seen in small children who are laughing at one moment, then crying at the next. Clients with a labile affect can show a rapid change in feelings from one minute to the next.

LANGUAGE

A client's manner of self-expression is one of the factors noted in the mental status examination. Here we note the presence of speech disturbances such as stammering or **echolalia** (a persistent repetition of one's own or the other person's words and phrases), as well as the volume and pressure of speech.

FORM AND CONTENT OF THOUGHT

In testing this area we note how coherently and logically a client is able to express himself or herself and how well the client can pick up a train of thought when interrupted. Often some chronic mentally ill persons are unable to follow a train of thought. They change topics rapidly and seem unable to think a subject through. When the changing topics are somehow connected, their manifestation is known as a **flight of ideas.** But when the changing topics seems to have no connection or underlying rationale, the symptom is known as **loosening of associations.**

In examining a client's thought content, we note the presence, or absence, of such positive symptoms of mental illness as agitation, hallucinations, and delusions.

POSITIVE, NEGATIVE, AND SOCIAL FUNCTIONING SYMPTOMS

We classify symptoms of mental illness into three categories: positive, negative, and social functioning symptoms (Strauss *et al.* 1974). Although these symptoms manifest themselves differently, in line with a person's cultural background, they are nevertheless present and their validity has been established in cross-cultural studies (Moscarelli *et al.* 1987). In the United States, for example, a person may experience an auditory hallucination as the president's voice coming from the television set, whereas in an underdeveloped third-world village the voice may be that of a deceased ancestor emanating from a tree.

Positive symptoms, also referred to as **expressive symptoms,** consist of unusual behaviors that reflect a positive expression of the client's psychotic state. Delusions and hallucinations are prime examples of positive symptoms.

Negative symptoms, also called **deficit symptoms,** include such passive manifestations of mental illness as apathy, listlessness, excessive tiredness, and a short attention span. Negative symptoms are the result of the energy drain caused by the illness. When clients lose much of their interest in the world around them, when they can't seem to concentrate, when their vocabulary becomes diminished and they have problems expressing abstract ideas or complex feelings, they are displaying negative symptoms. The loss of physical energy coupled with the disturbances in thought processes are bound to affect a client's social functioning. Often negative symptoms and problems in social functioning are associated with one another and displayed together. In fact, not long ago social functioning deficits were referred to as negative symptoms. But they are not one and the same.

Social functioning symptoms are the problems that many chronic mentally ill persons have in maintaining and caring for themselves. The most typical problem is an inability to work in the competitive workplace. Other deficits center on the ability to perform a wide variety of housekeeping tasks, relating to others, raising children, shopping, taking care of personal needs, and the use of social, educational, and medical services. Persons who are most seriously ill display severely disabling negative symptoms as well as serious social functioning deficits. It seems that many of the persons who suffer from this symptom combination were raised in conditions of extreme poverty and received little attention and stimulation from their families (Pogue-Gelle and Harrow 1985).

Hallucinations

Hallucinations are distorted or totally unreal sensations experienced as though they were real. These sensations are transmitted through one or several of the five senses: hearing, taste, smell, sight, and touch. Because they

76

seem so real and persistent, and because they are rarely pleasant, hallucinations are the most terrifying experiences for many chronic mentally ill.

DSM-III-R refers to five kinds of hallucinations:

1. **Auditory hallucinations** are most frequently encountered among mentally ill clients. Clients report hearing nonexistent voices clearly and loudly. These voices may talk to them, sing, or just produce nonsensical sounds. The voices can haunt the person from place to place and from day to night. Sometimes the voices tell the client that he or she is unworthy and has sinned. Less frequently voices praise the client, and tell of the great deeds the client will accomplish: "You will save the world from destruction." "You will become emperor of the United States."

   Command hallucinations, or voices ordering clients to kill or harm themselves or someone else are also auditory hallucinations. There is great agreement that clients experiencing command hallucinations should be hospitalized and only released under careful conditions after these symptoms have been controlled.

2. **Gustatory hallucinations** affect the sense of taste. Clients report nonexistent, often unpleasant taste sensations such as tasting spoiled food or dishwater.

3. **Olfactory hallucinations** are connected to the sense of smell. Those who suffer from these symptoms believe they are smelling nonexistent odors, such as noxious gases when the air around them is clear, or the odor of coffee and other foods when these are not around.

4. **Visual hallucinations** consist of seeing nonexistent objects. Pleasant visual hallucinations reported by clients include having clearly seen Christ or an angel; while unpleasant, indeed terrifying, hallucinations are those of shape-changing and threatening demons.

5. **Tactile** or **somatic hallucinations** produce sensations of feeling unreal objects, texture, and temperatures. Clients may feel a wooden table as a freezing block of ice, or their dry bedsheets as wet and slimy.

Delusions

Delusions are illusory beliefs that are only minimally related to external reality. They usually reflect a person's values, fears, anxieties, and wishes. Mild forms of delusions occur in many non–mentally ill persons, as for example delusional jealousy. This is the not uncommon suspicion, bordering on certainty, that one's lover is unfaithful. When delusions are symptoms of mental illness, they pervade a person's thoughts to such an extent that they guide most of the person's actions.

The following three delusions are often encountered among the chronic mentally ill:

1. Delusions of **grandiosity.** These delusions involve an exaggerated belief in one's power and influence. For example, Greta Smith—a 60-

year-old, impoverished, and gravely disabled patient in a nursing home—is firmly convinced that she owns the home and controls what goes on there. Henry Williams, a 40-year-old schizophrenic who was neither able to complete high school nor hold a job, believes that he is engaged to Elizabeth Taylor and that he owns several movie studios in Hollywood. These delusions are comforting. They provide the illusion of mastery and power in an otherwise drab, troubled, and helpless life.

2. On the other hand, **persecutory delusions** and **delusions of reference** can be upsetting and troubling. Clients who experience them believe that objects, persons, and even events single them out for harm and trouble. The following are typical of delusions of reference: Sheila Harmon, a 29-year-old client of Middlestate Community Mental Health Center, believes that when football players go into a huddle they speak about her. Harris Jones, another client of the Center, is not troubled by his delusions of reference. Jones is convinced that a television game show hostess addresses all her remarks to him alone, and, in fact, has promised to marry him.

    Typical of persecutory delusions is the belief of a client that the F.B.I. watches every step he or she takes both day and night and is out to ''get him'' for some monstrous, unspecified transgression.

3. **Delusions of being controlled** have it that one is merely a puppet under the control of someone else's power and will. Some decompensating patients demonstrate this delusion dramatically when they declare that angels, or the devil, speak through them, send messages through them, and control their every act. Some believe that nothing they do is the result of their own will—that an external force guides them and decides their fate.

Because the flare-up of positive symptoms is profoundly disturbing, it is often accompanied by agitated behavior, such as rapid pacing and speech, inappropriate laughter, cursing, hitting, or head banging. Much of this behavior will subside as symptoms are brought under control with medications and other social and medical interventions.

But there are persons with paranoid delusions, who, even though they experience hallucinations and delusions, seem composed and coherent. They may calmly discuss such delusions as enormous harm and persecution by others, and then, when they have enough trust in the therapist, may outline a bizarre plan for ''getting even'' and seeing to it that ''justice is done,'' as illustrated in the following case.

> When Fred Parkman, accompanied by his mother, was brought into the emergency room of the Midtown General Hospital, he was in an acute state of his illness and incoherent. To get information about Fred, the hospital social worker interviewed his mother. Mrs. Parkman calmly told the worker that her son had been in the best of health until treacherous relatives and neighbors be-

gan to persecute him. For example, said Mrs. Parkman, one particular neighbor had put an evil spell on Fred so that all his food turned rancid. Relatives cursed him and took away his money and clothing. Incompetent doctors did not believe her story, and thus made matters worse. Finally, Mrs. Parkman said that she was in the process of bringing legal action not only against neighbors and relatives, but also against doctors, a judge, the hospital chief of service, and the governor of the state. As the interview progressed, it became clear that Mrs. Parkman suffered from a full-blown delusional system. But, because her outward behavior was generally within normal limits, she had never before come to the attention of mental health professionals.

The Current Illness

In our inquiries about a client's current illness, we want to know when and how it began, the conditions that tend to precipitate decompensation, and the family's history of mental and other illnesses. This information is needed both for treatment planning and the prevention of future decompensations.

Conditions Surrounding Onset

Inquiries regarding onset of a mental illness include the following:

1. *Sudden or gradual onset.* We want to know whether the client's first decompensation came like "a bolt out of the blue" or whether symptoms developed gradually and insidiously over a span of months and years.
2. *First appearances.* How did the illness first manifest itself? Was the client agitated? violent? Did the client withdraw from social contacts? stop talking to family and friends? lapse into inertia? What was the nature of the patient's positive symptoms?
3. *Client's living conditions prior to the onset of the illness.* Questions should probe for any pressures and problems in a client's environment that might have triggered the illness. We take note of the client's and the family's social and economic circumstances, the neighborhood in which they live, their relationships with family, friends, individuals, and organizations in the community with a special focus on changes that may have occurred in the year prior to the onset of the illness.

History of Illness

In taking the history of the current illness we essentially note the pattern of decompensations and the nature of its symptoms. The history should include:

1. Age at first onset
2. Date of each decompensation
3. Date and place of each hospitalization

4. Names of attending doctors, if available
5. Medications (by name) and other medical interventions while hospitalized and in the community
6. Side effects, especially which of them the patient can tolerate or is unable to tolerate
7. Any medical intervention that either did not work or seemed to be particularly effective

Family History of Physical and Mental Illness

A history of the family's physical and mental illnesses is obtained from both the patient and members of the family. The following information is needed:

1. Are the patient's parents alive and well? If not well, what ails them? If dead, what did they die of and how old were they at the time of their death?
2. Are siblings, uncles, and aunts alive and well? If not well, what ails them? If dead, what did they die of and how old were they at the time of their death?
3. Are grandparents alive and well? If not well, what ails them? If they are dead, what did they die of and what was their age at the time of death?
4. Does any relative have the same problem that the patient has?
5. Is there any psychiatric, emotional, or medical disorder that several members of the patient's family have?

USING THE DSM-III-R

The data we have gathered so far will be needed to categorize and label the patient's illness. To do so, we have to know how to use the current edition of the *Diagnostic and Statistical Manual of Mental Disorders*, the *DSM-III-R*. This manual represents an effort by the psychiatric profession to arrive at uniform diagnoses—in other words, to assure that when mental health professionals refer to a psychiatric label such as delusional (paranoid) disorder they have in mind similar symptoms and history of the illness.

HISTORY OF THE MANUAL

The current *DSM-III-R* has gone through four previous editions. The first, *DSM-I,* appeared in 1952. That was a relatively short manual designed to be carried in a coat pocket. Because the aim of the first edition was primarily that of arriving at some uniformity in psychiatric nomenclature, it listed mainly the names and categories of mental and emotional disorders. *DSM-II,* published in 1968, was more ambitious. It expanded the listing and description of major mental disorders.

The two third editions, *DSM-III* and its revision, *DSM-III-R,* represent a quantum leap in extensiveness over the two previous editions. The current *DSM-III-R* concerns itself not only with symptoms of mental illness but also with physical illnesses and environmental factors that contribute to a disorder, as well as the client's adaptive social functioning. *DSM-III-R* is explicit in highlighting important features of each psychiatric disorder, such as its essential features, age at onset, impairments that may result from the disorder, predisposing conditions, prevalence among the general population and within the sexes, and its occurrence within families. A wide spectrum of disorders is listed, from the most disabling mental illnesses to the emotional problems most students have, at one time or another, with their studies.[1]

Disorders are classified along five axes. Only the cumulative information drawn from all the axes results in a differential diagnosis. The axes are as follows:

Axis I

Axis I focuses on clinical syndromes plus those conditions that are not attributable to a mental disorder but that nevertheless become the focus of psychiatric attention or treatment.

Clinical syndromes constitute the major mental illnesses and disorders, such as schizophrenic, mood, and delusional disorders. Each of these syndromes is discussed in separate sections where the various types or manifestations of the disorder that are specific to the syndrome are described, listed, and coded. For example, the section on schizophrenic disorders not only discusses the schizophrenic syndrome as a whole, but also its manifestations in such types as paranoid schizophrenia (295.3x), undifferentiated (295.9x), catatonic (295.2x), and the like.

Conditions that are the focus of attention but that do not stem from a mental disorder include the so-called "V" problems such as marital problems (V61.10), parent-child problems (V61.20), other interpersonal problems (V62.81), occupational problems (V62.20), and the like.

Axis II

Axis II deals with personality disorders, including antisocial disorders that are found mainly in adults and occasionally in children and adolescents, as well as developmental disorders that are encountered mainly in children and adolescents.

---

1. Study problems are listed in *DSM-III-R* as "309.23 Adjustment Disorder with Work (Academic) Inhibition. This category should be used when the predominant manifestation is an inhibition in work or academic functioning occurring in a person whose previous work or academic performance has been adequate. Frequently there is also a mixture of anxiety and depression. *Example:* inability to study or to write papers or reports" (p. 331).

Axis III

Axis III is concerned with any physical disorders and conditions that are important to the understanding and treatment of the client. Only physicians are qualified to complete this axis.

Axis IV

Axis IV focuses on the severity of a client's psychosocial stressors during the past year. Stressors are evaluated by the degree of their severity along a seven-point continuum that ranges from none (1) to catastrophic (7). For example, getting a traffic ticket may be seen as a minor (2) stressor while a devastating natural disaster such as a fire that results in the client's losing all possessions and incurring a grave physical injury is evaluated as catastrophic.

An Axis IV evaluation takes into account changes that the stressor precipitated, how much of the stress was under a client's control, and the number of stressors that acted on the client during the past year. For example, we may have a client who has had a longstanding marital conflict (a moderate stressor). That conflict may have cumulated in his learning that his wife had taken a lover (a severe stressor). The couple's decision to embark on a divorce is another stressor. The divorce proceedings may turn into a bitter and acrimonious process (a severe stressor) that results in the client's losing custody of his two children and possession of his home, a further extreme stressor.

Axis V

Axis V evaluates a client's highest level of adaptive functioning during the past year. Ratings are made along a five-point continuum, ranging from Superior (1) through Good (3) to Poor (5). Adaptive functioning is a composite of the client's social relations, occupational functioning, and use of leisure time.

The design of the *DSM-III-R* is that of a decision tree, where a more severe condition must be ruled out first before a less severe disorder is accepted. The decision-tree process first requires that the presence of an organic disorder be ruled out before one can consider the presence of a mental disorder. For example, the presence of a brain lesion can produce hallucinations, loose associations, and other symptoms of mental illness. The treatment of brain lesion disorders is more drastic and quite at variance with the treatment of mental illness. Therefore, the clinician should not assume mental illness without first having ruled out the presence of organic causes. Second, the presence of a chronic psychotic disorder has to be ruled out before a diagnosis of a transient psychotic disorder can be made. Finally, psychotic disorders have to be ruled out before a diagnosis of an emotional disorder can be made.

Because nonphysicians cannot make diagnoses of organic disorders (Axis III), they are also not in a position to make a diagnosis of a mental disorder entirely on their own. When they participate in formulating *DSM-III-R* diagnoses they should do so as members of a diagnostic team, or, at the very least, in consultation with a physician. To do otherwise is not only unethical, but makes nonphysicians vulnerable to malpractice litigations (Kutchins and Kirk 1987).

SCHIZOPHRENIC DISORDERS

The concept of schizophrenia is difficult to define, in part because we still do not have the technology to diagnose the illness accurately through the presence of clear-cut physical symptoms, such as identifiable abnormalities in the brain. We primarily diagnose schizophrenia from a person's behavior and reaction to antipsychotic medications. To make matters more difficult, signs and symptoms of mental illness differ from one person to another so that each presents us with a unique expression of the illness.

Historical Definitions

One of the first to grapple with the definition of schizophrenia was the physician Kraepelin (1919). Kraepelin, who studied only hospitalized patients, observed that the illness predominantly made its first appearance when the patients were fairly young, in their teens or early twenties. Therefore he called the illness **dementia praecox,** or the insanity of the young. Kraepelin also noted that as the illness progressed, each decompensation left patients increasingly impaired, particularly in their ability to think and to relate to the world around them.

Later, the Swiss physician Bleuler (1950) renamed dementia preacox **schizophrenia** and broadened its previous definition. Bleuler also studied hospitalized patients, and did not follow the careers of numerous persons who were discharged into the community, in line with the policies of Swiss mental hospitals at the turn of the century. Bleuler's diagnostic concept was based on the "Four A's": (1) Loosening of *associations,* (2) flatness of *affect,* (3) *ambivalence,* and (4) *autism.* He included in his "group of schizophrenias" mild manifestations of the illness—such as acute decompensations that may have occurred only once during a patient's lifetime, with relatively little impairment—as well as the severe, recurrent, debilitating form we now know as chronic schizophrenia. Bleuler's broad, inclusive definition stirred up many debates around the causes of schizophrenia, its treatment, and the signs and symptoms that distinguish it from other disabilities. At one extreme of these debates are those who claim that schizophrenia is really not an illness, but a sheer construct used by society to control deviants (Szasz 1961).

Today, clinicians and serious researchers generally agree that schizophrenia is an illness but that it cannot be diagnosed from one psychotic episode alone. A diagnosis of the illness can be made only from a pattern of schizophrenic signs and symptoms as displayed over a period of time. The usual course of schizophrenia is marked by acute episodes presenting such symptoms as delusions, hallucinations, incoherence, illogical thinking, and disorganized behavior. These episodes, also known as the "active phase" of the illness, leave most but not all patients increasingly impaired.

Decompensations are usually followed by a **residual phase,** where the psychotic symptoms have subsided. Some symptoms, such as loosening of associations, may persist but in a less severe form. In the residual phase many persons show a flat affect and an impairment in some area of functioning. Some regularly attend and perform satisfactorily in school prior to a decompensation; and yet for many school attendance may become irregular and their schoolwork may deteriorate even during the residual phase. The diagnosis of schizophrenia requires a broad, biopsychosocial perspective that concerns itself not only with patients' signs and symptoms but also with their social functioning over time (Carpenter 1987).

Current DSM-III-R Criteria

DSM-III-R defines schizophrenia more narrowly than the first two editions. This was in part a response to the fact that American psychiatrists used to overdiagnose schizophrenia. Where British psychiatrists diagnosed depressive or bipolar disorders, American doctors tended to diagnose schizophrenia. The overdiagnosis also turned out to be, for many patients, the wrong diagnosis. The incorrect treatment these patients received actually made their condition worse (Pope 1983).

Another important but controversial change in *DSM-III-R*'s diagnosis of schizophrenia is the stipulation that the illness inevitably involve a deterioration from a previously higher level of functioning. This criterion will probably be changed in the next edition. It has been disputed in a thirty-year longitudinal study known as "The Vermont Study" (Harding *et al.* 1987). Researchers involved in that study contacted 118 patients from the Vermont State Hospital who had been released to the community during the first wave of deinstitutionalization in the mid-1950s. While hospitalized the study group had been seriously ill, "backwards," poorly functioning patients, most of whom had been diagnosed as suffering from schizophrenia. After being released from the hospital, all ex-patients were provided with individualized community care services so that they were not just "dumped" onto an indifferent community.

With the help of the patients' original, extensive hospital case records, the researchers rediagnosed them using current, stringent criteria. The surprising finding of the Vermont study is that one-half to two-thirds of the patients did not continue to deteriorate but actually improved from their functioning level of thirty-two years ago! About one-fifth did not need rehospitalization, and almost one-half had held relatively stress-free jobs such as custodians.

The current manual has changed schizophrenia from a catchall diagnosis to a more precise diagnostic entity. In fact, the new diagnosis is so stringent that many patients who have positive symptoms of schizophrenia but have not met other criteria, such as the minimum six months duration, cannot be given the diagnosis and thus are excluded from receiving financial and other benefits (Andreasen 1987).

Conditions with a more favorable prognosis that were previously considered schizophrenic now have a different classification. For example, when a person does not exhibit a recurrent pattern of psychotic symptoms the illness may be classified as a **schizphreniform disorder.** Disorders that are characterized only by a withdrawal from others and disturbed thinking may currently be classified as **personality disorders,** such as paranoid or schizoid personality disorders.

The current diagnosis of schizophrenia requires

1. that schizoaffective disorders and mood disorders with psychotic features first be ruled out
2. the presence of characteristic psychotic symptoms during the active phase such as delusions, hallucinations, loosening of associations, catatonic behavior, or flat or grossly inappropriate affect
3. continuous signs of the disturbance for at least six months
4. a deterioration from a previous level of functioning
5. an onset that usually occurs during adolescence or childhood
6. an impairment in daily functioning

Types of Schizophrenic Disorders

Five types of schizophrenic disorders are listed: (1) catatonic, (2) disorganized types, (3) paranoid, (4) undifferentiated, and (5) residual.

Diagnostic criteria for the **catatonic type** center on various manifestations of catatonia: stupor (a marked decrease in reactivity to the environment and/or reduction in spontaneous movements and activity) or mutism; negativism (an apparently motionless resistance to all instructions or attempts to be moved); rigidity (maintaining a rigid posture against efforts to be moved); excitement (apparently purposeless excited motor activities); and posturing (voluntarily assuming inappropriate or bizarre postures) (*DSM-III-R* 1987, p. 196).

The **disorganized type** is characterized by "incoherence, marked loosening of associations or grossly disorganized behavior, and, in addition, flat or grossly inappropriate affect" (p. 197). Patients with catatonic and disorganized types of schizophrenia have the greatest difficulties in functioning. They often need help with many basic activities, such as getting in and out of bed, getting dressed, using toilet facilities, and eating nourishing food.

There are two diagnostic criteria for **paranoid type** schizophrenia: "A. Preoccupation with one or more systematized delusions or with frequent auditory hallucinations related to a single theme, and B. *None* of the following: incoherence, marked loosening of associations, flat or grossly inappropriate affect, catatonic behavior, grossly disorganized behavior" (p. 197). The case of Mrs. Parkman, described on page 78, is typical of this disorder.

In diagnosing an **undifferentiated type** of schizophrenia the patient must not meet the criteria for paranoid, catatonic, or disorganized type but has "Prominent delusions, hallucinations, incoherence, or grossly disorganized behavior" (p. 198).

Choosing the **residual type** diagnosis rules out "prominent delusions, hallucinations, incoherence, or grossly disorganized behavior" but requires "continuing evidence of the disturbance, as indicated by two or more of the residual symptoms listed in criterion D of Schizophrenia" (p. 198).

MOOD DISORDERS

Mood disorders are severe mood disturbances that are accompanied by manic or depressive episodes that harmfully affect a patient's behavior. *DSM-III-R* lists two categories of mood disorders, bipolar and depressive.

Bipolar Disorders

Previously known as "manic-depressive" and "bipolar affective," **bipolar disorders** are typified by the presence of both depressions and manias.

Manic Episodes

To diagnose a **manic episode** there must be a "distinct period of abnormally and persistently elevated, expansive, or irritable mood." During such episodes a person may talk excessively, become increasingly active, and need less sleep and rest. At the height of the manic episode the person usually feels elated, "on top of the world," and full of energy.

To classify as pathology the mood disorder must be so severe as to "cause (a) marked impairment in occupational functioning or in usual social activities or relationships with others, or to necessitate hospitalization to prevent harm to self or others" (p. 217). In this condition a person may believe that he or she is invincible and omnipotent. The patient may buy two or three expensive new cars at a clip, give away all of his or her clothes, quit his or her job, or stay up all night furiously writing voluminous diaries or books.

The "Chinese menu" part of the diagnostic criteria for a manic episode requires at least three of the following seven symptoms to be present (p. 217):

1. Inflated self-esteem or grandiosity
2. Decreased need for sleep
3. More talkative than usual or pressure to keep on talking
4. A subjective experience that thoughts are racing
5. Easily distractable
6. Increase in goal-directed activity either socially, at work, or at school, or psychomotor agitation
7. Excessive involvement in pleasurable activities that have a high potential for painful consequences

Depressive Episodes

With the subsidence of the manic state a period of equilibrium may ensue during which the person returns to normal functioning. This state, however, usually does not last very long. It is often followed by a **depressed** state, during which the person loses interest in life, cannot experience pleasure, and feels worthless. At the bottom of the depressed state the person may experience delusions, feel hated by everyone, believe that he or she is the ugliest person in the world, that food will rot in his or her mouth. In such a state a person may become immobilized, mute, irritable, and morose.

To make diagnosis of a bipolar disorder, *DSM-III-R* stipulates that the criteria for both a manic episode and a major depressive episode be met. Diagnostic criteria for **major depressive episodes** stipulate that they neither be the result of organic problems nor of a patient's normal depressive reaction such as the death of a loved one. Delusions or hallucinations should not last for more than two weeks. At least five of the following nine symptoms must be present (p. 222):

1. A depressed mood
2. Markedly diminished interest in pleasure in life
3. Significant weight loss
4. Daily insomnia or hypersomnia (sleeping too much)
5. Daily psychomotor agitation or retardation
6. Daily fatigue or loss of energy
7. Feelings of worthlessness, guilt
8. A daily diminished ability to concentrate
9. Recurrent thoughts of death

PSYCHOTIC DISORDERS NOT ELSEWHERE CLASSIFIED

If the signs and symptoms of a person's mental illness do not fit into the classification of organic mental disorders, schizophrenia, mood disorders, or delusional disorders, we check the category "psychotic disorders not elsewhere classified." This class contains four particularly significant diagnostic categories: schizophreniform disorders; brief reactive psychosis; schizoaffective disorders; and induced psychotic disorders. There is also a residual category, **atypical psychosis,** that is reserved for disorders that do not meet the criteria of any other specific psychotic disorder.

A person who meets all the diagnostic criteria for schizophrenia except for duration of the illness may be diagnosed as having a **schizophreniform disorder.**

A **brief reactive psychosis** describes the sudden onset of a psychotic disorder that should be present for at least a few hours but not more than two weeks. This disorder can be brought on by major life stresses or crises that would cause some distress to anyone. After the passing of this disorder, there is a complete return to the previous level of functioning. The following vignette illustrates this disorder.

> Sarah Major, a 22-year-old college junior, became pregnant by a classmate with whom she did not wish a further relationship. She decided to have an abortion. Shortly after she made the decision and arranged for the abortion, Sarah hallucinated the presence of her dead grandmother, who urged her not to have the abortion. Sarah went to see a therapist at the college's counseling center. She told the therapist that she had seen and heard her grandmother very clearly. She experienced profound dread at the presence of this "vision," but nevertheless decided to go through with her decision. Sarah never had a recurrence of her "vision," but to this day insists that she had seen and talked with her grandmother.

A **schizoaffective disorder** "represents one of the most confusing and controversial concepts in psychiatric nosology" (*DSM-III-R* p. 208). In the earlier *DSM-III* this was the only listed disorder that did not include specific diagnostic criteria because the manual's author could not reach an agreement on its typical characteristics. In the current manual, schizoaffective disorder is classified as a condition whose characteristics are almost like those of schizophrenia, or of a mood disorder, and which is not caused or maintained by an organic condition. Current diagnostic criteria include the following:

A. A disturbance during which, at some time, there is either a Major Depressive or a Manic Syndrome concurrent with symptoms that meet the A criterion of Schizophrenia.

B. During an episode of the disturbance, there have been delusions or hallucinations for at least *two weeks*, but no prominent mood symptoms.

C. Schizophrenia has been ruled out, *i.e.* the duration of all episodes of a mood syndrome has not been brief relative to the total duration of the psychotic disturbance (p. 210).

The classification of **induced psychotic disorder** is more familiarly known as "folie à deux" or a "shared paranoid disorder." The disorder typically results from a close relationship between two or more persons, one of whom has a mental disorder, usually of a paranoid type. The important aspect of the relationship is that the non-mentally ill person begins to accept the other's delusional system, making it his or her own. The following case history exemplifies this condition.

> Henry and Samantha Harris have been married for 40 years. They have worked their own produce farm since the time of their marriage. An only son, Tim, now 36 years old, is a minister who lives several states away from his parents and who has not seen them for five years. When he recently visited them he found that both parents had isolated themselves from friends and neighbors. Both now believe that aliens have taken over Earth and are poisoning all food and water supplies. Mr. and Mrs. Harris eat only what they themselves grow.

They distill their water several times before using it for cooking and drinking. They did not want to let Tim into the house, fearing that he had become contaminated by the alien invaders.

SUMMARY

As every experienced clinician knows, it is a rare client who can be neatly diagnosed in one category or another. Most clients who present a mixture of symptoms are known as "dual-diagnosed" patients. Dual diagnoses may include such combinations as schizophrenia *and* mental retardation or substance abuse. Mentally ill persons who are also substance abusers pose especially vexing problems in diagnosis. It is difficult, if not impossible, to tell whether their symptoms are the result of substance abuse or whether, and how, substance abuse symptoms overlie and exacerbate a mental illness.

There are other problems in formulating an accurate diagnosis. One is predicting the future course of the illness. An accurate prediction of future behavior for any individual is always difficult. It is especially difficult when we deal with the uncertainties of mental illness. Yet predictions about the future course of a mentally ill client's illness must be made. They aid in the development and implementation of long-term treatment plans and in securing of financial and other material benefits, and they are frequently required in legal proceedings, such as involuntary commitment hearings, where the law requires that future dangerousness be predicted, and the like. This and other problems inherent in the diagnostic process are discussed in the next chapter.

CHAPTER 6

PROGNOSES AND
RELATED PROBLEMS

A PREDICTION OF the likely course of an illness or the outcome of contemplated treatment is called a **prognosis.** Since predictions importantly influence treatment plans, they should be included in all clinical assessments. Our treatment strategies will be different for persons who have a high likelihood of relapse than for others whose mental illness is not as severe. We plan differently for persons who are more likely not to take their medications as prescribed, for those who have a high likelihood of acting out, and for those who may withdraw from all human contact.

In practice prognoses, though made on the basis of experience and research findings, are often merely educated speculations. There are very few 100 percent certain predictors, although some prognostic factors, particularly those based on extensive experience and research, lead to greater accuracy than others. Since research on outcomes of the treatment of chronic mental illness is relatively new, predictions of who will benefit from which treatment under what conditions should be always made tentatively and with caution.

PREDICTING THE LIKELIHOOD OF RELAPSE

Five factors seem to differentiate patients with a high probability of relapse from others—all of which should be taken into account in the development of a prognostic statement:

1. Noncompliance with taking antipsychotic medications
2. A pattern of previous relapses
3. Acceptance of the sick-patient role
4. The nature of the onset of the illness
5. A highly critical and intrusive family

The weightiest factor is a patient's compliance with the antipsychotic medication regimen.

MEDICATION COMPLIANCE

One reason for the phenomenon of "revolving door" patients, who go in and out of the hospital, is noncompliance in the use of medications. In the hospital the patient is restored from an active psychotic state to a condition of stability: delusions, hallucinations, and agitation subside. The patient is then discharged. However, should the patient fail to take prescribed antipsychotic medication, there is a very high likelihood of decompensation and rehospitalization. Studies show that where antipsychotic medication is withdrawn from persons who had been successfully maintained on it, more than seven out of ten will experience a relapse within the year (Anderson *et al.* 1986; Hogarty *et al.* 1976; Johnson *et al.* 1983).

The regular use of antipsychotic medications is the most effective and potent way to restore and stabilize the functioning of the majority of chronic mentally ill persons. There are, however, exceptions to this general rule. About one-third of all mentally ill persons who are on antipsychotic medications will relapse within the year. At the same time, a few mentally ill persons who are not on medication may not relapse for over a year or more (Hogarty *et al.* 1974; Hogarty 1984; Van der Kolk & Goldberg 1983). Although the reasons for these paradoxical outcomes are not yet fully known, there is increasing evidence that those who tend to relapse even when they are on good medication regimens suffer from a more severe form of mental illness, a lack of social supports, and more characterological disturbances than others who do not relapse as often (Keefe *et al.* 1987).

HISTORY OF RELAPSE

The best predictor of future behavior is a pattern of past behaviors. Those who have shown a pattern of violent acting-out behavior in the past tend to repeat their violent acting out (Monahan 1984). This also tends to be the case in the flare-ups of positive symptoms of mental illness. Those who in the past have experienced decompensations that necessitated hospitalization will, in all likelihood, decompensate again. Kirk's (1976) review of studies that examined relapse factors among the mentally ill concluded that patients who are susceptible to frequent relapses tend to continue this pattern, regardless of the care with which their medication is administered and in spite of compliance with medical and social interventions.

The frequency and severity of a person's past relapses is also an indicator of the severity of illness. The more seriously ill persons will have had more admissions to mental hospitals in the same period of time than others who are judged to be less seriously ill (Strauss and Carpenter 1977). The patient who has been hospitalized ten times within the past two years is considered to have a more severe form of illness than the patient who has the same diagnosis but who has had only two hospital admissions during the same time. For hospital workers this is an important datum: the more severely ill patients tend to need longer periods of hospitalization before they are restored than those with less severe forms of illness (Moller *et al.* 1986).

The prognosis is quite poor for those who have had 40 or more hospital admissions during their lifetime necessitated by psychiatric decompensations (Geller 1986). Many of these persons may not be able to function at all outside of an institution. In all likelihood their illness has undercut most of their coping capacities so that they require the structure of an institution for the rest of their lives. Long-term relief from illness flare-ups is unlikely for these seriously ill persons.

ACCEPTANCE OF THE SICK-PATIENT ROLE

Some persons dislike everything connected with being sick. These patient-role refusers take to bed only as a last resort, when they can no longer remain upright. They tend to accept medical care only when they are sure that it will hasten their recovery and prefer not to be ministered and fussed over by others. If slightly improved, these sick-role refusers bound out of bed or sign themselves out of the hospital and attempt to return to their daily activities.

Some chronic mentally ill persons are sick-patient-role refusers. They tend to resist being hospitalized, preferring to be treated as outpatients. But once hospitalized, they want to be discharged as soon as possible. In order to achieve their goal they will follow their psychosocial treatment program because they want to feel better and resume their lives outside the hospital as expeditiously as they can. Still, they often draw the line at taking part in recreational and social activities that seemingly don't contribute to a rapid restoration of their health. A one-year longitudinal study of chronic mentally ill patients in a large Veterans Administration hospital found that sick-role refusers were far less likely to be rehospitalized than patients who participated actively in ward activities and community-based therapies (Fontana and Dowd 1975).

Sometimes sick-role refusers are regarded as "difficult" by mental health professionals. They may question and even challenge the expertise of their helpers and the efficacy of their prescriptions. This is not to suggest they tend to refuse to take their antipsychotic medications. On the contrary. Their desire to return to a normal state as soon as possible impels many to accept their medications in spite of distressing side effects.

Sick-role refusers are less likely to be readmitted to mental hospitals than "good patients" or those who in the hospital tend to do what they are told to do, who are more interested in recreational than in therapeutic programs, and who want to be catered to as much as possible (Brown *et al.* 1972; Fontana and Dowd 1975).

One explanation for the good prognoses of sick-role refusers is that they are unwilling to accept the "secondary gain" advantages that are inherent in the patient role. Those who are perceived as "sick" are allowed a rest from work, school, paying bills, cleaning the house. When bedbound, their meals are brought to them and they become the focus of attention. These secondary gains often outshadow the pleasures of being well and reinforce the continuation of the sick-patient role.

CONDITIONS SURROUNDING THE ONSET OF THE ILLNESS

Mental illness sneaks up stealthily on some, and with others it suddenly makes its first manifestation like a "bolt out of the blue," quite unexpectedly. It first appears in some persons when they are in their teens, while in others it surfaces at a later age. Both the nature of its first onset and the age when it occurred are powerful indicators of the severity of the illness and prognostic factors (Falloon 1984; Moller *et al.* 1986; Westermeyer and Harrow 1984).

Persons who have had a slow, imperceptible onset are more at risk than those who experienced the sudden one. Where the first signs are insidious, such as lessening attention span, growing irritability, desire to seclude oneself, a gradually increasing neglect of one's personal appearance and responsibilities, the illness will also tend to be more severe and long-lasting. The severity of an illness is judged by the strength and persistence of both its positive and its negative symptoms.

The earlier the first appearances, the more serious the illness is likely to be. An early appearance affords the chance to do more psychic damage and to interrupt the crucial growth and development that takes place during the teen years and early twenties. A person whose crucial early development is interrupted by the onset of mental illness will be less likely to "catch up" and function as well as those whose illness appears in their thirties or later, when they have already learned the skills that are needed to get along in their world.

"Expressed Emotion" in the Family

The classic studies of Brown and colleagues (1972) demonstrate that there tends to be a high relapse rate for patients who have extensive face-to-face contact with their families (over 35 hours per week), who are dissatisfied with them and frustrated by them, and who express this with criticism. Patients with such families are more at risk than those who spend less time with families that are more accepting and tolerant. The overinvolvement of families with their mentally ill members is familiarly known as the *E.E.,* or expressed emotion, factor. This factor, which is discussed in more detail in chapter 15, is currently under much debate. On one hand, advocates for the families of the mentally ill claim that expressed emotion is a spurious phenomenon that is used by mental health professional to continue to blame families for the mental illness of its members (Hatfield *et al.* 1987). On the other hand there are those who believe that the many controlled studies on the effects of expressed emotion are persuasive enough to be a valid predictor of the course of mental illness (Mintz *et al.* 1987).

A Nonpredictive Factor: Hospital versus Community Functioning

There is a factor, once in vogue, that should no longer be regarded as valid. This is the prediction of a person's functioning in the community on the basis of functioning in the hospital, especially during a first hospitalization. A major review of studies that followed the behavior of hospitalized mentally ill persons from hospital to the community concluded that no relationship existed between behavior in these two different settings (Anthony *et al.* 1978). Some persons who were quiet and compliant in the hospital tended to act out in the community and were noncompliant with medication and other psychosocial interventions. Others who were oppositional in the hospital had a good record of treatment compliance in the community. Still others acted in the community as they did while hospitalized.

This should not surprise us. Mental hospitals and other closed institutions are self-contained worlds where residents give up their freedom to come and go as they like in return for prepared meals, shelter, routine, and the provision of medical care. Staff approves of "good" patients and openly rewards them just as it overtly disapproves of patients who don't follow the rules. Rarely does a client receive this kind of care, attention, and reinforcement in the community. Some clients who flourish in a hospital setting can't manage in an open, unstructured community setting. Unless we have a record of a patient's pattern of posthospital adjustment, we cannot predict from hospital adjustment how a patient will function in the community.

PROBLEMS PRESENTED BY CLINICAL DIAGNOSES

It is a serious matter to classify persons who suffer from mental and emotional problems by assigning them a diagnostic label that will determine where, by whom, and how they will be treated. We assume that diagnoses will be made by expert professionals with thoughtfulness, care, and sensitivity. But not all professionals who develop diagnoses are equally competent.

CARELESSNESS AND OVERMEDICATION

A recent study of the diagnostic practices at the Manhattan State Psychiatric Hospital in New York City has produced troubling findings of misdiagnoses (Lipton and Simon 1985). The researchers in that study set out to review the charts and reexamine and reevaluate the diagnoses of 131 randomly selected mentally ill patients. Among the findings was the fact that 80 percent of the case records did not contain documentation that could justify patient's diagnoses. For example, the presence of schizophrenia was documented with only one or two criteria instead of the minimum six as specified by the *DSM-III*. In the process of reexamining patients and stringently following accepted diagnostic criteria, the researchers found that only 16 of 89 diagnoses of schizophrenia were valid. The other, misdiagnosed patients actually suffered from mood disorders, organic conditions, and other disorders.

Why such a remarkably high incidence of wrong diagnosis? One explanation is the careless way in which clinical assessments were made. Mental health professionals are often called on to process too many cases in too short a time. Instead of resisting and protesting their overload assignments, they try to do the best they can with too much in too short a time. The result is less care and attention to the many and complex problems presented by each person.

There is also the problem of overmedication. Patients in Manhattan State and other psychiatric hospitals are often routinely overmedicated in order to manage them more effectively, calm them, and make them easier to care for. But heavy doses of antipsychotic medication not only injure the patient, they also mask the symptoms and signs of the illness, which tends to make accurate diagnosis more difficult.

Three additional factors are associated with misdiagnoses: the YAVIS, labeling, and diagnostic-trends factors, all of which exert a subtle but powerful impact on diagnoses and social functioning assessments.

THE YAVIS FACTOR

Every practitioner has some clients who are preferred over others. Clients who are perceived as cooperative, motivated to change, and interesting are often the favorites. Most likely they are bright, not too old, articulate, and attractive. They may even validate the practitioner's expertise by showing more improvement than do other clients. The acronym commonly used to describe these clients is YAVIS: Young, Attractive, Verbal, Intelligent, and Successful.

This acronym was coined by a sociologist who observed a remarkable attraction of therapists to this group of clients (Schofield 1964). Schofield noted that most of the YAVIS clients were young, single women who were fairly sophisticated city dwellers. None were seriously mentally ill. These are the "walking worried," or persons who tend to be pleasant to work with, enhance a therapist's self-image, and are able to pay the going fee. In turn, they receive the best prognoses and treatment.

Link and Milcarek refer to the YAVIS's preferential treatment as the Matthew Effect (1980). According to the Gospel of St. Matthew, "Whosoever hath, to him shall be given, and he shall have more abundance; but whosoever hath not, from him shall be taken away even that he hath." In their extensive study of hospitalized patients, Link and Milcarek found that the closer a patient approaches the YAVIS configuration, the more likely that patient is to receive attention from mental health professionals to the detriment of less attractive patients, who may have more serious mental disabilities and are more in need of care and attention. The limited resources of the hospital were allocated to those who needed them the least.

YAVIS clients tend to belong to a higher socioeconomic class than do the sicker, poorer, and more difficult clients. Many studies, beginning with the research of Hollingshead and Redlich (1958), have shown that clients from lower social classes tend to be diagnosed as having more severe mental illnesses than those who come from higher social strata. Thus a discriminatory sequence of events occurs. Attractive and affluent clients are assigned relatively mild diagnoses and good prognoses and receive more attention and better treatment. Unattractive, poor, inarticulate, and difficult clients tend to be diagnosed more pessimistically, receiving poorer prognoses and treatment.

THE SCHEFF AND SZASZ LABELING THEORIES

The assigning of diagnostic labels remains a controversial issue that first emerged during the 1960s. One of the originators of the labeling concept was Thomas Scheff (1966), a sociologist who theorized that psychiatric labels help to maintain or even cause mental illness by creating a self-fulfilling prophecy of illness and disability. Scheff argued that a person who is assigned a mental illness label such as "schizophrenic" will be treated as sick and incompetent. In turn, that person will begin to act more and more mentally ill. The label itself has created an effect.

Scheff believed that mental illness is merely a form of deviance from societal norms. People who behave bizarrely and unpredictably may not be breaking laws, but their behavior is clearly out of line with social expectations. A society that is unable to tolerate persons who behave unpredictably and bizarrely yet is unwilling to press criminal charges against them will solve its dilemma by referring to them as mentally ill. In turn, the mental illness label will determine the labelee's self-image and guide the manner in which others will relate to him or her.

Scheff further postulated that when an allegedly mentally ill person wanted to break away from the assigned role and act as other people do, this desire to change would be thwarted by powerful, complex social forces of reward and punishment. The would-be "healthy" person would be haunted by the mental illness label when trying to get a good job, get married, enlist in the armed forces, or join a social club. However, the person will be rewarded for staying in his sick role with financial, medical, and other social support. The Scheff theory concludes that the "mentally ill" person who realizes that society has made it impossible to become "normal" will not only revert to deviant behavior but will also tend to find solace by acting progressively worse.

Understandably Scheff's theory, also known as the Societal-Reaction Theory, caused much debate among mental health professionals. In 1961 Thomas Szasz, a psychiatrist, published his notion that there was no such entity as mental illness but merely a "myth." Unlike a "real" illness, it has no organic manifestations such as fevers, rashes, measurable blood disorders, and the like. Szasz concurred with Scheff that mental illness is nothing more or less than deviant and unusual behavior that society needed to control. The forms of control are mental hospitals and other institutions where the mentally ill can be segregated, often for an indefinite period. Szasz advocated the total abolishment of psychiatric labels for the "so-called" mentally ill who were, in reality, only experiencing "problems in living" (Szasz 1963).

The Szasz-Scheff theory especially appealed to those who, during the turbulent 1960s, were eager to attack any systematic approach to social and personal problems that they regarded as reflective of the values of "the establishment." They gladly accepted an approach that suggested that the mental health establishment and its concepts was part of a malignant conspiracy to institutionalize those who were deviant, bizarre, and a nuisance to society. As the seductive notions of myth and labeling took hold of the popular imagination, sociologists, anthropologists, and other social scientists began to examine the ideas and attempted to sort out the truths, the half-truths, and the nontruths implicit in this bold attack on the mental health system.

One of the first to attack Scheff's theory was Walter Gove (1970), a sociologist who submitted Scheff's theory to a factual analysis and found it substantially invalid (1970). Later, a compelling analysis was presented by anthropologist Jane Murphy (1976).

Murphy reasoned that if Scheff's theory were valid, mental illness either would not exist or would not take the same form in isolated preindustrial societies that have not yet learned to apply our diagnostic labels. Her investigations led her to the isolated villages of Eskimo and Egba Yoruba tribes. Members of these tribes had not been exposed to Western psychotherapeutic approaches and knew nothing about mental illness labels.

After members of the studied tribes learned to trust her, they introduced Murphy to persons who acted oddly and unpredictably, who heard nonexistent voices, and who were unable to get along with others. One such person

97

was a young man who would not clean himself or conform to the rules of his clan. He spent most of his time on an anthill outside of the village. This man, and others like him, exhibited the signs and symptoms of schizophrenia. The tribe members had never heard of "schizophrenia" but they clearly considered such persons crazy, not merely deviant.

Murphy also found that the incidence of mental disorders in the groups she studied was about the same as it is in our culture. She concluded that "Rather than being simply violations of the social norms of particular groups, as labeling theory suggests, symptoms of mental illness are manifestations of a type of affliction shared by virtually all mankind" (Murphy 1976, p. 1027).

Another study tested the proposition that the mental illness label prevents the labelee from breaking out of the mold and changing life-style (Weinstein 1983). It was reasoned that when labeled persons feel unhappy enough about their assigned mental illness role to the point that they tried to break away from it, they would bitterly resent not only the label but also their role and the treatment accorded to them by mental health workers. The study reviewed other mentally ill persons, who were directly interviewed about their feelings about having been assigned a psychiatric label, about their patient role, and about receiving mental health services. According to the findings, most mentally ill persons did not feel stigmatized by their labels or their illness. Their attitude toward mental illness was actually more favorable than that of nonpatients. Moreover, they did not believe that any significant obstacles had been placed in their way when they tried to resume normal activities. If there is a stigma attached to a mental illness label, it is transitory, posing no serious problems to the labelee.

But, even though the Szasz-Scheff labeling contentions have been shown to be invalid, it must be acknowledged that labeling can create problems. Two problems are prominent: reification and differences in interpreting the same concept.

Reification: The Incarnation of a Concept

Labels should be convenient shorthand expressions for complex manifestations. They take the place of lengthy, cumbersome descriptions of illnesses. In no way can a psychiatric label describe the person who suffers from the illness, or the unique configuration of a person's disorder. Unfortunately labels tend to take on a life of their own, so that persons who have received a diagnostic label become, in the eyes of some, the incarnation of the label. Schizophrenics differ among themselves as much as do diabetics, school teachers, the unemployed, housewives, and the like. When we confuse a label with a person, accurate assessment and treatment become impossible.

There is another danger of reification in the indiscriminate use of psychiatric labels that has been noted by Levy (1981). Mental health staff may establish a deep gulf between themselves and the clients they are supposed to help when they begin to differentiate between "them" and "us." The "them" not only are considered sick but also take on an aspect of untrust-worthiness and incapability. On the other hand, the "we" are perceived as ca-pable, expert, and trustworthy. As "we" differentiate and separate from "them," the preconceptions about our clients take over, blinding us to their uniqueness and potential. Such preconceptions partially explain why long-tenured staff in some settings have given up on what they considered to be "hopeless cases"—and newcomers were able to effectuate significant restora-tion.

DIFFERENCES IN INTERPRETATION OF THE SAME CONCEPT

The American Psychiatric Association, through its diagnostic manual, *DSM-III-R*, has made a major effort at bringing about uniformity in diagnostic in-terpretations. Nevertheless, psychiatric labels still hold different meanings among professionals and nonprofessionals alike. For example, a lay person may have an image of a "schizophrenic" as someone with a "split," or dual, personality, or as an uncontrollably violent person. Some professionals are just as ignorant or confused about the concept of schizophrenia. For exam-ple, a psychoanalytically oriented therapist may think that the "schizo-phrenic" compartmentalizes feelings and suffers from massive identity confusion. Many family therapists claim to have "cured" schizophrenics—they may simply have in mind clients who don't readily communicate their feelings and who experience a period of behavior strange enough to warrant a brief confinement to a mental hospital (Simon 1987). But such persons may not have lost any of their functional or mental capacities nor met other *DSM-III-R* criteria for a diagnosis of schizophrenia.

These differences in interpretation indicate that it is necessary to define diagnostic terms as precisely as possible in communications with professional and lay persons alike. We cannot assume that others have the same under-standing of a clinical label as we do.

DIAGNOSTIC TRENDS

There are fashions and fads in psychiatric diagnoses just as in everything else. Some diagnoses have been more in use during some periods than others. For example, in the 1930s and 1940s "neurosis" was the favored and most often used diagnosis. Today neurosis is not even included as a classification in the *DSM-III-R*, and its use among mental health professionals is steadily declin-ing. By contrast, the diagnosis of schizophrenia has gained in popularity since the 1970s, while mood disorders have become more prominent in the 1980s.

Among the first to take account of these trends was sociologist Jeffrey Blum, who analyzed case records of all patients discharged from a single Vet-erans Administration hospital during the years 1954, 1964, and 1974 (Blum 1978). Blum compared the diagnoses that were made in these three decades and found that they had noticeably changed over time. For example, diagnoses of mood disorders, schizophrenia, and situational reactions increased between 1954 and 1974 while diagnoses of neuroses and psychophysiological disorders decreased, all at statistically significant rates.

Does this mean that mental illnesses have a cyclical existence or that over time psychiatrists tend to diagnose the same phenomena differently? The case records in the Blum study indicated that patients' symptoms of mental illness had not changed but remained substantially stable over time. However, the *interpretation* of these symptoms by mental health professionals had changed. The explanation for this phenomenon may be that therapists tend to diagnose conditions they think they can treat successfully. Thus, in the early 1950s, prior to the introduction of antipsychotic medications, there was little that could be done to alleviate schizophrenia. But psychiatrists were confident that they could cure neurotic disorders through psychoanalytic therapies. As a consequence, they may have recognized fewer cases of "intractable" schizophrenia and more cases of mood disorders that seemed to be more amenable to treatment. The revolution in psychopharmacology has now provided psychiatrists the tools to successfully treat the previously untreatable. Their increased confidence may also have resulted in an increased diagnosis of these conditions.

Finally, increases in knowledge resulting from followup studies and "treatment-response" research have resulted in changes in diagnostic categories. It is not uncommon, for example, that a psychiatrist may base a diagnosis on the manner in which a patient responds to an antipsychotic medication. Thus, a patient who displays symptoms of mania that do not respond to a specific medication such as lithium carbonate may therefore not be diagnosed as having bipolar or manic mood disorder but another condition where the symptoms of mania are present. Accordingly, response to medication helps to determine the more precise nature of the illness!

SUMMARY

Blum's study serves to remind us that a diagnosis is not always the final word, engraved in marble, unchangeable and unchallengeable. Some diagnoses are engraved in ice that will melt at the first sign of warmth. All clinical diagnoses and social functioning assessments are profoundly influenced by diagnostic trends, the received wisdom, prejudices, and perceptions of mental health professionals, and the rapidly expanding knowledge of mental illness.

Finally, there are numerous changes that occur naturally with the passage of time. The health of clients changes, circumstances change, therapists change, and interventions change. Diagnoses and assessments should allow for flexibility and change. The acid test of their quality is the effectiveness of the interventions that result from them.

CHAPTER 7

SOCIAL FUNCTIONING ASSESSMENTS

SOCIAL FUNCTIONING ASSESSMENTS have a broader scope than clinical diagnoses in that they stress a client's patterns of behavior in relation to the environment: family, friends, work, school, self-care, and the use of community resources. These patterns provide a fuller in-depth understanding of strengths, weaknesses, and potential for change. The social functioning assessment also evaluates areas in which a client's environment supports or militates against his or her illness and functional problems and focuses on the client's motivation and opportunities for improving the situation. Such an assessment provides the basis for interventions whose focus is on helping the client to get along better in a variety of circumstances: with his or her family, living arrangements, in the workplace, the neighborhood, in exercising a religion, and the like. As social workers, we not only help a client change behavior and feelings but also intervene in the environment to further his or her functioning.

The social functioning assessment begins, like the clinical diagnosis discussed in chapter 5, with a systematic observation of the client's appearance, manner of self-expression, and behavior toward the interviewer and others. But the focus of the social functioning assessment expands to include observations of the client's interactions with family and transactions with land-lords, friends, schools, employers, shopkeepers, and neighbors. We evaluate the extent to which the client's behavior adheres to or violates the social norms of the community, and the extent to which others accept the client's behavior and illness.

There are many ways of categorizing and measuring social functioning. All mental health facilities use forms designed to evaluate their clients' social functioning. These range in complexity from relatively simple intake and ad-mission protocols to more elaborate rehabilitation and progress surveys. The data categories for these forms have been derived from researchers that have examined the social functioning of all classes and types and have produced in-struments used to evaluate social functioning. The most popular of these in-struments are the Anthony Rehabilitation Model (Anthony 1980, 1984) and the Liberman (1982) Model, both of which will be discussed in this chapter.

SOCIAL SKILLS ASSESSMENT

The concept of social skills describes a client's ability to obtain what he or she wants and needs. These skills range from basic levels of obtaining survival ne-cessities to high levels of conceptualization of complex situations and achieve-ment. Many chronic mentally ill persons tend to be deficient in exercising social skills for two main reasons. First, most chronic mental illness appears early in life, during adolescence or in the early twenties, periods that are sig-nificant for an individual's social development. During this time adult skills are learned, such as dating, getting along with members of the opposite sex, assuming new, more mature roles in relation to one's family, the give and take of friendship, the discipline needed to pursue higher education, living on one's own, obeying laws and community norms, and earning a living. But as mental illness emerges, these developmentally related learning processes are retarded and sometimes halted altogether. Second, the havoc that mental ill-ness plays with thinking processes and memory tends to destroy much of what has already been learned and makes further learning difficult or impos-sible.

APPEARANCE

Often persons with a chronic mental illness appear clumsy at getting what they want. Indeed, they often do not know what they want or need for pur-poses of survival. For example:

> Celia Howe, a 25-year-old woman diagnosed as a chronic schizophrenic, used to come to the Middle State Community Mental Health Center wearing light summer clothes on cold winter days. When asked why, she responded that they were very pretty and her favorite clothes besides.

Harry Marsh, another client, was extremely docile and passive. He would quickly do what others told him but could not bring himself to make the simplest request, such as asking for permission to leave an activity in order to go to the toilet.

One of the worker's most important therapeutic tasks is to help the client to learn and retain social skills. This is accomplished through the identification of a client's personal and environmental resources that can be called on for skill training. The following vignette illustrates how a treatment team built on Celia Howe's personal strength so as to train her to wear suitable clothing:

Among Celia Howe's strengths, as identified by her treatment team, was an ability to make and keep friends. She had a long-standing friendship with Mary Quinn, another Center client. Celia also loved to grow houseplants, which flourished under her care—another strength. Mary Quinn, who knew how to dress, was asked to discuss with Celia what clothing to wear each day, to help her pick appropriate clothing from her wardrobe, and to shop for clothing with her. Then the team instituted a behavioral reward system for Celia. For each day that she wore appropriate clothing to the Center, Celia received a token, and for every ten tokens she received a small pot of African violets, her favorite houseplant. Within two months Celia was able to select suitable clothing on her own.

In assessing social skills, we look at (1) communication skills, or how well a client can convey wants and needs, (2) problem-solving skills, or how well a client can think through a situation that poses difficulties and decide on a course of action, and (3) functional skills, or how well the client carries out the tasks needed in a variety of roles.

COMMUNICATION SKILLS

There are two components to all communications: verbal and nonverbal. **Verbal content** consists of words that are actually spoken or written and the literal meaning of the message they are intended to convey. **Nonverbal content** consists of the facial expressions, body movements, and intonations that accompany verbal content. Over three-quarters of all spoken communications consists of nonverbal content that conveys more about the meaning than the verbal content, as in a threatening tone of voice or a look that accompanies a one-word command such as "Stop!" (Truax and Carkhuff 1967).

In assessing communication skills, we necessarily observe both verbal content and the nonverbal factors. It is critical that we not only hear what the client says but also how it is said.

Assessing the verbal content of communications is identical with that made in clinical diagnoses (chapter 5), where we observe how clear and realistic a client's self-expression is.

BEHAVIOR

In assessing nonverbal communication we observe the ease, or lack of it, with which a client talks. We consider the appropriateness of facial expressions, body movements, and intonations. To illustrate: A client may discuss a serious illness of a close friend while smiling and chuckling. Another may never look directly at the person with whom he or she is talking. Some clients stammer, fidget, and scowl without provocation. Restless, high-strung clients may walk away from the speaker while the latter is in the middle of a sentence. These behaviors are quite naturally distressing to others.

Liberman (1982) identified seven subcategories involved in communication processes that are useful in identifying problems a client may have with self-expression. Each of the seven is assessed in terms of its appropriateness to the speaking situation.

1. *Eye contact*. We evaluate whether and for how long a client can look directly at the person who is speaking to him or her.
2. *Posture*. Facing the speaker, a certain amount of relaxation and appropriate mobility of one's head, arms, legs, and hands are signs of an appropriate posture.
3. *Speech disruptions*. These include too much coughing, distracting harrumphing, or clicking of the tongue or teeth.
4. The *duration* with which words and sentences are spoken and the length between them. We determine whether the pauses between words and sentences are too long, making the messages interminably long and boring, or whether the speaker's words and sentences run together and tumble over one another so that they cannot be understood.
5. The presence or absence of appropriate *smiling*.
6. *Loudness* or volume of speech.
7. *Speech intonation*, or the way a client modulates, and by tone accents, what is said.

Table 7.1 Nonverbal Communication Skills

Areas of Communication	Positive Skills Indications
1. Eye contact	Looks in eye; does not stare
2. Posture	Open, relaxed, to speaker
3. Speech disruptions	Few or no disruptions
4. Duration	Pauses between words and sentences long or short enough to be understood
5. Smiling	Pleasant; fluid, not frozen
6. Loudness	Moderate
7. Intonation	Accents and tone variations

SOURCE: Data derived from R. P. Liberman, "Assessment of Social Skills," *Schizophrenia Bulletin*, Vol. 8, No. 1 (1982), pp. 62–83.

PROBLEM-SOLVING SKILLS

The ability of clients to solve problems in living will depend on how they receive and process information. Faulty thought processes and memory deficits can result from a number of causes, including the mental illness itself, antipsychotic medications, or from street drugs and alcohol. Problems resulting from faulty information processing can be alleviated by the use of skill training procedures that include the modeling, in incremental stages, of the way problems can be solved and rehearsing these stages with the client around problems that are important to them, either on an individual or small-group basis (Kelly 1982). The following vignette illustrates problem-solving skill training.

> *William Jackson, a 33-year-old member of the South Beach Club, a rehabilitation center for mentally ill young adults, was eager to date but unable to bring himself to ask women to go out on dates with him. Physically Jackson's shyness demonstrated itself by his inability to look at others, especially women, directly in the eye, not speaking clearly and directly to others, and finally, of not knowing how to phrase a request for a date.*
>
> *Because dealing head on with the problem of shyness would have been too difficult and threatening for Jackson, his counselor, Martha Hayes, discussed it in terms of the above skill deficits. In order to encourage his problem-solving ability, Hayes encouraged Jackson to set his own skill-training priorities with the ultimate aim of being able to ask a female club member for a date. Jackson said that he wanted to learn how to speak better to others. Hayes then modeled for Jackson how to look people in the eye, and with the help of a mirror encouraged him to practice this skill alone, and later in one of his activity groups that he especially enjoyed. There, group members soon caught on that Jackson was to be rewarded with smiles, praise, and cheers for increasingly lengthy eye contacts.*
>
> *When, after three weeks, Jackson had learned the eye-contact skill, Hayes began to model, with the use of hand puppets, how one can ask a woman for a date. All group members, but especially Jackson, enjoyed this "date game." They practiced for four entire sessions the tone of voice and phrasing that would get them a date. Finally, Jackson thought he was ready to take the plunge. His carefully rehearsed "I want to take you to a movie tonight. Will you come?" produced results with a female club member, who happily accepted a date with him.*

Jackson was able to persevere through his skill training by keeping in mind his goal: being able to date. This required that he be able to *remember* his goal, that his memory be more or less intact. Most chronic mentally ill persons experience memory problems, caused either by their illness or use of antipsychotic medications (Marcus *et al.* 1988). Memory problems can be identified in the mental status examination, discussed in chapter 5, and other psychological tests. In addition to formal memory tests, the impact of memory on problem-solving skills can be evaluated informally during the course of an ordinary interview.

First, we want to know how well a client can recall recent events. This is important, because in order to even think about a problem it is necessary to remember the problem and the situations in which it occurred. If short-term memory is deficient and distorted, problem solving will be equally deficient and distorted.

We evaluate a client's short-term memory by requesting a discussion of a very recent event, one that may have taken place only a few hours earlier, but that seemed important or may have posed difficulties for the client. We probe for specific details of the event: what actually happened, the place where it happened, the people who were involved, what was said, by whom, to whom, what the client said, thought, and felt.

Second, we assess the manner in which the client thinks about the event in terms of the present and the future. Whatever the adequacy of the client's short-term memory, he or she has thoughts about what is happening in the immediate present and what the result of his or her actions could be. We ask the client what consequences he or she expects from the recalled event, what he or she would like to do now about it, and whether there are any other ways of addressing the situation. The client's answers will reveal not only how well he or she can remember and think about situations, but also the presence of situational problems, emotional problems, realism, flexibility, and imagination. The following case history exemplifies a problem with short-term memory that was confounded by other problems.

Evelyn Herr, a 31-year-old chronic mentally ill woman, is a client at the Western Psychiatric Rehabilitation Center. She lives with an older sister who is a bank accountant. The sisters bicker constantly, mainly because Evelyn often accuses her sister of hating her, of stealing her clothing, and of spreading false gossip about her in the neighborhood. Evelyn frequently tells her case manager that she wants to move away from her sister and live in a place of her own. The sister agrees that she and Evelyn have a difficult time living together and would prefer that Evelyn move away.

When a new group home opened in town, the case manager made an appointment for Evelyn to be interviewed by the home's director as a preliminary step to being admitted. However, on the appointed day Evelyn was not at home when the case manager called for her to take her to the interview. In fact, Evelyn had gone to visit a friend in another part of town. Evelyn also did not keep a subsequent appointment claiming her alarm clock failed to go off. At length she told the case manager that she actually loved her sister and that there was no problem between them. She saw no reason to leave. The sister, however, now insisted that Evelyn move out. By this time, however, the group home was filled.

The case manager was not sure whether Evelyn denied problems between herself and the sister as a result of faulty memory or her fear of living on her

own for the first time in her life. In a conference with the sister and when con-
fronted by the facts as presented by her, Evelyn reluctantly admitted to having
started many unnecessary fights, thus revealing that her memory was not as
bad as it may have seemed. Still, her solution was to try to work things out by
"trying to be sweet and extra good." However, the sister was now adamant
that Evelyn move out of her apartment within the month. Evelyn then said
that she would move back in with her parents. In providing this solution, she
seemed to have forgotten that the parents had long insisted that they would
not, and could not, live with her.

Evelyn denies her problems or provides unrealistic solutions to them. Memory-skill training began by the case manager's helping Evelyn to remember the numerous events that led up to the current crisis. At the point that the client agreed that she had to start looking for other housing, Evelyn was helped to remember how to be on time for appointments. The case manager gave her a series of boldly lettered notes to "jog the memory." The reminders in the notes included setting the alarm clock, laying out her clothing the night before, when to eat breakfast, and at what time the case manager would call on her. As it turned out, Evelyn actively participated in what turned out to be a successful search for housing.

FUNCTIONAL SKILLS

In assessing functional skills, we evaluate the manner in which a client takes care of himself or herself, relates to others, works, learns, and uses leisure time.

A useful scale for evaluating functional skills is the Specific Level of Functioning Assessment (SLOF) Scale developed for use with mentally ill clients by Schneider and Struening (1983). In this scale, reproduced as figure 7.1, skills are categorized as physical functioning, personal care skills, interpersonal relationships, social acceptability, activities, and work. Each skill area is rated on a five-point continuum, with 5 representing the highest performance and 1 the lowest. For example, in the area of personal care skills the highest area of performance (5) is designated as "totally self-sufficient" and the lowest (1) as "totally dependent" in such skills as toileting, eating, personal hygiene, dressing, grooming, care of own possessions, and care of own living space.

In applying the social acceptability category of the SLOF Scale to Evelyn Herr, we would rate her as follows: a 2 in the area of "verbally abusing others" because she does so frequently. She would rate 5 in "physically abuses others" because Evelyn has never lashed out at anyone. She gets a 5 for "destroying property" for the same reason.

The SLOF Scale highlights Evelyn's problems and strengths, and as such becomes the foundation on which a treatment plan can be drafted. By completing the form at various intervals, such as every four or six months, the

Figure 7.1. Level of Functioning Assessment

Instructions: Circle the number that best describes this person's *typical* level of functioning on each item listed below. *Be as accurate as you can.* If you are not sure about a certain rating, ask someone who may know or consult the case record.

Mark only one number for each item. Be sure to mark all items.

Self-Maintenance

A. Physical Functioning	No Problem	Problem, But no Effect on General Functioning	Slight Effect on General Functioning	Restricts General Functioning Substantially	Prevents General Functioning
1. Vision	5	4	3	2	1
2. Hearing	5	4	3	2	1
3. Speech Impairment	5	4	3	2	1
4. Walking, use of legs	5	4	3	2	1
5. Use of hands and arms	5	4	3	2	1

B. Personal Care Skills	Totally Self-Sufficient	Needs Verbal Advice or Guidance	Needs Some Physical Help or Assistance	Needs Substantial Help	Totally Dependent
6. Toileting (uses toilet properly; keeps self and area clean)	5	4	3	2	1
7. Eating (uses utensils properly; eating habits)	5	4	3	2	1
8. Personal hygiene (body and teeth; general cleanliness)	5	4	3	2	1
9. Dressing self (selects appropriate garments; dresses self)	5	4	3	2	1
10. Grooming (hair, make-up, general appearance)	5	4	3	2	1
11. Care of own possessions	5	4	3	2	1
12. Care of own living space	5	4	3	2	1

Social Functioning

C. Interpersonal Relationships	Highly Typical of This Person	Generally Typical of This Person	Somewhat Typical of This Person	Generally Untypical of This Person	Highly Untypical of This Person
13. Accepts contact with others (does not withdraw or turn away)	5	4	3	2	1

	Highly Typical of This Person	Generally Typical of This Person	Somewhat Typical of This Person	Generally Untypical of This Person	Highly Untypical of This Person
14. Initiates contact with others	5	4	3	2	1
15. Communicates effectively (speech and gestures are understandable and to the point)	5	4	3	2	1
16. Engages in activities without prompting	5	4	3	2	1
17. Participates in groups	5	4	3	2	1
18. Forms and maintains friendships	5	4	3	2	1
19. Asks for help when needed	5	4	3	2	1

D. Social Acceptability	Never	Rarely	Sometimes	Frequently	Always
20. Verbally abuses others	5	4	3	2	1
21. Physically abuses others	5	4	3	2	1
22. Destroys property	5	4	3	2	1
23. Physically abuses self	5	4	3	2	1
24. Is fearful, crying, clinging	5	4	3	2	1
25. Takes property from others without permission	5	4	3	2	1
26. Performs repetitive behaviors (pacing, rocking, making noises)	5	4	3	2	1

E. Activities	Totally Self-Sufficient	Needs Verbal Advice or Guidance	Needs Some Physical Help or Assistance	Needs Substantial Help	Totally Dependent
27. Household responsibilities (housecleaning, cooking, washing clothes)	5	4	3	2	1
28. Shopping (selection of items, choice of stores, payment at register)	5	4	3	2	1
29. Handling personal finances (budgeting, paying bills)	5	4	3	2	1

	Totally Self-Sufficient	Needs Verbal Advice or Guidance	Needs Some Physical Help or Assistance	Needs Substantial Help	Totally Dependent
30. Use of telephone (getting number, dialing, speaking, listening)	5	4	3	2	1
31. Traveling from residence without getting lost	5	4	3	2	1
32. Use of public transportation (selecting route, using timetable, paying fares, making transfers)	5	4	3	2	1
33. Use of leisure time (reading, visiting friends, listening to music)	5	4	3	2	1
34. Recognizing and avoiding common dangers (traffic safety, fire safety)	5	4	3	2	1
35. Self-medication (understanding purpose, taking as prescribed, recognizing side effects)	5	4	3	2	1
36. Use of medical and other community services (knowing whom to contact, how, and when to use)	5	4	3	2	1
37. Basic reading, writing, and arithmetic (enough for daily needs)	5	4	3	2	1

F. Work Skills	Highly Typical of This Person	Generally Typical of This Person	Somewhat Typical of This Person	Generally Untypical of This Person	Highly Untypical of This Person
38. Has employable skills	5	4	3	2	1
39. Works with minimal supervision	5	4	3	2	1
40. Is able to sustain work effort (not easily distracted, can work under stress)	5	4	3	2	1

	Highly Typical of This Person	Generally Typical of This Person	Somewhat Typical of This Person	Generally Untypical of This Person	Highly Untypical of This Person
41. Appears at appointments on time	5	4	3	2	1
42. Follows verbal instructions accurately	5	4	3	2	1
43. Completes assigned tasks	5	4	3	2	1

Other Information

44. From your knowledge of this person, are there other skills or problem areas not covered on this form that are important to this person's ability to function independently? If so, please specify.

45. How well do you know the skills and behavior of the person you just rated? (Circle one)

Very Well		Fairly Well		Not Very Well at All
5	4	3	2	1

46. Have you discussed this assessment with the client? (Circle one)   Yes   No

    If yes, does the client generally agree with the assessment? (Circle one)   Yes   No

SLOF Scale becomes an instrument that helps us to evaluate the effectiveness of our interventions. An unchanged score in a deficient skill area we had been working on means, in all likelihood, that the intervention we chose to remedy the problem has not been successful and that we must now select another approach.

Another method of assessing social functioning is the Anthony Scale (see figure 7.2), which was specifically developed by Professor William Anthony to help in the rehabilitation of mentally disabled persons (Anthony 1979, 1980, 1984). It has the merit of being easy to understand and apply.

The Anthony Scale is presented in a 3×3 form with one axis designated for personal characteristics and a second for the areas of living where these characteristics are played out. The personal characteristic axis consists of three elements:

1. The "P" area deals with the presence or absence of important physical capacities and weaknesses, such as the ability to groom and dress oneself, to do house cleaning, to cook, and the like.

Figure 7.2.   Client Diagnostic Planning Chart

Name *Ms. Smith*

Situational Problems: *Does not interact with anyone in her neighborhood.*

Rehabilitation Goals: *Increase amount of interaction between Ms. Smith and community residents.*

Environment	Strength/Deficit	Physical Skills	Emotional Skills	Intellectual Skills
Living Environment *apartment & neighborhood*	+	*Housework* *Grooming* *Driving a car* *Using public transportation*	*Listening*	*Budgeting* *Shopping* *Cooking*
	–	*Physical fitness*	*Conversing* *Telephoning*	*Scheduling time* *Identifying interests* *Making decisions* *Setting goals*
Learning Environment *not applicable*	+			
	–			
Working Environment *not applicable*	+			
	–			

Note: Words in italics are filled in by the practitioner.

SOURCE: William A. Anthony, "The Rehabilitation Approach to Diagnosis," in L. Stein, ed., *Community Support Systems for the Long-Term Patient,* New Directions for Mental Health Services No. 2 (San Francisco: Jossey-Bass), pp. 30–31. Used with permission.

2. The "I" area assesses the capacity to perform intellectual activities including the ability to think about and solve a problem and to analyze a situation and its alternatives. Evelyn Herr had difficulties in this area.

3. The "E" area focuses on the appropriateness with which a client expresses emotions. Here we assess a client's interaction and relationships with others, such as adroitness in making and keeping friends, and behavior at emotionally significant occasions such as birthday parties and funerals. Some clients have problems in relating to their parents but are able to have a few friends. These friends are often also

112

mentally ill or "street people" whose relationship with the client may be tenuous and casual. Some clients believe that the drug dealers and others who prey on them are their friends.

The above skill areas are rated in the context of three environmental situations. The first is the "L," or living environment, which includes places of residence and recreational settings. The second is the "LE," or learning environment, such as a school and other settings where learning takes place. The third area is known as the "W," or working environment. It includes the noncompetitive as well as the competitive workplace. The presence of skills is designated with a plus sign and their absence with a minus sign.

Three different environments are stressed because skill behaviors may vary from one setting to another. For example, a client who never loses his temper—an emotional skill—at the supermarket where he works as a checker may not be able to control himself at home where even the most modest and reasonable request from a parent produces a temper tantrum.

The Anthony Scale has a dual focus in that it highlights supportive and deficient factors in a client's environment as well as in the client's own social functioning that are in need of improvement. For example, Evelyn Herr's "L" (living) environment with her sister would be identified with a minus sign, as would be her "I" and "E" personal characteristic areas.

Like the SLOF scale, the Anthony Scale flags a client's strengths and deficiencies, the necessary underpinning for realistic treatment goals and treatment planning. Likewise, when administered at regular intervals, the Anthony Scale can tell us how effective our interventions have been, and in what areas we need to rethink and change them.

FAMILY FUNCTIONING AND DATA

As discussed in chapter 15, families of mentally ill persons can either help or harm them by providing or withholding emotional or material supports. Families can play a critical role in determining the course of the client's illness. For that reason, case records should contain all relevant information on the family. At the very least, the following information should be developed.

1. Names, addresses, phone numbers, and relationship to the client of family members who live nearby
2. Names, addresses, phone numbers, and relationships of family members who do not live nearby but who have been in contact with the client and who have helped within the preceding year.
3. A checklist of those members of the family about whom the client has said that he or she can "trust them and turn to them in time of trouble."
4. A checklist of family members who can be counted on to provide material help and who rely on the client for material and other help.

113

For the young persons who still live with their families or whose parents are still relatively young and accessible, much more information is needed. All members of the immediate family should be seen at the point of admission to a hospital or in the initial interview at the community agency. Families who are involved early on in planning are also more likely to play a participatory role with mental health professionals than are those whose involvement is delayed or who are altogether left out of the process.

FIRST FAMILY INTERVIEWS

In first family interviews we focus not only on what is said but also on how family members relate and interact with each other. Who speaks on behalf of the family? On behalf of the client? In what manner is the client discussed? We note the family's emotional state. Do they appear to be overwrought? emotionally exhausted? Are they critical of the client? Do they blame themselves for what has been happening to the client? Does the family seem to be hiding a family secret? Does the family live by a myth such as "In our family we always love one another, stand by one another, and never lose our tempers"? Do family members tend to ramble on without providing needed information? Are there strong currents of patience and caring?

During first interviews we may assess a family's expressed emotion (EE) quotient using the Camberwell Scale described in chapter 15. Expressed emotion, or a family's acceptance of and direct involvement in a client's life, is a significant factor in determining the course of a client's mental illness. Some families show their excessive attention to a client not by being pleasant and caring but by treating the client harshly or demeaningly and complaining about the client to the interviewer. They appear to be "locked in" to the client and the illness, exhausting themselves by caring for the client at the cost of other social contacts and activities. These families tend to rank high on their expressed emotion quotient and may need support such as that found in the psychoeducational approaches and support groups discussed in chapter 15.

THE ENVIRONMENT

Environmental influences outside of the family also play a significant role in determining a client's course of mental illness. The impact of the environment will vary from person to person. For example, a critical comment by a nurse may be taken in stride by one client, totally ignored by a second, but deeply upset a third. By the same token, life in a deteriorating inner-city environment may exacerbate the illness of some but have no effect on others. In fact, some may actually flourish in a "slum" kind of environment where they may feel more accepted. In comparing themselves to some deviant slum dwellers, a chronic mentally ill person may feel less different and more "normal."

Therefore, we should not automatically assume that what we think of as a "good" environment is also good for the client and that a "bad" environment is, by definition, harmful. Still, environmental factors provide additional clues to the puzzle of what may have precipitated a client's illness and what determines its current course. Environmental factors that contribute to or maintain a client's illness can be classified in three types. First, added situational stress; second, lack of supports; third, the loss of already existing supports.

The first, **added situational stress,** may be difficult to detect. On the surface, nothing may seem to have changed: a client continues to live in the same place for years and engages in the same activities, but the client's felt stress level rises. Perhaps one of the client's friends, or an employer, or even a case manager has changed the expectation placed on the client's performance. A friend may want to borrow money. An employer may expect increased productivity or promptness. The case manager may be involving the client in more intense and demanding treatment. Added situational stress factors include

1. Unrealistic expectations from others
2. Death or illness of someone close
3. Changes in household composition
4. Moving
5. Institutionalization
6. Recent disagreements, arguments, and fights with important others, such as with landlords and roommates.

Lack of support and **loss of support** are easier to detect. Supports are friends; family; familiar faces in the neighborhood; and material, educational, and medical assistance. These factors, known as support networks and social networks, are discussed at length in chapter 16. Knowledge about them is vital in social functioning assessments and treatment planning. The presence or absence of a connectedness to various parts of the social network tells us much about a client's (1) ability to get along with others and to ask for and get help, (2) sense of belonging to a community, and (3) social resources in general. This information helps us to plan which areas of the network need to be shored up, such as friendship and recreational activities, which the client can count on for help, and which the worker should mobilize on behalf of the client's welfare.

Basic data relating to these networks is, as a rule, included in fact sheets and case records. The following is a useful way of organizing network data:

1. Names of household members other than family members
2. Names, addresses, and phone numbers of important friends, acquaintances, and professionals
3. Names and addresses of others readily recalled by the client

4. Information relating to the client's religious affiliation such as the name of the place of worship and the clergy
5. Social service organizations that have helped the client in the past or with whom the client has had dealings

Information for the support network fact sheet is ordinarily obtained in initial interviews (Garrison and Podell 1981) and corrected and expanded during subsequent contacts with the client and the family. It goes without saying that no one in a client's support system should be contacted without the knowledge and consent of the client or guardian.

SUMMARY

As a first step in developing treatment plans that will enable our clients to live satisfying lives outside of institutions and to keep the occurrence of their mental illness to a minimum, we develop clinical diagnoses and social functioning assessments. These are our attempts at obtaining answers to complex questions. What precipitated the client's illness? What environmental factors exacerbate it? maintain it? What does the client need to function and get along better? Who and what in the client's environment can be enlisted in the struggle to optimize health and keep the client's illness at bay? What are the client's strengths? weaknesses? What does the client want? How motivated is the client to fulfill wants? We can only map out partial answers to these questions. There can be no exhaustive or "correct" answers to these multifaceted, difficult questions that form the basis of effective interventions.

We obtain answers to our questions through a systematic gathering of relevant data and impressions, and by organizing them in such a way that they serve as a useful guide in treatment planning. As such, the process of assessment does not stop but continues for as long as we work with the client.

APPENDIX 7A: Outline for a Social Functioning Assessment

I. The Client's Own Functioning
  a. Communication Skills
    1. *Verbal content.* What does the client say? Does the client express hallucinations and delusions? Do the client's thoughts logically follow one another? Does the client jump from one subject to another seemingly without connection?
    2. *Nonverbal factors*
      i. Eye contact. Is the client's eye contact appropriate or does the client stare or not look others in the eye? For how long can the client maintain appropriate eye contact?
      ii. Facial expression. Does the client's facial expression match the content of what he or she says? How animated is it?

    iii. Speech. Is the client's speech pressured? too loud? too quiet? Are there speech problems such as stuttering, too much hesitation, a rate of speech too fast or too slow to be clearly understood? Are the client's intonations appropriate or is everything said in a monotone?

b. Problem-Solving Skills
1. *Recall of recent events.* How well can the client remember what happened 10 minutes ago? Can he or she recall important events that took place one hour ago? one day or a week ago? Can the client recall what took place, where, who was involved, who wanted what from whom and what the client said or thought at the time?
2. Can the client identify problems that are important to him or her?
3. Is the client able to think through steps that must be taken in order to address the identified problem?

c. Functional Skills
1. *Grooming and personal care skills.* Is the client able to keep clean? To comb his or her hair and brush his or her teeth? Does the client use the toilet appropriately? What are the client's eating habits? table manners? Is the client able to get dressed, and to dress according to seasonal and weather conditions? Can the client recognize and avoid common dangers, such as obeying traffic regulations, taking care in using electrical appliances, cooking appliances, dangerous cleaning compounds, and so forth?
2. *Health care skills.* Is the client able to take his or her medication regularly? Does the client keep appointments with his or her therapist, physician, dentist, and other health care providers? Can the client tell when something is physically wrong? Can the client monitor his or her own signs of decompensation?
3. *Interpersonal relationships.* Does the client form relationships with others or withdraw? Does the client pick fights, threaten or act provocatively? Can the client participate in group activities? Is the client dependent, compliant, rebellious, or too passive?
4. *Learning skills.* How well does the client follow directions? How well can the client read? write? Can the client study in a classroom with others? How well and how much can the client learn independently? How well can the client complete assignments and other learning tasks?
5. *Work skills.* Does the client have any skills that can lead to competitive employment? How much supervision does the client need when working? Can the client go to work on time? Complete work assignments? get along with supervisors and coworkers?
6. *Household skills.* Can the client clean his or her room? How neat is the client? Can the client cook, shop for groceries, wash dishes,

wash clothing? Does the client take care of his or her finances? Can the client use the telephone?

7. *Leisure activity skills.* What are the client's recreational and leisure activities? Are these solitary activities or something that can be done with others? Are they active, *e.g.*, sports, or passive, *e.g.*, watching television?

8. *Navigational skills.* Can the client take public transportation? Does the client easily get lost in his or her neighborhood? in a new neighborhood? in a large building?

9. *Social acceptability skills.* Does the client break laws that result in incarceration? Does the client destroy furnishings and personal property, be it his or her own or others'? Does the client take things from others without permission? Does the client masturbate, urinate, or defecate in public? Does the client cling to others, following them around and otherwise intruding on their personal space?

II. The Functioning of the Client's Family

a. *Members and their helpfulness to client.* Who are the members of the client's immediate family? With whom does the client live? With which members of the client's extended family (uncles, aunts, cousins) does the client have a special relationship? On whom can the client count for what?

b. *Socioeconomic data.* What are the occupations of the family members? their education? Is their income sufficient to meet their basic needs? What is the source of their income, *e.g.*, welfare? What kind of neighborhood do they live in?

c. *Health history.* Who else in the family (include grandparents) has had mental illness? What were the symptoms of that illness? What treatment was received?

d. *Involvement with client.* How well does the family accept the client's mental illness and the client's behavior? How much time do they spend with the client and what do they do together during the time spent in actual face-to-face contact? What do they do for the client?

e. *Current family relationships.* How well do family members get along with one another? Is there open communication among them? Do family members tend to help each other and stand by each other in difficult times?

III. The Environment

a. *Living situation.* Does the client live in an apartment, a house, a room, a group home, or an institution? Does the client's living arrangement meet basic hygienic standards? If the client does not live with his or her family, what kind of relationships does the client have with others, including staff and other residents?

b. *The neighborhood.* Does the client live in a neighborhood where there is a high crime rate? Are illegal drugs openly sold? Is there access to public transportation? to medical and psychiatric care?

c. *Changes.* What has changed in the client's environment that contributes to situational stress?

d. *Involvement with others.* Does the client have friends, and what can they do for the client? Do family members have friends and belong to social groups? What is the relationship of the client and his or her family to others?

e. *Involvement with community organizations.* To what organizations do the family members belong or are they known to, including religious organizations, the legal system, social agencies, and recreational organizations? Which organizations have helped the client in the past, and can they help in the future?

PART III

Care in the Hospital: Admission, Treatment, and Discharge

CHAPTER 8

PSYCHIATRIC CRISES AND EMERGENCY SERVICES

G ERALD CAPLAN, one of the originators of contemporary crisis theory, defined a crisis as a severe upset of a person's usual emotional state that could be caused by either physiological or psychological forces (Caplan 1964). To create a crisis, these forces must be so powerful, unexpected, or unusual that they unbalance one's ordinary coping capacities, leaving a person unable to function in one's normal manner. These forces are known as stressors.

CRISES AND STRESS

For most of us a crisis is a painful, emotionally upsetting state during which we feel anxious, depressed, and helpless. Workers may not be able to go to work, students may not be able to concentrate on their studies and go to class, mothers may not be able to care for children, and the like. However, since crisis states tend to be self-limiting events, they usually subside even without interventions within four to six weeks (Lukton 1982). When they pass, we usually recover our emotional balance and get on with our lives.

But this is not ordinarily the case for chronic mentally ill persons for whom a crisis is often a disabling, traumatic event. For most, a psychological crisis precipitates a decompensation, or the flaring up of hallucinations, delusions, and thought disorders that exacerbate an already severely limited ability to relate to others and care for imperative personal needs. While undergoing a crisis, most chronic mentally ill persons substantially lose their functioning capacities.

Given enough stress, each of us has a breaking point. None of us is immune from the loss of coping capacities caused by crisis. But the amount of tolerable stress varies from person to person. One of the characteristics of severe mental illness is the vulnerability to stress. Even a relatively low level of stress that the non–mentally ill person ordinarily takes in stride can cause a psychiatric crisis. Crises have been brought on by having been slighted by a friend, a demanding sexual relationship, and being criticized for not getting good grades or having a job. Even overly high expectations from therapists can become the unbalancing force (Kanter 1985).

Crisis-producing stressors, particularly those made up of the additive effects of seemingly inconsequential events, are frequently not readily perceived by others. It may have taken a long time for the stress to build to a breaking point even when, superficially, it appears that the crisis suddenly overwhelmed the client without apparent cause as illustrated by the following vignette.

Irene Fitch, 24, has had three psychiatric hospitalizations since her first admission six years before. She has been diagnosed as having a schizophrenic disorder of the paranoid type. Since her last hospital discharge fifteen months ago, Ms. Fitch has been living with her parents and holding a part-time job as an assembly-line worker in a nearby food-processing company. Two months ago, as she was helping her mother unpack groceries, she dropped and broke a bottle of soda. When her mother jokingly called her "butterfingers," Ms. Fitch accused her mother of "always putting her down" and making her life miserable. That night, unable to sleep, she smoked two packs of cigarettes, a habit she had been trying to stop. Although she continued to dwell on her mother's "unfair accusations and insults," Ms. Fitch made every effort to behave politely toward her mother. This effort at self-control required a great deal of energy. She continued on her job but became increasingly morose and self-absorbed.

Several weeks after the bottle-breaking episode, Ms. Fitch could not find her house keys when she returned from work. She became convinced that her parents must have hidden the keys from her to punish her for her clumsiness, but she would not confront them with her suspicion, fearing that if she were to do so they would only deny everything and humiliate her even more. Ms. Fitch continued to lose sleep and stopped taking her antipsychotic medications.

At work the following week she thought she heard her coworkers talking and snickering about her. Feeling a rising panic, she left her work and started to go home. As she crossed a street against a traffic light, a policeman shouted at her to watch where she was going. At that, the stress reached the breaking point and Ms. Fitch's crisis fully erupted. She began to scream incoherently at the policeman and tried to hit him with her fists and purse.

CRISIS SERVICES

A psychiatric crisis can be a life-threatening situation. While in a state of decompensation, some mentally ill persons may become immobilized to the point where they will not eat, get dressed, use the toilet, or communicate with others. When left untreated, some may curl up in a fetal position or assume rigid postures from which they cannot be budged. There are others who become so agitated that they drain their energy by constant nervous pacing, incessant talking, and sleeplessness. Many report that their thoughts seem to race so fast that they cannot keep up with them, causing them to lose all ability to attend to what is going on around them. The more they lose their attentional ability, the more agitated they become. Serious suicide attempts are made by some who are caught up in this painful vicious circle.

Some people appear to be dangerous when they shout obscenities, pick fights, or even threaten physical harm to others and to themselves. There are in fact persons who, during a psychiatric crisis, become capable of acting out their symptoms dangerously.

For these reasons, psychiatric crises are regarded as emergencies that call for quick intervention aimed at a rapid restoration. The sooner the primary symptoms of mental illness are brought under control, the more likely that further psychological deterioration and erosion of a person's social skills can be prevented (Kane 1987).

HOSPITAL CRISIS SERVICES

Crisis interventions for the mentally ill are provided through either formal or informal structures. The **formal** structures include the emergency rooms and crisis wards of general and psychiatric hospitals. **Informal** structures include mobile emergency units or individual psychiatrists who deliver care to a person's own home and to other nonhospital settings.

Stays in hospital emergency rooms are relatively short, ranging from a few hours or overnight. Should the emergency room staff determine that a patient undergoing a psychiatric crisis needs longer emergency care for observation or acute care treatment, the patient may be transferred to the hospital's crisis ward or unit. Most patients stay only two weeks in a crisis ward. From there they are either discharged to their homes or transferred to another inpatient care facility such as the hospital's psychiatric ward or a mental hospital.

The most traditional and accessible crisis services are provided by emergency rooms in general hospitals. Emergency rooms are known for their round-the-clock services where anyone who needs immediate help can be seen by a doctor without needing a prior appointment. For city dwellers—particularly for the poor, socially isolated, and chronic mentally ill persons—emergency rooms have become "drop-in" clinics where they expect help for all their health problems as well as for counseling and advice on a variety of problems in daily living. Because most emergency rooms provide these services, they are becoming increasingly popular, increasing the number of patient contacts at a rate of more than 11 percent each year (Bassuk and Birk 1984). More than eight out of ten of all emergency room patients come from the lowest socioeconomic groups and present the widest variety of problems (Bassuk and Birk 1984; Solomon and Gordon 1986).

Triage

Because only a small proportion of persons who present themselves to the general hospital's emergency room actually need its intensive and very costly services, the first decision that emergency room staff must make deals with identifying those persons who need its resources the most and, of these, who need them most urgently. This decisionmaking process is known as **triage.** Triage decisions involve two steps. The first is the sorting out of the conditions that most require the emergency room staff's immediate intervention. The second consists of deciding on the most appropriate disposition, or referral, for its patients. In a triage decision, for example, a person who was seriously injured in a car accident will be treated before someone who is assaultive but who can be temporarily restrained. The disposition for the injured patient may involve immediate major surgery in the operating room, while the assaultive patient may be medicated and transferred to the psychiatric ward for observation and adjustment of medication.

Patients who present less serious problems such as a cold or a minor infection have to wait until the more serious cases are attended to. This often means that they have to wait for many hours until seen by a physician.

The Gatekeeper to the Mental Health System

Emergency rooms are known as gatekeepers to the mental health system because for most mentally ill persons they provide access to other mental health services. For many they are their first point of entry to psychiatric hospitals, community mental health centers, and other organizations that make up the extensive network of mental health services.

Before their illness has been formally diagnosed but beyond the point where their caretakers are able to cope with their behavior, mentally ill persons are usually taken to these general hospital emergency rooms. Later, after the diagnosis of mental illness has been established and accepted, persons experiencing subsequent crises may be directly admitted to mental hospitals or provided with community-based psychiatric crisis services (Stroul 1987).

Emergency Room Assessments

In the emergency room a patient is usually met by a member of the emergency team, which is made up of an attending physician, a medical resident, a nurse, a social worker, and an aide. The team member's first responsibility is to make the patient as comfortable as possible and obtain information that can be used to develop an assessment, which includes a clinical diagnosis. The emphasis is on speed: assessments must be developed as rapidly as possible so that a disposition can be made for each patient as soon as possible. In such a hurried environment, assessments may not always be accurate or elegant. They are often based on minimal data, such as a patient's presenting complaint, current behavior, physical condition, and, whenever possible, a history of the complaint. When the presence of a psychiatric crisis is suspected, a psychiatrist, usually an attending psychiatric resident, is consulted. As a rule, each team member makes a substantial contribution in formulating the initial diagnosis and in providing emergency care.

Assessments made in the emergency room are critical to subsequent treatment. For example, a patient who presents symptoms resembling those of mental illness may not be mentally ill and therefore doesn't need admission to a psychiatric ward. Some conditions, such as alcoholism or the use of such chemicals as LSD or PCP ("angel dust"), can mimic mental illness. An accident, the improper use of over-the-counter medications, or withdrawal from sedative-hypnotics may be the cause of the presenting condition. The following case illustrates how other conditions can be mistaken for mental illness.

> Clara Hopkins, a 34-year-old, never-married bookkeeper, was brought to the emergency room by a friend. Ms. Hopkins was markedly upset and agitated. The friend insisted that she was crazy and "out of control."
>
> Ms. Hopkins reported that two months ago "the scales fell off my eyes" when she began to realize that her neighbors and coworkers were plotting to "have me undone." She also began to hear voices. The voices were becoming increasingly clear, loud, and insistent, threatening her with torture and death. Finally, when she could no longer bear it, she asked her friend for help. The friend persuaded her to come to the hospital's emergency room.
>
> Ms. Hopkins expressed herself coherently and had more awareness of her developing psychotic condition than most mentally ill persons do. Although she was appropriately oriented, she had problems in recalling events that took place just a few hours earlier. The attending resident thought that this difficulty might have been associated with her high level of anxiety. There were no indications of an organic disorder, such as headaches or visual disturbances.
>
> The history revealed that this was Ms. Hopkins's first psychotic episode. She had completed junior college and was a steady worker who lived alone and supported herself for the past fifteen years. Ms. Hopkins told the social worker who was taking the history that six months earlier she had moved to a larger apartment in a different part of town. She complained that the new neighborhood

was noisy, with unabating traffic day and night. Ms. Hopkins mentioned the great trouble she had sleeping through all the noise. She tried over-the-counter sleeping pills, but they did not help her to sleep. When asked how she managed to stay awake on her job, she said that her friends let her sample their prescription medicines as well as "uppers" they had and thought would help her to sleep. The emergency room team suspected that Ms. Hopkins's symptoms were caused by the mix of the medications and nostrums she had been ingesting.

Ms. Hopkins was voluntarily admitted to the general medical inpatient unit, where she was detoxified. In four days she stopped hearing voices and her delusions stopped. She returned to her home and job without further symptoms.

Once it is decided that a patient has a mental illness, a differential diagnosis is required. For example, other mental illnesses such as paranoid disorders, schizophreniform disorders, and schizoaffective disorders are easily mistaken for schizophrenia during a crisis.

Emergency Room Assessment Protocols

Psychiatric emergency room assessments usually follow this pattern:

1. The gathering of information that will shed light on the presenting problem
2. Obtaining information about a patient's social and economic resources
3. A mental status examination
4. A physical examination
5. Relevant laboratory tests, such as X-rays and blood and urine tests (Hyman 1984).

It is imperative to obtain as much information from as many persons as possible. Patients in a state of decompensation are often unable to tell their stories fully, credibly, and coherently. In such instance help from families, friends, case managers, and other professionals should be secured. Inquiries should touch on the following areas:

1. *Information about onset.* What were the first signs and symptoms leading to the current crisis? When were they first noticed? What stressful factors precipitated the crisis at this time?
2. *Social history of illness.* Has the patient had similar crises prior to the current one? What precipitated them? Was any stress factor that precipitated past crises similar to the one that brought on the current crisis? How has the patient and the family tried to cope with the stress factor? What was the patient's level of functioning prior to the onset of the crisis?
3. *Medical history of the illness.* What medical and psychiatric treatment did the patient receive for this mental illness? Which treatments were and which were not effective? In discussing the ineffectiveness of past

128

treatments, we ascertain why the patient or members of the family believe certain treatments did not work. What were the side effects of previous treatments?

4. *Other medical history, including drug and alcohol use or abuse.* Does the patient drink, and if so, what is the daily alcohol intake? Does the patient use illegal drugs? over-the-counter drugs? Does the patient have health and dental problems? Have there been recent changes in the patient's health?

5. *A family history of mental and physical illness*

6. *Living arrangements.* With whom does the patient live? If not living with family members, does the patient live alone? in a halfway house or some other group residence? Does anyone look after the patient? Have there been recent changes or problems in living situation?

7. *Current employment history.* Where does the patient work, if at all, and what kind of work does the patient do? How steady is the patient's work record? Have there been recent changes or problems in the work situation?

8. *Financial and other material resources.* What is the amount of the patient's income and what are its sources? Have there been recent changes or problems in financial situation?

A mental status examination includes the following areas of inquiry:

1. *Appearance and behavior.* How appropriate and neat is the patient's clothing, hair style? How appropriate is the patient's behavior in relation to circumstances? Are there noticeable unpleasant odors?

2. *Level of consciousness.* Is the patient alert, stuporous, or comatose? How does the patient react to what is going on? If the patient experiences any pain, how does he or she react to it?

3. *Attention.* How good is a patient's ability to concentrate? How aware is the patient of stimuli in all sensory areas, such as smell, vision, and touch?

4. *Mood and affect*—as discussed in chapter 5.

5. *Memory.* Does the patient know his or her name, age, where he or she is, the reasons for coming to the emergency room? Does the patient know what time it is? what day of the week, month, and year it is? How well is the patient able to repeat something that the interviewer says? Can the patient remember what happened ten minutes ago? more remote events?

6. *Language.* Here we evaluate any speech disturbances and the volume and pressure of a patient's speech.

7. *Form and content of thought.* How coherently and logically is the patient's self-expression? When interrupted, how well can the patient return to the subject matter? Does the patient express such symptoms as hallucinations and delusions?

Decisions regarding where to send a patient for subsequent treatment are not easy to make. For example, some mentally ill persons present themselves to the emergency room in an acute state of alcohol intoxification. The emergency room team must decide whether detoxification should be given precedence over treating the psychiatric crisis. Are there facilities where both treatments can proceed simultaneously? Is a patient's condition so serious as to warrant involuntary commitment to a mental hospital? Is the patient's condition stable enough to warrant returning home? Where can the patient get the best care and treatment that the condition warrants?

Referrals to Community Resources

Only one-third of mentally ill persons who come to the attention of the emergency room are subsequently admitted to psychiatric wards or to mental hospitals (Ellison and Wharff 1985). The others may need inpatient medical services or referrals to shelters, outpatient psychiatric and medical services, substance abuse facilities, welfare, and the like. It is not unusual that patients cannot readily be discharged to the community because of the lack of supportive services—and at times discharges are not effectuated simply because team members don't know about the existence of needed resources. Churgin (1985), who observed the practices in various emergency rooms, noted that those emergency room staff who knew the most about community-based services also tended to make the most discharges to the community and the fewest transfers to psychiatric inpatient care. It was often the emergency room's social worker who shared her knowledge of community resources with other staff members and who was in charge of contacting families and arranging for housing, welfare, and outpatient medical and psychiatric care.

It takes time to make effective referrals to the community from the emergency room, but the pressured atmosphere of the emergency room will not affect the manner in which referrals are made if one expects patients to actually follow through on them. Emergency room patients tend not to follow through on rushed, hastily made referrals, especially when they are only given such "hard data" as the name and address of an organization and a date for their appointment (Solomon and Gordon 1986). Patients do tend to follow through, however, when a team member takes the time to discuss their thoughts and feelings about linkages that are about to be made. It helps when we ask whether the patient has previously used a resource, such as a halfway house facility or an outpatient psychiatric clinic. What was the patient's pattern of clinic attendance? Were the services satisfactory? If not, what would make them satisfactory? Does the patient see any obstacles to using the resources? Are there others among the patient's acquaintances who have used the resources? What was their experience? If the patient does not want to use a resource, are there other suggestions? Does the patient know what will happen if he or she decides not to use a resource?

Backup Emergency Services

The Psychiatric Emergency Service of New England Medical Center, a 24-hour component of the hospital's general emergency room, requires the completion of patient–service provider linkages (Ellison and Wharff 1985). In addition to providing the usual diagnostic emergency care and referral services, emergency room staff continue their contact with patients even after their discharge, facilitating and completing their linkages with community services. The Psychiatric Emergency Service also provides backup services at times when community mental health agencies are closed, such as evenings, weekends, and holidays. Backup services include the evaluation of unexpected changes in a client's behavior, adjustment or provision of medications, and help in effectuating hospitalizations. The following case history is an example of a backup emergency room service.

> *Estelle James, 62, had been living in a community residence for mentally ill persons since her discharge from a mental hospital two years earlier. She took lithium for a bipolar mood disorder and had been functioning fairly well on her medication. A week prior to her admission to the Psychiatric Emergency Service, Ms. James had become increasingly irritable and angry. In an unaccustomed manner she began to pick fights with other residents and staff. Her case manager feared that Ms. James's condition might escalate into a full-blown manic episode. He tried to reach her psychiatrist, but the latter was out of town.*
>
> *The social worker took Ms. James to the Psychiatric Emergency Service for help, where Ms. James was seen within the hour. A mental status examination revealed that she was confused and disoriented and had difficulty in focusing her attention. A diagnosis of delirium was suggested. The medical examination showed, however, that Ms. James had hand tremors and walked stiffly and mechanically. This suggested lithium toxicity resulting from too high a dosage. She was referred to a psychiatric ward, where her lithium toxicity was cleared up within a week. Ms. James was returned to her residence, restored.*

NONHOSPITAL CRISIS SERVICES

Many acutely mentally ill persons don't need the elaborate and expensive medical facilities of general or mental hospitals in order to recover from their crises. Since the 1960s there has been a growing trend to provide psychiatric emergency services outside of hospitals. These include the inpatient wards of community mental health centers, which may keep patients experiencing psychiatric crisis for a limited time, such as two weeks or less. Patients are sent to hospitals only if their condition does not improve within a given period.

There are also crisis services that are not part of a community mental health center or hospital. Prominent among these are the California Psychiatric Health Facilities (PHFs), established by the California legislature in 1978 specifically to fill the gap in many counties' psychiatric emergency services economically. PHFs provide 24-hour emergency care to all patients who are not so physically ill as to require admission to a general hospital. The cost of maintaining a patient in a PHF is less than one-half that in a hospital (Moltzen *et al.* 1986).

But this daily saving is offset by patients' longer stays. Whereas patients average 8.2 days in acute-care wards, those in PHFs average 9.5 days (Rappaport *et al.* 1987). It is not clear whether acute-care ward patients or PHF patients receive better quality of care, but PHF patients are provided with a broader range of services, including vocational and educational services. Moreover, PHF patients are not discharged until linkages to community agencies are completed. The following is a vignette of a completed PHF service linkage.

Paco Hernandez, a 30-year-old unemployed farm worker, was brought to a PHF by a friend. Hernandez was actively hallucinating and attempted to disconnect and tear out all wirings to lamps and telephones because he was "afraid of the evil current." The friend explained that he and Hernandez had only recently arrived from another state looking for work. The friend described a history of mental illness that had been controlled with antipsychotic medications. Although Hernandez was given medication several months earlier in another town, he had run out of his pills.

When Hernandez was admitted, the friend explained that he was about to move to another town, leaving the former without any family or acquaintances.

A mental status examination and Hernandez's behavior resulted in a diagnosis of schizophrenia. Hernandez was admitted to the acute-care unit and, with the help of antipsychotic medications, his symptoms were brought under control within six days. Hernandez was fatalistic when he learned that his friend had left him behind in a strange town. He said he knew that sooner or later this would happen. The social worker introduced him to a local priest who was interested in helping migrant workers. The priest located a family who would take Hernandez as a boarder but could not do so for another week. Arrangements were also made for Hernandez to be seen as an outpatient in a community mental health center. Hernandez appeared hesitant, and a discussion revealed that he was afraid about what would happen to him as an "outpatient." With Hernandez the social worker visited the Community Mental Health Clinic and introduced him to the psychiatrist and to the new social worker who would be working with him.

Hernandez remained in the PHF, participating in a Spanish-speaking therapy group until his residence became available. A followup at six months revealed that Hernandez had followed through on his treatment and was pleased with his living arrangements. He also held a part-time job as a gardener.

OTHER ACUTE-CARE ALTERNATIVES

Hospital and non-hospital-affiliated emergency services such as those above accept all patients experiencing psychiatric crises, regardless of whether they are harmful to themselves or others. There are other services that will accept persons in a state of decompensation, provided they are not suicidal, homicidal, or drug and alcohol users.

Polak *et al.* (1979) report on a system of private homes around Denver, Colorado, where psychiatric nurses and other specially trained persons accept and care for patients in their own homes. Patients in these homes are seen by psychiatrists, social workers, and volunteers from a regional community mental health center. The average stay of patients in these private crisis-treatment homes is two weeks.

In Madison, Wisconsin, the Training in Community Living (TCL) psychosocial rehabilitation project aims to maintain mentally ill persons in their homes during crises whenever possible. Among its service components, TCL has a mobile emergency unit staffed by a team of emergency workers. The mobile unit is equipped to visit patients on a 24-hour basis, make quick diagnoses, and provide emergency care. When patients do not respond as hoped for or when they are too violent for home treatment, the unit facilitates their admission to a mental hospital (Stein and Test 1979).

PRACTICE PRINCIPLES

Being taken to an emergency room and experiencing the attention of the team is in itself therapeutic for most patients in crisis. It is reassuring for the patient to know that the condition is being attended to and will be properly treated. But it is not enough for crisis team members to formulate accurate assessments and arrange for appropriate treatment. They also need to know how to work with patients in crisis so as to facilitate the restoration of their coping abilities. Several principles for doing so are discussed below: forming an alliance, recognizing the client's concerns, setting realistic goals, and identifying supporting strengths.

FORMING AN ALLIANCE

The disorientation and anxieties brought on by a psychiatric crisis terrify most people. Even though they may protest that they wish to be left alone, psychiatric emergency room patients need a reassuring, calming human contact during their crisis. It is important for an emergency room professional to take the time to spend the time with patients, talking to them and responding to their fears with reassurance and information. We may ask why we should do this, especially when it appears that the patient is not paying attention or is not aware of what is going on. Yet it is not unusual for patients to recognize the professional who held their hand and soothingly talked to them when their contact with reality is regained. And even when the comforted patients do not seem to recognize the professional after restoration, they tend to establish a therapeutic alliance in a shorter period than others for whom the effort was not made. Gorton and Partridge (1982, p. 6) report the following case that illustrates this point.

> *A 42-year-old woman was brought to the emergency unit the day after the death of her mother, with whom she had been living. She was markedly regressed at home, sitting silently in the corner and refusing to eat. In the emergency unit she was motionless, staring at the floor and saying nothing. A psychiatric resident thought that she must be a catatonic schizophrenic or that she was in a psychotic depression that would require long-term hospitalization.*
>
> *His supervisor suggested a different plan, and the woman was put into an overnight bed. Each hour until he turned in, the resident would visit her and tell her how sorry he was to hear that her mother had died. The client did not acknowledge his presence until the following morning, when she greeted him saying "My mother has just died. I need to go home and help with the funeral."*

Forming the therapeutic alliance is tantamount to forming a professional relationship that is based on mutual trust and respect. Where such an alliance is present, the professional and the client work well together for the benefit of the client. Emergency room patients who have established this relationship will be more likely to cooperate in their subsequent treatment and follow through on referrals.

THE CLIENT'S IMMEDIATE CONCERN

Paying attention to a patient's immediate concern not only helps to alleviate a sense of helplessness but may also avert potential problems. Patients want to know what will be happening to them. They worry about the medical treatment they are getting. They ask where their friends and relatives are. Those who have pets seem especially worried about how their pets will be cared for during their absence. They may need clothes and toilet articles from home. In their rush to formulate assessments and make referrals, clinicians sometimes overlook these practical concerns that are important to patients.

SETTING REALISTIC GOALS

As in all areas of practice, emergency room work demands setting realistic, doable goals for patients. Short-term interventions call for goals that can be accomplished during the limited period of time the patient is with us. An example of an unrealistic goal would be to expect that a patient's symptoms will be brought under control during the relatively short stay or that major social and financial problems can be solved. Goals that can be attained may include the following:

1. Reassuring a patient about a transfer to another part of the hospital or another facility
2. Providing information to the family about the patient's condition
3. Obtaining information from family and friends that will help in formulating the diagnosis
4. Helping the patient to pay overdue bills
5. Involving the family in treatment planning
6. Mobilizing friends and family who can help at this time

SUPPORTING STRENGTHS

Few emergency room patients are absolutely and *totally* helpless. Most can do a little something for themselves, such as washing up, combing their hair, putting on an article of clothing, or using the toilet. It is important not to do for patients what they can do for themselves. Taking over functions that patients can perform only helps to reinforce and prolong their helplessness. It is good practice to encourage them to do as much for themselves as they can, even when their efforts seem clumsy and take extra time.

It is not unusual for patients to want advice about their personal problems. Tempting as it may be, such advice should be withheld. Emergency room work does not allow enough time to get to know patients in any meaningful way. To give advice for problems whose dimensions we cannot begin to understand can at best be useless and at worst harmful and counterproductive. However, time permitting, we can help patients explore options that could lead to a systematic way of addressing their problems and eventually solving them. Taking patients' concerns seriously can bolster their self-esteem and speed their regaining control over daily activities.

SUMMARY

Psychiatric crises are always serious conditions that require rapid, intensive interventions. These interventions are ordinarily provided through emergency rooms of general hospitals. Emergency room teams perform three vital functions:

1. They diagnose a patient's condition and decide whether ER services are appropriate for an individual patient.
2. They provide emergency treatment that includes skills in crisis intervention techniques.
3. They effectuate appropriate referrals.

Emergency room work demands a knowledgeable and skillful application of the principles of crisis intervention. The most important subsequent decisions for treatment of patients involve the extent of further inpatient care versus discharge to their home or other community-based, noninstitutional living arrangements.

FOR DISCUSSION AND THOUGHT

You are a member of a treatment team in the psychiatric emergency room of a large urban hospital. Three persons have just been brought in by the police.

Patient A is an old, emaciated-looking woman who has been found wandering on the streets, carrying several plastic shopping bags filled with rotting fruit and dirty clothing. She is incoherently muttering to herself and unaware of what is going on around her. She seems to have trouble breathing, exhibits a palsied shaking, has open sores on her legs and feet.

Patient B is a large middle-aged man, totally naked. He is generally quiet when left alone, but will scream when anyone tries to come near him. According to the police, patient B undressed himself while walking on a crowded street, shouting "someone will have to die."

Patient C is a young woman who tried to commit suicide by jumping out of her fifth-story apartment window. She appears depressed and refuses to talk with anyone. The police report states that patient C has three children, all under the age of six, who are temporarily being cared for by neighbors who knew of no relatives who could care for them. Her apartment was found in a state of disarray. She had put up a fierce struggle when the police stopped her from jumping.

Your team must decide which patient should be given first priority for emergency treatment, who is to be second, and who third.

1. What further information would you want for each patient before you can make your decision? Remember, there are no relatives whom you can contact *at this time.*

2. On what criteria do you base your decision for each patient?

3. Provide your reasons for your criteria.

4. What disposition would you recommend for each patient?

5. What are your social work treatment goals for each patient?

6. Discuss how, given enough time, you would implement one or more of your chosen treatment goals for each patient.

CHAPTER 9

HOSPITAL-BASED PRACTICE: ADMISSIONS AND TREATMENT PLANNING

T HE GREAT MAJORITY of chronic mentally ill persons are cared for in general and psychiatric hospitals during the acute phase of their illness. In spite of the fact that one of the stated goals of the deinstitionalization movement has been the elimination of public mental hospitals and despite the predictions that mental hospitals are no longer viable (Demone and Schulberg 1975), public mental hospitals are still with us and continue to serve important functions (Ames 1983). In theory, it is possible to shift the functions of mental hospitals to general hospitals, community mental health centers, and innovative living quarters that provide long- or short-term asylum in the community. But as a practical matter, such a shift would be very costly, requiring community facilities to add staff and substantially expand physical plants. It is not clear that the benefits entailed in such shifts would outweigh the expenses.

Moreover, public mental hospitals usually provide amenities that are simply not available elsewhere, such as large, protected grounds and a wide range of treatment, rehabilitation, and recreational facilities. Many such hospitals provide a range of services that short- or long-term patients need, such as beauty parlors and barber shops, clothing and gift shops, snack bars, and the various activity rooms. Public mental hospitals tend to be self-contained "worlds" that provide an ambience and services that the cramped quarters of general hospitals and community facilities cannot provide. In addition to short-term restorative treatment, the public mental hospital provides long-term treatment and care for the most fragile and helpless patients, especially those for whom there is no suitable community-based facility (Lawrence *et al.* 1988).

GENERAL FUNCTIONS OF MENTAL HOSPITALS

Patients who have a favorable prognosis, or those who can be restored to a greater or lesser degree of independent functioning, are best served by short-term intensive inpatient care. Studies have demonstrated that this kind of treatment can restore a patient more quickly and effectively and maintain wellness for longer periods of time than is the case with lengthy hospital care (Talbott and Glick 1986). Much of this treatment is provided in general hospitals, even by hospitals that do not have psychiatric wards (Kiesler and Sibulkin 1987).

In hospitalizing a mentally ill client we keep two major goals in mind. The first is to bring the patient's symptoms of mental illness under control through the provision of somatic treatment, such as antipsychotic medications. The second is to restore social functioning to the extent that the patient can return to and survive in the community. To accomplish these objectives, hospitals should perform the following functions (Glick *et al.* 1984; Stein and Test 1980):

1. Provide intensive short-term care aimed at obtaining a diagnosis and providing restorative treatment
2. Provide longer-term care for patients whose illness does not readily respond to treatment—and for patients who have been involuntarily committed by the courts, for as long as they are both mentally ill and dangerous to others or themselves.
3. Provide long-term asylum for patients who cannot be returned to the community in the foreseeable future, either because they are too dangerous or too helpless, and where the prognosis of restoration is poor.
4. Provide short-term protection of families and the community where patients have become temporarily dangerous.

CAUSES FOR ADMISSIONS

There are four reasons chronic mentally ill persons are admitted and readmitted to hospitals. The first and most frequent reason for rehospitalization is, in fact, not a psychiatric crisis but lack of adequate community supports. According to a recent study conducted at St. Elizabeths Hospital in Washington, D.C., as many as 60 percent of all rehospitalized patients are not admitted because of a psychiatric decompensation. Rather, they return to the psychiatric hospital because of a physical illness for which they could not find medical care in the community. These patients sought out the shelter of the hospital because they did not have suitable housing and were without family or friends who could look after them (Harris *et al.* 1986).

The second most common reason is the involuntary admission of patients who are considered to be dangerous to themselves or to others. The third is transfers from jail or prison of those found "not guilty by reason of insanity" or who have manifested serious misbehavior resulting from mental illness while in confinement. The fourth, least frequent reason for hospitalization is admission of persons who are experiencing a decompensation or an uncontrollable flare-up of their psychiatric symptoms.

These days it is difficult for a mentally ill person to gain admission to a public mental hospital as a voluntary patient. There are economic and legal reasons for this. Operating on restricted budgets, state hospitals prefer to admit those who can most profit from their services. For example, they are unwilling to admit patients who may sign themselves out before treatment has had a chance to take effect. Hospital staff have learned that many voluntary patients, or those who have not been committed through legal procedures, often exercise their legal rights to be discharged after only a few days' stay.

Prominent among these premature self-dischargers are the young, high-energy, high-demand persons. Many of them were pressured by families or well-meaning others to seek admission to hospitals. They themselves have no appreciation for the seriousness of their illness or how vexing their behavior is to others. Often, shortly after they are admitted, these patients learn through the grapevine how easy and how smart it is to insist on a legal right to discharge. Hospital administrators prefer not playing the revolving door game with some of these voluntary patients, and choose not to admit them in the first place.

Furthermore, as some state commitment statutes are loosened, more judicially committed involuntary patients now require beds. Thus there are fewer spaces available for voluntary patients.

INVOLUNTARY HOSPITALIZATION

Practitioners should be familiar with those statutory standards and procedures that are applicable to involuntary hospitalization, because a large proportion of chronic mentally ill persons are confronted with this situation at one time or another. (See Appendix 9A.)

A state can exercise its power to involuntarily commit a mentally ill person either through its police power or its **parens patriae** authority. Until the 1970s, a *parens patriae*, or medical model approach, prevailed. Under this approach, the state takes a paternalistic, protective role toward the mentally ill, acting on their behalf just as it does for children and other helpless persons. Most state laws originally embodied the *parens patriae* philosophy in providing that anyone who was mentally ill and in need of care or treatment could be committed to a mental hospital against his or her will and for an indeterminate period of time. This was often accomplished merely by obtaining a written statement from two psychiatrists to the effect that the patient needed to be hospitalized. Such recommendations to hospitalize were forwarded to courts who approved them routinely, in a *pro forma* manner. Under the guise of helping, many mentally ill persons were unnecessarily committed to hospitals and confined for excessively long periods of time.

This paternalistic approach gave way to formal judicial procedures that were based on a view that hospitalization is a serious deprivation of a person's liberty. In the 1970s lawsuits were brought to challenge paternalistic statutes on the ground that they were too vague and ambiguous. Under such statutes almost any person who was deemed to be mentally ill could be confined. These legal reforms emphasized and gave an added impetus to the deinstitutionalization movement that was well underway at the time.

Legal reformers urged that the police power be the primary basis for involuntary commitment. Under this power the state has the right to deprive a person of liberty mainly in order to protect others, rather than for the person's own benefit. Thus the mentally ill cannot be hospitalized against their will for "their own good," but only if they are physically dangerous to themselves or to others. The dangerousness approach culminated in a landmark Supreme Court case decided in the mid-1970s, O'Connor v. Donaldson (1975). This case concerned a chronic mentally ill man, Donaldson, who had been confined for 15 years without treatment in a Florida mental hospital and who had not been dangerous at any time. The court noted that if Donaldson could survive without danger in the community, either by himself or with the help of others, it was unconstitutional to keep him confined. The court emphasized Donaldson's right to liberty.

Originally, under the police power approach, dangerousness was defined as physical violence. But many states have since expanded the term to include harm to property or to emotions. Thus a mentally ill person who frightens others by threats or behavior, even though he or she has not yet acted out, may be considered to be "dangerous" and committed to a hospital involuntarily. Also, many states regard "gravely disabled" persons who cannot provide for their own food, clothing, shelter, or medical care as dangerous to themselves. (See Appendix 9B.)

When a Patient Should Be Admitted

Although a practitioner may have made every reasonable attempt to prevent a client's rehospitalization and to keep the client in the community, this is not always possible. The flare-up of the signs and symptoms of mental illness

140

may make hospitalization imperative at one time or another. Inpatient care is usually the treatment of choice under the following circumstances:

1. *Controlling the signs and symptoms of mental illness*—to bring under control symptoms that have resulted in the following behaviors:
   a. Unmanageability at home and in the community, such as assaultiveness, exhibitionism, making threats, refusal to eat, destroying property, and the like
   b. Suicidal or homicidal threats and ideations
   c. Delirium
2. *Treatment planning*—to observe a person in a controlled environment in order to prescribe or redesign medical and psychosocial treatment. This is usually necessary for those who do not respond to their medications and other treatments, for persons who seem unable to follow their prescribed treatment, and those for whom "nothing seems to work."
3. *Monitoring*—to provide close monitoring for persons who have been placed on major new medication regimens. This includes the monitoring of blood and urine levels of patients on lithium and changes in types of antipsychotic medications.
4. *Detoxification*—to detoxify persons either from prescribed medications or from substance abuse
5. *Treatment for resistant and refractory conditions*—to provide somatic treatment for persons whose positive and negative symptoms are cause for concern and who resist being treated in the community. This includes those who have a pattern of decompensation because they refuse to take their medications, or take them in grossly inappropriate ways, or who altogether fail to keep appointments with their therapists.
6. *Hospital-specific treatment*—to provide treatments that cannot be given anywhere except in a hospital setting, such as electroconvulsive therapy.

CONTRAINDICATIONS FOR ADMISSION

Some patients cannot and would not benefit from mental hospital care. We should not waste scarce hospital resources on them, nor waste their time and their own resources. Researchers have identified the following situations in which hospitalization not only is not needed, but also is often contraindicated for the patient, the family, or the community (Glick *et al*. 1984; Talbott and Glick 1986):

1. To provide a temporary place to stay for persons who are awaiting court hearings or who are trying to avoid criminal charges
2. To adjust medications where the stringent observations and monitoring processes available in hospitals are not needed, as for example in relatively minor dosage adjustments

141

3. To attempt a scattershot of treatments with the hope that "something will work"
4. To use hospitalization as a punitive measure
5. To attempt to "cure schizophrenia," "straighten out" a character disorder, or engage in other treatment that sound research tells us will not work
6. To administer therapies that have not worked in the past or that are not available in that particular hospital

TREATMENT PLANNING

From the moment a mental health professional first sees a newly admitted patient, treatment plans based on tentative first impressions begin to take shape. These plans continue to develop until they are refined and finally formalized during meetings with the treatment team. The treatment team considers relevant data bearing on the formulation of diagnoses and treatment plans. Unfortunately, and all too often, in its eagerness to conclude its work as efficaciously as possible, a team may fail to take fully into account the patient's own feelings about being hospitalized and wishes regarding treatment.

CONSIDERATION OF A PATIENT'S FEELINGS AND WISHES

The struggle to restore a patient is half won at the point where he or she willingly agrees to, and does, cooperate with the treatment. To facilitate cooperation between patient and staff, we should pay attention to and respect a patient's feelings and wishes about the contemplated treatment. Often this is not possible for those newly admitted patients who don't realize what is happening to them.

Bizarre behaviors, violent outbursts, reality testing losses of new "admits" tend to scare and prejudice staff. Some staff members continue to treat patients as incompetent long after they have been restored. Firsthand accounts of patients show that many carry bitter memories of their experience in the mental hospital (Allen and Barton 1976). They are especially hurt when they are treated by mental health professionals as if they were puppets rather than as thinking and feeling human beings. Professionals who seem coolly efficient but who pay no attention to patients' feelings, requests, and opinions are particularly disliked. Patients also resent having their questions answered in professional jargon that is incomprehensible to them, and by getting tentative and inconsistent answers. When the professional does not communicate clearly and openly with patients, the latter begin to believe that their true situation is deliberately being kept a secret, and that it therefore must be much worse than they already feared. Under these circumstances, neither staff nor hospital treatments can be trusted or accepted with equanimity.

Admission Interviews

While not losing sight of what patients and their families think and feel about hospital treatment, initial contacts require that we conduct a structured interview in order to obtain the data needed to develop a diagnosis and treatment plan. In most hospitals these assessment protocols are lengthy and exhaustive. (See Appendix 9C.) In general, the following guidelines are useful for members of an admission or treatment team in conducting "first contact" interviews with the patient, the family, or others:

1. Review the circumstances that caused the current admission.
2. Inquire how the patient feels about being hospitalized. It is especially important at this time to demonstrate empathy with the patient's feelings.
3. Discuss the various treatment options that can be made available. Here we also should explain and discuss possible benefits and side effects of each option.
4. Discuss with the patient the probable length of stay in the hospital.
5. Tell the patient where (which building, what wing, which ward) he or she will occupy in the hospital and who will be in charge of treatment.
6. Inform the patient and the family of their legal rights.
7. Ask about what kind of treatment the patient received in the past, which treatments worked and which did not. What are the patient's treatment preferences?
8. Ask about any matters that have to be attended to at home while the patient is hospitalized. Do rent and other bills have to be paid? What will happen to pets and household plants? What about the patient's employer? Should anyone be notified? Is there anyone who could help the patient with these matters? Is there anything that the patient wants the social worker to do?

Assessment and Treatment Principles

Assessment and treatment planning begins as soon as the patient is admitted. Although the assessment and treatment planning principles are discussed in detail elsewhere in this book, let us briefly review those that are most applicable in the admission process.

The social worker's most important contribution in the *assessment process* lies in identifying and analyzing the following four areas:

1. The social, economic, and cultural factors that affect a patient's psychosocial functioning (chapter 7)
2. The environmental factors that may help to maintain or exacerbate a patient's illness, such as overly intrusive, censorious family members, overly high expectations from a teacher, employer, or therapist, lack of adequate housing and other social support

143

3. The strengths of the patient and the family. Here we identify environmental resources such as a concerned, helpful family, the patient's social skills, and material resources.
4. The material and social supports a patient will need upon discharge.

In treatment planning, the treatment team should follow the following principles:

1. Involve the patient and the family in the planning process as soon as possible.
2. Set realistic goals, suited to the expected length of the patient's stay, the patient's motivation, resources, and most important needs.
3. Develop the treatment contract with the patient, and, if need be, the family or guardian.
4. Follow the principle of the least restrictive alternative.
5. Start discharge planning at the time of admission.

SUMMARY

When the positive symptoms of a chronic mental illness flare up, many persons are best cared for in a hospital. There, the symptoms of their illness can be brought under control as rapidly as possible and patients can be kept from harming themselves or others or destroying property. The process of admitting a patient to a hospital should never be taken lightly, or done solely "for the patient's own good." An involuntary hospitalization is nothing less than depriving a person of liberty, even if done with the best of intentions. Moreover, not every mentally ill person needs the inpatient services of a hospital. In this chapter we have reviewed the functions of a mental hospital, the legal approaches involved in involuntary hospitalization, the criteria by which we can distinguish who will and who will not profit from hospitalization, and the major practice principles involved in assessing and treatment planning for newly admitted patients.

APPENDIX 9A: STATE LAWS

Inasmuch as the laws of each state are different, practitioners should first become familiar with the precise law of their state. Statutes dealing with civil commitment are usually found under such captions as "Mental Health" or "Public Health." These statute books usually contain references to cases that have interpreted various statutory provisions. Librarians can be helpful in finding the appropriate statutes. Local and state bar associations usually have libraries that contain statutory material—lawyers' offices also have statutory material, as do most public libraries. Each hospital and community mental health center should have at least a volume that contains mental health statutes.

Some states, of which Wisconsin is one, publish their mental health statutes in handbooks that can be obtained from the state agency responsible for mental health and mental retardation.

Several publications provide up-to-date information about new developments in mental health law. The best of these is the *Mental and Physical Disability Law Reporter,* published by the American Bar Association, 1800 M Street, NW, Washington, D.C. 20036-5886.

Another useful publication is the *Mental Health Law Reporter,* published by Business Publishers, Inc., 951 Pershing Drive, Silver Spring, Maryland 20910.

Finally, an important textbook on mental health law is that of Professor Alexander W. Brooks: *Law, Psychiatry and the Mental Health System* (1974, with a 1980 supplement). This book organizes the law in this field and contains a bibliography of relevant books.

APPENDIX 9B: PETITIONS FOR INVOLUNTARY ADMISSION

Petitions for involuntary psychiatric commitment should be made by a responsible person who has personally observed the patient's behavior. The petition consists of a written statement that clearly and concretely describes the client's dangerous behavior. The Emergency Commitment Office of a Pennsylvania Mental Health, Mental Retardation, Drug and Alcohol Program requires that the client's dangerous behavior must have occurred within 30 days of the filing of the petition, and, according to a memorandum issued on January 14, 1988, must meet at least one of the following criteria:

A. Clear and present danger to others shall be shown by establishing that within the last 30 days the person [the client] has inflicted, or attempted to inflict serious bodily harm to another and that there is a reasonable probability that such conduct will be repeated. A clear and present danger of harm to others may be demonstrated by proof that the person has made threats of harm and has committed acts in furtherance of the threat, or

B. The person has acted in such a manner as to evidence that he/she would be unable, without care, supervision, and the continued assistance of others, to satisfy his/her need for nourishment, personal or medical care, shelter, or self-protection and safety, and that there is a reasonable probability that death, serious bodily injury or serious physical debilitation would ensue within 30 days, unless adequate treatment were afforded under the act, or

C. The person has attempted suicide and there is a reasonable probability of suicide unless adequate treatment is afforded under this act. For purpose of this subsection, a clear and present danger may be demonstrated by the proof that the person has made threats to commit suicide and has committed acts in furtherance of the threat to commit suicide, or

D. The person has substantially mutilated himself/herself or attempted to mutilate himself/herself and that there is a reasonable probability of mutilation unless adequate treatment is afforded under this act. For purposes of this subsection, a clear and present danger shall be established by proof that the person has made

145

threats to commit mutilation and has committed acts in furtherance of the threat to commit mutilation.

APPENDIX 9C: SAMPLE ASSESSMENT OUTLINE

The following is an assessment outline, used by one New Jersey state mental hospital, that must be completed for newly admitted patients. The completion of the assessment protocol is, as a rule, the responsibility of the Social Work Department.

PATIENT NAME:
DATE OF ADMISSION:
UNIT RECORD NO:
DATE OF BIRTH:
UNIT AND WARD:
DATE OF ASSESSMENT:
AUTHOR:

1. Last Assessment Dated: _____

2. Patient's Legal Address on Admission: _____

_____
       STREET   CITY   COUNTY   STATE   ZIP

3. Service Area: _____ 4. County of Origin: _____

5. Current Commitment Status: _____

6. County of Commitment on Admission: _____

7. Legally Responsible Person: _____ Yes _____ No

           If Yes, Specify: _____ Power of Attorney

                           _____ Legal Guardian

                           _____ Other: _____
                                              Specify

Name: _____

Address: _____
           NO. & STREET   CITY   STATE   ZIP

Home Telephone Number: _____
                           AREA CODE   NUMBER

Work Telephone Number: _____
                           AREA CODE   NUMBER

8. Emergency Contact Person—Relationship: _____

Name: _____

Address: _____
           NO. & STREET   CITY   STATE   ZIP

Home Telephone Number: _____
                           AREA CODE   NUMBER

Work Telephone Number: _____
                           AREA CODE   NUMBER

9. SOURCES OF INFORMATION (Sources used to complete this
   assessment. Include name, address, telephone number, and a comment
   on the reliability and relationships of each):

_____

_____

_____

_____

10. DESCRIPTION OF PATIENT (Gender, age, race, marital status, general appearance, any distinguishing characteristics or behaviors, including handicaps and communications barriers):

_____

_____

_____

_____

11. REASON FOR HOSPITALIZATION(S) (Describe significant social stressors occurring within period preceding this admission, community intervention attempts and the patient's perceptions, if possible. Also include information on previous hospitalizations. Address history of injurious behavior to self or others):

_____

_____

_____

12. CULTURAL INFLUENCES (Identify ethnic, language, and religious background of the patient. Assess the cultural influences on the patient's life):

_____

_____

_____

_____

13. FAMILY OF ORIGIN (Include parents' & siblings' names, a statement of family stability and the nature of patient's dependence on family of origin. Comment on the type and quality of all family relationships):

_____

_____

_____

_____

14. EXTENDED FAMILY (List all significant family relationships and explain the nature of the relationships, i.e., grandparents, grandchildren, aunts, uncles, etc.):

_____

_____

_____

_____

15. CHILDHOOD AND ADOLESCENCE (Where patient was born, who raised patient, and any significant events):

_____

_____

_____

_____

16. EDUCATION (Grade completed, academic success or problems, reading and writing deficits, special training):

_____

_____

_____

17. SOCIAL ADJUSTMENT (Quality of peer group relationships throughout relevant stages of development. Include comment on sexual attitudes and concerns):

_____

_____

_____

_____

18. SIGNIFICANT EMOTIONAL AND PHYSICAL HEALTH FACTORS OF FAMILY MEMBERS (Include major medical incidents and history of substance abuse by family members, suicidal attempts, and psychiatric disorders and treatment):

_____

_____

_____

_____

19. MAJOR STRESSES & LOSSES IN THE FAMILY (Significant and anniversary dates, e.g., deaths, moves, separations, and their meaning to the client):

_____

_____

_____

_____

20. MARITAL RELATIONSHIPS (List marriages [legal and nonlegal] and note quality of relationships. Include spouse's name and a statement assessing the quality of the marriage and patient's age at marriage termination/reason for termination.):

_____

_____

_____

21. CHILDREN (Names, ages, location, and quality of patient's parental relationships):

_____

_____

_____

_____

22. SIGNIFICANT NONFAMILIAL RELATIONSHIPS (Names of friends and influence and quality of relationships):

_____

_____

_____

23. DRUG AND ALCOHOL HISTORY: PATIENT'S HISTORY OF USE (Include a description of use and in cases of known abuse, indicate approximate date of onset, previous treatment, and problems related to past or current use):

_____

_____

_____

24. CONSTELLATION OF FAMILY GROUP NOW (If different from family of origin. List currently involved family members. Discuss quality of these relationships):

_____

_____

_____

25. LIVING ARRANGEMENT PRIOR TO ADMISSION (Describe type of housing and neighborhood, length of residence, number in household, and whether patient can return. Describe patient's initial response to alternate living situation, if applicable):

_____

_____

_____

26. EMPLOYMENT HISTORY (Types of work, length of jobs, etc.):

_____

_____

_____

_____

27. MILITARY HISTORY (Include V.A. claim number):

_____

_____

28. RETIREMENT, IF APPLICABLE (Why, when, and adjustment to):

_____

_____

_____

29. FINANCIAL STATUS (List source of income by amount and person who handles funds or a statement of lack of income and rationale. Include an assessment of patient's and/or other's ability to manage funds appropriately):

_____

_____

_____

_____

30. LEGAL STATUS (Describe patient's legal status, include charges and municipality, power-of-attorney or legal guardian, if any. If Krol, state charges and status. Describe influence of legal status on hospitalization and discharge plan):

_____

_____

_____

31. TYPICAL DAILY SCHEDULE, PRIOR TO HOSPITALIZATION (Describe use of leisure time during typical 24-hour period. List hobbies, special interests, or talents as stated by patient/family/others):

_____

_____

_____

_____

32. PATIENT AND FAMILY ATTITUDES/EXPECTATIONS TOWARD ADMISSION, TREATMENT, AND DISCHARGE (State patient and family reaction toward hospitalization, include direct quotes and state patient and family rationale. Include family's willingness to help by their active participation in ward team meetings and family counseling, and Wednesday Evening Family Groups. Indicate extent of influence of these factors on discharge planning):

_____

_____

_____

_____

_____

_____   _____
DATE   SIGNATURE & TITLE

CHAPTER 10

MEDICAL TREATMENTS: PSYCHOTROPIC MEDICATIONS AND ELECTROCONVULSIVE THERAPIES

M EDICAL TREATMENTS, most particularly psychotropic medications and electric shock therapies, are the most rapid and potent means of controlling the signs and symptoms of mental illness. The use of psychotropic medications in the treatment of a wide spectrum of conditions ranging from sleeplessness to major chronic mental illness has grown exponentially since these drugs were first introduced in the early 1950s. Virtually every mentally ill person who has been in the mental health system has, at one time or another, been treated with at least one type of antipsychotic medication.

Antipsychotic medications have largely replaced previous somatic treatments such as electroconvulsive therapies and have been responsible for the elimination of other treatments, such as insulin coma and hydrotherapy. Moreover, largely because of the introduction of these medications, the deinstitutionalization of many previously "incurable" patients from mental hospitals was made possible. In 1956, when the antipsychotic agent

152

chlorpromazine (Thorazine) was first introduced in the United States, the census of patients in state and local mental hospitals was at a high of 558,900. The following year the patient count began to diminish. It stabilized in the late 1970s at its current low of 116,000 (Kiesler and Sibulkin 1987).

Electroconvulsive therapies (ECT) continue to be used, but not as widely as before the introduction of antipsychotic medications. Although ECT continues to be surrounded by controversy, it is clearly the treatment of choice for severely depressed persons who do not respond to medications and other interventions.

Because of the steadily growing use of medical treatments, it is necessary for nonmedical mental health professionals to know enough about them in order to understand what is happening to their clients. It is necessary to be familiar with which medical interventions are most appropriate for which conditions in order to be able to recognize short- and long-term side effects and to weigh the costs and benefits of these treatments for the client. This is not to say that social workers and other nonmedical professionals should do the doctor's work, acting as a handmaiden. Only doctors should prescribe medication, discuss with patients alternate medical treatments, and predict the effects of medications and other therapies. Nevertheless, nonmedical mental health professionals have a significant role in the administration of medical treatments that will be discussed in this chapter.

This chapter will provide an overview of the most generally used medical treatments, emphasizing their benefits and their costs or risks. We will focus in particular on antipsychotic medications and lithium, drugs that are most commonly used to treat the chronic mentally ill, as well as the administration of electroconvulsive therapy. Finally, we will analyze the role of social workers and other nonmedical professionals in this area.

PSYCHOTROPIC MEDICATIONS

The term **psychotropic medication** applies to all drugs that are used to influence moods and mental functioning in the treatment of mental and emotional disorders. These medications are widely prescribed by physicians. Studies show that approximately 10 percent of all hospitalized patients and the same proportion of all ambulatory outpatients receive psychotropic medications of one kind or another (Haggerty *et al.* 1986; Koch 1984).

These medications are categorized according to their functions and according to the class of chemicals to which they belong. There are three broad categories. Category One, which covers the most commonly used medications, includes antianxiety agents, sedatives, and hypnotics used in the treatment of minor anxieties, depressions, and insomnias. Category Two consists of antidepressants used in the treatment of major depressive disorders. Category Three includes psychotropic and antimanic medications that are used to treat major mental illnesses such as the schizophrenic disorders and manic conditions.

New varieties of these drugs are constantly being developed, and their use is increasingly accepted and even expected as a concomittant to psychiatric treatment by the general public. According to a survey conducted by the National Center for Health Statistics, physicians named 136 psychotropic drugs that they prescribed for approximately 10 percent of their ambulatory office patients in the period of one year (Koch 1984).

ANTIANXIETY, SEDATIVE, AND HYPNOTIC MEDICATIONS

Antianxiety medications, sedatives, and hypnotics are often referred to as "minor tranquilizers." These drugs are prescribed for minor anxieties and occasional loss of sleep. By themselves they do not affect the symptoms of major chronic mental illnesses, but some clients receive them in addition to other medications such as lithium or antipsychotic medications because drugs from this category can help to induce sleep and act as anticonvulsants and muscle relaxants.

There are two drug groups in this category. The first are **glycerol derivatives.** The second are the **benzodiazepines.** The following are the most commonly prescribed drugs:

1. *Glycerol Derivatives*
   Meprobamate (Equanil, Miltown)
   Tybamate (Solacen, Tybatran)
2. *Benzodiazepines*
   Chlordiazepoxide (Librium)
   Lorazeparm (Ativan)
   Chlorazepate (Tranxene)
   Flurazepam (Dalmane)
   Temazepam (Restoril)

These drugs do not produce side effects, but they can become addictive for those who believe that they need them in order to sleep or relax. Tolerance to these drugs increases as they are used. After an initial three to four weeks, patients often find that their dosages have to be increased in order to produce the original effects.

ANTIDEPRESSANTS

Antidepressants are increasingly used in the treatment of major depressions. Major depressions, also known as clinical or psychotic depressions, occur to approximately 25 percent of the general population at one time or another (Lobel and Hirschfeld 1985). When such depressions last for long periods, especially during adolescence, they may foreshadow the emergence of a major mental illness such as schizophrenia.

Severely depressed persons experience a significant change in mood. They no longer experience and find pleasure in things they previously enjoyed, such as food, music, people, parties, or nature. This inability to feel pleasure is known as **anhedonia.** Depressed persons tend to feel demoralized and hopeless, unworthy and ineffectual in relation to their work and personal relationships. They avoid friends, relatives, parties, and other active socialization.

The physical symptoms of clinical depression include disturbances in sleeping and eating and in the digestion of food. Depressed persons may not easily be able to fall asleep. Once asleep, they may awaken in the early morning hours, such as at 3 A.M., and not be able to fall asleep again. These wakeful hours are often taken up with brooding about the unfairness of life, thoughts that only serve to exacerbate depression. Some depressed persons experience constipation or diarrhea. Some overeat, gorging themselves on junk food. Others lose their appetite altogether, and cannot bear the sight of food, finding the notion of eating repugnant, virtually starving themselves.

A severe depression may lift after only a few days but may also endure over many months. The longer a depressive state lasts, the more life- and health-threatening it becomes. Fifty percent of all persons experiencing severe depression are thought to recover spontaneously within a year. But their depression seriously disrupts their lives. Antidepressant medications can lift most clinical depressions within one to two weeks.

Should antidepressant medications fail to produce desired results within a few weeks, however, their administration ought to be discontinued and other forms of treatment should be sought, including individual or group psychotherapy. Some persons who do not respond to an antidepressants may have to turn to electroconvulsive therapy (ECT).

There are two classes of major antidepressants:

1. *Tricyclics (TCA)*
   Imprimamine (Tofranil)
   Amitriptyline (Elavil)
2. *Monoamine Oxidose (MAO Inhibitors)*
   Phenelzine (Nardil)
   Tranylcypromine (Parnate)

ANTIPSYCHOTIC MEDICATIONS

The Discovery of Antipsychotic Medications

Prior to the discovery of **antipsychotic medications,** also known as **neuroleptics** (drugs effecting a reduction of nervous activity) or major tranquilizers, the positive symptoms of mental illness could be controlled only by the most unpleasant and often harmful techniques, such as straitjackets, hydrotherapy, insulin coma, and electroconvulsive therapies. For example, **hydrotherapy** (consisting of cold and warm baths) was prescribed for agitated hospitalized patients. Patients were immersed for several hours in long bathtubs filled with cool or alternately running cool and warm water. A tarpaulin

155

was stretched across the top of the tub, only allowing patients' heads to portrude.

Such interventions worked only for short periods for the vast bulk of mental patients. Because most remained unable to care for themselves and acted out in unpredictable, bizarre, or destructive ways, they were confined in mental hospitals for most of their lives. When antipsychotic medications were first introduced to the mental health system, they seemed to usher in a new era of treatment.

The first antipsychotic medication, chlorpromazine, a synthetic antihistamine belonging to the phenothiazine category, was developed in France in 1951. This drug was originally intended by its developers to prevent postoperative complications resulting from surgical shock and to increase the effectiveness of anesthetics (Swazey 1974). One of the developers, the French physician Henri Laborit, suggested in 1952 that the drug be administered to psychiatric patients, in conjunction with barbiturates, in order to induce a continuous sleep of several days' duration. This sleep treatment, or "hibernation therapy" as it was then called, became popular with psychiatrists who used it to calm agitated behavior in neurotic and psychotic patients. During its first clinical trials it became apparent that this new drug was also effective in controlling psychotic agitation. Mentally ill patients who previously had been unable to sleep for weeks, even months at a time, were helped to sleep with the administration of chlorpromazine (Swazey 1974).

In 1953 chlorpromazine's property of controlling positive symptoms of mental illness was discovered. This discovery was made by a Canadian psychiatrist, Heinz Lehman, who observed that the continuous administration of chlorpromazine controlled hallucinations and delusions in even the most severely ill, backward patients. As reported in an interview many years later, Lehman still recalled vividly the excitement he felt at the time he realized chlorpromazine's potential:

> We thought we were just treating excited states with CPZ (chlorpromazine) and attributed the improvement that the schizophrenics showed to that effect of the drug. But then, about three months after the trial had ended, we discovered that some of the chronic, back-ward schizophrenics had been accidentally left on large doses of CPZ. And incredibly, to us, four or five of these back-ward patients were getting better. No one believed that a pill could cause remission in schizophrenia, and we seemed to be getting the best results with chronic paranoids, the group most refractory to treatment (Swazey 1974, p. 157).

Lehman foresaw that with a continuous administration of chlorpromazine, positive symptoms of mental illness could be controlled for long, if not for indefinite, periods of time. Patients could now be discharged from psychiatric hospitals and, with the aid of medication, be maintained in the community. This development ushered in the deinstitutionalization wave of the 1960s.

At first antipsychotic medications were greeted with uncritical acclaim by psychiatrists and other mental health professionals who, until very recently, regarded antipsychotic medications as among the most harmless of all drugs (*e.g.,* Torrey 1983). They were also seen as the instruments that would lead to the eventual closing of all mental hsopitals and a new millennium in the care of the mentally ill. Both assumptions, as we now know, have proven to be quite wrong.

The Effectiveness of Antipsychotic Medication

The effectiveness of antipsychotic medications is attributed to the fact that they block the transmission of the chemical dopamine along neural pathways in the brain. We still do not know why this blocking action is so effective in reducing hallucinations, delusions, agitation, and even, in some instances, clinical depression. What we do know is that the medications help the mentally ill person to restore contact with the external world and thus render the person receptive to other psychotherapeutic and social interventions. For example, patients who previously heard loud and insistent hallucinatory sounds and voices may continue to hear them, but in a more muted and less disturbing fashion.

By themselves, antipsychotic medications do not enable patients to behave in better ways. They do not and cannot restore functional capacities that either never existed or were lost as a result of a psychotic episode, as, for example, the ability to form reliable and reciprocal relationships with others or to work in a competitive environment as one did prior to the onset of illness. Moreover, these medications do not "cure" the illness. They simply effect a degree of restoration while the medication is in the bloodstream.

The elimination of medications from the body is uneven and varies from patient to patient. Some of the medications are eliminated within 10 to 30 hours, while others remain in the system for several months (Donaldson *et al.* 1983). Once the medication is out of the system, the overwhelming majority of persons decompensate and revert to their psychotic condition. One analogy to the use of antipsychotic medication is the case of the diabetic for whom insulin is not a "cure." Insulin must be taken on a continuing basis. The same is true of antipsychotic medications.

Medications are not equally effective for all. For example, it has been estimated that from 10 to 20 percent of mentally ill persons may not suffer a relapse over a 30-month period even after discontinuing medications (Anderson *et al.* 1986). On the other hand, about 10 percent of the chronic mentally ill will not benefit from any medications or other treatment (Donaldson *et al.* 1983). Even though medications restore some, their effect is temporary for many. A review of medication studies has shown that 40 to 50 percent of all mentally ill patients risk a relapse every two years, in spite of taking antipsychotic medications either orally or by injection (Anderson *et al.* 1986).

157

The Classes of Antipsychotic Medications

There are six classes or families of antipsychotic medications, all of which perform the same functions and have the same side effects, but which exert different effects on different patients. For example, the absorption rate of each medication in the intestinal tract varies among individuals. This will determine how soon and how completely the medications will act. Two other factors are potent predictors of medication effectiveness: the patient's premorbid functioning and the way in which the illness first manifested itself. Favorable predictors are good premorbid functioning and an acute onset of the illness. Insidious onset of illness, poor functioning prior to the illness, and many episodes of decompensation do not bode well for the effectiveness of medications (Fenton and McGlashan 1987).

Antipsychotic drugs should be selected on the basis of the side effects that a person can tolerate and their past effectiveness. Sometimes the selection of the most appropriate drug is a trial-and-error process. Some persons are comfortable and feel few unpleasant side effects in taking a particular drug but become extremely uncomfortable with another.

The following are the six classes of antipsychotic medications and some of the most commonly used and well-known drugs they include:

1. *Phenothiazines*
   Chlorpromazine (Thorazine)
   Fluphenazine (Prolixin)
   Trifluoperazine (Stelazine)
   Thioridazine (Mellaril)
   Mesoridazine (Serentil)
   Perphenazine (Trilafon)
2. *Butyrophenones*
   Haldoperidol (Haldol)
   Triperidol
   Benzeperidol
3. *Thioxanthenes*
   Chlorprothixene (Taractan)
   Thiothixene (Navane)
4. *Oxoindoles*
   Molindone (Moban)
5. *Dibenzoxazepines*
   Loxapine (Loxitane)
6. *Rauwolfia alkaloids*
   Rauwolfia Serpentina (Raudixin)

Antipsychotic medications are classified as either **high-** and **low-dosage** or **high-** and **low-potency** drugs. For example, Thorazine is a low-potency drug that must be taken in relatively high doses in order to obtain desired results. Haldol, on the other hand, is a high-potency medication for which relatively low doses are needed in order to bring psychotic symptoms under control. For example: 100 milligrams (mgs.) of Thorazine produce the same effects as 2 mgs. of Haldol. Daily dosages of Thorazine range from 400 to 1600 mgs., while those of Haldol range from only 5 to 100 mgs. Low-dosage, high-potency drugs include Prolixin, Haldol, and Navane. High-potency medications are more favored than low-potency ones for two reasons: First, they take effect more rapidly than the low-potency drugs, particularly when delivered through intramuscular injections. Second, they produce fewer extrapyramidal and anticholinergic side effects.

SIDE EFFECTS OF ANTIPSYCHOTIC MEDICATIONS

For years following the discovery of antipsychotic medications there was little awareness among practicing psychiatrists of the harmful side effect of these drugs. Side effects caused by medications were, and still are, commonly mistaken as part of the mental illness itself, because they often mimic the signs and symptoms of the illness (Weiden *et al.* 1987).

Very often these medications block the immediacy of one's perceptions and feelings of the outside world. Users feel as if they were watching others from inside a bell jar, giving up some of the quality of their lives (Diamond 1985). In the past, when patients complained that medications made them feel dysphoric or unwell, and wanted to discontinue taking them, mental health professionals did not take these complaints at face value. Resistance to medication and to other treatment regimens was regarded as characteristic of the irrationalities, irritabilities, and defensiveness of the mentally ill. Patients were told that medications were good for them, that the "therapeutic doses" prescribed by the doctor could only help and certainly would not be harmful. When patients became more urgent or vehement in their resistance to medications, their dosages, ironically, were often increased. Increases in dosage only served to speed up the development of harmful and irreversible side effects such as tardive dyskinesia, discussed below.

It was not until the early 1970s that the psychiatric profession began to recognize the serious risks involved in the administration of antipsychotic medications. The likelihood that a medication user will develop adverse side effects, including irreversible tardive dyskinesia, tends to increase in proportion to the length of time medication is taken and to dosage strengths. Chronic mentally ill persons who are required to remain on long-term maintenance dosages are at far greater risk of developing side effects damaging their physical, mental, and social functioning than are those who take medications only for limited periods to control acute episodes. Since large doses are not necessarily more effective than smaller ones in both acute and maintenance treatment, prudent medication administration calls for a "least is best" strategy (Donaldson *et al.* 1983).

With most persons, side effects last only for a short period, appearing when medications are first administered. But there are others for whom harmful side effects remain and become progressively worse.

159

Side effects can generally be categorized as anticholinergic and extrapyramidal. **Anticholinergic** side effects emanate from the autonomic nervous system, over which we have no conscious control and which influences digestion, perspiration, blood pressure, and the like. **Extrapyramidal** side effects stem from the central nervous system, which is responsible for motor behavior and over which ordinarily we do exercise some control. Bodily behaviors that are normally under our conscious control include walking, standing, sitting, hand and finger movements, facial movement such as focusing one's eyes, smiling, frowning, moving one's tongue, and talking. But patients who are affected by extrapyramidal side effects lose control over one or more of these motor functions.

At least a third of patients on antipsychotic medications experience extrapyramidal side effects, most of which appear at the beginning of their treatment, after which the side effects gradually abate. Those patients whose side effects remain unchanged after several weeks should be considered for a change in medication or dosage (Bassuk *et al.* 1983).

Extrapyramidal Side Effects

There are four groups of extrapyramidal side effects. The first are the **dystonias**, which are characterized by jerky movements and problems in speaking and focusing one's eyes. In some cases the eyes tend to roll backward, causing much anxiety and distress.

Second are the **Parkinsonian** side effects, known as such because they resemble the symptoms of the physical disorder known as Parkinsonism. Here we find signs of muscular rigidity, tremors in the limbs, an expressionless, masklike face, and a lack of spontaneity in feeling and movement. Patients afflicted with Parkinsonian side effects often have difficulty in speaking. They speak slowly, slurring their words. Because their faces lack expression, and their movements are stiff and mechanical, they resemble mannequins, an appearance that is particularly distressing to the afflicted person.

The third major side effect is known as **akathisia.** The major symptom of akathisia is a physical restlessness that is characterized by nervous pacing, shaking of arms and legs, and the bouncing of feet. This restlessness is commonly accompanied by agitation and anxiety.

The fourth and most troubling side effect is **tardive dyskinesia,** a condition regarded as irreversible for many. This condition is characterized by grotesque movements of the face, lips, tongue, and jaw. The tongue produces snakelike, rolling movements that result in drooling and an inability to talk clearly. There are jerky limb movements and rubbing finger motions, as if the patient were rolling a never-ending supply of pills. Many afflicted persons cannot walk normally, but shuffle or walk with jerking motions. For some, the problems brought on by tardive dyskinesia are worse than those of their mental illness.

Anticholinergic Side Effects

The most typical side effects experienced by patients shortly after they begin taking their antipsychotic medications are **dry mouth** and **drowsiness.** In some cases these side effects gradually disappear within two to five weeks. In others they persist. When the drowsiness remains, patients feel that they are sleeping their lives away. When the dry mouth persists, patients suffer from frequent thirst and from difficulties in speaking.

The side effects known as **akinesia** consists of a lack of spontaneity coupled with drowsiness. Patients who suffer from akinesia also complain of extreme weakness and muscle fatigue. They find it difficult to get out of bed in the morning. Families, and even hospital staff, often make the mistake of thinking that this drug-induced lethargy is a form of laziness that can be overcome with training and through the exercise of will power. Since some patients are, in fact, lethargic and withdrawn even without medications, it is difficult for those who do not know them to differentiate drug-induced side effects from the regressive behavior caused by their illness.

There are **sexual problems.** Men may experience an inability to ejaculate normally and their sperm is discharged into their bladder. Women's menstrual cycles may become disrupted or stop altogether. Both men and women may become anorgasmic, or unable to experience orgasm. There are urinary problems, in which some persons experience difficulties in the frequency and amount of their urination. Some may also stop urinating altogether, a situation that is clearly life-threatening.

Dysphoria

Some anticholinergic effects can drastically change a patient's moods. Some begin to feel gloomy, anxious, sad, and depressed. Others report that they feel as if inside a bell jar, and the world seems muted, distant, and disconnected. Emotions are not experienced keenly but become severely blunted, resulting in **dysphoria,** or the loss of pleasure in everyday living. Dysphoric patients describe their feelings of unwellness in the following terms: "I feel that I am caged in in my own head," "Everything is now gray," "I don't like to eat. Food tastes like mush, like nothing," "Why do I feel so jittery and can't get rid of this feeling?" "I feel dizzy and get the blahs. Nothing to do but lie down and sleep."

These mood changes become destructive to social and interpersonal relationships. Dysphoric patients no longer want to relate to friends and family. In fact, they may lash out at those who reach out and try to help them, creating a harmful reciprocal effect. Friends and relatives start to think that the patient no longer wants to see them and that their presence is a burden. Feeling rejected, they break off essential contact—probably just at the time when the patient was most in need of their support.

Intellect and Memory

Antipsychotic drugs can affect the intellect and memory. Studies show that after taking antipsychotic medications, a substantial number of mentally ill persons cannot learn or exercise judgment as well as they could previously (Hammond and Joyce 1975). Many patients retreat into an intellectual vacuum. They may stare for hours at a television set even after regular broadcast hours, when a test pattern replaces the picture.

The effects on memory are often unnoticed by clinicians (Marcus *et al.* 1988), especially among older persons in whom memory loss is often regarded as an expected development of the aging process. Nevertheless, the prolonged administration of antidepressant and antipsychotic drugs, especially when several types of these medications are given simultaneously, can seriously, and at times irreparably, damage a person's memory.

Children are particularly vulnerable to side effects. They develop tardive dyskinesia and anticholinergic side effects, including nausea, vomiting, and anorexia sooner and at a significantly higher rate than do adults (Gualtieri *et al.* 1984). It is generally recommended that antipsychotic medications be used for children and youths under 16 only when absolutely necessary and then only in the smallest dosages for the shortest possible periods of time.

Neuroleptic Malignant Syndrome (NMS)

Some persons seem to be allergic to antipsychotic medications and develop very bad reactions to them, no matter how small or large their dosages. One such reaction is classified as **neuroleptic malignant syndrome.** The presence of this disorder can be manifested by the presence of muscular rigidity due to prolonged contraction, fever, instability in walking and other movements, and other dysfunctions of the central nervous system (Baldessarini 1985). NMS can cause profuse perspiration and affect pulse and respiration and heart rhythm rates. The symptoms of this deadly disorder can develop rapidly and without any warning after drugs are administered. When the symptoms of NMS are left untreated, irreversible brain and muscle damage will result. Also, death can result among 10 to 20 percent of afflicted persons (Baldessarini 1988). The treatment of NMS is unequivocal: an immediate withdrawal of all psychotropic drugs at the first suspicion of its presence.

LITHIUM AND ITS SIDE EFFECTS

Discovery and Effectiveness

The discovery of the effectiveness of lithium as a treatment for manic conditions came about by chance in the late 1940s. Lithium is a naturally occurring salt, related in some ways to common baking soda. As a form of salt, it was tested on diabetic patients as a salt substitute, one that would not affect blood pressure the way ordinary table salt does. In the course of its "trial run'' as a salt substitute, lithium was tested in mental hospitals. Patients used it freely on their food—and some died as a result. Others, however, ceased being manic and agitated. The Australian physician John Cade had the perspicacity to realize lithium's potential and subject it to controlled medical trials (Cade 1949). It was not until the mid-1960s that lithium came into general use in the United States for the treatment of manic conditions (Johnson 1984). Its main use is in controlling manias and as a stabilizing maintenance medication for patients with bipolar disorders. If properly administered and monitored, lithium has fewer harmful side effects than any other psychotropic medication. Nor is there a significant risk of addiction. However, it is potentially a very dangerous drug. The dosage that produces the desired therapeutic effects is very close to the toxic dosage.

Lithium can help approximately 80 percent of patients suffering from bipolar disorders. Only 20 percent of its users tend to relapse while on the drug. There is also growing evidence that lithium is helpful in treating some schizophrenic conditions and that, if taken in conjunction with antipsychotic medications, it can benefit many chronic, poor-prognosis patients (Donaldson et al. 1983).

Side Effects of Lithium

Most users do not feel unpleasant side effects. However, too much lithium will result in minor side effects, or even—in extreme cases—death. Dosages have to be adjusted for each patient for the smallest effective amounts. The first signs of side effects stemming from too much lithium are tremors in the limbs, usually in the arms, when the user is at rest (Carroll et al. 1987). If the lithium dosage is increased, the tremors worsen. There is thirst, diarrhea, and ataxia. The white blood cells can also be affected and a wide variety of cardiac complications may ensue (Prakash 1985). When lithium levels reach the toxic stage, thinking slows down. Patients will appear disoriented and confused. If caught in time, most lithium-induced side effects can be reversed either by reducing the dosage or eliminating its use entirely.

There is some evidence that lithium can affect memory and motor speed—the speed with which persons can walk and perform tasks. These are not permanent effects. When lithium is withdrawn, patients' memory and motor speed return to their normal level (Plasky et al. 1988; Shaw et al. 1987).

Because of lithium's potential toxicity, those using it should be evaluated prior to treatment and then regularly and carefully monitored thereafter by means of urine and urinary function tests. It is often recommended that this be done in a hospital. Persons who are just starting a lithium regimen should be monitored on a weekly basis until stabilized on optimal dosages. Once stabilized, lithium levels should be checked once a month. Every four to six years, lithium drug holidays are scheduled to avoid the possibility of kidney damage.

POLYPHARMACY

It is generally considered poor practice to administer two or more antipsychotic drugs or two or more antianxiety drugs at the same time. This practice is known as polypharmacy. Polypharmacy does not result in better results for the patient. On the contrary. The mix of drugs only increases the risk of toxicity and contributes to an increase and buildup of harmful side effects. Moreover, the practice of polypharmacy confuses and complicates efforts to identify the drug that caused the most harm and that had the best effect. In spite of the dangers associated with it, polypharmacy is still practiced, often by poorly trained doctors or others who have not kept up with advances in psychopharmacology.

MEDICATION AVOIDANCE

Although some patients do not mind taking their "meds" (a few seem actually to enjoy taking them), there are a substantial number who find it exceedingly difficult to tolerate side effects. In hospitals, some patients successfully resort to ruses in which they pretend to take their medications while actually throwing them away. The most common practice is "cheeking," involving the concealment of pills in the cheek and spitting them out later. Patients in the community often stop taking their medications and then, feeling guilty for not following "doctor's orders," terminate altogether their contact with outpatient psychiatric and medical services.

To cope with these problems, the practice of long-acting intramuscular injections (depot medications) of antipsychotic drugs such as fluphenazine or Prolixin is becoming increasingly common. The effect of these injections can last as long as two weeks. But patients who receive these injections often complain bitterly about how unwell they feel under their effect. Ironically, they find that their side effects are even more unpleasant than those of oral medications.

ELECTROCONVULSIVE THERAPY (ECT)

ECT is the treatment of choice for persons with severe depressive states who have not responded to other therapies, including medication. ECT has the advantage of taking effect more rapidly than antipsychotic medication on, for example, depressed persons for whom the risk of suicide and self-mutilation is imminent. A practical aspect of the use of ECT is that it often results in significant recovery from depression within the time period covered by third-party payments. Since private hospitalization is extremely expensive, the quick-acting aspect of ECT becomes important.

THE DEVELOPMENT OF ECT

Electroconvulsive therapies were first introduced in 1938 by an Italian psychiatrist, Ugo Cerletti, who named the treatment "electroshock" therapy. Dr. Cerletti had observed that depressed persons who also suffered from epilepsy emerged from their depressions after epileptic seizures. Electroshock therapy, which imitated the seizures of grand mal epilepsy, also appeared to be most effective in providing rapid relief from serious depressive episodes, although no one understood then or understands now the biological mechanism involved (Fink 1979).

Nevertheless, Dr. Cerletti's findings were incontrovertible. After a short period of convulsions and unconsciousness induced by the electric current, patients whose depressive states had brought them close to death emerged from their treatment with a sense of physical and emotional well-being. ECT was introduced in the United States in 1940, a decade before the introduction of psychotropic drugs (Thompson and Blaine 1987).

In its earliest phase, the administration of ECT involved the risks of such injuries as transient memory loss, spinal injuries, and bone fractures resulting from unchecked convulsions. Nevertheless, psychiatrists welcomed the new treatment modality with open arms and virtually uncritical appreciation. The treatment was dramatic in bringing about rapid improvement in patients who had failed to respond to other interventions.

But the success of ECT also led to abuses. As a result, in the 1960s electroshock became the focus of medical and political controversy that continues to this day.

ECT, without having first been subjected to careful laboratory and field testing, was administered indiscriminately for a wide variety of conditions, including many types of social, emotional, and mental problems that did not respond to ECT. Moreover, ECT was administered to patients who routinely presented behavioral problems to mental health professionals, such as psychopaths, alcoholics, and youngsters who were considered to be delinquents. But ECT did not "cure" psychopaths of their antisocial behaviors. It did not stop alcoholics from drinking. It did not reform delinquents, nor did it control the symptoms of schizophrenia and other mental disorders. Patients who were needlessly subjected to ECT began to regard this form of treatment as punishment (Breggin 1979).

Shock therapy fell into disrepute. Not only was there disappointment at ECT's lack of effectiveness, in treating conditions unrelated to severe depression, but also a public outcry at what was perceived to be a punitive and barbarous treatment that could irreversibly wipe out whole stores of memory.

Articles appeared in prestigious and influential magazines, such as *The New Yorker*, written by persons who claimed that ECT had made them lose all memories of their professional training and experience. The vivid film *One Flew over the Cuckoo's Nest* depicted ECT as a form of punishment by a mean-spirited nurse and doctor. Some mental health professionals condemned the use of ECT as an archaic form of "brain blasting" that severely and permanently damaged the brain (Breggin 1979; Friedberg 1977).

These hostile reactions caused drastic curtailment in its use both in the United States and in Great Britain (Beveridge and Renvoize 1988; Thompson 1987). In Berkeley, California, for example, the use of ECT was actually banned in 1982 by a municipal ordinance, which was later struck down by a court as unconstitutional. Research on this significant form of treatment came to a virtual halt.

Costs and Benefits

ECT is now coming back into favor. Many of the physical injuries originally caused by ECT no longer occur due to improvements in its administration. Recently, a panel of experts assembled by the National Institutes of Health cautiously acknowledged that ECT should be used as a "treatment of last resort for some types of severe depressions." The report conceded that the risks of serious side effects are relatively low, and that no other medical interventions, including antipsychotic medications, have proved to be superior in providing relief for depression (Holden 1985).

The administration of ECT can be more closely controlled than is the case with antipsychotic medications. Also, it no longer carries its original risks. Prior to the administration of ECT, patients are given mild sedatives and injections of muscle relaxants that have eliminated the convulsions that had resulted in fractures. In fact, the only way that attending staff can note that the electric current has taken effect is through a slight twitching of the patient's toes or fingers.

Loss of memory has also been minimized by attaching electrodes to one rather than both brain lobes. Researchers report that in instances where memory losses do occur, most completely clear up within seven months after treatment (Weiner 1984).

The typical number of sessions of electroshock administration needed varies from six to twelve. If by the twelfth session expected results have not been realized, the treatment is usually discontinued. Once a patient's depression has lifted, an antidepressant medication is often given, which tends to maintain the gains of ECT. Maintenance medications are prescribed to accompany supportive and insight-oriented psychotherapy. This dual treatment approach seems to be the most effective way to prevent the recurrences of depression. But clinicians have noted that once patients have experienced the dramatic relief accorded by ECT alone, many will discontinue medical and psychotherapeutic treatments, thinking themselves to be permanently cured. This may be true for only a small group of elderly patients. Others, who have not learned to protect themselves with situations that trigger their depressions, tend to relapse.

The effects of ECT are cumulative and could result in permanent loss of some areas of memory. A good treatment principle is not to let any person have more than 30 ECT treatments over the course of a lifetime.

THE ROLE OF THE SOCIAL WORKER IN THE ADMINISTRATION OF MEDICAL TREATMENT

Does the social worker have a role in relation to these medical interventions? This is a subject that involves the jurisdiction, or the turf, of medicine, the most powerful profession in the mental health system. Doctors prefer not to be scrutinized or challenged on their own turf. They are trained to be in charge of patients, to do what they regard is best for patients, and to give orders to patients, nurses, and others. The law reinforces this approach, giving doctors authority that other mental health professionals do not have. Because of this power structure, other professionals, including social workers, tend to fall in line and carry out doctor's orders.

But those who obediently do what they are told to do by doctors must ask themselves whether they are indeed helping their clients or simply protecting their own interests. Doctors, especially in the public sector, are neither infallible nor consistently conscientious or meticulous in caring for their patients. They too are human. Social workers, in protecting and furthering their clients' well-being and interests, are compelled at times to question or to challenge doctors and other professionals involved in the care of their clients. This can be a formidable undertaking. There are risks involved in challenging and opposing one's colleagues and other professionals with whom one works, especially those who have more power, authority, and status. Moreover, a worker does not always receive positive recognition for having engaged in internal advocacy. Yet social workers acting as independent peer professionals whose aim is to assure the best treatment for their clients eventually may receive more respect from doctors than those who behave as their obedient handmaidens.

Minimizing Harmful Side Effects and Maximizing Benefits

The taking of preventive measures is still the best policy in minimizing long-lasting destructive side effects (Simpson *et al.* 1986). Careful drug prescription, the lowest possible dosages, drug holidays, and the observation of patients' reactions to their medications can minimize harmful side effects and retard the emergence of tardive dyskinesia.

Long-lasting, late-appearing, harmful, and ultimately irreversible side effects can be minimized in two ways. First, clients should be involved as much as is feasible in planning and following their own medical treatment. Second, practitioners should contribute toward exercising the quality control of medical interventions.

INVOLVING CLIENTS IN PLANNING FOR THEIR MEDICAL TREATMENT

This practice principle, discussed in chapter 4, applies more in the area of medical treatments than in others since the health of the client is intimately at stake. It is for the doctor, who prescribes medical treatment and who is ultimately held responsible for its efficacy, to involve the patient in this area of treatment planning. But the social worker cannot always rely on the doctor to provide full and clear explanations to the patient and the family of what can be expected from medical procedures or what alternate courses of treatment are available. This is particularly the case in the delivery of public mental health services where the patient is not only mentally ill but also poor, often uneducated, lacking in initiative, and ignorant of what to expect from the doctor.

Where chronic mentally ill persons are fully informed by doctors who have sympathetically treated them over a period of time, they tend to adhere to their medical regimens and benefit from them more than those persons who are treated in a perfunctory manner by a succession of psychiatrists (van der Kolk and Goldberg 1983).

What should social workers do when they find that the doctors in their organizations give little time to their patients and do not involve them in treatment planning? The first reaction of many practitioners is to help the doctors by doing part of the job for them. After all, social workers are experts in involving clients in planning.

But social workers should ask themselves three fundamental questions:

1. Do I have the proper training? Do I have the expertise to discuss with my clients all the important aspects of and alternatives to this medical treatment?
2. Am I prepared to accept the legal consequences stemming from not having provided full information to my client?
3. Should I relieve the doctor of responsibility for involving the patient more fully in treatment planning?

The answer to the first two questions is obviously negative. But the answer to the third question is not clear. A doctor who wants to see as many patients as possible may prefer to delegate those aspects of practice that are not considered "pure medicine" to someone else. Such delegation frees the doctor to carry out the more technical aspects of the work, leaving time-consuming explanations and efforts to get to know the patients to "lesser" professionals. Yet the latter aspects are precisely those that lead to the establishment of a stronger relationship between the patient and the doctor. Many doctors want a good relationship with their clients, although whether their desire for good doctor–patient relationships is the same for public as for private patients is a serious question. Additionally, as demonstrated by van der Kolk and Goldberg (1983) cited above, patients who have formed a relationship with their doctors tend to comply more with medical regimens than whose who have not.

In the final analysis, doctors must be held accountable for fulfilling their responsibilities toward their patients. In most instances they need a reminder from social workers or others of what is needed for them to involve patients in treatment planning and in the administration of medical interventions.

MAXIMIZING COMPLIANCE

Sometimes people who wholeheartedly cooperate in their treatment planning fail to follow through on their regimen. This is especially the case when they do not receive thorough and individualized instructions on following treatment regimens. Many also need ongoing encouragement from peers and professionals to continue their adherence.

It has been demonstrated that most of us—almost eight out of ten persons—fail to take medicines as prescribed: incorrect quantities, or at the wrong times, or in incorrect sequences (Rusch 1985). Noncompliance is even higher among mentally ill persons, where nine out of ten may be noncompliant.

Nevertheless, the level of compliance can be significantly increased when clients are given the following information as soon as their treatment begins.

1. *The names* of their medications and other treatments (If possible, patients should be given names that they can understand and pronounce.)
2. *The reasons* they are given each medication or other treatment; what the hoped effect of the treatment is to be; when they can expect the effect to take place
3. *How often, how much, and in what sequence.* In the case of medications, patients have to understand how, in what time sequence, and in what quantities they are to take them. It is a good idea to check the patient's understanding of the instructions by having the patient repeat them.
4. *Where* medications and supplies can be obtained. Unless the patient knows where to obtain them, names and addresses of drugstores, surgical supply stores, and so forth need to be supplied.
5. *Payment.* If medications and supplies are covered by insurance or government programs, information should be given about how patients can obtain them.
6. *Side effects:* what short- and long-range side effects patients can expect and whom to contact on a regular and on an emergency basis to report serious and unforeseen side effects
7. *Contraindicated foods and drugs:* what kinds of food, alcohol, and other drugs are to be avoided

8. *What to do and whom to call* when problems arise. Patients may be worried when they miss a dose, take too much medication, or eat or drink something that they believe may cause harmful interactions with their "meds." Hot-line numbers and other emergency and regular phone numbers should be given to the patient in writing.

Medication compliance can also be improved through the use of regular group meetings. Olarte and Masnik (1981) report excellent results they obtained using "coffee groups" that consisted of severely impoverished and culturally deprived chronic schizophrenic persons. These groups met at least once a month for an hour and a half at their community mental health center, where participants discussed their concerns about medications with co-therapists and other group members. In session after session, instructions were patiently reviewed and prescriptions changed where necessary. Group members developed cohesiveness and helped each other to adhere to their prescribed treatments.

QUALITY CONTROL

Social workers can take an active role in assuring for the client the best quality of treatment. This involves the monitoring of the client's progress and ascertaining the factors in the client's environment that interfere with medical treatment.

Monitoring Treatment Progress

Social workers are in a good position to monitor their clients' progress with their course of medical treatment. Through regularly scheduled contacts with clients and their families, they are able to note changes in physical and social functioning and to clarify which symptoms are medication-induced and which part of the illness. In most settings practitioners also have access to those client medical records that can alert them to inappropriate treatments, such as polypharmacy, and to those treatments that in the past have had deleterious effects or have not worked.

Environmental Factors

The most commonly used and consistently harmful environmental factor that interacts harmfully with psychotropic medications is alcohol. Many young mentally ill persons also use street drugs such as cocaine and heroin and will trade their antipsychotic medications with other mentally ill persons. It has been estimated that up to 60 percent of the young "chronics" use street drugs and alcohol (Bachrach 1987). The mixing of psychotropic medications with other agents will either neutralize the effects of the psychotropics or interact with them in such ways as to cause serious physical harm and personality changes. It is often impossible to distinguish the role played by the illness and the role played by alcohol and other drugs in causing these changes. Some patients who are ordinarily friendly and tractable become aggressive and oppositional when they drink or use street drugs. For others, an already low energy level drops even further, rendering them extremely passive, withdrawn, and unwilling to participate in any therapeutic activities.

Patients who drink and use street drugs most often deny this. But family members and social workers who know these patients usually can tell when new factors have been added to the client's usual behavior. They are in a position to find out about the nature of the client's substance abuse. The treatment team should know as much as possible about the nature of a patient's substance abuse in order to plan for the most effective and least harmful medical care.

Other environmental factors that affect the success of medical treatment include the family's and friends' attitudes toward treatment, the accessibility of the psychiatrist, doctor, and drugstore, financial resources, and sometimes someone to remind the patient to take medications or report for a checkup.

THE INTERACTION OF DRUGS AND SOCIOTHERAPY

A social worker, Gerald Hogarty (1984), made one of the most important contributions to research dealing with the effectiveness of antipsychotic medications and psychosocial interventions in the forestalling of relapse among chronic mentally ill persons. Hogarty followed persons who were discharged, in fairly good condition, from psychiatric hospitals over a 40-month period. He found that over one-third would relapse, no matter what kind of treatment they received and how well they followed their regimens. A substantial group was able to forestall relapse by taking their medications as prescribed. Moreover, persons whose relapses occurred less frequently than those of others were those who received typical psychosocial treatment consisting of supportive therapy and the provision of social resources (Hogarty *et al.* 1974; Hogarty 1984). Persons who did not significantly profit from psychosocial treatment were those who had little insight and were conceptually disorganized, overly anxious, and too quickly aroused.

Hogarty's findings were replicated by others (*e.g.*, Falloon and Liberman 1983) and clearly indicated that the most potent treatment at our disposal is a combination of medications and psychosocial interventions. But the benefits of this treatment approach last only as long as the psychosocial interventions are in place. Once the interventions are discontinued, patients tend to deteriorate in relation to their illness and their functioning capacities. Thus, a long-term supportive relationship with a social worker or similar mental health professional in combination with a conservative administration of appropriate psychotropic medications appears to be the keystone in maintaining mentally ill persons at their optimal health and functioning.

SUMMARY

In this chapter we have reviewed some of the most commonly used medical treatments of major mental illness, their side effects, and social workers' roles in assuring the best treatment for their clients. This is an area where the roles of doctors and social workers can, but need not, overlap and conflict. Even though social workers need to develop knowledge of medical interventions, they have to do so primarily to secure good treatment for their clients, and not to relieve doctors of their responsibilities by acting as their assistants.

CHAPTER 11

TREATMENT
PROGRAMS

Hospital-based therapies are delivered in the context of the hospital's environment, or its *milieu*. When this environment is deliberately designed to be a major treatment component, it is known as a *therapeutic milieu,* which in and of itself is considered to contain curative properties. A group that is involved in milieu-focused treatment and participates in decision making around selected aspects of members' treatment is known as a **therapeutic community.** In the hospital, such a group of patients, usually from one ward, is known as the **patient government.**

A BRIEF COMPARISON OF MILIEU AND BEHAVIORAL THERAPIES

Milieu therapy is an integral part of a therapeutic milieu. It ordinarily consists of group activities aimed at such goals as increased insight, self-expression, self-esteem, and the development of behavior responsive to the feelings and needs of others.

Milieu therapies are not confined to hospitals and other residential treatment settings. Many day treatment and rehabilitation centers make use of the total environment in caring for their clients.

Today, many hospitals also use the treatment approach known as the **token economy,** a form of behavior modification. Both token economy and milieu therapies are based on the notion that human behavior tends to respond more to external environmental influences than to internally produced wishes and drives. For that reason, both treatment approaches aim at producing changes in the environment that will result in changes in an individual. Apart from these similarities, there are profound differences between these approaches.

For example, the theory that undergirds a therapeutic community approach to treatment is based on the **sociogenic** theory of pathology, namely that psychopathology can be treated through a 'constructive' change in the environment.

This statement is typical of the broad, vague outlines of the therapeutic community approach. Practitioners are left to their own creativity for day-to-day applications. As we will see, this nonspecificity has lent itself in many institutions to subversion and misuse, where the most basic principle of the therapeutic community, namely that treatment always be humane and sensitive to a patient's feelings, has been ignored.

On the other hand, behavior modification approaches such as that exemplified in the token economy are concrete and specific. Here the focus is on precisely defined and measurable behavior that can lend itself to change by means of a specific technology. According to B. F. Skinner, one of the originators of modern behavior modification theory, the ultimate goal of behavior modification practice is to make interventions as technologically precise and predictable as are the physical sciences (Skinner 1971).

This does not mean that behavior modification should be carried out in a mechanistic, insensitive manner. Indeed, Skinner also postulated that in order to be successful, behavior modification therapies must fully apprise a person of the proposed treatment and take into account the person's wishes and feelings in relation to the therapy. But these treatment principles also have, in some instances, been ignored and subverted.

THE THERAPEUTIC COMMUNITY

Below we outline the history of the therapeutic community approach, and its theory and practice in modern settings.

Origins of Milieu Therapy

The concept of "milieu therapy" is credited to Maxwell Jones (1953), who envisioned using a patient's environment as the primary mode of treatment. The treatment was originally developed to "cure" such character disorders as sociopathy. It was intensive, costly, and best fitted to institutions where even furnishings and food lent themselves to the accomplishment of therapeutic objectives. Staff-to-patient ratio was high, at times two to three staff members for each patient. All staff members, including such laypersons as gardeners, cooks, and janitors, became an integral part of therapy. Everyone was responsible for maintaining a permissive, egalitarian atmosphere. There were frequent group meetings with patients, who were encouraged to express themselves freely and openly. Patients were expected to formulate rules governing their own behavior. In this way a therapeutic environment was created in which, it was hoped, the damage of past experiences could be undone and healthy growth fostered.

Shortly after its introduction, milieu therapy became enormously popular in the United States and hailed as one of the most important developments in the care of mentally ill patients (Rioch and Stanton 1951). Two reasons account for its popularity in a period just prior to the introduction of antipsychotic medications. The first was that therapeutic tasks could now be distributed among all mental health professionals. The second was its humane approach to treatment.

The distribution of therapeutic functions that formerly had been the exclusive preserve of psychiatrists was eagerly welcomed by nonpsychiatrists such as social workers and nurses. They became more satisfied with their jobs and with their increased status than heretofore when their inpatient treatment responsibilities were primarily those of custodian or doctor's assistants.

Hospital administrators also envisioned advantages. They expected that the new treatment approach would render patients more manageable and compliant without the expenditure of additional funds. Where private mental health care facilities required a high staff-to-patient ratio, public hospitals did not see any reason to increase their existing, already low ratio.

At the height of its popularity there was a widely accepted belief that in milieu therapy "it does not matter what you do as long as you do *something*" (Cumming and Cumming 1962, p. 2). Routine activities such as playing cards with patients or accompanying them to activity and dining rooms were now considered to be milieu therapy. According to contemporary observers, even patient neglect could be interpreted as milieu therapy:

> In the past few years the term "milieu therapy" has become so popular that few hospitals will admit to *not* supplying a therapeutic milieu. Some hospitals, for example, record the treatment given to a psychotic patient who has received little more than three meals a day and a bed each night as milieu therapy (Cumming and Cumming 1962, p. 1).

Today the form and function of the therapeutic milieu is more focused and circumscribed. The following functions have been identified (Gunderson 1978; Gutheil 1985; Leeman 1986):

1. To provide a predictable *structure* in terms of time, place, staff, and other residents
2. To provide clear, published *limits* in order to contain acting out and other undesirable behavior

175

3. To provide a *supportive* atmosphere that is designed to foster self-esteem and help residents to feel better about themselves. Support should emanate both from staff and from other residents.

4. To provide a *stimulating* environment that encourages residents to become involved in therapeutic, rehabilitative, intellectual, physical, and recreational activities

5. To foster both the growth of *responsibility and autonomy* in each resident through appropriate social skills training and a realistic expectation toward the resumption of responsibilities

SOME ASPECTS OF A HOSPITAL'S THERAPEUTIC MILIEU

A therapeutic milieu is one in which the environment does not hinder but furthers the aims of treatment. For example, prisonlike, sterile, dark, and otherwise depressing surroundings should be avoided, and warm, homelike spaces that invite relaxation and stimulation should be fostered.

The milieu should also be responsive to the special needs of its users. For example, most patients are disorganized and disoriented when first admitted to a psychiatric hospital. They need practical and clear signs to help them get around and become oriented. For this reason, most hospitals provide directional and identification signs on doors, in hallways, and rooms used by patients. Staff wear identification tags highlighting their names. Clocks and calendars aid in orientation to time while readily available mirrors help to remember, reaffirm, and monitor one's body image.

Self-care supplies are an important part of the structure. There should be ample supplies of soaps, shampoo, toothbrushes, combs, hairbrushes, and cosmetics to establish an atmosphere of giving as well as providing basics for self-care social skill training.

PATIENT GOVERNMENT

Although patient government was regarded in the 1960s as a new form of treatment for mentally ill persons (Hyde and Solomon 1950; Jacobs 1964; Gerhardt 1968), there are no discernible differences between it and the therapeutic community. In both instances the central intervention is a limited form of self-government.

The objectives of patient government have been described as follows:

A. To promote the general welfare and to strive for better conditions in the patient community. To strive for self-improvement and to cooperate with one another in order to promote better mental health for all.

B. To strive for a closer relationship with the Hospital Staff and to work with them toward a more complete program of self-help and self-improvement; to inaugurate programs of patient activities that will serve to help the Hospital Staff in their efforts to promote better Mental Health in the Patient Community (Jacobs 1964, p. 55).

The concept of the therapeutic community developed at about the time that antipsychotic medications were introduced in mental hospitals. Psychiatrist Maxwell Jones coined the term especially for the treatment of hospitalized mental patients. He defined it as follows:

> The therapeutic community is *distinctive* [emphasis in original] among other comparable treatment centres in the way the institution's total resources, both staff and patients, are self-consciously pooled in furthering treatment. This implies above all a change in the usual status of patients. In collaboration with the staff, they now become active participants in the therapy of other patients, and in other aspects of the overall hospital work—in contrast to their relatively more passive, recipient role in conventional treatment regimes (Jones 1959, p. 200).

This makes it clear that the most important objective of a therapeutic community is to provide patients with frequent and close interactions with staff and a voice in their own treatment. Three factors are involved. The first is an accepting but structured atmosphere. The second is caring and attentive staff. The third is group therapy as the primary treatment vehicle. Unless each of these factors is present, treatment may be ineffective or harmful.

The Atmosphere

One popular axiom of psychodynamic theory in vogue at the time of the therapeutic community was that mental and emotional problems could be "cured" when patients were enabled to express their innermost thoughts and feelings and that this could be accomplished within an accepting, permissive, and understanding environment.

Although we now know that "ventilation" of feelings cannot cure major mental illness, we still foster patients' disclosure as part of the overall treatment process. Self-disclosure is a necessary condition for the kind of self-exploration that seeks answers to why it is we do what we do, and whether and how we can change. It provides an impetus for change and helps to maintain gains. We also believe that self-exploration is best carried out in an accepting, permissive atmosphere. Moreover, where patients are encouraged to talk about their feelings, experiences, and hopes, staff will tend to develop greater understanding and sensitivity toward them.

But an overemphasis on self-disclosure and limitless permissiveness are both impractical and potentially harmful. A balance must be struck between permissiveness and overregulation. No one has the right to give vent to unhindered self-expression, especially of the kind that transgresses on rights of or deeply offends others.

There have been situations where overemphasis on self-disclosure and confrontation has caused more harm than good. In a hospital we work with a captive audience. Some patients may prefer not to disclose sensitive information about themselves. When pressured to "tell all for their own good," they could lapse into depression, withdraw, or revive the symptoms of their illnesses. Johnson and Parker (1983) provide the following illustration:

A 17 year old was admitted [to an inpatient setting] because of multiple substance abuse. With confrontation he revealed his homosexuality, which he had never revealed to his family. He was encouraged by the openness of the milieu to tell his family. When he did so, he was so rejected by them that he subsequently became disorganized and fearful, and had pejorative hallucinations. His acute symptoms subsided when he was given antipsychotic medications, but reappeared several weeks later when a reduction in medication was attempted (p. 171).

Staff

Early theorists declared that the attitude and behavior of staff toward patients in a therapeutic community is infinitely more important than their academic credentials or experience (Rioch and Stanton 1951). Although this proposition has been proven to be unworkable in practice, we still expect all staff members to show, and not just feel, patience and kindness toward patients. Everyone who comes in contact with patients plays a role in the total therapeutic "push." If even one staff member is rude, unkind, or abusive to a patient the best work of other therapists can be undone in a moment.

Patients and staff have a powerful impact on each other. Thus staff's morale and conscious use of self are crucial aspects in treatment. A depressed, burned-out, or angry therapist is bound to communicate those feelings to patients whether by deed, word, or affect. Low staff morale will be reflected in the low morale of patients, their feelings of hopelessness, and a fatalistic attitude toward treatment. Where patients and staff interact as frequently as they do in the therapeutic community, a good staff morale should be fostered. Staff should be supported in their work, given recognition for work well done, and protected from morale-eroding activities such as inordinate amounts of paperwork.

Staff's Role in Groups

The therapeutic community approach is based in large part on group processes in which, theoretically and ideally, all members have equal decision-making powers (Moline 1977). But in practice, as each group member knows, staff members have the most power. The latter can override all other group members when it comes to treatment decisions and know much more about treatment and discharge planning. It is important that staff members be candid about their role in the group, including their veto and protective powers. For example, they can exercise veto powers in clearly disruptive ventures such as overnight visits in wards of the opposite sex. They help to prevent group members from being hurt through verbal or physical attacks, through scapegoating, or through tacit exclusion. They help to facilitate group processes by helping each member to speak and be heard and providing the appropriate structure and continuity.

Group Processes

The decisionmaking powers of patient group members are limited. For example, they cannot decide to remove staff members from their positions in the group or their posts on the ward or hospital. They cannot vote on who is to be discharged or how to allocate material resources to hospital units. But they should make decisions regarding certain self-government aspects of their own units. They can decide what rewards should be given for good behavior and what sanctions should be taken for the breaking of group rules. Most importantly, therapeutic community groups can decide on, plan, and implement activities aimed at self-development and recreation such as the following:

1. Appointing someone to take attendance at meetings
2. Birthday parties
3. Card games and card tournaments
4. Physical exercise, including calisthenics, jogging, and aerobic dancing
5. A "local" or ward newsletter
6. A buildingwide newspaper
7. Outings to favorite fast-food places
8. Appointing patient-mentors who help to advise newcomers
9. Appointing liaison committees to bring concerns or suggestions to hospital administrators

Scheduling the frequency of meetings should take into account treatment goals and the wishes of group members. In group homes where residents may remain for an indefinite time, the schedule of meetings is more leisurely than it is in time-limited hospital units. In long-term residences, once-weekly meetings are the norm, while in intensive therapeutic settings daily meetings are sometimes scheduled.

When Group Meetings Are Contraindicated

Some patients prefer groups to individual therapy, because they feel less exposed and are not expected to talk as much. But group treatment is not for everyone. Some, such as persons who have a severe schizophrenic illness, are unable to tolerate the pressure and stimulation inherent in group meetings. When forced to participate in therapy groups, they tend to decompensate in spite of medications and other hospital treatment (Van Putten 1973). Their desire to withdraw should not necessarily be interpreted as harmful or regressive. Withdrawal may be a form of protection against stress. It is better to err on the side of caution by not pressuring reluctant patients to participate in group meetings or to make self-revelations that go against their feelings.

BEHAVIOR MODIFICATION PROGRAMS

A major tenet of behavior modification is that successful treatment outcomes depend substantially on the expertise of the therapist rather than on the motivation or insight of the client. Where treatment goals are not attained, clients are not accused of having been uncooperative or insufficiently motivated. Instead, the therapist returns to the "drawing board" to rethink and redesign treatment goals and their implementation. Success is considered to be the result of accurate observation of events that either precede or follow specific behaviors, and in knowing how to rearrange these events so as to bring about desired changes. The **token economy** program is one such procedure whose success in mental hospitals has been amply documented (Kiesler and Sibulkin 1987). In order to understand both the strengths and limitations of this approach, let us briefly review its underlying concepts.

CONCEPTS AND BASIC PRINCIPLES

The Law of Effect and Positive and Negative Reinforcers

Behavior modification is based on the assumption that most, if not all, behavior is learned. Therefore, behavior can also be unlearned or changed. This approach is based on the so-called **Law of Effect,** developed by the American psychologist Thorndike (1911), who had been conducting experiments on cats and other animals. Thorndike observed that the frequency of his subjects' actions, or behaviors, could be attributed to the impact, or effect, that the result of their behavior had on them. He further noted that the animals tended to repeat behavior that brought them pleasure and avoided actions that resulted in pain or discomfort. Eventually they associated their activities with the satisfaction or discomfort to which they had originally been exposed.

> Of the several responses made to the same situation, those which are accompanied or closely followed by satisfaction to the animal . . . will be more firmly connected with the situation, so that when it recurs, they will be more likely to recur; those which are accompanied or closely followed by discomfort to the animal . . . have their connection with the situation weakened so that, when it recurs, they will be less likely to recur. The greater the satisfaction or discomfort, the greater the strengthening or weakening of the bond (Thorndike 1911, p. 55).

We provide pleasurable consequences, or rewards, to those whom we want to behave in certain desired ways. These rewards, known as positive reinforcers, serve to increase or strengthen desirable behavior. On the other hand, when we want to help someone to decrease or eliminate destructive or inappropriate behavior, we make use of negative reinforcers. There are three types of negative reinforcers. The first is **aversion,** which involves arranging for an unpleasant consequence to occur as a result of undesirable behavior. The use of physical punishment and verbal reprimands are examples of aversion techniques. The second is **extinction,** where neutral, not unpleasant, consequences are meted out for inappropriate behavior. A refusal to pay attention (a positive reinforcer) to the behavior is an example. The third type of negative reinforcer is **response cost,** the taking away or withholding of positive reinforcers as a way of making the performance of undesirable behavior unpleasant.

Reinforcers can be material or social. Material reinforcers include such items as food, candy, tokens, stars, or grades. Reinforcers that are necessary to sustain life, such as food and water, are known as primary reinforcers. Secondary reinforcers are not basic, life-sustaining necessities, but may become associated with them. Money is an example of a secondary reinforcer, since it is associated with acquiring basic needs such as food, shelter, and clothing. Money is also used to purchase amenities such as luxury foods, movie and concert tickets, vacations, and the like.

Social reinforcers are personal signs of approval, including attention, smiles, nods, pats on the back, and praises such as "Nice!" and "Well done!" Social reinforcers are secondary since they are not absolutely necessary to existence. They are, however, the basic building blocks of self-esteem. More than material reinforcers, social reinforcers send us a message to the effect that we are worthwhile and capable, and that someone cares for us.

When a behavior modification program is first started, reinforcers are meted out on a regular basis, immediately following each performance of desirable behavior. Both positive and negative reinforcers should be given immediately after the occurrence of a behavior in order to produce desired results. The need for timing reinforcements immediately with the occurrence of behavior is based on the Law of Association-by-Contiguity. Later on, when the program is well established, behavioral gains are maintained by providing reinforcers at variable intervals.

The Law of Association-by-Contiguity

This law posits that when a behavior takes place in close association with certain **stimulus events** it will become associated with the event. Stimulus events can be objects and actions that contribute to the performance of certain behaviors. For example, a cigarette smoker who habitually smokes while talking on the telephone or drinking a cup of coffee will associate smoking with coffee and telephones. The latter become the stimuli that set off the cigarette smoking response. The immediate pleasure that the smoker experiences from the cigarette not only strengthens, or reinforces, the smoking habit but also causes the smoker to associate the smoking of cigarettes with the pleasure experienced, such as relaxation. Similarly, automobile drivers learn to associate green traffic lights with "Go—right away" and red ones with "Stop—right away."

Categories of Behavior

Behavior is classified into two categories. The first is **operant** behavior. This is behavior that is voluntarily exercised and under our conscious control, such as talking, walking, getting dressed, eating, and the like. Most of our operant behavior is shaped by its consequences, or the satisfaction or displeasure it gives us.

The second form of behavior is known as **respondent** behavior. This consists of involuntary, automatic reflex responses to internal or external stimuli and is not under our conscious control. Salivating at the sight of food and an unreasonable fear of exams are examples of respondent behavior. This form of behavior is shaped by the stimuli that precede its occurrence. For example, the food becomes the stimulus that elicits the response of salivation.

Ethical and Clinical Issues in Behavior Modification Programs

In view of the fact that behavior therapy is largely in the hands of the therapist, three ethical issues must be kept in mind. The first concerns the use and usefulness of negative reinforcers. The second deals with the patient's informed consent. The third is concerned with the individualization of treatment plans.

Only positive reinforcements contribute to the psychological well-being and improved functioning of mentally ill patients (Kanfer and Goldstein 1986). The use of negative reinforcers, especially of aversive techniques, or punishment such as isolation rooms, scoldings, drastic withdrawal of privileges, electric shocks, medications, or other physical punishment is not only clinically unsound but must be avoided at all costs. It has been known for quite some time now that in both the long and short runs aversive techniques have proven to be more damaging than helpful (Rachman and Teasdale 1969). Unlike non–mentally ill individuals, who may voluntarily subject themselves to aversive therapies for such problems as alcoholism and overweight, the hospitalized mentally ill are usually neither in a position to understand nor able to resist these interventions. Even when applied by skilled and caring staff, they stifle a person's striving toward autonomy and dignity. When administered by untrained or uncaring staff, they can become an exercise in cruelty and sadism as illustrated in the following legal case:

> Two patients who had been involuntarily committed to Midwest Psychiatric Hospital brought legal action against the officials of the state, alleging that as a part of a behavior modification program they had been subjected to injections of the drug apomorphine, without their informed consent. The drug caused vomiting that lasted from 15 minutes to an hour. The use of apomorphine was an aversive technique administered for such violations as not getting out of bed on time, giving cigarettes to other patients without permission, or for swearing or lying. A federal court observed that this aversive technique, if administered to an unconsenting patient, was cruel and unusual punishment rather than effective psychiatric treatment. Its ruling permitted the use of such an approach only after a patient had given written, informed consent for each application and where strict safeguards protected the patient during the administration of the drug (Knecht v. Gillman 1973).

Professional ethics and legal mandates dictate that we should obtain informed consent from our clients before embarking on any major treatment. Clients should know what treatment entails, its probable results, and whether alternative modes of treatment are available. Yet persons who are hospitalized because of a flareup of their illness are usually incapable of understanding the aims, let alone the processes, of behavior modification. And they may not want to change the way they act. Moreover, few patients have the necessary assertiveness to persist in refusing a form of treatment that is objectionable to them. Most tend to accept treatment passively, not because they want to, but because they are expected to. By and large, patients don't want any trouble and want to avoid hassles. It is important to identify persons who have strong objections not only to a behavior modification program but to any other form of treatment. These persons must be enabled to avail themselves of other, more acceptable types of treatment, as illustrated in the following vignette:

> *A token economy program is in effect for patients in the forensic unit of the Northwest State Psychiatric Hospital. Harriet Grey, the social worker assigned to the women's ward of the forensic unit, noted that three patients resisted participating in the program. Instead of earning privileges, they had privileges taken away from them for such behaviors as not getting out of bed on time and creating disturbances in the dining room. Ms. Grey knew that each patient was capable of better performance and that the removal of privileges, such as visits to the hospital's snack bar, made them increasingly angry and depressed. In discussing the situation with the patients, Ms. Grey found out that each had her reasons for not wanting to go along with the program.*
>
> *In discussing this situation with the treatment team, it was decided not to expect these women to participate in the reward and privilege withdrawal system of the program. However, the "resisters" were to meet in a discussion group that stressed personal concerns as well as their reasons for not wanting to do what everyone else was doing. The patients' resistance to the token economy program was reframed as a strength. After three months of group meetings, the behavior of all three women had noticeably improved. They said they were now ready to participate in the token economy program, but only "for the fun of it."*

Although many wardwide behavior programs operate under similar rules, they must still be individually designed for each patient, bearing in mind the patient's strengths, the severity of the illness, and the patient's preferences and dislikes. Material rewards, such as special snack-bar privileges, should be chosen in cooperation with each patient. Sanctions for undesirable behavior must also be individualized and discussed with each patient. For example, one person may find it unpleasant to have ground privileges withdrawn for a limited time period, while this sanction may be meaningless to others.

TOKEN ECONOMY PROGRAMS

Token economies derive their name from tokens that are used as reinforcers for desirable behavior. Tokens consist of any light, distinctive material, such as

183

brightly colored plastic strips, that can be readily dispensed and carried. They are used as an exchange vehicle to buy material goods and privileges and must be earned for clearly stipulated and understood standards. Tokens can also be taken away for unacceptable behavior as "token charges." In addition to such fines, undesirable behavior can also be dealt with by not receiving attention from staff or by being confined to a "time out" room.

Token economy programs can significantly increase the self-sufficiency and decrease disruptive behavior of hospitalized mentally ill persons (Kiesler and Sibulkin 1987). This may be accounted for, in part, by the fact that these programs require that staff pay continuous attention to patients so that they can monitor their behavior. Staff must know when to give out or withhold tokens, when to charge a fine, and when to collect tokens that patients want to trade in for rewards. Because social reinforcements are important in this treatment approach, staff must also be friendly, warm, and supportive.

One of the most successful and widely applied token economy programs is the **social learning approach,** developed by psychologists Gordon Paul and Robert Lentz (1977). The first principle of the program stipulates that patients should never be forced to participate in their program, but their participation should be encouraged by making it as pleasurable as possible.

> In the fully operative token economy almost every behavior of the resident either gains or costs tokens. . . residents performing very minimal levels of behavior do not receive many reinforcers. As residents move up through the step levels, they gradually earn more tokens, thereby acquiring access to more reinforcers in all areas. . . .
> Residents are not forced to do anything with the exception of not performing blatant violations of unit rules. Rather, after the residents' initial sampling of available backup reinforcers, regular programmed consequences and their free choice within the token system guide them in the direction of more appropriate behaviors (Paul and Lentz 1977, pp. 76–77).

The cornerstone of the program is staff who are thoroughly trained in basic concepts of social learning theory and programmatic procedures. For example, staff must know how to take note of each resident's behavior so that desirable behavior can be immediately reinforced. Social reinforcers, even more important to patients than tokens, should be generously and warmly provided when appropriate. Behavior should be shaped toward desired ends by reinforcing partial approximations of the target behavior. For example, if the target behavior for a temporarily incontinent patient is that the patient urinate only in the bathroom, the patient will be provided with tokens for just walking in the direction of the bathroom (the approximate behavior), even if the patient doesn't quite "make it" and is unsuccessful in retaining urine.

Patients who are best served by the social learning program include the following:

1. Those whose symptoms of mental illness have not yet been brought under control

184

2. Those who have poor self-directional and planning skills
3. Those who have problems with self-care and social skills
4. Those who are unrealistic or delusional about themselves and their own capacities
5. Those who display largely undesirable behavior, in spite of the medications and other treatments they are receiving

The ways in which patients can earn and spend their tokens must be well known to both staff and patients. (See Appendix 11-1.) Records of token exchanges and patient progress should be recorded immediately to ensure their accuracy.

TEACHING SOCIAL SKILLS

Treatment plans for hospitalized patients include strategies for the development of those skills that can be learned during a patient's projected length of stay. The goals of such training should be concrete and attainable. Most often these goals focus on self-care and basic interpersonal skills that help patients to get along better with staff and other residents and in following institutional routines. The attainment of basic skills is also important in preparing patients for returning to the community.

Just as in token economy programs, social skill training requires that target skills be clearly specified and each step taken toward their achievement be recognized and suitably reinforced by staff. The training proceeds in small, incremental steps from simple to more complex skills. A modest and attainable goal in the area of self-care skills is, for example, teaching a patient to brush his or her teeth. Although tooth brushing seems like a simple activity, for many persons afflicted by mental illness it is a complex activity, consisting, as it does, of numerous subroutines. First, one has to know when to brush one's teeth and where. One must learn to distinguish one's own toothbrush from others, to know where toothbrushes and toothpaste are kept, and to return them to their proper places. One has to know how to put the right amount of toothpaste on the brush. Finally, one must know how to brush the teeth and rinse the mouth. The token economy system, discussed in the next section, facilitates each step of this training.

A serious skill deficit observed among chronic mentally ill persons is an inability to talk easily and clearly with others. Many of these persons can be taught good conversational skills, seemingly a complex goal. But again, a conversational skill consists of simpler subcomponents. Kelly (1982) identified four subcomponents of conversational skills:

1. *Eye contact.* This is a skill that can be measured by the number of times and length of time that a person looks the conversational partner in the eye.
2. *Appropriate affect.* This skill consists of maintaining an appropriate emotional tone and responsiveness in an interaction.

3. *Conversational questions*. This is the ability to ask questions that will elicit information from and about the conversational partner.
4. *Self-disclosing statements*. These are statements to the partner about oneself that convey information about one's activities, interests, wishes, and the like.

Others have identified the subcomponents of conversational skills somewhat differently. Wixted *et al.* (1988) see conversational skills as consisting of the following three areas, in each of which subcomponents can be identified:

1. *Initiating conversations*
   Initiating a brief conversation with an acquaintance
   Initiating a brief conversation with a stranger
   Social telephone calls
2. *Maintaining conversations*
   Asking questions
   Providing information
   Social reinforcement
   Social perception
3. *Ending conversations*
   Timing
   How to break off
   Goodbyes
   Judging when the partner wants to leave

The subcomponent skills for the ''initiating a conversation'' area are as follows:

1. Making contact, such as smiling at the other and saying ''hello,'' speaking the other's name
2. Asking a general question, such as ''How have you been?''
3. Asking a specific question or answering a question from the other (Wixted *et al.* 1988, p. 12)

Although social skill training can proceed in any setting, hospitals and other residential facilities provide a uniquely intimate perspective on a person's daily habits as well as motivation and ability to learn new skills or hone up existing ones.

SUMMARY

The relatively short stay of most hospitalized patients is a deciding factor in the treatment goals we choose. The goals must be fitted to the hospital's resources and environment and have a twofold aim: to help patients live more comfortably in the institution, while preparing them for life on the outside. This chapter reviewed some of the most commonly used treatment approaches which, of course, are also used in other settings. It is important to remember that given the "wrong" conditions—such as untrained or uncaring, burned-out staff, overwork, and serious lack of resources—each approach can be subverted to the extent that it can no longer be considered either effective or ethical treatment. With the right conditions, hospital-based treatment can contribute much to patients' health and well-being.

APPENDIX 11A: SAMPLE TOKEN ECONOMY PROTOCOL

The following is an example of a protocol that outlines the ways in which tokens can be earned and spent in a token economy.

EARNING TOKENS

1. *Getting up on time*   1 token each morning

2. *Appearance*   1 token 3 times per day
   Clean fingernails
   Hair combed
   Teeth brushed
   Clothing buttoned, zipped, tucked
   Clothing neat and clean
   No odor

3. *Making beds*   1 token each morning
   Sheets tucked in
   Blanket straight and neat
   Bedding not soiled
   Everything put away properly

4. *Mealtime behavior*   1 token each meal
   Tray properly returned
   No stealing or grabbing
   Courteous table manners
   Proper use of utensils
   Proper use of hands
   No gulping
   No sloppiness

5. *Bathing*   1 token 3 times a week
   Obtain and return soap and towel
   Soap and rinse head area
   Soap and rinse upper half of body
   Soap and rinse lower half of body

6. *Interpersonal skills*
   Informal interaction (includes
   responding to requests, to

187

conversation, intiating requests
and conversation, cooperating
with others.)   1 token 2 times per day

Small group meeting attendance   1 token 2 times per week

Small group meeting participation   1 token once a week

SPENDING TOKENS

1. *Ward environment use*
   Quiet day room   2 tokens per class period
   Courtyard/patio   2 tokens per class period
   Refrigerator   2 tokens per class period
   Extra bath or shower   1 token per request

2. *Unit facility use*
   Store   1 token per request
   Canteen   2 tokens per request
   Unscheduled time in game room   5 tokens per class period

3. *Program resource use*
   Special catalog purchase   2 tokens per request
   Solitary games   2 tokens per class period
   TV/VCR use in bedroom   20 tokens per request

4. *Other*
   Use of personal radio   2 tokens per class period
   Late bedtime   20 tokens per request

FINES

1. Minor infractions of unit rules that do not violate other people's rights: these include use of goods or facilities without paying required tokens, an off-unit absence without prior explanation and approval

Consequence: time out for a 15-minute period and a 5-token fine

2. Major infractions that violate other people's safety and rights and that, in the community, could result in an arrest: these include stealing, creating a fire hazard, damaging things, excessive swearing

Consequence: time out for a 15-minute period and a 10-token fine

3. Assaultive behaviors, including direct physical attacks on others, attempts to cause physical harm, and direct threats to cause physical harm

Consequence: time out in seclusion for 24 hours and a 25-token fine

FOR DISCUSSION AND THOUGHT

1. Is it possible to offer both milieu therapy and a token economy approach simultaneously in the same unit? Give your reasons for either choice.

2. It has been argued by some that shaping behavior through a behavior modification program is a form of "brainwashing," or patient manipulation. Do you agree? If so, what are your reasons? If not, what are your reasons?

Note to the instructor: Divide the class in two groups, according to their disagreement or agreement with the statement. Each group can develop rationales for its position, then report back to the class as a whole for an open discussion.

3. Why is intensive psychotherapy not used more often with patients who are hospitalized in state hospitals? in psychiatric wards of general hospitals?

CHAPTER 12

DISCHARGE FROM
THE HOSPITAL

IN THIS CHAPTER we will discuss two aspects of discharging patients from psychiatric hospitals. The first is the criteria used in determining whether a patient is sufficiently restored for discharge. The second is discharge planning, the process of making arrangements for placement of the about-to-be-discharged patient within the community. While the psychiatrist plays a major role in determining the patient's readiness for discharge, the social worker's contribution to the decisionmaking and planning is crucial.

Discharge planning, or the preparing of the patient for life outside the hospital and linking the patient to needed resources in the community is, as such, an important therapeutic activity (Blazyk and Canavan 1985). Indeed, it can be considered the keystone of all other therapies. If carried out completely, the discharged patient will adjust well outside the hospital. If done poorly, the best hospital-based treatment will founder shortly after the patient's release.

ASSESSING READINESS FOR DISCHARGE

Three factors should be taken into account in assessing the patient's readiness for discharge: achievement of inpatient treatment goals; the patient's desire to be discharged; and the availability of community supports.

ACHIEVEMENT OF TREATMENT GOALS

When the acute signs and symptoms of a mental illness have been brought under control and the patient is restored to precrisis functioning capacity, major inpatient treatment goals have been achieved. In general, patients are considered restored when their contact with reality has been reestablished, when their behavior is once more mostly under their volitional control, and when they are no longer deemed to be dangerous to themselves or others.

The following criteria are commonly followed in evaluating whether a patient has been sufficiently restored to be able to manage outside the hospital:

1. *Orientation to time and current events.* Does the patient know who he or she is, where he or she is, and what time of day or season it is? Does the patient know what kind of treatment he or she has been receiving? Does the patient recognize the treatment staff? Does the patient know when mealtimes are, when bedtime is, when recreational activities—such as films, social hours, and dances—are offered by the hospital or in the ward?

2. *Orientation to immediate past and future.* Does the patient know where he or she came from? who his or her family members and friends are? Does the patient know where he or she will go upon discharge and what he or she will do?

3. *Self-care behavior.* Is the patient able to wash, brush teeth, bathe, and shower? Does the patient get dressed without assistance? Does the patient use toilet facilities appropriately? Can the patient attend popular and pleasant activities without assistance or does the patient need to be escorted? Can the patient stand in the cafeteria line and select food without assistance? If not, how much assistance does the patient need? Can the patient feed himself or herself? If so, does the patient use eating utensils appropriately?

4. *Relationships with others.* Is the patient able to ask for what he or she wants from staff and other patients? Can the patient hold conversations that are understood by others? Does the patient physically or verbally fight with others? How does the patient generally get along with roommates, with others on the ward and in the dining and activity rooms?

5. *Obeying rules.* Does the patient understand and obey the house and ground rules of the hospital? Does the patient go off the grounds or out of the ward or building without permission? Does the patient consistently ignore rules? If the patient breaks rules, is it because of not being able to understand them, or for other reasons?

6. *Behavior during outings.* Does the patient behave appropriately when taken on predischarge outings, such as to fast-food restaurants, on walks in town or in parks, on shopping trips and the like?

7. *Behavior during a weekend or other limited leave.* If the patient is permitted to leave the hospital for a limited period of time, does he or she over-

191

stay the leave without notifying the hospital? How does the patient behave toward family or others with whom he or she visits during leave? Does the patient engage in harmful activities such as excessive drinking or taking of illegal drugs?

8. *Restoration to predecompensation level of functioning.* Unless one has known the patient prior to the crisis that caused hospital admission, it is difficult to judge whether the patient has been restored to the precrisis level of functioning. But the patient's family, friends, or case managers who have known him or her for a length of time may be able to tell when the patient is well enough to be discharged and is on the way to recovery.

Moreover, psychiatric hospitals are no longer in a position to keep patients for the indefinite length of time that is required for a precrisis restoration to take place. Nowadays we expect that community care will pick up where hospital care left off in the process of restoring mentally ill persons.

9. *Legal criteria.* Legal statutes in many states refer to a patient's discharge readiness as a "restoration" or "stabilization." Although legal criteria for discharge vary from state to state, there are some standards that most hold in common. For example, in most states a patient is automatically eligible for discharge if he or she no longer meets the criteria for involuntary commitment, such as dangerousness or being severely disabled by reason of mental illness. Most courts require that a patient be discharged when he or she reaches the restored or stabilized condition described in the statute. In order to prevent unnecessarily prolonged hospitalization, many state statutes provide for periodic judicial reviews that are designed to save both time and material resources.

Except for the legal criteria, it is not necessary for a patient to meet all the others in order to be assessed ready for discharge. What matters is that a patient be well enough to avail himself or herself of and benefit from the medical, psychiatric, and social care that the community has to offer.

WHO SHOULD NOT BE DISCHARGED

Although hospital treatment can restore many, there are always some for whom that is not quite possible. These persons can be classified into two groups. The first consists of those who, although not showing much improvement, have achieved a level of functioning that makes it possible for them to be discharged to a maximum-care facility such as a nursing home, where care is available that enables them to function to the best of their capacity. The second consists of those whose impaired functioning makes it necessary for them to remain in the hospital.

We should be especially careful before discharging patients who are over 65 years of age, are physically frail, have cognitive impairments, or have spent much of their lives in mental hospitals. Such patients who are transferred to other settings, even to good nursing or boarding homes, have been shown to have significantly higher mortalities than have similar patients who remained in the hospital (Gopelrud 1979). For many of them, the mental hospital has become the only home they know and the place where all their friends and acquaintances are. When such long-term elderly residents are forcibly discharged, they may feel uprooted from everything familiar. In nursing homes, where most of this group have been reinstitutionalized, many may become so lethargical and depressed that they develop serious illness that often culminates in their death (Craig and Shang 1981).

The second group consists of persons for whom it is difficult or impossible to find an acceptable residence and for whom longer term asylum in the mental hospital appears to be the only reasonable option (Christ 1984). This group includes persons who, unless placed in restraints, physically assault others, remain self-destructive and suicidal, destroy furniture and clothing, have uncontrollable fits of screaming, refuse to eat or drink, or refuse to move from their beds or chairs. It is not uncommon that other facilities refuse to accept or keep them. Although they do not need a hospital's intensive and expensive care, these persons have to remain hospitalized until such time as a suitable community setting becomes available.

A New Jersey Supreme Court case is illustrative of the problem the second group of patients can pose:

A number of patients in New Jersey state mental hospitals who had been institutionalized for decades were determined by a state court to be no longer committable. Legally, these patients were eligible to be discharged. But hospital staff took the position that these patients should not be released because they were incapable of functioning independently and self-sufficiently in the community. The trial judge created a category to fit these patients, which he designated as "Discharged Pending Placement," or "DPP." In other words, although the patients were technically "discharged" they remained in the hospital indeterminately because they could not be placed.

The "limbo" status of DPP resulted in some hospitals having as many as 60 percent of all patients classed as DPP. This resulted in a legal challenge of the DPP status that was eventually brought to the New Jersey Supreme Court. That court ruled that in order to make the discharge process more effective and efficient, judicial "placement hearings" for each DPP patient had to be held at least every six months. The purpose of the hearings would be to monitor the progress of discharge planning. What placement opportunities could be made available to the patient? Which placement alternatives had been investigated? Why were placement alternatives not considered to be suitable? The court ruled that the following factors should be considered:

1. *The patient's clinical condition*
2. *The length of the patient's stay in the hospital*
3. *The potential harm to the patient if additional time is spent in the hospital*
4. *The type of facility to which release would be appropriate*
5. *The range of available facilities*
6. *The restrictions that would be imposed on the patient in each such facility*
7. *The extent to which each such facility comports with the patient's expressed desires*
8. *The realistic opportunity the patient will ever have of being fully discharged from the facility in question (In Re S.L. 1983)*

The above criteria are useful in both discharge planning and in justifying a lengthy hospital stay for difficult, hard-to-place patients.

RESISTANCE TO DISCHARGE

Many patients feel ambivalent about leaving the hospital. On one hand, they are eager to get away from institutional routines and demands. On the other, they are afraid to leave an environment that provides structure, amenities, and respite from the pressures of the outside world. Often they worry about what will happen to them in the community, especially about not having enough money to pay for basic necessities, not having a decent place to live, not getting needed medical care, and not being able to work (Ewalt and Honeyfield 1981).

Some hide their anxiety by making up stories about loving families and fine homes and jobs waiting for them on the outside. This is illustrated in the following vignette.

Joe Gould, a 45-year-old, never-married patient, was restored to functioning capacity after six weeks in Harborview Psychiatric Hospital. Gould could have been discharged sooner had it not been for a physical illness he developed during his hospital stay. He developed typical "flu" symptoms, including fever, headaches, aches, and pains. When Gould discussed discharge plans with his social worker, he mentioned that he had been invited by a well-to-do sister to move into her large home in a nearby affluent neighborhood. He vividly described the sister's husband, a stockbroker, their three children, and their pet dog.

The social worker was puzzled. Gould's description sounded too much like the kind of idealized family shown on television "sit-coms." Moreover, his case record did not mention family members or recent contacts with them. Further discussions about his family resulted in Gould's making numerous contradictory statements until he sadly acknowledged that actually he had lost contact with his sister fifteen years earlier and didn't even know whether she was still alive. But he was so terrified of "life on the outside" that he made up stories of

194

a loving, idealized family. It became clear that because of his anxiety, Gould had partly feigned and partly developed real symptoms of physical illness in order to delay his discharge.

Unlike Gould, many patients are reasonably candid in describing their worries about not being able to return to families or not having anything or anyone to return to. These worries should be confronted, explored, and resolved, especially where the patient shows signs of resistance in participating in his own discharge planning.

We recognize resistance when a patient becomes unusually vague, apathetic, or even hostile in discussing discharge plans. The plans of resistant patients may be full of contradictions, and glaring omissions such as addresses of friends, family members, or organizations that are supposedly going to help. Some patients show their passive resistance by altogether avoiding any discussion of discharge or by claiming that they have no idea what they will do after leaving the hospital. Apathetically they may accede to whatever the discharge worker proposes.

Unless their resistance is recognized and worked through, the outlook for a satisfactory adjustment to community living is poor for these patients. It has been demonstrated that patients who do not actively and willingly participate in their discharge plans are much more likely to decompensate and return to the hospital before the year is out than those who leave the hospital with plans that they helped to draft and approve of (Smith and Smith 1978).

Resistance to discharge can be worked through in a three-stage process. First, we bring examples of resistance to the patient's attention, if possible as they occur. This should be done in a nonthreatening manner so that we can proceed to the second stage, where we inquire about the reasons for resistance. The third stage consists of a serious examination of each reason. Here we avoid brushing aside any of the reasons as inconsequential and avoid providing premature or unwarranted reassurances such as "All the residents of Mrs. White's boarding home are happy there." In the above case of Joe Gould, the social worker had handled stage one by confronting him, in a friendly manner, with his inconsistencies: "But only yesterday you told me that your sister owns a blue Mercedes and today you tell me she owns a blue Cadillac. Does she change cars the way I change my dress? The way she lives, she does not seem real to me."

When Gould was able to admit to his fabricated story, the worker empathized with his fear of the "life on the outside." One by one she discussed his fears, which ranged from not having meals served to him in the hospital's cheerful dining room to becoming homeless because of high rents and his own lack of resources. All of Gould's fears had some basis in reality and none was solely a symptom of his illness. It took several weeks and many contacts with the community mental health center's liaison worker to work out discharge plans that were somewhat satisfactory, but not entirely reassuring, to Joe Gould.

Availability of Community Support

Discharged patients who do not have adequate support awaiting them in the community tend to be noncompliant in following through on psychiatric treatment, especially medications. They decompensate more rapidly and severely than those whose supports are adequate (Caton *et al.* 1984).

What are the supports needed by about-to-be-discharged patients? A study conducted among social workers in two large state mental hospitals in Ohio showed that every patient needed some kind of service, with a minimum of 2 different services to a maximum of 27 services per person. Table 12.1 is a partial listing of patients' service needs, in order of their frequency, derived partially from data in Solomon *et al.* (1984).

Evidently persons with mental illness need individual counseling almost as much as they do medications. A partial explanation may be that mental illness tends to erode self-esteem and creates problems in personal relationships, work, managing of one's finances, and the like. Supportive counseling helps to address these issues. But the mere provision of counseling services is not enough. One of the themes of this book is that, as a group, chronic mentally ill persons need a full spectrum of material, medical, and educational services to support their functioning in the community. Linking them to services is one of the most important aspects of the discharge worker's responsibilities.

DISCHARGE PLANNING

Discharge planning is usually handled in social service departments. It requires anticipating and identifying the patient's posthospitalization needs

Table 12.1
Postdischarge Needs of Psychiatric Patients

Services	Needed by % of Patients
Psychotropic medications	90
Individual counseling	85
Leisure activities	67
Socialization and self-help groups	53
Public assistance	52
Help for household members	48
Help with financial management	45
Family and substance abuse counseling	43
Job placement	42
Vocational adjustment and training	38
Food stamps	36
Placement in a therapeutic environment	35
Further education	26
Marital and family counseling	19

SOURCE: Data derived partially from P. Solomon, B. Gordon, and J. M. Davis, "Assessing the Service Needs of the Discharged Psychiatric Patient," *Social Work in Health Care*, Vol. 10 (Fall 1984), pp. 61–69.

and linking the patient to necessary and appropriate community resources. The time and effort invested in careful discharge planning invariably pays off in protecting a person against decompensation and rehospitalization. Moreover, the person who has participated in preparing for his or her own discharge will not feel that he or she is being dumped without a safety net. The actively participating patient is more likely to comply with the recommendations and prescriptions of mental health professionals than other patients who have not become involved in the process.

DISCHARGE PLANNING FUNCTIONS

Discharge planning involves the following functions:

1. *Identifying needed community resources.* Here we identify the material, medical, and social resources that a patient will need after discharge. Our primary concern centers on the patient's basic needs, such as housing, finances, and ongoing social, medical, and psychiatric care.
2. *Linking.* Linking involves the actual referral to the identified resources, assuring that the patient will have the opportunity and be in a position to avail himself or herself of their services.
3. *Consultation.* Discharge planners consult with patient, family, hospital staff, family physician, and community agencies about aftercare services and resources. There is much that the patient and others want to know. *Where* are the services? For example, in what part of the county or city is the boarding home where the patient will live after discharge? How far away from the patient's home is the community mental health center or the nearest drugstore? *Who* staffs the services? Who is going to be the patient's psychiatrist, social worker, and rehabilitation counselor at the community mental health center? *When* will the patient be contacted by the social worker, or when is the patient expected to keep an appointment that has been made? *How much* of the cost of community services is the patient expected to assume? For example, how much will the copayment of the patient's medication be? What is the cost of public or other transportation, rent, and so forth?

THE DISCHARGE PROCESS

The Early Start

The discharge process involves the functions we have discussed so far in this chapter. The actual process of planning for a patient's discharge should have started when the patient was first admitted. There are two reasons for this. The first is that the sooner that problems related to discharge are identified, the quicker they can be worked on and satisfactory solutions found. The second reason concerns finances. All hospitals have come under pressure from health insurance companies and government funding organizations to limit the stay of patients in order to contain costs. One way of assuring cost containment is to not keep patients any longer than is necessary. We can speed their discharge by having discharge plans in place at the time the patient is restored (Schrager *et al.* 1978; Schreiber 1981).

Financial Considerations

In private psychiatric hospitals the length of a patient's stay and the treatment the patient receives tend to be geared to the span of insurance coverage. Most policies provide for only six weeks of care for mental illness. Staff in private hospitals therefore have only six weeks within which to devise and implement discharge plans. In public mental hospitals where inpatient services are reimbursed by public funds such as Medicare or Medicaid, stays may range from five to twelve weeks or more.

Hospitals that receive funds from the federal government are required to comply with standards set by the Professional Standards Review Organizations (PSROs). PSROs were originally established by a 1972 amendment to the Social Security Act. The statute has two objectives. The first is to control the quality of patient care. The second is to oversee the costs of general hospital care. PSRO policy is explicit in stipulating when the discharge process should begin, when patients are to be prepared for discharge, and arrangements for their posthospital care:

> Where problems in post-discharge care or discharge placement are anticipated, discharge planning should be initiated as soon as possible after admission to the short stay hospital. Discharge planning should include both preparation of the patient for the next level of care and arrangement for placement in the appropriate care setting (U.S. Department of Health, Education, and Welfare 1974, p. 13).

Diagnostic Related Groups (DRG) Funding

When mentally ill patients are cared for in general hospitals, either for a physical condition or for mental illness, their length of stay is determined by the primary diagnosis that caused their admission. Patients are grouped by diagnostic criteria, known as Diagnostic Related Groups, or DRGs. Under DRG regulations hospitals receive reimbursement on the basis of how long an average patient would need inpatient services for a given condition. When a patient's stay is less than the time stipulated by DRG criteria, the hospital is nevertheless paid for the entire length of the anticipated stay and benefits financially. On the other hand, should the patient require a longer stay, the hospital is not reimbursed for the additional time and must assume the additional cost. On the whole, DRGs are a good arrangement for hospitals because the hospitals receive advance, or prospective, payments from public or private funding sources as determined by each patient's DRG.

Psychiatric hospitals are still exempt from the DRG prospective payment system. There is good reason for this. As shown in a recent study, it is almost impossible to predict with accuracy the length and cost of psychiatric inpatient services when based solely on diagnostic categories (Schumacher *et al.* 1986). The course of mental illness is closely tied to numerous complex and unpredictable factors that constitute each patient's unique psychosocial functioning.

Identifying Needs

Foreseeable discharge problems should be identified as soon as possible. The earlier we can anticipate difficulties that may prevent a patient from being discharged the sooner we can get started on working out solutions for them. This is especially indicated for those problems that usually require much time in finding a satisfactory solution, such as locating suitable housing. Some hospitals have special housing units who concentrate solely on arranging for appropriate housing. Others rely on community mental health center liaison staff for housing arrangements. Sometimes the community-based housing liaison worker is a full-time member of the hospital's treatment team, who begins to plan for a patient's discharge shortly after admission.

A simple checklist that provides a quick overview of patients' resources and anticipated needs is helpful.

1. *Housing.* Does the patient have a home to return to? Is the home adequate? If not, is other housing available? If new housing is needed and is available, what arrangements have to be made and how long will they take?
2. *Income and financial resources.* Does the patient have the means to pay for lodging? for food, clothing, and other necessities?
3. *Work.* Does the patient have a job waiting? If so, does the patient need help in returning to it?
4. *Medical and psychiatric care.* What kind of posthospital medical and psychiatric care will the patient need? Will the patient require treatment for alcoholism or other substance abuse? Where can the patient obtain such treatment? Does the patient have a doctor in the community? Is the patient known to a community mental health center? What arrangements have to be made to refer the patient to needed treatment?
5. *Compliance with antipsychotic medications.* Of particular concern is whether the about-to-be-discharged patient will continue to take antipsychotic medications, assuming that the medications are necessary to prevent decompensation. Does the patient have a previous pattern of medication noncompliance? If so, the reasons for noncompliance must be addressed and some solution devised.
6. *Social services.* Does the patient have a case manager? Is the patient known to social agencies, such as psychosocial rehabilitation centers and clubhouses?

7. *Family and friends.* Who are family members and friends who have helped the patient in the past? Can the patient count on them after discharge? in what ways?

Linking

There is an art and science of successful linkage of patients to needed resources that is discussed in the next chapter, "Case Management." Linkages to community services for patients are made either by hospital staff or community liaison workers who actively participate with hospital treatment team members in discharge planning, although they are not involved in making decisions regarding readiness for discharge. They do have a say about the kind of housing for which a patient may be suitable, and about the patient's acceptability for therapeutic, rehabilitational, and recreational services. Community liaison workers interview the patient and the family in the hospital and introduce the patient to the new community-based therapists, boarding home operator, and others with whom linkages are being established.

Those who carry out the linking process should develop an expertise in many roles, including that of therapist, broker, advocate, and diplomat in addition to having thorough knowledge of community resources and the quality of their service delivery. This knowledge and expertise cannot be learned from books or organizational manuals. It can only be developed over time. It takes time to get to know who provides what services where, and which clients can benefit most by various service providers. Over time the worker will also develop a network of other mental health professionals who can assist in locating suitable services and arranging referrals. In the discharge planning role, the worker provides a bridge for the patient in returning to the community and smoothes the patient's path to a reasonably independent, healthy, and dignified life. Without the community liaison worker's expertise, the best treatment of medical and other staff would soon be undone.

SUMMARY

Discharge planning is complex. It demands not only a great deal of knowledge about community resources, but also an expertise in playing the role of broker, advocate, educator, mediator, and enabler. The worker is often subjected to conflicting goals advanced from various quarters. Families and patients may have goals that differ from those of funding organizations, those of the community, and those of the hospital's professional staff—often presenting the worker with ethical dilemmas (Abramson 1981). Adequate discharge planning requires that all the service needs of each patient be taken into consideration and dealt with. Certainly, mental health workers should raise objections to and resist discharging patients for whom basic supports such as housing and financial help have not been assured.

FOR DISCUSSION AND THOUGHT

You are planning for the discharge of George Ramirez, a 25-year-old chronic schizophrenic patient. Prior to his latest admission, Mr. Ramirez lived with his widowed mother, who supports herself as a saleslady in the cosmetics department of a large department store. The patient has been in the hospital for seven weeks. The treatment team agrees that he has been sufficiently restored to leave the hospital.

You are told by the chief of the social work department that under a new hospital policy the ward in which George is a patient has to be closed out as soon as possible. Since, because of lack of space in the hospital, it will be difficult to relocate patients from the ward into other hospital wards, most patients will have to be discharged. Since Mr. Ramirez has been evaluated as ready, his discharge should take place as soon as possible.

You interview Mr. Ramirez. He tells you that he will be happy to return to his mother's apartment, even though she is "always on my case" and makes his life difficult. He does not want to consider other housing alternatives.

You interview Mrs. Ramirez, the patient's mother. She tells you that under no circumstances does she want George to return to her. Their relationship has been very strained. His behavior makes it impossible for her to sleep. Mrs. Ramirez tells you that she will not be able to stay in her job should her son return.

George cannot be discharged if he has no home awaiting him. The only available housing suitable for him is a boarding home. But the boarding home operator does not accept patients from your hospital who do not come willingly.

Discuss the following questions in small groups. After a given period of time, each group will report the results of their deliberations back to the class as a whole.

1. What other information will you need to proceed on this case?
2. How will you proceed with Mrs. Ramirez?
3. How will you proceed with George Ramirez?
4. Do you want to interview them singly or together? Discuss your reasons for whatever choice you make.
5. Are there organizations in your community, or that you know of, that could help George and Mrs. Ramirez? If so, discuss the type and quality of services provided by these organizations.
6. Would you advocate that George remain longer in the hospital? If so, what reasons would you present to the chief of social service?
7. How much time will you need to effectuate George's discharge?

PART IV In the Community

CHAPTER 13

CASE
MANAGEMENT

A<small>S WE DISCUSSED</small> in chapter 1, the deinstitutionalization of the mentally ill in the 1960s and 1970s resulted in the discharge of many thousands of chronic mentally ill persons into communities that were not prepared or willing to accept them. The full spectrum of material, medical, and social supports that had previously been provided to the chronic mentally ill in hospitals were either not available or, when available, widely scattered and inaccessible. The result was suffering, deterioration, and decompensation for many, leading to the well-known "revolving door" phenomenon.

Currently, there is some agreement that the revolving door can be slowed down when mentally ill are served by case managers who, through caring, long-term personal relationships with their clients, have the basis for providing and coordinating services needed by each. Noninstitutionalized mentally ill persons who receive case-management services are more likely than others who do not have a case manager not to be socially isolated, to live more independently, to function better at work, and to enjoy a better quality of life in general (Anthony *et al.* 1988; Goering *et al.* 1988; Intagliata and Baker 1982; Perlman *et al.* 1985).

In this chapter we will examine those events that gave rise to the need for and development of case management services and will examine the functions and practice principles that guide the case manager's role.

HISTORICAL BACKGROUND

The need for case management virtually did not exist only a short time ago, when most chronic mentally ill patients were confined in mental hospitals for long periods of time, often for the balance of their lives after commitment. All the services needed by patients were provided within the hospital. Patients who were discharged were usually released to the care of members of their family or to other sheltered living arrangements where their vital needs continued to be provided within a structured setting. The discharge process was invariably a simple procedure, consisting mainly of ensuring that the patient would arrive safely with the next caretaker. Little planning took place. Discharged patients were given a list of community-based agencies that they were expected to contact on their own, despite their known disabilities. Since not many chronic mentally ill patients were discharged, little thought was given to aftercare.

Social workers in mental hospitals were caught up in the excitement generated by the idealism of deinstitutionalization. Most welcomed the large-scale discharge of patients, believing that care in the community was bound to be better than that provided by even the best hospitals (Flomenhaft *et al.* 1969). But as we now know, discharged patients had few coping skills for managing in communities that were not prepared to care for them. Community agencies had yet to learn to offer outreach and support to persons facing the difficult transition from hospital to community.

The lack of outreach especially posed formidable obstacles for deinstitutionalized persons. For example, three out of four failed to keep initial appointments with community-care clinics and were, for all intents and purposes, lost to the service delivery system (Kirk and Therrien 1975). Most drifted from bad to worse, tending to live in substandard housing and neglecting basic dietary, health, and hygienic needs. When readmitted to hospitals, the condition of many of these neglected persons was worse than ever.

These bitter lessons taught mental health professionals the importance of discharge planning and vigorously reaching out to help mentally ill persons in the community. It was also clear that someone in the community had to be responsible for helping mentally ill persons to avail themselves of its various scattered and fragmented resources. That "someone" became known as the **case manager.** In the Community Support Program (CSP), developed by the National Institute for Mental Health, case managers are regarded as key to all other services. Their responsibility includes ensuring access to and coordination of services such as help in obtaining financial, medical, and other resources; the protection of their legal rights; and counseling (Turner and TenHoor 1978).

CASE MANAGEMENT AND SOCIAL WORK

The goals of community case management are threefold: (1) to help clients lead satisfactory lives outside of an institution; (2) to help sustain client's psychosocial functioning; and (3) to prevent deterioration and relapses. These goals are almost identical with core goals of the social work profession. Over thirty years ago, a major paper defining the nature of the social work profession proclaimed that

> Social work seeks to enhance the social functioning of individuals, singularly and in groups, by activities focused upon their social relationships which constitute interaction between individuals and their environments. These activities can be grouped into three functions: restoration of impaired capacity, provision of individual and social resources, and prevention of social dysfunction (Boehm 1958, p. 18).

Today, the articulated goals of social work remain strikingly similar to those of case management, reflecting the profession's dual focus on the individual and his or her environment:

1. To help people change their competence and increase their problem-solving and coping abilities
2. To help people obtain resources
3. To make organizations responsive to people
4. To facilitate interaction between individuals and others in their environment
5. To influence interaction between organizations and institutions
6. To influence social and environmental policy (N.A.S.W. 1981, p. 6)

Case managers, just as social caseworkers, stand at the interface between the individual client and the environment, mediating between the two for the benefit of clients. They provide services whose functions, it has been averred, "can legitimately be claimed as one of social work's core technologies" (O'Connor 1988, p. 97).

CASE MANAGER ROLES

The concept of case management with mentally ill persons has as its roots functions that were first carried out by paraprofessionals in mental hospitals. It originally appeared in 1969 in writings concerned with cost-effective ways of providing better care for hospitalized patients (Polanka 1969; Willard 1970).

THE PARAPROFESSIONAL ROLE

Ward aides were to be given the new responsibilities to which the title of "case manager" was appended. They were now charged with ensuring that each patient followed a prescribed daily routine. The increased sphere of responsibilities of these case managers included overseeing the patients' following their prescribed diets, proper dress, washing, and reporting for therapy and activity sessions. In this way case managers helped to relieve professional staff of relatively routine and menial work (Kriauciunas 1974).

After a few years, the case manager role was introduced in community mental health centers. Here, too, it was perceived as basically a role for paraprofessionals who would take direction and supervision from professionals (Broekma *et al.* 1975). Essentially they were expected to ensure that linkages between clients and services were completed and monitored. Sometimes they were also expected to give limited help and advice in problems of daily living. But in general, paraprofessional case managers were to relieve the professionals of much of the work that the latter considered neither challenging nor rewarding (Johnson and Rubin 1983).

It made little difference what the educational credentials of case managers were. They could be high school or college graduates, B.S.W. social workers, members of the clergy, occupational therapists, nurses, nurses' aides, and so forth. Many administrators reasoned that by tapping into a large paraprofessional manpower pool, there was some assurance that case management services could be provided wherever and whenever needed (Ozarin 1978).

THE PROFESSIONAL ROLE

Meanwhile, psychiatrists, social workers, and other mental health professionals who had been providing long-term care to chronic mentally ill persons recognized that the "new" case management role was one that they had been carrying out all along. Some expressed concern about delegating it to paraprofessionals, fearing that the splitting of service provisions from therapeutic responsibilities would add more fragmentation to an already uncoordinated service system and weaken the therapeutic alliance between therapist and client. An eloquent advocate for this point of view is psychiatrist H. Richard Lamb, who regards the coordinating and monitoring of the service provision to patients as part and parcel of the conscientious therapist's normal duties:

> Among the most important parts of therapy are assessing the patient's ego strength and capabilities, discussing his preferences with him, making the referral and providing ongoing monitoring and liaison. To help the long-term patient establish a satisfactory and satisfying life in the community usually requires a person who provides support and encouragement, has a thorough understanding of the patient, and has earned the patient's trust. For these reasons, those who perform case management functions should be referred to as "therapist–case managers" rather than simply "case managers." This view does not mean that the therapist–case manager should be doing in-depth psychotherapy; in many instances it may be contraindicated, as generally the most meaningful psychotherapy with long-term patients is dealing with the realities and day-to-day issues of life and survival in the community (Lamb 1980, p. 763).

Moreover, argues Lamb, the delegation of case management functions to paraprofessionals complicates service delivery and adds an unnecessary layer of personnel in already unwieldy bureaucracies. Time-consuming activities that professionals cannot afford, such as accompanying clients on lengthy visits to clinics and governmental agencies, could be delegated to aides on an as-needed basis.

The sphere of responsibilities of professionals is broader than that of paraprofessional case managers, notably in the areas of assessment and therapeutic activities. Moreover, because professionals have been trained to act more autonomously than paraprofessionals, they can devote more time to direct client contact and less in obtaining advice and guidance from supervisors. The following list, taken from an activity accountability form, reflects the daily tasks of M.S.W. case managers in one large New Jersey organization:

1. *Assessment*
   Intakes: telephone, office, and home
   Emergency screenings
   Family interviews
   Data gathering from other agencies and records
2. *Planning*
   Formulate service plans with team or others in agency
   Arrange and attend case conferences with other agencies
3. *Linking*
   Arrange appointment with other agencies
   Take client to other agencies
   Meet with clients and staff from other agencies
4. *Monitoring*
   Discuss progress with clients, other agencies
   Read progress notes
   Discuss progress with families
   Conduct continual followup
   Monitor medications
   Monitor client's behavior, health, grooming, and social skills
   Monitor client's housing
5. *Mediation*
   Intercede in interpersonal problems and disputes
   Intercede for client to obtain services
6. *Psychotherapy*
   Group and individual therapy
   Crisis intervention
7. *Evaluation*
   Developing individualized evaluation protocols
   Administering standardized pre- and posttests
   Participating in agencywide research endeavors
   Statistical analyses

DISTINCTIVE CASE MANAGEMENT FUNCTIONS

The above-listed functions include just about everything that most M.S.W., direct-practice social workers are expected to do regardless of their client populations. But as case management is evolving as a specialized role, the frequency and emphasis with which the various functions are performed is changing. For example, individual and group counseling, or therapies designed to change the behavior of the individual, are performed less frequently while those associated with environmental change are emphasized. Table 13.1, developed partially from data found in D'Ercole *et al.* (1988), lists the frequency with which full-time case managers carry out their function, and is illustrative of the evolving and increasingly specialized role.

Table 13.1 makes it clear that case managers' most distinctive functions are in the area of linking of clients to services, monitoring their progress, and aggressive outreach. Although little time appears to be devoted to research activities, the evaluation of one's own practice effectiveness is a crucial component of practice.

LINKING CLIENTS TO SERVICES

Linking clients to resources and services is a complex process. To effectuate good matches, the following steps are needed:

1. Assessing a client's need for services
2. Assessing a client's capacity to use services
3. Identifying appropriate resources
4. Knowledge of how to obtain identified resources
5. Ensuring that linkages are completed
6. Monitoring continuing need and quality of services

Table 13.1
Time Allotment of Case Manager Functions

Activity	% of Total Time
Supervision: Discussing clients with supervisor	17.82
Monitoring: Checking with client to see how he is doing	13.12
Home visits	11.59
Consultation: Discussing client with staff providing services	10.20
Telephone to family and others	5.6
Documentation: Reviewing and updating medical/psychiatric charts	(not measured)
Outreach: Home visits and encouraging clients to call with any problems	4.5
Contact with clinics to check on clients' attendance	3.4
Counsel: Helping clients in crisis advice giving	3.1
Assessment: Assessing needs for a particular service	2.1
Linkage: Arranging for clients to receive a service	1.8
All other functions: Including participating in research activities	26.3

SOURCE: Data derived from A. D'Ercole, E. A. Peters, and C. Robinson, "The Effectiveness of Case Management: A Controlled Clinical Trial Study," unpublished mimeographed report. Bronx, N.Y.: Albert Einstein College of Medicine.

The social functioning and need assessments discussed in chapter 7 serve to identify a client's needs for services. But once these needs are identified, we still have to find out whether and how a client can make use of the available resources. In the following section we will examine how to evaluate a client's capacity to use existing services and ways of increasing motivation and cooperation in using them productively.

Assessing Capacity

A wrong referral is always counterproductive to the aim of helping each client to become as autonomous as possible. Sometimes a miscalculated linkage can socialize a client into an unnecessarily dependent role. One can also err in the other direction by thinking that a client is more resourceful or functional than is actually the case.

For example, it is unwise to link a dependent person who has a pronounced tendency to shy away from most relationships with a fast-moving, high-expectation rehabilitation program. Conversely, we should not refer a relatively independent, well-functioning, and active person to an agency where most clients are severely regressed and most activities geared to such capacities.

To evaluate the factors that contribute to a client's autonomy, we assess his or her social functioning and self-image. We ask the following questions:

1. How realistic is the client in relation to his or her mental illness?
2. If the client has other problems, such alcohol or substance abuse, how realistic is the client in assessing their nature and effect?
3. How realistic is the client in assessing the impact he or she has on family members, friends, employers, and others?
4. What does the client think he or she can do and cannot do?
5. How realistic is the client in relation to future plans for himself or herself?

The most reasonably self-directed persons are usually those who are the most realistic and optimistic about their condition. When their illness can be satisfactorily brought under control, they should be supported in their aspirations. Our expectations should be much more modest for those clients who are less realistic and have already reconciled themselves to a dependent "sick-patient role."

Figure 13.1 is a useful schema that helps us to match client to resources along the autonomy dimension. The schema has been developed by Kanter (1985). Clients are classified along two dimensions. The first is their acceptance of the role of mental patient, where the benefits associated with the illness, such as financial benefits, and attention from family and mental health professionals have shouldered aside most strivings toward leading an autonomous, fairly normal life. The second is development: whether it has regressed or has been arrested as a result of mental illness. Regressed development refers to functioning that had once been at a higher, more skilled level and that, be-

211

Figure 13.1   Mental Patient Role and Development

Social Role

	Group 1	Group 3
Development	"Mental Patient" role	Non-"Mental Patient" role
	Arrested development	Arrested development
	Group 2	Group 4
	"Mental Patient" role	Non-"Mental Patient" role
	Regressed development	Regressed development

SOURCE: Joel S. Kanter, ed., *Clinical Issues in Testing the Chronic Mentally Ill,* New Directions for Mental Health Services No. 27 (San Francisco: Jossey-Bass), p. 72. Used with permission.

cause of the trauma of the illness, is now lost. By contrast, arrested development refers to inadequate functioning where a higher, more skilled level was never attained, where the normal pattern of emotional growth and skill development never took place.

Clients in Group 1 are those whose development has been arrested early in their lives and who, most likely, have accepted the patient role for as long as they can remember. Since they are functionally impaired, they need long-term help in many areas. Group 1 clients do best when matched with agencies that can provide structured long-term help, and where staff is patient and understanding of their situation.

Group 2 consists of persons who had known a higher level of functioning and who have now accepted the role of mentally ill patient. The benefits they get from their patient role, such as governmental disability payments and access to mental health services, provide some sense of security. Yet they don't fully accept their illness, which makes them different from the friends they had known. Many young adults in this group prefer not to associate with other mentally ill persons, especially with those who are older and who are obviously frail, regressed, and suffering from severe medication side-effects such as tardive dyskinesia. Group 2 clients can benefit from supportive and rehabilitative services where other participants are functioning relatively well and where staff is optimistic and enthusiastic.

Group 3 clients are those who have not accepted the patient role but whose development has been impaired. Many possess few social skills, and many have been sheltered and overprotected by families or institutions. Although they are capable of learning new skills, their learning rate is often painfully slow and uneven. A serious problem with Group 3 clients is that should they accept the patient role they may altogether refuse to participate in learning activities. These persons tend to do best when they are linked to services that expect them to act as adults who are capable of growth and development, but who need enormous patience and understanding.

Group 4 clients, although regressed, have not accepted a dependent patient role. They represent the best possibilities for restoration. Most of them benefit from treatment approaches that combine careful medication administration with individual, group, and family counseling. Many Group 4 persons can be enabled to continue their education, accept employment, and live independently.

Motivating

Prior to undertaking the not inconsiderable effort of linking clients to a service, we should find out how motivated they are to make use of it. The best plans will founder when clients are either uninterested in or unable to make use of a particular service. Here, as in all other planning, success hinges on actively involving clients in the process. The following steps are helpful:

1. Begin with inquiring about the plans a client has for himself or herself, such as completing education, learning a trade, living independently, getting along better with family members or the opposite sex
2. Contribute realistic suggestions aimed at enhancing the client's life and forestalling relapses
3. Discuss points of disagreement between worker and client and work out realistic compromises
4. Develop a contract with the client specifying mutual goals
5. Identify the steps that need be taken and the service providers that can help the client to achieve agreed goals
6. Provide the client with data about service providers: eligibility requirements, location, transportation, the nature of their services, length of service
7. Discuss any of the obstacles the client can foresee in using the proposed services
8. Review what the responsibilities of each party will be in completing the linkage with a particular service provider

AGGRESSIVE OUTREACH

As discussed in chapter 4, outreach services are a necessary component of service delivery to mentally ill persons. As a rule, it is the case manager who is responsible for reaching out to clients by phone, home visits, or letters. Vigorous outreach can prevent evictions and homelessness, decompensations, and other harm. The following case is illustrative:

Carole Goldstein is the social work member of a case management team of the Metropolis Psychiatric Hospital. The team's clients are all served by the hospital's day treatment center, where they go five days a week, and its medical and psychiatric clinic. Late one day Goldstein learned that Laura Fielding, a 34-year-old, dually diagnosed client (mental illness and retardation), did not report for that day's activities. Goldstein telephoned Fielding, but received no answer. Goldstein began to suspect that something was wrong with her client and immediately drove to Fielding's boarding home. When Goldstein arrived, she found Fielding in her room, bruised from what seemed like a recent beating, and in the first stages of decompensation. Goldstein drove Fielding to the hospital, where she was immediately admitted and treated. Later it was learned that Fielding had been raped and beaten by another tenant while the couple who operated the boarding home were out.

EVALUATION OF ONE'S OWN EFFECTIVENESS

The evaluation of one's own practice effectiveness is an integral part of good clinical practice (Wood 1978). A systematically and objectively conducted inquiry into how effective therapies and services are for each client can inform practitioners whether their efforts are indeed fruitful, which approach is most suitable for which client, and when to change treatment methods, techniques, and directions. These evaluations, which can be designed by individual practitioners for individual clients, are known as single-system, or N = 1, research. This type of research is inseparable from practice in that it requires an accurate assessment of a client's situation and capacity, clear specification of treatment goals, and a precise statement about the chosen interventions designed to bring about these goals. In other words, building research into one's practice becomes a means of sharpening the clarity of one's thinking about practice.

There are other, not inconsiderable, benefits. When single-system outcome research is pooled we build on the critical clinical knowledge that aims to become more precise in matching interventions with individuals. It is a tool for quality assurance (Nuehring and Pascone 1986). It helps to justify our practice to administrative and governmental bodies that demand accountability for our clinical work and fiscal practices. Finally, and most importantly, the rigor required by practice research is also an impetus to our continued professional growth and development.

There are numerous methods that help practitioners to evaluate their practice, ranging from rigorous experimental designs that can tell us whether a client's behavior has changed in response to a given treatment, to systematized descriptive protocols that help monitor client progress and evaluate the success of service provision (Hersen and Barlow 1977; Jayaratne and Levy 1979; Hudson 1982). Single-subject designs should be chosen to fit into a client's situation so as to be least intrusive and most enhancing to the helping process.

Case managers are most likely to use those methods that help to track the success of resource provision. Foremost among these is the popular Goal Attainment Scaling method (GAS), a relatively straightforward way of evaluating whether and to what extent a client's wishes and the provision of resources have been met (Kiresuk and Sherman 1968). The scale has been found a reliable and valid outcome measure for both individual and family interventions (Woodward *et al.* 1978). It requires that each interventive goal be specified and its attainment described in each of five outcome possibilities that range from an outcome that is "much worse than expected" to "much better than expected." (See table 13.2.)

This form, which is also a research instrument, can tell at a glance what the goals of treatment for each client are, whether they were attained, and whether they exceeded or failed their expectations. When a case manager's goals are to link a client with a resource, the GAS can be drafted to provide information on whether and when the linkage took place, whether services were delivered as expected, and what effects services had on the client.

Table 13.2
An Example of a Goal Attainment Scale Used in
an Outpatient Department of a Community Mental Center

Client's Name:_____

Date of Goal Negotiation with Client:_____

Check ( ) Goal Levels for above date.

Followup Dates:_____   _____   _____

Attainment Level	Goals		
	1. Housing	2. Temper	3. Keeping Appointments
Much less than expected (–2)	Client is homeless	Daily temper tantrums	Fails to keep all appointments
Less than expected (–1)	Has to share room and cannot afford the rent	Temper tantrums twice a week	Is late for all appointments but keeps half
Expected level of goal attainment (0)	Has own room, within means	Can control tantrum, only one per month	Can punctually keep four out of five appointments
Better than expected (+1)	Own housekeeping apartment within means	Only one, brief outburst of temper, once every two months	Can punctually keep eight out of nine appointments
Much better than expected (+2)	One-bedroom apartment, within means, in nice part of town	No more uncontrolled, unexpected, and unjustified outbursts of temper	Can keep all appointments on time

SOURCE: R. Kiresuk, and R. Sherman, "Goal Attainment Scaling: A General Method of Evaluating Comprehensive Community Health Programs," *Journal of Community Mental Health*, Vol. 4. After exhausting every reasonable effort, we were unable to locate the copyright holder of record for this work. The current copyright holder is invited to contact F. E. Peacock Publishers regarding fees for using this work.

PRINCIPLES OF CASE MANAGEMENT

Five concepts undergird and guide the practice of case management:

1. Individualization of services
2. Comprehensiveness of service delivery
3. Parsimonious services
4. Fostering autonomy
5. Continuity of care

These principles span the functions of assessment, monitoring, linking with community resources, advocacy, ongoing treatment planning, and evaluation.

INDIVIDUALIZATION OF SERVICES

Individualization of services refers to the fitting of services to suit the need of the client in accord with the client's unique physical, mental, and social situation. The first principle requires that no two clients be treated alike. Wholesale treatment and care plans applicable to large groups of clients are the anathema of individualization.

Although superficially two persons may appear alike in respect to their diagnoses, age, sex, marital status, and racial and cultural background, they are not identical. People respond differently to medications, have different needs for housing, different capacities, different appetites for work, different recreational interests, and the like. The treatment plan for each person must reflect this uniqueness. It should also be altered as the client's life and circumstances demand change.

COMPREHENSIVENESS OF SERVICE DELIVERY

The second principle, **comprehensiveness of service,** is the best-known hallmark of case management. It refers to the linking, coordinating, and monitoring of the various resources needed by clients. In applying this principle, we ask ourselves what services are most appropriate for a client, which ones the client is most likely to use for what length of time, where to locate them, how to link or make a good "match" between the client and service, and how to monitor the progress of the match.

Case managers should be particularly adept in knowing about and obtaining resources for their clients. They have to become experts in knowing what services their communities have to offer, what services are available to clients outside of the immediate service area, how to work with staff from other organizations, and how to create and develop new resources when needed. The following is an illustration of the creation of new resources:

> *The Southern Midstate Community Mental Health Center served many elderly deinstitutionalized clients who had increasing problems in functioning.*

Many had developed disfiguring and disabling symptoms of tardive dyskinesia. Some were incontinent, others increasingly withdrawn and apathetic. Many of the boarding homes where these clients lived gave notice that, because of their problems, they could no longer house them. The director of the center and the case management team agreed that nursing homes were no solution. Instead, they placed an advertisement in the local paper, requesting responsible members of the community to provide foster homes for these clients. Staff expected that a few families and individuals would answer this ad. Their surprise was great when over 300 volunteers stepped forward. Out of this group the center staff was able to select enough families to house all their "difficult" clients.

Comprehensive resource provision is probably more important for the chronic mentally ill than for most other clients. Because of their profound anxieties, memory problems, and thought disturbances, these clients often cannot "do" for themselves or perform seemingly simple tasks that all of us take for granted. Even with carefully administered medications, many are helpless when it comes to budgeting, shopping, or obtaining financial help and housing. In following the principle of individualization, the type and extent of needed help will vary from client to client and from time to time.

PARSIMONIOUS SERVICES

The principle of **parsimony** requires that just the right amount of services be delivered and linkages made: not too few, not too many. To follow this principle, the case manager needs a thorough knowledge of existing and potential resources in order to create the right combination of services. Referrals should be parsimonious in that we select the fewest agencies that can provide the most and the best services. Clients should not be expected to report to more than two or three service organizations at one time. More than that actually creates an obstacle to service utilization. The logistics of keeping track of numerous dates and places for appointment are formidable and, in the end, so discouraging that many clients may stop using all services.

FOSTERING AUTONOMY

The fourth principle concerns the goal of **fostering and maximizing the client's autonomous functioning.** This principle requires that we maximize each client's freedom of choice in the selection of services. We should avoid inappropriate paternalism and overprotectiveness.

Inappropriate paternalism is exemplified by a worker who took charge of her client's budget, fearing that he was squandering money in treating his friends to snacks and drinks. But this client was, in fact, capable of managing his financial affairs. Treating his friends and being generous was important to him. He resented the worker's unwelcome intrusiveness.

217

CONTINUITY OF CARE

The fifth principle, **continuity of care,** pertains to providing services on a long-term indeterminate basis. As discussed in chapter 4, the assumption behind providing services on an open-ended basis is that there is no "cure" for chronic mental illness. Most clients will, to a greater or lesser degree, present problems caused by their illness for an indefinite period of time. It is unrealistic to expect that most chronic mentally ill persons will substantially recover after a brief period of treatment. Although the intensity of our service provision will vary with the peaks and remissions of these clients' illness, services should be available for as long as the illness hampers their functioning.

The Working Relationship

There are at least two reasons that a long-term relationship with a case manager is important to the client. The first is that it takes a long time, sometimes as long as a year, for the client to begin to trust the case manager to the extent that a therapeutic alliance becomes possible. The second is the obverse of the first. It takes a long time for case managers to get to know their clients well enough to work effectively with them.

Working relationships are formed when we accept clients as they are and show them warmth, patience, and understanding. This does not necessarily mean that we unquestioningly accept all of their behaviors, especially those that are clearly harmful to themselves and to others. The most commonly used treatment approach in a long-term helping relationship is that of supportive therapy (Rapp 1985; Roberts-DeGennaro 1987; Winston *et al.* 1986). In daily practice, supportive therapy aims to strengthen clients' self-esteem, lessen the stresses of their environment, and build up their capacities to cope with their illness, with others in their lives, and with the problems they are most likely to encounter. This approach is not aimed at developing insight in clients through an exploration of past events or in restructuring their personalities through other techniques.

In treading the fine line between providing supportive help and fostering independence, case managers should learn a great deal about their clients. They ought to know the patterns of each person's illness, his or her strengths, quirks, preferences, the important persons in his or her life, and the like. This knowledge cannot be acquired through a few contacts or simply by reading a case history, but only through a long-term relationship where each party learns to trust the other. Clients who know and trust their case managers most likely will turn to them for help when they encounter seemingly insoluble problems or begin to decompensate. The following vignette illustrates this point.

> *Karen Matthews is the case manager for Jerry Springer, a 36-year-old, 6-foot-tall, single schizophrenic client. Springer's illness has been fairly well controlled with medications and he has worked well with Matthews, whom he*

has learned to trust. One day Springer arrives at the mental health center where Matthews works, ranting, cursing, and threatening everyone within sight. Because of his size and threats, staff and other clients are obviously scared of Springer. Not so Matthews. The case manager realizes that although Springer has decompensated, he has nevertheless sought her out. He complies with her request that he sit down and wait, even though he continues to curse. Matthews then helps to get her client to a nearby hospital emergency room. While waiting over one hour to be admitted, Springer completely disrobes and continues his cursing, all the while sitting next to Matthews at her behest. Her presence has a relatively calming effect on him. After the admission procedures are completed and Matthews leaves, Springer turns into a "raving maniac" who now refuses to sit and tries to physically attack anyone who comes near him.

Unfortunately, case managers cannot always remain with their clients for an indeterminate period of time. The case history of Max Johnson typifies what can happen when a trusted case manager leaves.

After many months, Max Johnson, 25, diagnosed as having a schizophrenic disorder, began to trust and confide in Jeffrey Morgan, his case manager from the mental health center. Morgan had helped Johnson to find the kind of housing he wanted and got him much-needed eyeglasses. The case manager had spent many hours listening to Johnson's gripes and empathizing with his problems. Under his guidance, the client followed his medication routine and began studying accounting. However, after two years, Morgan had to move to another state. Before leaving, he introduced Johnson to his new case manager, hoping to ease the transition to a new worker. It didn't work. Johnson became sullen and depressed. He covered his hurt by telling the new worker that he never cared for Morgan anyway. He missed appointments with the new worker, picked fights with his family, and stopped taking his medications. It seemed that he wanted to withdraw into his world of psychosis. It took well over half a year before the client responded to the outreach efforts of the new worker and slowly began to establish a new relationship.

Although Johnson had a relatively long-term case manager in Morgan, discontinuity of services is more the norm in the mental health system (Bachrach 1981). Case managers, just as other mental health professionals, leave their jobs, are transferred to another caseload, or get promoted to a higher-level job. On the other hand, clients get new case managers when they are moved from community to hospital and back again. Among agencies there are often "turf" considerations that hinder the establishment of a long-term relationship between clients and their case managers.

Case Management Teams

One solution to the discontinuity-of-care problem is the case management team. Organizations that specialize in serving the chronic mentally ill such as the Training in Community Living program in Madison, Wisconsin, have developed such teams, in which clients can develop relationships with several team members at one time and each team member gets to know all clients served by the group. Should one staff member leave the team, there are other familiar faces to take up the slack and provide continuity. In the clubhouse model of continuity-of-care services such as Fellowship House in Miami and Fountain House in New York, clients become members of the organization and develop a sense of ownership in it. Their primary loyalty is given to "their" club, whose staff works in tandem to see to it that the various service needs of each member are met.

Case management teams include three to six staff members, who might be such diverse professionals as rehabilitation counselors, social workers, nurses, and in some instances psychiatrists or general physicians. All members participate in treatment planning for their clients and participate in assuming various case management functions.

Moreover, a team is in a better position than an individual to provide around-the-clock services. Members take turns being on call during evenings, weekends, and holidays, rotating vacation times so as to providing continuous coverage.

SUMMARY

Case management for the chronic mentally ill is a critically important role for social workers, embracing as it does the traditional values and direct-practice functions of the profession. As the role becomes more specialized, it also poses new challenges to practitioners, requiring a range of casework, groupwork, community organization, administrative, and research skills with an emphasis on service provision, monitoring, outreach, and a long-term supportive relationship between client and case manager.

FOR DISCUSSION AND THOUGHT

Supportive relationships and psychotherapy have been loosely and variously defined (Winston *et al.* 1986). Class members are to interview full-time professional staff in their field agencies and ask each interviewee to list three fundamental aspects of "supportive therapy." At the next class session, class members should share the results of their interviews.

1. Discuss areas of similarity enumerated by interviewees.
2. Discuss areas of dissimilarity.
3. Discuss divergent concepts, focusing on possible reasons for differences in opinions among the interviewees.

Johnson and Rubin, in their now well-known study (1983), found that most professional social workers would prefer not to be case managers for the mentally ill. Since that study was conducted over six years ago, attitudes may have changed in the meantime. Class members conduct the following experiment:

4. Interview professional staff in their agencies

5. Identify staff by profession (*e.g.,* social worker, nurse, psychiatrist) and educational degree.

6. Ask each staff member: "On a scale of 1 to 10, with 1 being the most and 10 the least desirable, where would you rate your desire to be a case manager for mentally ill persons? a psychotherapist for young persons who have problems associated with adolescence? for marital and family problems?"

7. Have each interviewee explain his or her rating for the case management role.

CHAPTER 14

HOUSING

Housing is crucial to the well-being of chronic mentally ill persons in the community. Good housing can mark the difference between health and illness, autonomy and dependency, and it has an effect on their self-image (Depp *et al.* 1983; Christenfeld *et al.* 1985; Kruzich 1986; Velzaquez and Mc-Cubbin 1980). Mentally ill persons tend to do better where they are accepted, treated with consideration and respect, and have good relationships with their neighbors. They deteriorate when they are shunned, treated impersonally, or stigmatized as "sick" people who can't think or act for themselves.

THE LAY OF THE LAND

But the key importance of housing notwithstanding, good options are scarce and difficult to come by. Also, the care of mentally ill tenants is largely left to chance and the good will of owners and operators of private housing, most of whom are motivated less by the desire to help than by the profit motive.

The housing area is substantially unregulated. There are few governmental licensure requirements or agreements with funding and service organizations. Only two states, California and Virginia, have some regulatory standards relating to the treatment of mentally ill residents in community housing (Peterson 1985). Most states have regulations that apply only to the physical plant and the handling of material objects, such as fire and safety regulations, cleanliness, food storage and preparation, ventilation, and the like.

Instead of a well-regulated and comprehensive spectrum of community housing, mentally ill persons still have to contend with an unpredictable and inadequate patchwork of facilities, such as unlicensed and unsupervised boarding homes. This situation is aggravated by a general scarcity of affordable housing. It is a difficult, challenging, and often time-consuming task to help a client locate a suitable place to live.

Sometimes there are pressures on the social worker to move mentally ill persons from one place to another and as quickly as possible. These pressures may come from the courts, mental hospital administrators, families, or neighbors. Statutes and courts require that hospitalized patients who no longer meet the legal criteria for involuntary commitment or retention be expeditiously discharged. Hospital administrators want patients discharged as soon as possible because of the high cost of inpatient care. Families who can no longer tolerate the behavior of a mentally ill relative insist that the social worker relocate him or her "right away." But the most invidious pressure comes from community residents who want to get the chronic mentally ill out of their neighborhood. Such neighbors often mobilize politicians and the media to achieve their aims. This approach has recently been labeled the NIMBY syndrome, or "Not In My Back Yard."

Withstanding such pressures takes courage, stamina, and ingenuity. In the process of matching clients to the right kind of housing, social workers must not only make use of clinical skills, but also the skills of a real-estate broker, mediator, advocate, and diplomat.

This chapter will examine the practice principles that are applicable in matching mentally ill persons to appropriate housing as well as the nature of some of the currently available housing options.

MATCHING CLIENTS TO HOUSING

Four principles are applicable in locating suitable housing. The first is responsiveness to a client's wishes. The second is making the right match of person to housing. The third is our familiar principle the least restrictive alternative. The fourth is the principle of "smallest is best."

THE CLIENT'S WISHES

The principle of fostering a client's self-determination by respecting individual goals, values, and wishes is stressed throughout this book. Its importance in finding housing should once again be underscored.

Our own personal values and ideas about what is the best housing option for a client may sometimes be in direct opposition to what the client wants.

This may be the case with persons who live in deteriorating neighborhoods and in unpleasant, cramped quarters, yet who refuse to move from surroundings that may appear to be harmful to them. Certainly, substandard housing can be harmful to clients' general health. They are more likely to contract infectious diseases and become prey to alcoholism and street drugs when they live in dangerous slums rather than in "better" areas. Moreover, vulnerable and helpless mentally ill persons run the risk of being mugged, exploited, and prey to alcoholism and drug dealers.

But when, in the course of two studies, mentally ill tenants of dilapidated, single-room-occupancy (SRO) hotels in a crowded, rundown urban neighborhood were asked how they liked their living arrangements, most of them answered that they were very satisfied (Cohen and Sokolovsky 1978). They relished their independence, such as having a room of their own where they can do as they please, come and go at will, and where no one expects much of them. Everything they need, restaurants, movies, shops, and medical care, is within walking distance.

Wherever feasible we should go along with a client's wishes when working on housing plans. But this is not always easy, as is illustrated in the following case:

> *Laura Martin is the social worker in the psychiatric unit of Metropolis General Hospital. One of her patients is Sarah Kaye, a 25-year-old, single woman who had been admitted several weeks earlier, diagnosed as suffering from an acute schizophrenic episode. There were bruises on Sarah's body and she also had a vaginal infection. When Sarah was restored, she told Martin that she was eager to return to her "family" as soon as possible. When questioned about her family, Sarah became evasive. The family address that she gave was in a notorious red-light district of the city. No one visited Sarah while she was in the hospital. When the social worker called Sarah's "home," a woman answered, who would only say that Sarah lived there and should come back as soon as possible. The social worker became increasingly concerned and confronted the client with her suspicions that her "home" was a brothel. But Sarah denied that she was a prostitute. Even though other housing options were offered to her, she adamantly insisted on returning "home."*

This case raises many troubling questions, some of which are presented in the end-of-chapter questions.

The Client's Characteristics

Mental illness leaves those it afflicts with varying capacities for coping with everyday tasks. In making a good match between a client and housing we must ask ourselves how much a client can do alone and how well the client can tolerate and relate to others.

The following factors should be taken into consideration:

Age

Problems can be prevented by not integrating older and younger mentally ill clients in close quarters. Many younger persons—especially those in their twenties and thirties—don't like to associate with older, clearly deteriorated persons. They tend not to participate in therapeutic and recreational programs that include older mentally ill persons. In congregate living situations, some may even insult and provoke fights with the older residents. This may be because some younger persons have not yet fully accepted the fact that they are mentally ill. They are afraid of being different and cannot stand being grouped with those older persons whose appearance and behavior clearly betoken a longstanding disabling mental illness. Quite understandably, the younger ones worry that they too may one day resemble these older persons who, in all likelihood, have spent most of their lives in mental hospitals.

On the other hand, older mentally ill persons also prefer not to associate with the younger set. They are uncomfortable with the restlessness, unpredictable eruptions of violence, and openly displayed sexuality that characterizes many of the "high-energy, high-demand" group. (Although many younger persons seemingly do display the politeness and other manners that the older ones value.) Older persons in congregate living facilities tend to worry that they may be physically assaulted or have their belongings stolen by the younger ones.

Housing History

Future behavior is best predicted from past patterns of conduct. When we estimate how a client will adjust to a new residence, we should find out how he or she managed in previous residences. We assess the following:

1. *Stability.* The length of time a client has remained in various residences. If there is a history of frequent moving, from one neighborhood to another or from one locality to another, what are the reasons?
2. *Preference.* Which of the past residences did the client like the most? the least? for what reasons?

Capacity for Independent Living

The manner in which a client is able to perform tasks involved in daily functioning (chapter 7) is a major factor in locating suitable housing. We evaluate how well and independently clients take care of their personal care needs, housekeeping chores, budget, and rent payments. For placement in congregate housing, or with roommates, we should know how well a client is able to get along with others. Finally, we should evaluate whether the client can live within prevailing legal and community standards.

Maluccio has conceptualized the match between client and housing along a dependence–independence continuum, as follows (Maluccio 1979):

1. *Independent housing.* This is housing for the client who needs minimal supervision and structure and prefers to live alone. This type of housing includes a client's own house, apartment, or room, or homes and apartments shared with others where there is no resident caretaker.
2. *Semidependent housing.* Included in this group is housing that can facilitate the transition from hospital to community or provide long-term accommodation. Semidependent housing provides some supervision through a resident caretaker, a set routine, and activities that provide structure and support. The homes of relatives, foster homes, and group homes are regarded as semidependent housing.
3. *Dependent housing.* This includes residences that primarily provide custodial care and secondarily medical care. Here residents are closely supervised and cared for. Nursing homes and rest homes are examples.

THE LEAST RESTRICTIVE ALTERNATIVE

The principle of the least restrictive alternative, as discussed in chapter 4, also applies in locating housing for chronic mentally ill persons. Least restrictive housing is that which provides the greatest freedom of movement compatible with functioning and treatment requirements. Independent housing provides the greatest freedom of movement; dependent housing the least.

The American Psychiatric Association has categorized housing options from the most to the least restrictive (APA 1982), listing in each category types of housing as variously named and known in different states. As can be seen by the following partial listing in each category, facilities known as **transitional care facilities** can range from highly to moderately restrictive:

1. *Nursing Facilities*
2. *Group Homes*
   Crisis Homes
   Group Foster Homes
   Halfway Houses
   Residential Care Homes
   Transitional Care Facilities
3. *Personal Care Homes*
   Board and Care Homes
   Boarding Homes
   Residential Care Homes
   Congregate Care Homes
   Social Rehabilitation Residential Programs
4. *Foster Homes*
   Family Care Homes
   Domiciliary Care
   Emergency Shelters
   Respite Homes

Shared Homes
Transitional Care Facilities
5. *Natural Family Placements*
6. *Satellite Housing*
Apartments
Cooperative Apartments
Sheltered Apartments
Cooperative Group Homes
Independent Living Projects
Independent Living with Aftercare
Transitional Residences
7. *Independent Living*
Lodgings
Single-Room-Occupancy Hotels

Care must be taken to ensure that a client is given the freedom that the accommodation promises. Some who are able to function fairly independently may be unduly restricted in what purports to be independent housing. This is illustrated in the following vignette.

Ms. Ellsworth, a 58-year-old widow, has received treatment for a chronic schizophrenic condition since she was 28 years old. She lived with her husband, whom she married before the onset of her illness, until his death a year ago. While she lived with her husband, Ms. Ellsworth functioned at a fairly high level. She was able to perform all household chores except for shopping and budgeting. Her history shows that she was a good wife and neighbor. But her husband's death represented a serious setback for Ms. Ellsworth. She decompensated and was hospitalized for six months. After her discharge, a friend offered to take her home and care for her there. As part of her discharge plan, Ms. Ellsworth was to report regularly to the outpatient clinic of a community mental health center for medications. The clinic's social worker attempted to interest her in the activities of the day treatment center, but Ms. Ellsworth, seemingly fearful, rejected all offers. The social worker then decided to visit the client at her home. During the home visit it was revealed that the "friend" kept Ms. Ellsworth locked in a small bedroom and allowed her to leave only at mealtimes and for brief visits to the center for medications. The ostensibly least restrictive housing turned out to be, in fact, the most restrictive setting for Ms. Ellsworth.

SMALLEST IS BEST

When a client has to be placed in semidependent or dependent housing, the setting that has the fewest residents and the most homelike conditions should be the residence of choice. In a smaller setting it is less likely that the client will be neglected and lost in the shuffle.

Persons who live in foster homes where the caretakers don't accept more than two or three residents tend to have more friends and be more accepted by their neighbors than those who live in larger privately operated residences (Sherman *et al.* 1984). Those in smaller, homelike housing tend to improve in most areas of their social functioning. By the same token, mentally ill persons who live in large, impersonal residences tend to deteriorate (Hull and Thompson 1981; Linn 1981).

To illustrate, Soteria, a small group home for chronic mentally ill clients in San Francisco, is known for its "smallest is best" approach. Soteria's rehabilitation program relies as little as possible on the use of antipsychotic medications. The facility accepts only 6 residents at a time. According to its directors, the program would not be as successful as it is were it not for its small size and homelike atmosphere (Mosher and Menn 1979).

Compatibility

When considering the placement of a client in a small facility (as for example a private home that is willing to accept one or two tenants), we also consider personal characteristics and preferences of both the prospective tenant and the landlord. For example, we would not want to match a heavy smoker with someone to whom cigarette smoking is odious, a compulsively clean person with an unrelentingly messy one, a highly gregarious person with someone who wants as little contact with others as possible. But sometimes compromises must be made, as illustrated in the following vignette:

> Mrs. Martha Herrington, a 60-year-old widow, heard through her church that the local community mental health center needed suitable housing for some of its mentally ill clients. Mrs. Herrington lived by herself in a large one-family home in a well-kept residential area. She thought it a good idea to share her home; this would not only help with some of her rising costs but also provide her with company. When Mrs. Herrington contacted the social worker at the mental health center whose responsibility it was to locate housing, she stipulated that her tenant should be a neat, quiet woman who did not smoke and did not drink. The social worker knew of a client, a Ms. Irene Smith, 55 years old, who seemed to fit Herrington's requirements. However, one month after Smith had moved in with her, Herrington complained that Smith was "impossible," describing her as both "too quiet" and "too vulgar." The social worker knew that Smith had a long-term schizophrenic illness mixed with a bipolar mood disorder. Smith regularly took antipsychotic medications that helped to control both disorders. But on the days when the client felt "down," she did not talk to anyone, and on days when she was "up," Smith talked very much, interspersing her conversations with vivid and street-wise curses and expressions. In order to help Smith remain in Mrs. Herrington's pleasant home, the social worker had to explain Smith's illness to the landlady, emphasizing the latter's fine qualities, such as her sobriety, honesty, and neatness. The social worker also helped Smith to spend more time at a day treatment center

where staff and other clients could more readily tolerate her agitated behavior on her "up" days. Since Smith was religiously devout, Mrs. Herrington was encouraged to take her along to her church services and activities. This turned out to be pleasurable for both women, who were able to draw closer together through their shared interest.

In the above vignette the social worker acted not only as a matchmaker between landlady and tenant but also as a mediator. Through a number of conferences, usually carried out in Mrs. Herrington's home, the two women learned to understand each other and live with each other in a more harmonious way.

COSTS AND BENEFITS OF HOUSING OPTIONS

This section will examine the characteristics, advantages, and problems of various housing alternatives, from the most independent to the most dependent.

SINGLE-ROOM-OCCUPANCY HOTELS (SROS)

Single-room-occupancy hotels tend to be older, delapidated buildings located in rundown areas of large cities. These hotels, which tend to have from 25 to 325 rooms (Eckert 1980), accept all comers if they can pay the rent, are ambulatory, and are capable of looking after themselves. Most of these hotels provide only a room. A few have dining rooms, recreational areas, elevators, or other amenities. The amenities provided by the typical SRO hotel include desk clerks and maid services.

Roomers in these hotels are completely on their own. Because SROs tend to be located in neighborhoods that have high crime rates, drug dealers, and numerous liquor stores, many of the chronic mentally ill who live there become victims of crime and drug and alcohol addiction. Yet, as mentioned before, many clients appear to be satisfied with their arrangements, preferring their independence and big-city anonymity to safer but more supervised housing (Cohen and Sokolovsky 1978).

FOSTER HOMES

Adult foster homes for mentally ill persons are not a new development. They have a long and consistently successful history, dating back to the early modern era, when the citizens of the small town of Gheel, in Belgium, began taking persons with mental illnesses into their homes.

In Gheel the mentally ill are treated as members of the family. They are expected to participate in family activities, to work, and to become as active in community affairs as their capacities permit. Except for the introduction of antipsychotic medications and the modern, psychiatric clinic, treatment of the chronic mentally ill has essentially remained unchanged since Gheel first started its foster care program in the seventeenth century.

Today the foster families of Gheel have access to services that should be available to foster families everywhere: crisis services on a 24-hour basis, outpatient clinics that provide a full spectrum of medical and psychiatric treatment, full and partial inpatient services, and professional outreach services (Carty and Breault 1967).

The first foster care program for the mentally ill in the United States was started in Massachusetts in 1885. This program was designed for patients discharged from mental hospitals who could not be returned to their own families and who needed continuing supervision and care (Segal and Aviram 1978).

The oldest continuing foster care program for the chronic mentally ill is operated by the Veterans' Administration. For thirty years the V.A. has been placing veterans who have a service-connected disability in foster homes that can accommodate from 1 to 5 residents. The veterans pay for this service with their monthly benefits. But their benefits are often not enough to cover the cost of care and have to be supplemented from personal savings or other public or private sources of income (Linn 1981).

A typical foster home does not accept more than 5 residents. The owner and operator is usually a middle-aged woman whose children either are grown up enough to work, have homes of their own, or are in high school. The foster mother's motivation for taking in chronic mentally ill residents is primarily altruistic. She wants to be useful and to help those who need her help the most. Like her Gheel counterparts, the foster parent treats her residents like members of the family, expecting them to participate in household, church, and neighborhood activities (Beaty and Seeley 1980).

BOARD AND CARE HOMES

Board and care homes came into existence in the late 1960s for the express purpose of housing the flood of newly deinstitutionalized patients. These homes are privately owned, have resident caretakers, and provide room and board on a long-term basis. Although the median number of board and care home residents is 50, some board and care homes accept as many as several hundred residents (H. Lamb 1979).

These large facilities have encountered the criticism that they are unsupervised and exploitative dumping grounds where mentally ill residents receive such inferior care that they often decompensate needlessly (Mendel 1974). Smaller facilities provide higher-quality care. The best care is found in homes sponsored by such nonprofit organizations as Horizon House, a psychiatric rehabilitation center in Philadelphia.

The quality of its staff makes the difference between the best and the worst board and care homes (Kruzich and Kruzich 1985; Kruzich 1986). In the best homes, staff members provide for residents a stimulating program of daily recreational and educational activities. They demonstrate to residents that they care about them by being interested in their opinions and listening to their problems. Where such a fine atmosphere is fostered, staff will also be satisfied with their work and remain on their jobs (Lamb 1981). This is in contrast to poorer-quality homes, where staff dissatisfaction and turnover are high.

Currently the number of board and care homes is declining. One reason is the increasing unprofitability of operating these homes due to rising real estate costs and taxes. Another is the difficulty homes have in hiring and retaining good staff. Staff turnover can be attributed to poor salaries as well as to the destructiveness and difficulties presented by many young mentally ill persons (Blaustein and Viek 1987). As discussed in chapter 2, many of these stay in any one place for only a short time, pick fights, mess up their rooms and the common living areas, and in general make life difficult for those around them.

As inadequate as some of the board and care homes are, their loss would be tragic for many who need the affordable living arrangements provided by this type of housing.

COOPERATIVE APARTMENTS

Cooperative apartments, known also as satellite housing, are sponsored by mental health organizations, such as a community mental health centers. These apartments are usually located in middle- and working-class residential neighborhoods and are occupied by 2 to 5 tenants.

Residents are responsible for paying rent and maintenance charges, performing housekeeping tasks, and providing their own groceries, furnishings, and clothing. The sponsoring organization's responsibility extends to leasing the apartment, selecting the residents, setting the conditions that govern eligibility for acceptance and tenants' continued stay, and providing supervision and crisis services.

Eligibility requirements usually include the following:

1. Following prescribed medical treatment
2. Having either a part-time job or being enrolled in an educational or rehabilitation program on a full-time basis
3. Cooperating with a case manager or some other mental health professional in working out current problems and preventing future problems related to congregate living (Burger *et al.* 1978; Goldmeier *et al.* 1977).

A major task for social workers and others who supervise cooperative apartments is to teach and help residents to get along with each other. Most often workers act in the roles of teachers, mediators, supervisors, and counselors. They teach residents how to cope with a tendency to be suspicious of others and to withdraw and isolate themselves from their housemates. They mediate the numerous bickerings among residents, such as quarrels over closet space, rotation of housekeeping tasks, ownership of snack food, snoring too loudly, and the like. They must supervise residents' continuing payments of rental and utility fees, check on their housekeeping and marketing habits, and periodically assess their general comportment with neighbors and others. In counseling roles, social workers will listen to and help residents to cope better with their personal problems.

HALFWAY HOUSES AND GROUP HOMES

Halfway houses and group homes are transitional residences that provide a bridge between mental hospitals and other, less-structured living arrangements in the community. Both settings provide trained resident caretakers, a homelike environment, and rehabilitation programs such as social skills training. Both accommodate from 5 to 50 clients.

The major differences between them are sponsorship and requirements for admission. Halfway houses are usually operated under the aegis of a psychiatric hospital and will admit only discharged hospital patients. Group homes, on the other hand, are operated by organizations other than mental hospitals, such as mental health centers and organizations of concerned parents. They are free to accept residents whether or not they come by way of the hospital route.

Neither facility will accept clients who cannot adhere to house rules, who have a past pattern of physical assaultiveness or lawbreaking, or who refuse to follow treatment plans.

Group homes, unlike most halfway houses, rely on untrained staff. This is partly for economic reasons and partly because residents can obtain professional services in outpatient clinics or through visits from their case manager, through daycare programs, and the like. The lack of professionals in group homes poses a problem in that it precludes on-site crisis intervention and intensive therapy programs (Cannon 1977).

NURSING HOMES

Nursing homes are long-term care facilities that provide medical and nursing care and such basic needs as shelter, food, and clothing. Special diets are available, as well as physical therapy, rehabilitation, and recreational services. Most nursing homes are privately owned, profit-making institutions.

The quality of services offered by different nursing homes varies enormously. Some homes relegate the most severely disabled and disturbed to back wards where the only form of "stimulation" is a television set that always seems to be turned on and to the same station. Others, most notably sectarian nursing homes, offer good care and stimulation. The quality of care in any given facility is largely determined by the philosophy and values of its administrators and the devotion and training of line staff.

Nursing homes will accept a wide range of patients, from the most helpless on one end to fully ambulatory patients who can take care of their personal needs on the other. During the deinstitutionalization move of the 1960s many of the most regressed patients were merely transferred from one institution (the hospital) to another (the nursing home). For many of these reinstitutionalized patients, the nursing home has become a permanent custodial residence, but one that often is not as carefully monitored and supervised as the hospital.

The average nursing home has 100 patients at any one time, of whom at least one-third are chronic mentally ill (Rovner 1985). Unfortunately, the majority of nursing homes provide few mental health services for these patients. Where psychiatric services are in evidence, only 7.5 hours per week are devoted to meeting the needs of all patients, barely enough time for the issuance of prescriptions (Shadish *et al.* 1981)!

For most residents the nursing home is their final home. Of those admitted to a nursing home, 75 percent remain there indefinitely, until they die (Shadish *et al.* 1981).

Nursing homes should be used as a last resort. They are clearly a very restrictive alternative. The following facts should be considered before a decision is made to place a mentally ill person in a nursing home:

1. Nursing homes provide the least freedom of movement and autonomy of all housing options (Dittmar and Franklin 1980a and b).
2. It is rare that a patient will leave the nursing home. The nursing home patient tends to become isolated from the rest of the community, loses interest in learning useful living skills, and deteriorate at a faster rate than those with similar disabilities but who have been placed in intermediate care facilities (Shadish *et al.* 1981; Shadish and Bootzin 1984).
3. Patients are excessively medicated and suffer needlessly from the side-effects of antipsychotic drugs. Even patients who don't need medications are forced to accept them. Overmedication serves the convenience of nursing home staff and renders patients sedated, listless, and docile (Segal *et al.* 1980; Shadish and Bootzin 1984; Waxman *et al.* 1985).
4. Patients get little care from psychiatrists, general medical doctors, and nurses (Dittmar and Franklin 1980a and b; Stotsky and Stotsky 1983).
5. Aides and paraprofessionals in nursing homes are poorly trained and poorly paid. They tend to be perfunctory, rough in feeding, dressing, bathing, and in tending to other needs of helpless patients. There is an extremely high job turnover among this level of staff, averaging 40 percent per year nationwide, and in some nursing home as high as 70 percent per year (U.S. Senate 1975a; Waxman *et al.* 1985).
6. In spite of mandated fire-prevention precautions, such as sprinklers and fire escapes, many nursing homes have had serious fires that have been fatal to their residents (U.S. Senate 1975b).

THE FAIRWEATHER LODGE MODEL

The Fairweather Lodge Model does not describe so much a type of housing as a manner of transferring mentally ill persons from a hospital to a community facility. The model was developed by the American psychiatrist George Fairweather, who, in his work in mental hospitals in the early 1950s, noted that many long-term patients who had satisfactorily stabilized in the hospital tended to relapse shortly after their discharge (Fairweather 1969 and 1980). Fairweather attributed this to the fact that when these patients left the hospital, they also left all their ward acquaintances behind, thus losing their major social supports. This situation could be remedied, reasoned Fairweather, by simultaneous discharge of groups of patients who had come to know one another while in the hospital and resettling them under the same roof.

This model, originally put in practice before the last wave of deinstitutionalization, appeared to have considerable merit. The discharged patients were supportive of one another and retained many of the skills they had learned while still hospitalized, such as self-care and gainful employment. Currently the model is adopted in many hospitals. It works like this: Prior to discharge, patients who have approximately similar coping skills are transferred to a separate ward. There they engage in group activities designed to foster getting to know another, to build supportive relationships with each other, and to learn skills they will need in the community. In the community setting—more often than not a house that has been leased in a residential neighborhood—the discharged persons become increasingly responsible for running their household and their own affairs. They set their own goals and household rules. In these settings the social worker will primarily act in the role of a consultant and rarely in that of a therapist or supervisor (McLaughlin 1988).

SUMMARY

One of the major challenges confronting the social worker is finding suitable housing for a chronic mentally ill client. Good housing in an acceptable location will contribute to a client's functioning, while poor housing that restricts freedom of movement and choice will contribute to regression and decompensation.

A sound match between client and housing is based on an accurate assessment of both. Workers who engage in this process are more than brokers who know what is realistically available for a client. In their role as clinician and enabler they help their clients reach the best decisions about where and how they want to live. They identify suitable existing housing or develop new options. They speak up on behalf of their clients to get them accepted by landlords and housing administrators. In congregate living arrangements, they mediate between the client and others. Finally, social workers make realistic compromises between the ideal and the real without sacrificing clients to expedient and destructive placements.

FOR DISCUSSION AND THOUGHT

1. Describe one of your current chronic mentally ill clients in terms of capacities, the severity of his or her illness, and treatment needs. How good is the match between the client and the client's housing? Discuss this in terms of such principles as the least restrictive alternative, "smallest is best," and dependent vs. independent housing.

Review the vignette of Ms. Sarah Kaye (p. 224).

2. You are the social worker for Sarah Kaye. You strongly suspect that she is a prostitute. Is it important that you either confirm or disconfirm your suspicion? Please explain your answer.

3. Do you think you have the right to prevent Ms. Kaye from returning to her "home"? Explain your reasons.

4. Suppose you have no choice but to let Ms. Kaye return to her "home." Is there any way in which you can be of help to her? Explain what you would do.

Review the vignette of Ms. Ellsworth (p. 227).

5. Using the least intrusive means, what would you do to verify that a housing option is as unrestrictive as it purports to be?

6. Could a situation similar to that of Ms. Ellsworth occur in your agency? Explain your reasoning.

CHAPTER 15

WORKING WITH
FAMILIES

An IMPORTANT WAY we can contribute to the welfare of the chronic mentally ill is to help their families. It is well established that intervention with families in combination with the administration of antipsychotic drugs has significantly reduced the severity and frequency of decompensations in addition to improving the quality of family life (Anderson *et al.* 1986; Falloon *et al.* 1981, 1982, 1984, 1985, and 1988; Ferris and Marshall 1987; Goldstein *et al.* 1986; Walsh 1988). To be effective, work with families must be responsive to their concerns and feelings. This may now sound like a truism, but until recently mental health professionals alienated families by leading parents to understand, directly or indirectly, that their offspring's illness was a product of their own shortcomings and of familial problems. Thus, therapists added insult to the injury of having a mentally ill family member by blaming families for the genesis of the illness.

This chapter will review and analyze theories that link families to the emergence and course of mental illness. We will also review two effective models of interventions with families of chronic mentally ill persons.

"BLAMING THE FAMILY" THEORIES

Mental health professionals tend to practice in keeping with theories that they were taught in their professional curricula and that are commonly accepted as "state of the art" knowledge. This body of knowledge helps us make sense about what is happening to our clients and how we can best serve them. Although today we rely on knowledge generated through research according to the patterns of scientific inquiry—such as randomly selected study samples, control and comparison groups, longitudinal studies, statistical analyses, and the like—this was not always the case. Until very recently most of the knowledge on which our personality theories and psychotherapy were based was produced from personal observations drawn from the limited practice experience of psychotherapists. Moreover, these observations were shaped by their biased perceptions of the world. For example, until the emergence of the women's liberation movement in the early 1970s therapists and social scientists could only perceive a world where men were the measure for what was "good" and "healthy." The family roles of mother and father were clearly and unequivocally delineated, with mother being charged with carrying out "expressive" responsibilities by taking care of the emotional needs of her family and housekeeping, while father's "instrumental" functions primarily consisted of setting rules and earning a living.

PSYCHOANALYTIC THEORIES

One of the great theoreticians of psychiatry was, of course, Sigmund Freud, an innovative and seminal thinker whose theoretical structure of psychoanalysis exerted the most powerful single influence on European and American psychiatry in the twentieth century. Freud, who had been trained as a physician, subscribed to the medical theory that prevailed at the end of the nineteenth century, namely that biological and neurological processes were at the root of mental illness. But Freud also posited the notion that the bulk of a personality and character were shaped by parents. In fact, he saw the influence of parents as so influential in a child's development that they could make the critical difference between offspring who were mentally "healthy" and those who were "sick." Moreover, pathologies within the family— especially those operating between the parents—could also produce pathology in children. For example, in his case analysis of "Little Hans," Freud concluded that a covert marital conflict between Hans's mother and father was the cause of their six-year-old son's paralyzing phobia of animals (Freud 1974).

Freud's theories and the practice of psychoanalysis that he developed were enthusiastically and, for the most part, uncritically accepted by American psychiatrists. Psychoanalysis held forth the promise of a cure of hitherto stubbornly "incurable" disorders. One leading American follower of Freud was Harry Stack Sullivan, who developed a reputation for successful work with hospitalized schizophrenic patients. Sullivan expanded on Freud's theory by positing that the behavior of family members, the patient's environment, and the development of mental illness were all intimately and inextricably linked (Sullivan 1953). According to Sullivan, success in treating schizophrenic patients depended on the therapist's relationship with them. A good therapeutic relationship was curative in and of itself because it could reverse and undo the pathology caused by parents. This is the sociogenic theory that views pathology as caused by social factors rather than by genetic or biological factors. It holds that the origins of serious mental illness are social in nature and can be found in the role the parents played in raising their children. This theory also holds that corrective environmental influences, or therapy, can "cure" pathology. This is really quite an optimistic view in holding that environmental causation can also be reversed through environmental factors and processes. In the case of mental illness, therapists became the agents of cure. This was the promise that was so hopefully and eagerly embraced by mental health professionals.

The sociogenic theories of Freud and Sullivan were soon augmented by those of others, most notably by the psychoanalyst Frieda Fromm-Reichman (1948), who was interested in the relationships of parents to their schizophrenic children. Fromm-Reichman noted that many mothers appeared to be inordinately involved with their mentally ill children. By contrast, the fathers in these families seemed to have relinquished both their spousal and parental responsibilities. They did not show an interest in their wives and children but devoted most of their energy and time to business and matters outside the family's realm. From the few families with whom she worked, Fromm-Reichman developed the "put-the-blame-on-mama" theory, positing that mothers of schizophrenic children are basically themselves immature and in need of endless supplies of emotional nurturance. At first these emotionally starved women turn to their husbands for satisfaction of their needs. But when the husbands don't satisfy the needs, the women then seek mothering from their own children, "smothering" the latter with unceasing attention in turn. Fromm-Reichman capped her fanciful theory by positing that those children who cannot escape mother's smothering would invariably develop serious emotional disturbances and mental illness such as schizophrenia. She went so far as to coin the term "schizophrenogenic" mothers, or mothers who "cause" schizophrenia. Outside of the few patients she worked with, Fromm-Reichman presented no empirical substantiation for her remarkable theory—which even more remarkably went unchallenged for many years.

CYBERNETIC THEORIES

In the 1950s, cybernetic theories of mental illness, inspired by the technological advances that followed World War II, emerged. These theories explain mental illness as a product of processes within families that are caused by all family members and affect them all. Family interactions are viewed as analogous to the working of a computer. The computer is a relatively closed system in which all parts are connected. Each part interacts with all other parts, influencing and being influenced by them in return. A family too can be regarded as a relatively closed system in which all members stand in interaction with each other and influence each other. Because the family "dance" involves everyone, individuals such as the mother are no longer to be regarded as sole pathogenetic actors. The family as a whole could now be blamed for the origins of pathology.

The Double Bind

Gregory Bateson, a communications specialist, is credited with originating not only the cybernetic theory of family interaction, but also the "double bind" concept of communication (Bateson 1978). Double-bind messages are no-win, "Catch-22" communications that inhibit independent actions on the part of a vulnerable family member that will ultimately result in the development of a serious mental illness.

To be considered double binds, messages have to be delivered on three levels. The first is at an overt level that consists of the actual spoken content of a communication. The second level is partially covert: here the overtly delivered message is contradicted by an unspoken message such as a facial expression, tone of voice, or bodily movement. Third-level messages are substantially covert and secret, consisting of a tacit understanding between speakers to the effect that second-level messages must never be openly noted, challenged, or discussed.

To illustrate: A father tells his daughter that she may go on a date with a particular classmate. This is a first-level message. But his tone of voice and facial expressions clearly convey to the daughter that he is quite worried about her dating and would prefer that she stay home. This is the second-level message. Now to the third level. One of the family rules is that no one must openly disagree with the father. The daughter knows that she must not challenge the contradiction between her father's spoken words and his nonverbal communication. This covert message puts the daughter in an exceedingly stressful bind that may begin by her not knowing what is real and what is not, and end up in mental illness.

Marital Schism and Skew

Theodore Lidz, a psychiatrist, further enlarged on the sociogenic theory of mental illness. He postulated that schizophrenia arises in families where parents who are deadlocked in marital conflict use their children as weapons in their struggle for power and supremacy (Lidz 1972; Lidz *et al.* 1957; Lidz and Fleck 1985). In these families there may be children who are so affected by the parental wars that they develop mental illness as a defensive response. Lidz originated the concepts of **marital schism** and **marital skew** to describe the dynamics of parental battles. Schism exists where the parents are bitterly, unreconcilably divided on most issues. Skew refers to a gross imbalance in the power relationship between husband and wife. One parent may wield disproportionate power that the other parent accepts passively, but with hostility. These bitter, never-ending struggles so disorient vulnerable, sensitive children that they take flight into mental illness.

Pseudomutuality

The psychiatrist Lyman Wynne, who developed the concept of **pseudomutuality,** carried the pathogenic "warring-parents" theory a step further. He theorized that it was not only the parental strife but also denial of its existence that caused mental illness (Wynne *et al.* 1958). Pseudomutuality can be recognized in certain family beliefs or "myths" that serve the purpose of papering over unpalatable feelings or realities such as anger, envy, shaky marriages, or scapegoated children. These myths are usually expressed in sunny superlatives such as "No one ever fights in our family"; "We all love each other all the time"; or "We always help each other." All negative thoughts, feelings, or actions of family members are suppressed and denied. But, continues the theory of pseudomutuality, such fictions can be maintained only at a great cost in terms of psychic energy and constricted relationships within and outside the family. Growing up in the make-believe world of pseudomutuality is so disorienting and the stress of having to maintain the family fiction so great that crippling neuroses and schizophrenia are bound to develop in sensitive individuals.

The Fused Ego Mass

The most complex cybernetic theory of the origins of schizophrenia was developed by the psychiatrist Murray Bowen (1960), who posited that mental illness results from the inability of family members to develop individual identities, or "differentiate" from the rest of the family. Schizophrenogenic families are characterized by a pathological emotional togetherness from which there is no escape. Family members tend to think alike and act alike, and they are afraid to venture away from family norms of "good," "bad," "right," and "wrong." The result is a family that so clings together that all members become, in Bowen's terms, part of a fused and undifferentiated "family ego mass." After several generations of being mired in an undifferentiated ego mass, schizophrenia is bound to emerge and flourish.

The "Mad Eccentrics"

Jay Haley, who teaches and practices family therapy, reports dramatic "cures" of schizophrenia (Haley 1980). All evidence to the contrary, Haley does not believe that schizophrenia is caused by biological or genetic factors (Haley 1988). His theory is, in many respects, similar to that of Thomas Szasz. (See chapter 2.) For Haley there is no such disease entity as schizophrenia. There is only strange and unpredictable behavior that tends to develop in children when parents fail to exercise authority over them. Haley considers the use of antipsychotic medications as counterproductive in the treatment of such "mad" or "eccentric" behavior. Instead, he prescribes family therapy of the kind that will enable parents to exercise authority in their own homes and help their children to become independent.

"Dirty Games"

Mara Selvini-Palazzoli is an influential Italian psychiatrist who founded the Milan Center for the Study of the Family. Her theory, like that of Lyman Wynne, argues that parents who are engaged in battle over issues of control are at the root of mental illness and emotional disorders (Selvini-Palazzoli 1986; Simon 1987). These parents play "dirty games" by manipulating their children to take sides in their unremitting maneuvers for control, while at the same time denying that such coalitions exist. According to Selvini-Palazzoli, schizophrenia is the predictable result of a child's attempt to take sides with one of the parents in these stalemated, destructive relationships. But in its attempts to help a parent, the child becomes figuratively torn apart by both. Selvini-Palazzoli claims to "cure" schizophrenia by giving her client families an "invariant prescription" that is designed to shake up the emotional equilibrium of the family system, put an end to "dirty games," and enable family members to "give up their symptoms." The prescription consists of a directive to the parents that they leave the family for various periods of time, without forewarning and without having any contact with them while they are gone. Such unexpected leavetaking on the part of the parents is designed to shake up rigid pathological processes within the family to the extent that the mentally ill member will be freed to become healthy.

EVALUATING TREATMENT SUCCESS CLAIMS

All therapists who subscribe to any of the above sociogenic theories of mental illness share the same treatment goal. They want to help families with mentally ill members become more "normal" or "healthy" according to whatever their definitions of normal and healthy may be, and in the process "cure" mental illness.

Today many mental health professionals are not so sanguine about the effectiveness of "straightening out the family" interventions. Psychiatrists who specialize in working with the persons who have a serious mental illness have noted that "blamed" families usually suffer and develop more problems as a result (Beels 1976; Terkelsen 1983). Most families are not persuaded that they need to be "straightened out" so that their mentally ill member can become well. Many—who are quite capable of reading the same publications that mental health professionals do—have guiltily accepted the "fact" that they caused their relatives' mental illness. Their inordinate burden of self-doubt and guilt, when fueled by even the most subtle "blaming messages" of a therapist, prevents the formation of a therapeutic alliance and the flow of the helping process. But family therapists who can't get families to cooperate often interpret them as destructively resistant to treatment. They then attempt to "rescue" the patient from the family. In doing so they worsen an already bad situation by producing a "conspiratorial split with the good staff and the treatable patient on one side and the bad family on the other" (Beels 1976, p. 251), producing even greater hurt and hostility in the family.

Even when families cooperate with the therapist's efforts to "normalize" them, the client does not necessarily get better or experience longer-lasting remissions. But families will eventually reject the therapist who has tried to change them. Many may then try, on their own, to undo whatever damage they believe may have been caused, becoming either too lenient or too strict with the client, thus botching up and worsening their situation (Terkelsen 1983).

How can we evaluate the validity of these conflicting approaches to practice? On one hand, influential therapists such as Bowen, Wynne, Haley, and Selvini-Palazzoli claim that their family interventions have been proved effective in the treatment of schizophrenia. But other therapists and researchers reject the notion of a "cure" of mental illness through family therapy. Even where "cure" is not the issue, there remain other claims of success that we should assess. What are we to make of reports that, as a result of successful family therapy, clients have stopped fire-setting, or have overcome a long-standing bed-wetting problem, or have returned to a productive life after years of inability to work?

In examining the success claims of any family therapy, we should scrutinize the following factors:

1. The validity of operational definitions
2. The selection of families to be treated
3. The objectivity of the study
4. The reporting of failures along with successes

THE VALIDITY OF OPERATIONAL DEFINITIONS

It is striking how often therapists report on their interventions with "schizophrenic," "borderline," and other disturbed individuals and families without specifying the criteria they have used to arrive at their diagnoses. But unless reference is made to a generally recognized diagnostic standard such as the *DSM-III-R*, we cannot assume that we know to which mental condition the reporter is referring.

Consider the following excerpt of a case study reported by Lidz on the treatment of a so-called schizophrenic young woman and her "typical" over-involved mother and distant father:

A college girl was admitted to the hospital after having been removed from a train bewildered and acutely delusional. I interviewed her parents when they arrived. In terms of the history alone, the girl's desperate condition sounded

much like a bolt out of the blue. She had been a fine student who was inter-
ested in writing, somewhat shy but sociable and well liked by her friends and
roommates. However, the session itself was replete with material familiar to
those who work with parents of schizophrenic patients. The mother did all the
talking, while the father remained silent (Lidz 1972, p. 620).

According to Lidz, after a brief period of hospitalization, the patient was
fully recovered and experienced no recurrence of symptoms. There was only
one delusional incident, and we have no way of knowing whether it was
caused by drugs, alcohol, lack of sleep, or some other causal agent. Given the
brief and nonrecurring nature of this young woman's "psychotic episode,"
we would not today diagnose her as "schizophrenic" using *DSM-III-R* standards.

Without a clear, straightforward, and commonly accepted diagnostic nomenclature, we are constrained to be wary of reported claims of successful interventions with "schizophrenic families" and should take such assertions
with a very large pinch of salt.

THE SELECTION OF TREATMENT FAMILIES

Most reports on successful interventions with families of the mentally ill do
not set forth the criteria on which the subject families were selected for study.
We should look for the following information:

1. Were treatment families selected at random by such means as using a
   table of random numbers? Was there some attempt at a random distribution, such as selecting every other family of a newly admitted hospital patient or community mental health center client? Or was every
   family accepted?
2. Did the treatment families get help in a public or in a private setting?
3. Did the study include families with such problems such as alcoholism,
   drug addiction, or mental retardation or were they excluded from
   treatment?
4. Did the study include families with serious physical health problems?
5. Did the families seek help on their own or were they ordered to do so
   by a court?
6. Was this a time-limited study that was funded by a grant?

Reports of successful family therapy often include only carefully identified and selected families whose profiles suggest a likelihood of success. But
success with hand-picked families is of limited significance for us. Practitioners cannot ordinarily pick and choose their clients. We work with whoever is
assigned to our caseload, including the involuntary, the violent, the substance
abuser, and the multiproblem client. We should neither expect consistently
successful treatment outcomes nor blame ourselves when the results of our
interventions are not as elegant as those reported by the "gurus" of family

therapy or by researchers who have large sums of money and excellently trained staff at their disposal.

THE STUDY'S OBJECTIVITY

Therapists tend to be subjective about their work. They are too close to the families with whom they work, too deeply involved and invested in what they are doing, to be able to judge objectively the effectiveness of both the process and outcome of their intervention. Therapists, especially those who work without a team, often do not recognize their own failures, or they rationalize them away as successes. In order to report clearly and objectively on the results of an intervention a study should be designed as rigorously as possible and analyzed with the help of researchers who do not have a personal stake in reporting favorable outcomes.

REPORTING FAILURES AS WELL AS SUCCESSES

Common sense tells us that a perfect 100 percent success rate in therapeutic interventions is in the realm of fantasy. Yet such a level of success is the impression one gets from the writings of many therapists who hope to dazzle us with the elegance of their interventions. Only a few studies report failures. Studies that report only successes must be read with a healthy skepticism.

EXAMPLES OF GOOD STUDY DESIGNS

Newer approaches in working with the families of the chronic mentally ill are being developed both by researchers and by therapists, often working in tandem (Falloon *et al.* 1984; Leff *et al.* 1983). These newer interventions are based on studies that meet our criteria for good research design, including matched comparison groups, specifications of how diagnoses are arrived at, the basis on which study families are selected, the number of failures and successes, and the length of time during which client improvement has been maintained. Two studies described below have added to our knowledge on the importance of interventions with families.

A three-year followup study was conducted that included all first-admission DSM-III–diagnosed schizophrenic patients at the Ventura Mental Health Center in California. For inclusion in the study patients had to have families who lived nearby. There were 104 patients who met the study's criteria. These were randomly assigned to four comparison groups. Each group received antipsychotic medications, controlled for varying dosages (from high to low dosages), but only two groups were exposed to a six-week course of crisis-oriented family intervention while members of the other two groups received individual and group therapies that the mental health center ordinarily provided for its mentally ill clients. After six months, not a single patient from the group that re-

ceived family intervention relapsed. After six months, not a single patient from the group that received family intervention with moderate medication dosages relapsed. But a relapse rate of 48 percent was recorded for those groups that were not given family intervention. The differences among the groups relating to relapses disappeared at the third followup. This may be attributable to the one-shot, short-term nature of family crisis intervention. The findings suggest that to maintain gains, work with families should be planned for a longer, possibly indeterminate, period of time (Goldstein and Kopeikin 1981).

A nine-month longitudinal study was conducted in the Los Angeles area by therapists and researchers from the University of Southern California. The subjects were 36 DSM-III–diagnosed schizophrenic clients who lived with their families. For inclusion in the study all families had to have a high EE [Expressed Emotion—discussed below] rating as measured by a scale that was both reliable and valid. Families were randomly assigned to two groups. Clients in each group received antipsychotic medications. Clients in the comparison group received one-to-one interventions. Those in the treatment group were exposed to home-based, behaviorally oriented family interventions. Both groups were treated for the same length of time and were seen by therapists at the same intervals to control for the therapeutic time factor. After nine months of treatment, there emerged statistically significant differences between the groups. Only two patients from the family-treated group were rehospitalized. Those who were rehospitalized were readmitted only once each and for a shorter period of time than those from individual therapy group, who had a total of fourteen rehospitalizations. Fifty-six percent of the family-treated group exhibited total symptom remission. But this was true of only 22 percent of the members of the one-to-one therapy group (Falloon et al. 1984).

The interventions in the above studies did not include the use of mystifying or paradoxical stratagems. Both are rooted in empirical research. The treatment approach of the Falloon *et al.* study was in fact an outgrowth of carefully conducted and thought-through empirical research.

THE "EXPRESSED EMOTION" (EE) FACTOR

Interventions with **high-expressed-emotion** families are currently enjoying the approval of many researchers, practitioners, and policymakers, though not the enthusiasm of the families themselves (Leff *et al.* 1983; Hatfield and Lefley 1987; Kanter *et al.* 1987). According to Hatfield, an eloquent spokeswoman for NAMI (the National Alliance for the Mentally Ill), expressed-emotion theories also blame families, not so much for causing as for determining the course of mental illness (Hatfield and Lefley 1987). Where certain patterns of intrafamilial behavior are identified as having any causal link to mental illness, the families can be said to be at fault.

Nevertheless, the findings derived from the so-called expressed-emotion studies have had an impact on practice; for example, on communication training, structured problem solving, the linking of families to self-help groups, and, in some instances, the policy of separating mentally ill members from their families. Let us now examine the nature of this relatively new concept, its validity, and its applications to practice.

THE CONCEPT OF EE AND PATIENT RELAPSE

In 1958 the British sociologist George Brown reported that a major factor associated with the relapse of chronic psychiatric patients was their overinvolvement with families who, in interviews with professionals, persisted in finding fault with them and in criticizing them (Brown *et al.* 1958). Brown noted that while many families tended to accept their relative's illness, others were notable for their expressed rejection, anger, and impatience. Mentally ill persons whose families expressed their negative emotions tended to relapse at almost three times the rate of those whose families seemed more accepting of them and their illness. Brown's work was subsequently replicated in other countries, including in the United States (Brown *et al.* 1962; Brown *et al.* 1972; Brown and Birley 1968; Leff and Vaughn 1985; Tarrier *et al.* 1988; Wing and Brown 1970).

Expressed emotion is measured with the Camberwell Family Interview Schedule (Berkowitz *et al.* 1981; Vaughn and Leff 1976). The schedule can facilitate early identification of families whose mentally ill member has a higher rate of decompensation than others.

In administering the schedule, the following five factors must be taken into consideration:

1. *Critical statements.* The actual number of unambigious statements of resentment, disapproval, and dislike that any family member makes about another household member are counted.
2. *Hostility.* The presence of hostility is defined as any rejecting statement made by a household member about any other member. It can also consist of a spontaneous outpouring of negative, critical comments.
3. *Dissatisfactions.* Statements of dissatisfaction in various areas of family life are counted and noted. These can include dissatisfactions with leisure activities, finances, and personal relationships.
4. *Expressed warmth.* This is noted from spontaneous positive comments about someone in the household. Positive comments can relate to being proud of someone's accomplishments, enjoyment of mutual activities, liking a family member's appearance, and the like.
5. *Emotional overinvolvement.* This is defined as any unusual concerns about the client by any household member, such as excessive attention to the client's hygienic, sleeping, and eating habits.

Care must be taken that, before predicting a person's chance of relapse or hypothesizing about the emotional atmosphere of the family, all of the following factors in addition to the above must be taken into consideration:

1. *Face-to-face contact*. The critical amount of time of contact between mentally ill persons and selected household members that affects relapse appears to be 35 hours per week.
2. *The taking of antipsychotic drugs as prescribed*
3. *Social isolation*. High-EE families tend to have fewer contacts with others outside of the family circle than did the low-EE group.

The schedule is administered during a regular family interview that, ideally, should be audiotaped or observed from behind a one-way mirror.

But is high expressed emotion the cause of relapse, or is it the result of a family's frustration with a serious and seemingly implacable illness? A recent British research endeavor seems to suggest that it could be causal (Tarrier *et al.* 1988). In that study families of community-based mentally ill persons were randomly divided among four treatment groups, two of which were specifically aimed at reducing hostility of families, as reflected by their EE ratings, through behavioral methods. In the one group where this goal was accomplished the relapse rates of the mentally ill member were indeed significantly lowered.

Still, as good as EE measurements may be, they still do not tell us anything about what families may want or need from the mental health professional.

WHAT FAMILIES WANT

When families of the chronic mentally ill were asked about what it was that they hoped to obtain from mental health professionals, they responded that they primarily wanted information, advice, and concrete help (Hatfield 1983; Hatfield and Lefley 1987). Families don't consider themselves to be a therapist's client merely because they have consented to an interview. They resent it when therapists want to change them through unasked-for therapies. They want to help their relative and expect that the therapist will treat them as responsible, intelligent adults. This, more specifically, is what they want:

1. *To learn about mental illness*. Families are interested in learning about the manifestations and the dangerousness of their relative's mental illness. They have questions about the hereditability of the illness and the chances of the illness afflicting others, especially young children, in the family.
2. *To learn about treatment*. Families of patients who are hospitalized for the first time in their lives want to know whether the illness can be "cured" and how it can best be treated. All should be told about the availability and effectiveness of various treatment options.
3. *Advice on coping*. Families want suggestions on how to cope with the relative's behavior on a day-to-day basis and during crises. What should they do when the client refuses to get out of bed, get dressed,

or get cleaned up? Should they insist that the client help with household chores? What should they do when the client becomes disruptive and destructive? when the client insists on drinking alcohol against the doctor's orders?

4. *Planning for the future.* There is a natural concern about what the future will hold for them and the mentally ill relative. What happens when the family can no longer care for the client?

5. *Meeting others with similar problems.* Families want to know what other families of the mentally ill are doing about their problems. In self-help and other family groups they can learn about the type of treatment that has worked best for others, how others live with the mentally ill members, where and how resources can be obtained, and the like.

6. *Concrete help.* Families need help in defraying the expenses involved in caring for the chronic mentally ill relative. Families need financial help, such as social security and welfare benefits. They want to know about housing options and support services. Some need time off from caring for their relative. They want someone to take care of their relative so they can get away for an evening, a weekend, or a vacation.

PRACTICE PRINCIPLES

The following guidelines for practice with families have been derived from empirical research. These principles can be applied in most approaches to working with families.

1. *See families as soon as possible and involve them in treatment planning.* When a patient is brought for inpatient services while in a state of crisis, it is likely that the family is in a state of crisis as well and will need support and reassurance. Moreover, the family can at this time provide vital information for the assessment of the patient. Families should be involved in the development of short- and long-term treatment plans. It is they who live with the patient and will be largely responsible for ensuring that the treatment plan will be implemented.

2. *Treat families as you would partners.* We should have no preconceptions about any family. Families of the chronic mentally ill are not villains, martyrs, or saints. Each is likely to be a cross section of all families, containing a mixture of strengths and frailties, of good and bad qualities. But some families can accept their mentally ill relative more than others do. What most will expect of the mental health professional is that they be treated with respect, taken seriously, and occasionally relieved of their caretaking responsibilities (Bernheim and Lewine 1979). They have valuable information to give about the patient, but they also want to receive information and advice (Mintz *et al.* 1987).

3. *Link families to support groups.* Families who want to meet others with whom they can share their problems should be referred to other fami-

lies of the mentally ill. Through self-help and support groups, families can develop new friendships, share experiences and advice, and participate in class advocacy. The largest and most influential of the self-help organizations is the National Alliance for the Mentally Ill (NAMI), a nationwide coalition of over 500 affiliates in fifty states. NAMI has state and local chapters. It conducts national and regional conferences, develops and distributes information about mental illness, and lobbies to extend the rights of and improve conditions for the chronic mentally ill and their families.

4. *Make ongoing professional supports available.* The gains of one-shot crisis-oriented help can soon become dissipated. Just as most chronic mentally ill persons require some form of help for an indeterminate time, families too may need occasional emotional and concrete support, advice, and guidance. Of course, when families request more intensive interventions for their own problems we should comply with the request. But such therapy should never be foisted on a family, even if well intended.

PRACTICE MODELS

The most effective models of intervention with families of the mentally ill are psychoeducational and behavioral. Behavioral intervention has been found to reduce client decompensations significantly and to prevent a decline in social functioning (Leff and Vaughn 1985), while psychoeducational intervention is acclaimed by both families and mental health professionals for its reasonable and supportive approach. Both models stress the education of families about mental illness and its management. In both models an appropriate administration of antipsychotic medications is a treatment keystone. The major difference between the two is that the psychoeducational model does not aim to change families, which is an objective of the behavioral model.

THE PSYCHOEDUCATIONAL MODEL

The major developer of the psychoeducational model is Carol Anderson, a social worker at the University of Pittsburgh School of Medicine (Anderson *et al.* 1980 and 1986; Anderson 1983). Another social worker, Kayla Bernheim, has expanded and extensively written about this model (Bernheim and Lehman 1985). Many hospitals offer this intervention because it is well suited to the needs and interests of families of newly admitted patients.

The model consists of four phases.

Phase I, Connecting with Families

This is the crucial phase of the model. Success at this stage will determine a family's participation in the following phases. In this first phase the clinician "connects" with the family by laying a foundation of a therapeutic alliance.

This is accomplished by seeing a family at the same time the patient is admitted or as soon after as is feasible. The clinician should empathically focus on the family's crisis and their hardships in living with and caring for the mentally ill member. The proposed treatment of the client is discussed, and families are involving in treatment planning. Their importance to the client's care and treatment is highlighted and stressed.

Phase II, The Survival Skills Workshop

This phase consists of a day-long workshop whose primary goal is to provide information about mental illness and its impact on the family. Workshops should start as soon as possible after an admission to the hospital or acceptance into a community rehabilitation organization. Morning sessions are usually devoted to presentations by mental health professionals about the nature of mental illness, its treatment, and its management. In the afternoon session, families are encouraged to discuss their feelings, concerns, and problems related to the mentally ill relative. Often these discussions revolve about how best to cope with the client's behavior and its impact on the family. Frequent problems include fatigue, exhaustion, depression, loss of privacy, a sense of loss, increasing friction between marital partners, and financial concerns (Pilisuk and Parks 1988). During the session, clinicians should stress the importance of maintaining relationships with other family and friends. Information about formal social supports and support groups such as NAMI should be provided at this point.

Phase III, Reentry and Application of Workshop Themes

After the florid phase of the patient's illness has subsided and the patient is able to participate, the original participants of the survival skills workshop (phase II) are invited to meet every third week for one year or more. There are two major objectives in this phase. The first is encouraging the patient to gradually resume responsibilities for his or her own welfare. The second is reinforcing families in their efforts at maintaining authority, in not having unrealistic expectations of the patient, and in maintaining their recreational activities and support networks.

Phase IV, Continued Treatment or Disengagement

When the goals of phase III have been reached, families are given the choice of involving themselves in traditional family therapy or terminating their contacts in favor of an occasional "booster" session.

BEHAVIORAL INTERVENTIONS

The goals of behavioral interventions are to reduce a family's hostility, lack of empathy, and overinvolvement with the patient. Interventions consist of communication training and structured problem solving. According to some studies, these approaches are especially effective in reducing the frequency of a patient's decompensation and in preventing deterioration of social skills (Falloon *et al.* 1984 and 1985; Goldstein *et al.* 1986). In order to gain the maximum cooperation of families in carrying out this training program, much of it takes place at home. The theory behind behavioral treatment posits that there is nothing inherently wrong with the family that has resulted in the dysfunctional behavior. There were only some slipups in the way they had been taught to behave, and these slipups can now be corrected through an educational approach that has no hidden agendas or "guru" therapists.

The Posture of Coach

First of all, a communication therapist assumes the posture of a coach. As such, the coach-trainer looks on family members as "team players," who have to be taught the "rules" of the "game." Focus on emotional problems or on feelings is to be avoided or minimized, but the errors of the players must be brought to their attention without fail and as uncritically as possible. The coach knows that it takes practice to produce desired results and enthusiastically urges the team to victory, rewarding it for a game well played.

Three Rules of Communication Training

There are two main objectives to communication training. The first is that each person assume responsibility for his or her own feelings, thinking, and experiences. This objective is achieved by the teaching of clear and succinct "I" statements (I think; I feel; I believe; I have seen; I want, etc.). By learning to use "I" statements, the trainee should also avoid attributing problems to someone else, such as "He did this to me" or "It is all his fault." The second objective is for family members to learn to listen to one another.

These are the rules of basic communication training:

1. Each family member (including the client) must make a statement to another about a situation that is causing problems. In describing the problem, the speaker is to refrain from making any judgmental or critical statement about the persons or situation that caused the problem.
   MOTHER: "Joe, I come home from work and I see you are still in bed. The house smells of your cigarette smoke and the sink is full of your unwashed dishes."
2. The speaker is to state how the problem has affected him or her, either in the way it was felt, thought about, or actually experienced.
   MOTHER: "Joe, this makes me feel angry and nauseated."
3. The speaker is to state what options he or she thinks are available to remedy the problem.
   MOTHER: "You should get out of bed by 8:00 A.M. and wash a dish after you have used it."

The Six Steps of Structured Problem Solving

When family members have learned to communicate their problems clearly, they should be further discussed so as to culminate in a solution that is acceptable to all concerned. The following problem-solving process is widely used by business, industry, and government decision-making bodies. It consists of six steps.

1. An agreement should be reached about the nature of the problem. In the case of Joe, who stayed in bed all day, it became clear that he did not appreciate the impact of his behavior on other family members. After some discussion, Joe agreed that he did stay in bed too much and that he messed up the sink with his dirty dishes. He agreed to stack his dishes in the dishwasher, but he could not agree to get out of bed. Had he done so, the problem-solving process could have skipped steps 2, 3, and 4. As it was, the family and Joe proceeded to step 2.

2. This step consists of brainstorming a solution to the problem. The family is asked to come up with at least three solutions, with each family member having a turn, round-robin fashion, at proposing one. Every solution is recorded without comment by a designated recorder. Joe's family came up with ten solutions, ranging from the impossible (drenching Joe with cold water while he is in bed) to the possible (enrolling Joe in a morning swim class at the YMCA, because Joe loves to swim).

3. In this step, three family members take turns in commenting on the advantages and disadvantages of each proposed solution. The recorder writes down each comment exactly as stated.

4. Actual decision making proceeds in this step, in which the family agrees unanimously, if possible, on the most acceptable solution. When unanimity or consensus cannot be reached, a majority vote is acceptable. In Joe's family there was a unanimous choice, that Joe be enrolled in the morning swim class.

5. This step is the implementation-planning part of the process. Here the family has to agree on the ways in which a chosen solution to a problem will be implemented. Joe has agreed to lay out his clothing the night before. His younger brother Henry has decided that he will wake Joe and see to it that he gets washed and dressed. Father has said he will prepare each day a favorite breakfast dish, provided Joe will rinse the dishes after eating. Mother has volunteered to provide transportation to and from the YMCA, where Joe will swim.

6. This step consists of reviewing the success and problems of the plan after it has been put into practice. In this case, Joe's mother reported to the social worker two weeks later that all had gone well except that Henry was becoming impatient about waking Joe each morning. Mother and the worker agreed that the time had come for Joe to try using an alarm clock.

The above model, just as others discussed here, relies to a large extent on a family's and the client's interest and active cooperation. Sometimes, when a family is not interested in a given approach, we must ask ourselves: Have we fitted the approach to the family's cultural background? Are we on the family's agenda or pursuing mainly our own interests? Have we been going too fast in our eagerness to get things done? Have we been underestimating their resilience and capacity and been going to slow to maintain their interest? Have our goals been realistic? And finally, have we done all we could to take their concerns seriously and involve them in the treatment process?

SUMMARY

This chapter has reviewed some of the influential theories that indicate the behavior of families in the genesis of chronic mental illness. Although families exert a powerful influence on the socialization of their members, there is now overwhelming evidence that they do not cause such illness as schizophrenia, although the stressful atmosphere generated in some families may contribute to a client's decompensation and play a role in the maintenance of exacerbation of the illness. This chapter has provided some guidelines for evaluating studies that claim to either "cure" or lessen the impact of mental illness.

All families are deeply affected and harmed by chronic mental illness. All need some form of emotional and social support. When families receive this support from the mental health system, they can become active and effective partners in the care of their mentally ill member.

FOR DISCUSSION AND THOUGHT

Note to the instructor: Telephone a nearby chapter of the National Alliance for the Mentally Ill (NAMI) or a similar support group of seriously mentally ill persons or their families to obtain permission for you and your students to attend one of its sessions. (You can obtain the address and phone number of a NAMI chapter near you by telephoning its Washington, D.C., headquarters: 703-524-7600.) Visit a session of a support group for the seriously mentally ill or their families. During the next class session, center discussion on the following:

1. What concerns did the participants raise?
2. What one concern affected you the most?
3. Discuss why it affected you.
4. If other participants offered advice on this particular concern, what was it?
5. Do you agree with the advice that was given? If you agree, justify your answer.

6. If you do not agree with the advice, what alternative solutions would you have offered?

As discussed in this chapter, there is a dispute between mental health professionals and spokespeople for NAMI and similar organizations over whether the concept of expressed emotion unfairly and unjustifiably blames the family for the course of their member's mental illness. (See Hatfield *et al.* 1987; Imber-Mintz *et al.* 1987; Kanter *et al.* 1987.) After having acquainted yourself with the literature on the subject, discuss the following:

7. Do interactions within the family, in your opinion, affect the number of decompensations of a mentally ill person? Justify your answer from both your own observations, drawn from your field practicum, and your readings.

8. Discuss the validity of the arguments presented by such representatives of NAMI as Agnes Hatfield.

9. If you believe that families are being unfairly blamed, provide the rationale for your position.

10. How would you convey to a family that you do not blame them for their member's mental illness?

CHAPTER 16

SOCIAL NETWORKS, SUPPORT NETWORKS, AND NETWORK INTERVENTIONS

SUPPORT NETWORKS play an important role in maintaining the health and emotional well-being of noninstitutionalized mentally ill persons (Flaherty *et al.* 1983; Gottlieb 1981; Morin and Seidman 1986; Turner 1981; Wittaker and Garbarino 1983). Families, friends, coworkers, neighbors, and social service organizations are all components of support networks, known also as **support systems.** The very presence of a support network can protect an individual from many harmful effects of such major life stresses as unemployment and can contribute to one's physical and mental health (Caplan 1974; Gore 1978; Holohan and Moos 1981). It can make a difference in how well one copes with daily problems such as living in a deteriorated, unsafe neighborhood (Tolsdorf 1976). It can also be the motivating force and encouragement needed to make appropriate use of medical and psychiatric services (Warren 1981). However, support networks are not always beneficent. The "wrong" type of friends may provide encouragement to drink excessively, use drugs, or engage in criminal activities. Because of its considerable effect on mentally ill persons, the analysis of social and support networks have become of interest to mental health professionals in that it contributes to assessment and treatment planning.

In this chapter we will examine the concepts of social networks as well as formal and informal support networks, emphasizing their characteristics and roles in relation to mentally ill persons. We will also examine the practitioner's role in working with support networks.

SOCIAL AND SUPPORT NETWORKS COMPARED

The terms *social network* and *support network* are often used interchangeably, but they are not the same. The term **social network** describes a sociological concept that refers to an abstract set of interconnected relationships clustered around a central, or **focal,** person. This network is often compared to a spiderweb. The spider in the central, or focal, part is linked through the strands of its web to others. The size of the web may be large or small, with strong or weak strands that are called network linkages. There may be many or few of these linkages. To shift the metaphor, sociologists view this structure the way engineers look at a bridge. A bridge can be strong or weak; it can serves a useful function; or it can be dangerous to those who use it. So it is with a social network. The concept itself is value-free. It is neither good nor evil, helpful nor destructive. It can only be described in terms of its structure, strength, and processes as these affect the focal person.

The concept of the **support network,** on the other hand, is closely linked to values. It refers to the individuals, groups, the organizations that cluster around the focal person in terms of their influence on him, such as good–bad, helpful–unhelpful, or functional–dysfunctional. These assigned network values pose difficulties both in theory and practice.

Values are elusive concepts. What is considered to be "good" and helpful by some may be regarded as "bad" or harmful by others. Let's take the example of a young man who considers his friends to be loyal and helpful companions. He can tell them anything and they will understand and uncritically continue to accept him. They can be counted on to lend him money, and to be with him when he wants companionship. But these friends are drunkards who support him in his heavy drinking. In terms of values, these friends may be "great guys" to our focal person, while to his wife they are "rotten ne'er-do-well's." To his therapist they are the "enablers" who reinforce his alcoholism.

As is usually the case, the composition of network members will change over time. For example, a person may give up drinking buddies in favor of abstemious friends from a support group. There can also be changes in the extent of supportiveness offered by network members to the focal person. Some who have originally been supportive may become destructive. And vice versa. For example, a loving and faithful husband, who had been a source of happiness and stability to his wife, may start an affair with another woman. If the wife finds out about this love affair, the marital relationship will in all likelihood suffer. Should she or the husband decide to terminate the marriage, the once supportive person may become the source of great distress. Because of these changing factors we should guard against hypothesizing about a person's future ability to withstand stress from the quality and composition of current network members.

PROPERTIES OF SOCIAL NETWORKS

Studies have shown that there are significant differences between the social networks of mentally ill and those of non–mentally ill persons (Hammer 1981; Hammer *et al.* 1978; Pattison *et al.* 1975; Tolsdorf 1976). The differences show up primarily in four characteristics: (1) network size and type, (2) network density, (3) durability, and (4) directionality.

NETWORK SIZE AND TYPE

The size of a social network refers to the number of others with whom the focal person maintains meaningful contact. In evaluating this characteristic we simply count the number of actual relationships that involve an emotional component and that are maintained either through personal contact, by telephone, or by mail.

The network type is either **subjective** or **objective.** Members of so-called objective networks are immediately available to the focal person and could be of help here and now. They may consist of family members, friends, neighbors, and acquaintances, as well as fellow members of organizations such as schools, social agencies, fraternal clubs, and churches with whom the focal person has an active relationship. By contrast, subjective network members are significant others whom the person has known in the past but with whom there is no actual relationship in the present. It can include dead and absent persons (Pattison and Pattison 1981). As a rule we don't count on subjective network members to provide material help. In our assessments we take both network types into account but distinguish between them.

The presence of objective network members can be elicited by such questions as:

1. With whom would you get in touch if you wanted to go out visiting or just have some fun?
2. Tell me who the persons are whom you see at least once a month.
3. To which organizations do you turn when you need to get some help?
4. To which people do you turn when you just need someone to talk to?

Subjective network members may be identified by such questions as:

1. Name all those persons who are important in your life, whether you like them or not. Where do these persons live now? How often do you see them?

2. Name all the persons whom you like the most. Where do they live now? How often do you see them?
3. Name all those persons to whom you feel close and know well. Where do they live now? How often do you see them?
(Pattison *et al.* 1975; Tolsdorf 1976)

The objective networks of persons with serious mental illnesses tend to be significantly smaller than those of the non–mentally ill. Where non–mentally ill persons may have twenty-five significant personal relationships, the mentally ill may count only twelve such relationships (Pattison *et al.* 1975; Sokolovsky *et al.* 1978). Also, objective networks of the non–mentally ill appear to be evenly divided among family members, friends, neighbors, and coworkers, whereas those of the mentally ill tend to consist mostly of persons from a single group, such as the family, or from the same setting, such as from the boarding home or mental health facility (Tolsdorf 1976).

Persons who have but few members in their objective networks are said to be socially impoverished. To many of them, even casual acquaintances become the most important significant others. This seems to be especially true of long-term mentally ill persons who may count janitors, waiters, and ward aides among the most important people in their lives (Cohen and Sokolovsky 1979). For such persons it is not so much the quality and consistency of a relationship that matters; rather, the physical proximity of others becomes the most important relational factor, whereas relationships with family or mental health professionals who are not seen as often fade in significance.

There appears to be an inverse relationship between the severity of mental illness and network size: the more severe the illness, the smaller the size of that person's social network (Lipton *et al.* 1981). We may account for this with three factors. The first is the regressive, illness-induced tendency of many mentally ill persons to withdraw from others and seek solitude. The second is their lack of social skills in forming and maintaining relationships. The third is an interactional factor and has to do with how others react to and relate with mentally ill persons.

It seems that some friends and family members who had been close to a person prior to the onset of mental illness tend to distance themselves after it makes its first appearance (Lipton *et al.* 1981). They may have become upset at the person's changed behavior; they may be afraid; or they may simply not know how to relate to the person. What matters is that many who have been important to the mentally ill person stop relating to him or her—ironically, just at the time when he or she is most in need of support from friends and others.

NETWORK DENSITY

Network density refers to contacts that network members have with one another that are independent of their contact with the focal person. A social network is said to be dense when a sizable number of the focal person's friends also know and communicate with the focal person's relatives. A dense network can also be referred to as a **close-knit** network. If, on the other hand, no one in the focal person's family knows his or her friends, and when few of a focal person's friends relate with one another, the network is described as **loose-knit.**

Network relationships tend to occur in definable groups, or **clusters.** For example, friends from one's college days will tend to be in touch with each other, forming a cluster. Similarly, coworkers tend to socialize with each other, forming another cluster. Family members will constitute yet another cluster, and so forth.

It has been observed that many seriously mentally ill persons have loose-knit social networks with few sizable clusters or connections among the clusters (Cohen and Sokolovsky 1979; Hirsch, 1980). Here too the network density is related to the severity of the illness, where persons with more severe forms of mental illness also tend to have more loose-knit networks.

NETWORK DURABILITY

Durability refers to the length of time that network members have known the focal person and one another. The lengthier the connection between the focal person and members of the network, the more durable the network is said to be.

Durability is also a social support factor. The longer network members have known the focal person, the more sensitive and accepting they will tend to be of his or her idiosyncracies and responsive to his or her needs. With old friends one has learned who can be counted on for what under which circumstances.

Networks of chronic mentally ill persons are often characterized by their absence of durability. This is particularly true for persons who drift from place to place and rarely, if ever, put down roots. (This lack of durability has also been noted among more settled persons, such as those who have lived in an institution for many years or long-term participants of day treatment programs [Froland *et al.* 1979; Henders *et al.* 1978].) Compared to other groups, seriously mentally ill persons have few longstanding friends. They also tend to cut off relationships with family members more frequently than others do (Hammer *et al.* 1978). The case of Joyce Brown, also known as Billie Boggs, is illustrative:

> *Joyce Brown gained media notoriety as a homeless woman who lived near a heating grate in Manhattan. There, to the annoyance of neighbors, she slept and performed all bodily functions. In newspaper and television interviews Brown claimed that she was homeless because she did not have the money to rent an apartment. What she didn't mention was that she had two sisters*

who had made a home for her, and who were willing to take her back and have her live with them in their middle-class homes in New Jersey. According to the sisters, Joyce was the one who took the initiative in leaving the family and who resisted all contact with them. Joyce Brown gave herself the fictional name of "Billie Boggs," claiming that this would prevent her family from finding her. In fact, the use of that name was based on her delusion that she was engaged to get married to a television personality by the name of Bill Boggs.

DIRECTIONALITY

Directionality describes the flow of communication and support between the focal person and members of the network. Directionality is reciprocal when the give and take between them is about the same. For example, we try to reciprocate favors with friends, put in a "good day's work" for the salary we receive, and pay for the services that we want.

In networks of the non–mentally ill, focal persons often give more than they receive. This is the case with parent–child relationships, where the flow of affection, care, and goods is primarily from parent to child. We call the direction of this flow **instrumental.** Where focal persons get more than they give, as is the case with children, the flow directionality is referred to as **dependent.** In networks of the mentally ill, the directionality of flow is more likely a dependent one.

Although many mentally ill persons accept about as much help as their non–mentally ill counterparts, unlike the latter they have difficulties in reciprocating (Cohen and Sokolovsky 1978). They tend to be deficient in the wherewithal needed to stand by and help others, be it with material or emotional support, through hard times, over any length of time, and with any consistency. This does not mean that they are unable to help their friends and families. In fact, even those who are very poor and very ill can be touchingly generous with their time, attention, and material goods. Many will even share their last pack of cigarettes and money with persons whom they barely know. But such help is sporadic and cannot be relied on (Estroff 1981).

In sum, networks of most seriously mentally persons ill appear to differ from those of the non–mentally ill by being (1) smaller in size, (2) marked by fewer relationships with friends and relatives, (3) having relationships primarily with persons who live in close proximity, (4) having fewer long-term friends, (5) having less interaction with close friends and family, (6) having fewer friends who know each other and who know family members and, (7) a more dependent directionality of the flow of help, favors, and services.

As intriguing as these findings are, they tell us more about the effects mental illness has on a person's relational network than they do about that person's unique needs for social, medical, and psychiatric services, the components of social support that will be discussed in the following section.

260

THE CONCEPT OF SOCIAL SUPPORT

The concept of social support is broad and elusive. Over the years it has been variously, loosely, and imprecisely defined (Schilling 1987). As described in the literature, social support includes such concepts as the **maintenance of one's identity, guidance, feedback, advice, task-oriented assistance, trust, value similarity,** and **concern** (Mitchell and Trickett 1980). It has been delineated as encompassing

> the emotional support, advice, guidance, and appraisal, as well as the material aid and services, that people obtain from the social relationships. In turn, this support is used to maintain identity and enhance persons' self-esteem and coping repertoire throughout their lives (Ell 1984, p. 134).

In an even broader vein, Beels, a psychiatrist who is interested in the problems of mentally ill persons, views social support as anything in the environment that will directly contribute to their physical and mental health (1981).

We know that some environments are more hospitable and supportive of fostering health and coping capacities than are others. For example, many persons who live in physically deteriorated neighborhoods tend to develop serious illness more frequently and to be emotionally less stable than others who live in better neighborhoods. Further, a significant number of persons who had enjoyed good health develop illnesses shortly after moving from a better to a deteriorated, slum neighborhood (Cassel 1974).

But even in the most run-down and unsafe neighborhoods there are persons who seem to flourish and who retain their physical and emotional health. What is it that seems to make the difference? Researchers who have studied the relationship of environment to health and illness have found, after controlling for such factors as social class, age, and ethnicity, that members of the healthier group also tended to have more satisfying relationships with friends, family, and neighbors (Caplan 1974; Cassel 1974; Kaplan 1976). These findings gave rise to the **well-being** theory of social support, which holds that supportive relationships, even when not immediately available—as is the case with friends who live at some distance—can be a buffer against stressful life events and protect our health and well-being (Steinglass *et al.* 1988).

Just as some neighborhoods are more conducive to well-being than others, so are some families, some groups of friends, some places of employment, and the like. As social workers we are particularly interested in identifying the factors in a client's environment that either strengthen or weaken capacity to cope and well-being. One of our most significant tasks is to make a client's environment more responsive to his or her needs, less stressful, and fuller of opportunities to live a satisfying, dignified life. We do so by easing stress in families, by linking clients to social resources and services, by mediating between clients and others such as landlords, shopkeepers, and teachers. Sometimes we even help clients to change their environments altogether by moving them to another living facility or area.

In our analysis of the social and potential sources of support in a client's environment we identify the individuals, groups, and organizations that contribute to the client's well-being and our helping processes. These supportive sources are often referred to as support networks.

FORMAL AND INFORMAL SUPPORT NETWORKS

We distinguish between formal and informal support networks. Family, friends, neighbors, loosely knit social groups such as card clubs, and social and fraternal organizations are all parts of informal support networks. By contrast, formal support networks are composed of public and private formal organizations that deliver such services as housing, money, counseling, education, and recreational activities. When there is some relationship among these organizations so that their services are fairly coordinated without undue gaps or duplication, we refer to this network as a community support system.

COMMUNITY SUPPORT SYSTEMS

The largest and best-known formal support network for the chronic mentally ill is the National Institute of Mental Health (NIMH). NIMH has been largely responsible for conceptualizing and funding other formal support networks, including statewide community support systems for the chronic mentally ill.

The role of the federal government in establishing and developing community support systems (CSS) is relatively new. The first CSS contracts were awarded by NIMH as recently as 1988.[1] The objective of these programs is to ensure the provision and coordination of a network of services for mentally disabled adults who can get along outside of hospitals and nursing homes. Ten service components are projected for the ideal support network (Turner and TenHoor 1978):

1. The identification of the population for whom the services are appropriate (This depends on an aggressive outreach program for those who are most in need of services.)
2. Assistance in applying for financial, medical, and other resources for which clients are eligible and to which they are entitled
3. Crisis stabilization services in the last restrictive setting (When out-

---

1. The first states to be awarded CSS contracts were Alabama, Arizona, Georgia, Maine, and New Jersey.

patient services cannot meet a client's treatment needs, hospitalization should be an available option.)

4. The provision of psychosocial rehabilitation services aimed at sustaining functional capacities and regarding the rate of deterioration of the chronic mentally ill. These services should include, but are not limited to, the following:

   Goal-oriented rehabilitation evaluation
   Training in community living skills
   Opportunities to improve employability
   Appropriate housing suited to a patient's condition
   Opportunities to develop social skills, interests, and leisure activities that provide a sense of participation and worth

5. Continuity of care service
6. Medical and mental health care
7. Backup support to families, friends, and community members
8. Involvement of community members in the planning of support programs and in selected aspects of service delivery, such as helping to make jobs and housing available for the population at risk
9. Establishment of procedures and mechanisms that protect the legal rights of the mentally ill, both in mental hospitals and in the community
10. Provision of case management that will help clients make efficient use of available services

The objectives of this coordinated, comprehensive support service network have not yet been realized. Except for a few model demonstration programs—such as the Training in Community Living program, which provides services for a limited number of mentally ill clients in Madison, Wisconsin (Test 1979)—most programs are fragmented. They lack clear and coherent policies from the federal, state, and local governments. Agencies, instead of cooperating, compete with one another for funds, clients, staff, and influence (NIMH 1984). This is especially detrimental to mentally ill persons, who as it is have great trouble finding their way through the Byzantine corridors of various uncoordinated bureaucracies.

Given the social, economic, and political structure of our country, solutions to the problem of fragmented and insufficient community services are not yet in sight. But significant attempts are being made to find solutions. For example, the Robert Wood Johnson Foundation, a private philanthropic organization, has recently funded projects on behalf of the chronic mentally ill in nine major cities of the United States.[2] These projects are specifically de-

---

2. These cities are Austin, Texas; Baltimore, Maryland; Charlotte, North Carolina; Cincinnati, Ohio; Columbus, Ohio; Denver, Colorado; Honolulu, Hawaii; Philadelphia, Pennsylvania; and Toledo, Ohio.

signed to provide better coordination of services, and they may serve as models throughout the country.

MUTUAL AID GROUPS

Mutual aid or self-help groups are partway between formal and informal support networks. They are a relatively recent phenomenon on the mental health scene, having been developed in response to needs that professionals did not meet and to the lack of understanding mental health professionals displayed in their treatment of the mentally ill and their families.

One of the largest of these groups is the National Alliance for the Mentally Ill (NAMI), which is mainly composed of relatives of mentally ill persons. NAMI has a threefold objective: (1) to share experiences and provide emotional support for its members, (2) to engage in advocacy activities that will extend the rights and entitlements of mentally ill persons, (3) to educate the public and other professionals about mental illness and its impact on the family and on others.

Most of these self-help groups have arisen spontaneously in response to needs that had not been met by mental health professionals. Group members decide on how their meetings should be conducted, on the fees, if any, that should be paid, and on their own goals and their implementation. Many support groups provide members with a sense of solidarity and purpose. When, and if, they avail themselves of the help of professionals the latter are called in as consultants on an as-needed basis.

PRACTICE WITH INFORMAL NETWORKS

When social workers link clients with services of formal and informal organizations they are said to be **networking.** Through these activities they may be accomplishing two objectives: the provision of resources and the expansion of a client's social network. The latter objective comes into play when clients are reunited with family members from whom they had been cut off, and when they are introduced to self-help, recreational, educational, and rehabilitative groups where new friends and acquaintances will be made.

NETWORKING

No one disagrees with the judicious provision of resources, without which many mentally ill persons could not get by in the community, but there are still unanswered questions about how many and which linkages present just the right mix of stimulation and resource provision for each individual. We know from studies such as that conducted by John Wing (1977) that too little stimulation will result in serious loss of functional capacities, while too much stimulation will result in decompensations. To what extent, if any, will the enlargement of a client's social network improve health and functioning?

264

When, in the course of service provision, will a client be made overly dependent on them? How will we recognize signs of oncoming overdependency? There are no empirical studies at this time that can guide the practitioner in tolerance of stress and stimulation. It also takes time to become acquainted with the type and quality of the various service providers that could be of help to our clients. Judicious networking, or the matching of individual clients to just the right number and types of organizations, is at first a trial-and-error process that should become increasingly well targeted in time.

INTERVENTIONS WITH INFORMAL CAREGIVERS

Mental health professionals have been advised to identify and work with "informal caregivers" (Gottlieb 1983 and 1985; Gottlieb and Schrotter 1978; Warren 1981; Whittaker and Garbarino 1983). It is argued that their jobs can be augmented and supplemented by "natural helpers" who are already in place and available to clients when the professionals are not around. These helpers can be landlords, barbers, dentists, shopkeepers, and others variously referred to as "natural neighbors," "folk support systems," "indigenous helpers," or "natural delivery systems."

The idea of recruiting informal caregivers to help the poor, sick, and mentally ill—and generally do some of the work that professionals had always performed—became popular during the 1960s and 1970s (Collins 1973; Lentz 1976). This seemed to be a good solution to the problem of the lack of professionals willing to work with these populations. Collins describes a project in which neighbors were recruited to provide, in consultation with professionals, limited help to distressed and mentally ill persons. These neighbors, organized under the rubric of Day Care Neighbor Service, helped with common-sense advice on day-to-day problems, with some tasks such as marketing, or just by looking in on someone (Collins et al. 1969). But these interventive experiments gradually petered out. Neighbors could not be relied on to provide services on a regular basis, and the quality of their services was spotty. There was also the question of confidentiality that neighbors, as lay persons, could not be expected to honor in all instances. Some persons to whom these services were provided saw this as a meddling in their affairs by neighborhood "busybodies" and preferred to go without this type of help. Moreover, and of great concern to professional caregivers, there is always the chance of a

> competitive relationship evolving between professional service providers and the more organized forms of support systems, in which each not only attempts to limit the other's sphere of influence in the human services but competes with the other for such resources as clients, political sanctions, funding, volunteers and media exposure (Gottlieb and Schrotter 1978).

Although there still is interest in recruiting natural neighbors into the helping process in some areas, there is still no empirically proven guide that could help in identifying, recruiting, and working with them and networks. We still know little about how to practice productively in this area, and we still have not answered many questions surrounding it (Schilling 1987). For example, should training be offered to the natural helper? If so, what type of training? Should the neighborhood bartender, who sympathetically listens to the troubles of customers, be trained in basic interviewing skills? If the bartender is willing to participate in training, how will the mentally ill customer benefit by it? On the other hand, the bartender may not want to work with the mental health professional who is attempting to enlist his or her help as a "key neighbor" (Collins *et al.* 1969). As it is, the bartender already enjoys a self-image as an expert in listening and dispensing advice for customers. The professional, eager to help the bartender become a better helper, may assume that he or she knows more about the helping process than the bartender does. The bartender, in turn, believes that he or she knows more about the "real world" and customers than the professional does. The two diametrically different approaches to helping, that of the professional and that of the "natural helper," are difficult to reconcile. They may, in fact, constitute worlds that can never meet (Hoch and Hemmens 1987).

At this time practitioners are well advised not to invest too much of their time or energy in a systematic recruitment of informal caregivers. When such efforts are undertaken, they should be done only after obtaining the client's full knowledge, assent, and cooperation.

NETWORK THERAPY

Another interesting recent development in direct practice with a client's informal support network is **network therapy,** first described by family therapist Speck (1967). Speck reports having observed in his work with families that members of support networks exercised enormous influence over client families. In some instances these members, even when living at some distance, were responsible for undermining or supporting therapeutic processes. The solution to the problem was to include kith as well as kin in a few family meetings. The results of this type of intervention were heartening, especially in working with problems of severe mental illness. Studies with comparison groups show that network therapy can significantly improve social functioning and reduce rehospitalization, case management efforts, and crisis intervention services for over two years after its introduction (Schoenfeld *et al.* 1985 and 1986).

The intervention itself is relatively straightforward, even though the logistics of convening a large group may, to the novice practitioner, appear formidable at first. Clients and their families are asked to convene network members who are both important in their lives and accessible. Meetings are attended by fifteen to thirty people, last about three hours, and require the participation of up to four therapists. One to five meetings are held for each network, the number of sessions being determined by the wishes of network members and their willingness to take on some responsibilities for a client's care (Erickson 1984; Halevy-Martini *et al.* 1984; Rueveni 1984).

The therapy consists of three phases: convening, connecting, and shifting the locus of responsibility to the network.

The first phase consists of assisting a client and the family to identify important persons in their lives such as relatives, friends, coworkers, neighbors, and professional helpers. The practitioner's role is to help the family make sure that a balanced group is selected so that each family member will have, during the meeting of the clan, an empathetic friend or relative present who will support him or her during the session. Family members cooperate in picking a convenient date and place for the meeting of the clan. The responsibility of extending individual invitations is shared between the family and the practitioners.

The second phase, that of connecting, takes place during the clan's first meeting. Here the group is encouraged to feel a sense of solidarity. The particular problem presented by a client is presented by the therapists, who encourage the clan to express their thoughts and feelings in relation to one another and to the presenting problem. Through group processes, the clan is then encouraged to work out ways in which the problem can be addressed by them or by others.

The final phase, namely that of shifting the locus of responsibility to the clan, may occur during the first or the last meeting. The therapists help the clan, in both large and small subgroupings, to work out implementations of their goals. The different perspectives that clan members bring to the problem and its solution identify interventive approaches that fit in with the group's cultural background, ways of coping, and resources; and they help the client and the family to cope more successfully with the problem.

SUMMARY

Social network and social support concepts help us to expand our focus and understanding of those environmental factors that can significantly affect our client's well-being. In practice, these concepts are useful in formulating assessments and treatment plans (Harris *et al.* 1987). Social work interventions with components of clients' support networks include work with their families, clans, support and self-help groups, other agencies, and, at times, with concerned members of a community. Interventions in this area of practice pose interesting new challenges to the practitioner.

FOR DISCUSSION AND THOUGHT

List all the members of your social network who are alive and that you can think of in 5 minutes.

1. What is the size of your network?

2. Is your network loosely or tightly knit? Give the reasons for your answers.

3. How many persons are in each cluster of your network (*e.g.*, the school cluster, the family cluster, the work cluster)?

4. Would you say your social network is durable? Explain your answer.

5. To whom, in your network, have you provided more help than was given? How do you feel about this? How do you think the recipient of your help feels about your giving?

6. Brainstorm how you would go about providing comprehensive services to the chronic mentally ill.

After you have come up with your plan, discuss foreseeable obstacles to its implementation from each of the following. (If you do not foresee any obstacles from any of the following sources, provide an explanation.)

    a. The agency in which you currently work, or in which you are doing your internship

    b. The town in which you live

    c. The government of the state in which you live

    d. The federal government

CHAPTER 17

ADVOCACY

ADVOCACY IS ONE of the most critical services provided by a social worker in the mental health system, especially in mental hospitals and nursing homes, where the well-being of patients heavily depends on the goodwill, humaneness, and expertise of staff. It is reassuring for the mentally ill and their families to know that they have access to a skilled advocate who can act to protect their fundamental human rights, with whom they can air complaints, and who will make representations on their behalf. This reassurance preserves for many clients a sense of autonomy, and for institutionalized patients it can act as an antidote to powerlessness.

Advocates for the mentally ill, such as lawyers, patient rights representatives, families, citizen advocate groups, and others, have taken actions that have resulted in many important reforms in the past twenty-five years. Advocates have become the monitors of the mental health system, surveying the welfare of clients, helping to ensure the protection of their legal rights, the provision and extension of material and service resources, and the prevention of abuse.

We tend today to take too much for granted the fact that advocacy for the chronic mentally ill is now a guiding philosophy and a basic component of practice. Given the current emphasis on advocacy, one might wonder why it was not an important function in the mental health system long before its ultimate emergence in the late 1960s.

THE EMERGENCE OF MENTAL HEALTH ADVOCACY

What historical forces created the current emphasis on advocacy? The answer depends to some extent on the fact that the 1960s and 1970s were a period of economic prosperity and rising social expectations. With World War II successfully concluded by the United States and its allies, Americans were optimistic about the future, believing there was little that the country could not successfully accomplish. We were ready to tackle the most difficult problems of all, poverty, illness, and injustice. President Lyndon Johnson declared war on poverty, deliberately invoking a minority slogan, "We shall overcome!" He signaled the federal government's readiness to address social problems that had long been neglected.

For the first time since the depression of the 1930s, attention was focused on increasing the entitlements and the political power of the poor, the sick, the disabled, and the disadvantaged. Reform movements expanded the rights of minorities, children, juveniles, women, consumers, criminal defendants, prisoners, and the mentally disabled. These activities received generous financial support from state and federal governments and from wealthy private foundations.

As we all know, the 1960s became a decade of social ferment. There was massive opposition to the unpopular war in Vietnam. There were inner-city riots, and there were marches, sit-ins, and other public demonstrations protesting poverty and demanding redress for minorities and other oppressed groups.

Many new organizations were created, including welfare rights groups and self-help groups for mentally ill persons and their families. Lawyers played an important role in developing a new body of public interest law that focused on the legal needs of the neglected and disadvantaged. As part of this movement, there emerged a body of brand-new mental health law, which received its greatest impetus in the 1970s and is still evolving.

Leading teachers and practitioners of social work began to ask themselves whether their profession had been sufficiently active and involved in its long-standing commitment to the poor and the disadvantaged. Many concluded that the profession had fallen behind, veering from its early concerns for the causes of the disadvantaged (Briar 1967; Grosser 1965 and 1967). From the 1930s, when psychoanalytic theory and therapies began to gain a stronghold on social work practice, until the 1960s, trained social workers seemed to serve the middle classes more assiduously than they did the poor. It was primarily the untrained, unskilled, and uneducated workers who ministered to clients of public welfare agencies and to the chronically ill.

In the late 1960s and early 1970s, however, leaders of the social work profession began to reverse this trend. They argued that social work's traditional commitment to the disenfranchised should be revitalized (Brager 1968; McCormick 1970). New policies and practice roles were necessary to further this objective. Social workers were urged to become "change agents" on behalf of the neglected (Levy 1972). Wherever policies, rules, and regulations were found to be hindering underprivileged clients from obtaining resources and entitlements, workers were encouraged to oppose, reshape, and reformulate them. The term **advocacy** was freshly minted to describe the functions of the new activist social worker who would implement the old values and new directions of the profession.

The National Association of Social Workers (NASW), through an ad hoc committee established by its Task Force on Urban Crisis and Welfare Problems, in 1969 adopted a general policy on advocacy for social workers announcing that it was the ethical duty of the social worker to practice advocacy on behalf of disadvantaged clients. In fact, advocacy was conceptualized as a vital and unequivocal component of the profession's code of ethics:

> [T]he social worker has an obligation under the Code of Ethics to be an advocate. That this obligation requires more than mere 'urging.' That under certain circumstances...the obligation is enforceable under the Code of Ethics (NASW 1969, p. 21).

NASW did not, however, provide an operational definition for advocacy. It was left to practitioners and theoreticians to devise their own ways in which advocacy would be carried out. Consequently, different interpretations and programmatic approaches to advocacy were advanced by various proponents. For some, the advocate was the "client's supporter, his advisor, his champion, and if need be, his representative in his dealings with the court, the police, the social agency and other organizations" (Briar 1967, p. 28). For others, the advocate engaged in changing agency policies, programs, and procedures (Patti 1974). The concept was also interpreted as the profession's responsibility to focus the public's attention on the unmet service needs of clients (Siporin 1975). All these various approaches have merit and are valid. They are embraced in the conceptualization of advocacy that is presented in this chapter.

THE ADVOCACY ROLE DEFINED

Social workers play many roles. As social brokers, they link clients to needed resources. As therapists, they assess their clients' problems in relation to environmental and cultural factors and develop and implement appropriate treatment plans. As mediators, they effectuate agreements and understandings between their clients and others. As teachers, they instruct and model socially adaptive skills and behaviors. As advocates, they monitor the rights and entitlements of their clients and, in keeping with current definitions of social work advocacy, focus on influencing decision makers in favor of an individual client or of a group of clients (Kutchins and Kutchins 1978; Sosin and Caulum 1983; Gerhart and Brooks 1983; Weissman *et al.* 1987).

Advocacy involves the presentation of a demand on behalf of clients to a decision maker or decision-making group that have heretofore ignored or resisted the fulfillment of a client's entitlement or right. As conceptualized here, the advocacy role comes into play only where the provision of service is refused, resisted, or inadequately offered by the provider and where arguments and appeals must be presented in order to obtain them.

Under this conceptualization, certain characteristic social work activities sometimes referred to as advocacy are not advocacy. For example, while advocacy is closely linked to gaining client access to needed services (Lurie 1982; Solomon *et al.* 1984), the routine linking of clients with available services is not advocacy. It is social brokerage, even where the practitioner must cut through red tape or make applications for services that the client cannot obtain for himself or herself.

Where practitioners propose and argue for different psychosocial interventions or psychiatric treatments with doctors, staff, and treatment teams who agree with and acquiesce in these arguments, they are really not performing advocacy. They are, rather, performing treatment functions and acting in the role of therapist.

Where workers teach clients to advocate on their own behalf and advise them of their rights, they are performing teaching functions, not advocacy functions.

Where workers identify obstacles to and gaps in effective service delivery in their own and other agencies and engage in reformist efforts, they are acting as organizational reformers and not as advocates.

THE FUNCTIONS OF ADVOCACY

Current definitions of advocacy emphasize the advocate's function of influencing decision makers in favor of one's case or a cause:

> [Advocacy is] Pleading a case or a cause, one's own or another's. . . in an appropriate forum. . . to accomplish a specific goal (Kutchins and Kutchins 1978).

or

> An attempt, . . . by an individual or a group to influence another individual or group to make a decision that would not have been made otherwise and that concerns the welfare or interests of a third party who is in a less powerful status than the decision maker (Sosin and Caulum 1983).

In essence, then, advocacy is an activity in which a request is presented to a decision-making body with the aim of obtaining a favorable decision. The request can be made by advocates on behalf of others or on behalf of themselves. A significant part of the difference between advocacy as defined here and that in previous representational approaches is actually one of emphasis. Today's advocates see their representation as usually involving clients' rights and entitlements and not merely privileges or favors that can be handed out at the discretion of decision makers.

CLIENTS' NEEDS, RIGHTS, AND ENTITLEMENTS

The needs, rights, and entitlements of the mentally ill have received much attention from lawyers who have brought massive right-to-treatment class-action litigations against entire state mental health systems with the objective of improving hospital conditions (*e.g.*, Wyatt *v.* Stickney 1972). These efforts were aimed at both the clinical and liberty needs of the mentally ill. Litigations have focused on such issues as physical conditions in hospitals, the ratio of professionals and other staff to patients, the need for treatment plans, and the dignity, privacy, and other liberty interests of the mentally ill. These litigations, and legislation enacted in their wake, established a substantial body of new rights and entitlements that still remain to be fully enforced. An important responsibility of mental health professionals is to ensure that these newly created rights do not become a dead letter, but rather are implemented and even enlarged upon where necessary and feasible. As the lawyers who have brought major class action cases leave the scene, the task of social workers and other mental health professionals becomes one of day-to-day implementation of rights and entitlements.

What are the major client needs and entitlements? The mentally ill need decent and specialized housing suited to their functional capacities, including nursing homes, halfway houses, cooperative living arrangements, and the like. They need access to financial resources, such as Social Security or categorical welfare supports. They need psychiatric and physical care and a variety of educational, rehabilitational, vocational, and recreational services. Most importantly, chronic mentally ill clients need durable, long-lasting relationships with helpers who can provide linkages with services. These helpers are known as therapists, case managers, and case management teams, and they should remain with their clients for an indeterminate period of time, providing the continuum of care and services known as continuity of care.

In addition to care and treatment needs, there are "liberty interest" needs for privacy, dignity, freedom of movement, and autonomy. Persons who are competent to do so should be able to make decisions for themselves. They should be able, or enabled, to decide where to live, what treatment to accept or reject, with whom to associate, and the like. Clients should have a right to freedom of movement where possible, a right to be treated with dignity—as human beings and not as mere cases to be dealt with—and finally, a right to privacy. These rights have been translated by statutory and decisional laws into such specific rights as the right to vote, to communicate freely by letter or phone, to have a voice in medication programs, and to protest and negotiate treatment. But these rights are not self-enforcing. They become meaningful only when workers monitor and implement them.

THE LEGAL AND UNION MODELS OF ADVOCACY

The advocacy model practiced in the mental health system is more in accord with the legal than the union model. In the legal model, clients' cases and causes are presented through oral or written demands and arguments. The model relies heavily on persuading decision makers through the marshaling of facts, data, and reason. The model rests on an assumption that in an ordered society civil arguments are more effective than a show of force.

The union model includes the persuasion-through-reason steps but ultimately relies on the use of social, economic, and political pressure. The union model bargains with the threat of public demonstrations, strikes, protest marches, picketing, and sit-ins. The use of such pressure and force to obtain an objective is not within the legal model of advocacy.

In fact, the union model, which presupposes reasonably equal distribution of power between bargaining parties, is not applicable in the struggle for patients' rights. Employers may own factories and plants, but labor controls the work force. Even though each has power over the other, strikes and other shows of force are weapons to be used as a last resort.

Patients and mental health professionals, on the other hand, have no such power. They cannot participate in physical demonstrations or exert sufficient force to win significant gains. For mental health professionals, it is difficult enough to further their own objectives as unionists, let alone to use force on behalf of their clients. The most important rights that the mentally ill possess at this time are those that were given them by law through the applications of the legal model of advocacy.

SPECIALIZED KNOWLEDGE AREAS FOR ADVOCATES

Advocacy for the mentally ill requires a command of two specialized bodies of knowledge and skill. The first is knowledge about the nature and character of mental illness. The second is a broad and general familiarity with pertinent statutes, regulations, and judicial decisions (and the rationale underlying them) that establish the rights of the mentally ill.

KNOWLEDGE OF MENTAL ILLNESS

Advocates should be knowledgeable about the nature of mental illness, its etiology, the extent and manner in which it incapacitates the individual, its manifestations, and its impact on others who are immediately affected, such as families, mental health staff, and communities. They should be able to identify each client's capacity to make decisions, to work, to learn, to relate to others, and to seek assistance from others. This knowledge is necessary in order to identify the validity of needs and grievances of one's clients and to credibly present their claims to decision makers.

Some mentally ill persons are too withdrawn, fearful, anxious, and dysfunctional to make their needs known either to their helpers or to others, even when their problems threaten to overpower them. Others tend to exaggerate and to call to the attention of their social workers every petty concern, no matter how trifling or insignificant. Those with paranoid disorders may be so suspicious of others that they conceal their problems, fearing that asking for help would only result in more trouble for them.

Persons who have lost their decision-making capacities during the florid phase of their illness tend to regain them, either fully or partially, after they have been restored. For example, some persons who vigorously resist antipsychotic medications while in a state of decompensation may become grateful for the enforced administration of drugs once the symptoms of their illness has been brought under control. Others refuse to take medications under the best of circumstances. Still others believe that the more medications they take, the better their health will be and demand excessive dosages of drugs from their doctors (Gutheil 1982).

In order to understand whether clients first of all have a "case" for which advocacy is called for, it is necessary to distinguish between impairments in judgment and decision making that stem from mental illness and behaviors that reflect otherwise "normal" character traits.

KNOWLEDGE OF LAWS, RULES, AND PROCEDURES

Social workers–advocates should be generally familiar with the laws, rules, and regulations that affect their clients and themselves. They are, of course, not expected to be as conversant with law and its applications as are lawyers. But practitioners should be generally familiar with state statutes, constitutional law, important cases, and the regulations of their state mental health department. This body of knowledge is not as inaccessible as is often thought.

Many states have so-called patient bills of rights that include a right to prompt and adequate treatment for any physical ailment, to clean and seasonal clothing, to receive visitors, not to have mail or telephone calls censored, and the like. In the community, the rights of the mentally ill include rights to medical and psychiatric treatment, nondiscrimination in housing and employment, protections against unreasonable eviction, voting rights, and the like.

For example, in New Jersey hospitalized patients have the following rights:

- To vote in all elections
- To make contracts, to make a will, to hold or transfer property
- To marry
- To acquire or retain a driver's license
- To receive schooling if between the ages of 5 and 20
- To be free of unnecessary or excessive medication; if a voluntary patient, to refuse all medication
- To be free from shock treatment, psychosurgery, or sterilization without express and informed consent after consultation with counsel or other persons of one's choice
- To be free from corporal punishment

- To a safe, sanitary, and humane living environment
- To participate in the development of one's treatment plan and be informed of one's condition and progress
- To receive prompt and adequate treatment for any physical ailment
- To know and be involved in plans for one's discharge from the hospital, including plans for meeting one's financial, medical, and mental health needs in the community
- To privacy and dignity
- To the least restrictive conditions necessary to achieve the purposes of treatment
- To keep and use personal property
- To wear one's own clothes
- To have storage space available for private use
- To regular physical exercise several times a week
- To go outdoors at regular and frequent intervals
- To practice the religion of one's choice or abstain from religious practices
- To be informed of the itemized costs of the services one receives and how these costs will be paid
- To know any financial limitations placed on the duration of services
- To mail and receive unopened correspondence
- To have access to letter-writing materials, including stamps
- To have access to a telephone; to make and receive confidential calls
- To receive visits from family members, friends, and others of one's choice at reasonable times
- To refuse visits from those one does not choose to see
- To receive visits from one's personal physician, attorney, and clergyman at reasonable times

All patients are given these rights in writing, usually in the form of a pamphlet. They are also informed where to make complaints about violations of their rights, such as to members of their treatment team, the hospital's chief executive officer, a special hospital-based patient advocate, advocates from the Department of Human Services, the Central Office of the Division of Mental Health and Hospitals, and the Department of the Public Advocate.

Some rights are more difficult to interpret than others. For example, the right to refuse visits from persons whom a patient does not want to see is easier to implement than the one granting "suitable opportunities to be with members of the opposite sex." In one hospital a group of male patients insisted that the latter right permitted them to be with female patients, or with their girlfriends and wives, alone and undisturbed, so they could engage in sexual activity. On the other hand, hospital officials interpreted this right as providing patients only with supervised opportunities for socialization in dining and activity rooms.

Violations of rights do not always fall neatly into existing laws or regulations. Ingenuity is sometimes called for in determining which rule should be invoked in order to respond to a particular problem. The following case of the "closed pharmacy" is an illustration of the creative use of an existing statute that was called into play to provide new rights for hospitalized patients.

> *Carl Andrews, a newly admitted patient, became very agitated because he could not take the medication that, at home, he had become accustomed to taking on a daily basis. The social worker on the admissions unit found out that even though Andrews was given a prescription by the admitting psychiatrist, it could not be filled because the hospital pharmacy was closed on weekends. Andrews had been admitted on a Saturday and therefore had to wait for two days, until Monday, before receiving his "meds."*
>
> *On looking into this problem, the social worker found out that other patients were also adversely affected by the weekend closing. She brought this directly to the attention of the hospital director, urging him to keep the pharmacy open every day. The social worker argued that a state statute that guaranteed patients a right to treatment suited to their condition should be interpreted as requiring that the pharmacy be open at all times. The director responded to this argument by instituting a weekend "on call" staff. There was a modest additional expense to the hospital, but considerable benefit to the patients.*

STEPS IN IMPLEMENTING THE ADVOCACY ROLE

Five steps are involved in advancing the claim of a mentally ill client. The first is to identify the validity of the client's grievance. The second is the identification of the scope of the problem. The third is identifying the appropriate decision maker. The fourth is to determine the manner in which a claim is presented. The fifth is evaluating and minimizing the risk.

IDENTIFYING THE COMPLAINT AND ITS VALIDITY

Outreach and Ethical Dilemmas

Because some mentally ill clients are unable to make their problems known, social workers must reach out actively to identify them. Outreach services are the first step in problem identification and a vital component in mental health advocacy (Willetts 1980).

Severely withdrawn persons or those experiencing the acute, florid stages of their illness may be unable to make their needs known. It is necessary to identify and reach out to these persons and, often without their knowledge or consent, advocate on their behalf. This, naturally, raises an ethical dilemma. Should representations be made on behalf of clients who have not given their consent to such representations? Would they have wanted advocacy services were they in a position to make a reasoned choice?

This problem particularly arises in dealing with some homeless mentally ill who resist any kind of confinement or having regulated living conditions imposed on them. Left to their own devices, they prefer to live on the street, risking malnutrition, molestation, and even freezing to death. Most police in big cities are now specifically charged with picking up the homeless on very cold nights and transporting them to public shelters, despite their protests. Do these clients understand the consequences of their refusals? Should their rejection of shelter be taken seriously? Some shelters for the homeless are dangerous places where defenseless mentally ill persons can be abused and robbed.

The failure of some persons to take their medications results in decompensation, which in turn may lead to abusive and destructive behavior. Should these persons be forced to take their medications or should their rights to refuse medication be honored, assuming they are competent and not dangerous while refusing?

Should housing violations, such as the presence of rats, stopped-up toilets, and unsafe stairs, be reported to the authorities even where clients, fearing eviction, specifically ask the social worker not to make such reports?

These ethical dilemmas must be resolved on a case-by-case basis. Advocates must evaluate their clients' competence to make decisions and honor them where feasible. But what is feasible? If a client has lost the ability to make a decision, the social worker has to consider what the client would have wanted were he or she still competent. Further, the rights of a client must be balanced against the rights of others—families, neighbors, coworkers, and others.

The following case history illustrates how one advocate's good intentions backfired.

> *Marianne Browne, the case manager for Frank Coleman, was called by a neighbor who lived in the same building. The neighbor, who knew of Coleman's illness, became concerned when Coleman refused to leave his room and stopped answering the phone and doorbell. Upon entering Coleman's small apartment with the help of a policeman, Browne found Coleman cowering under a table, hallucinating and unable to communicate rationally. The case manager noted that the building in which Coleman lived was in disrepair. There were falling plaster, broken windows, and poorly lit halls strewn with garbage. She was accustomed to such sights, but this time her composure was upset by a big rat that scurried out of Coleman's kitchen.*
>
> *After Coleman was admitted to the psychiatric hospital, Browne lodged a complaint with the board of health about unsanitary conditions in Coleman's apartment building. The owners of the building decided that rather than fix the building, they would sell it. All tenants received eviction notices. When Coleman was restored, he became angry at his case manager when he found out about her advocacy activities. He told her that because of her "meddling" he not only lost his home but also his friends.*

As discussed elsewhere in this book, outreach is so important that it should be included in regular workload plans. This is especially so for patient advocates who are responsible for preventing abuse and protecting patients' rights. In some hospitals, patient advocates make it a point to leisurely "walk through" their assigned wards at regular, daily times known to the patients. These advocates will stop for brief chats with some patients, read the charts of others, and make themselves accessible to all. Case managers in community-based agencies set aside a special time during which they telephone or visit clients who have failed to show up for appointments.

Real or Imaginary Complaints

Because of the mood swings, ambivalence, irrationality, memory problems, and inarticulateness of mentally ill clients, it is sometimes difficult for the worker to judge the seriousness of a complaint. The problem is compounded where rational complaints ("the food they give me is so bad that I cannot bring myself to eat it") are intermingled with irrational ones, ("because they put poison in everything they serve here"), or where complaints are expressed with inappropriate affect.

Workers who are familiar with their clients can often tell whether a complaint is real or irrational. They learn to interpret metaphorical expressions as well as changes in a client's appearance and behavior that are not necessarily illness-related. Rapid weight loss and poor grooming, for example, may be signs of neglect by caretakers. Unaccustomed timidity, fear, or depression may indicate physical and verbal abuse.

Where a problem is suspected, its validity should be checked out. Evidence must be gathered that separates fact from speculation. For example, one can only hypothesize physical neglect from weight loss or poor grooming. Proving neglect requires such evidence as corroborating statements of other residents or staff or a similar appearance among other residents.

Time is of the essence when one attempts to verify complaints of physical neglect and abuse. If too much time is permitted to elapse between the complaint and the investigation, important evidence may be lost and witnesses no longer available.

IDENTIFYING THE SCOPE OF THE PROBLEM

Once a problem has been recognized and identified, it should be determined whether it pertains only to the complainant or has broader impact on others as well. This raises an important issue that has practical as well as ethical implications. Should the advocate engage in "case" advocacy, which affects only one individual, or in "cause" advocacy, which affects an entire group or class of clients?

Cause Advocacy

Cause advocacy, sometimes referred to as class advocacy, is the changing or reforming of the structures, rules, or practices affecting groups or classes of

279

clients. The cause may be a small or a large one. It may involve the operation of an entire state system, one hospital, or just one ward of that hospital.

Small-scale, or **micro** cause, advocacy, ordinarily affects a circumscribed unit, such as a hospital, a ward, a boarding home, or a daycare center. It does not require the expenditure of time and material resources that are called for by large-scale class actions that involve legal litigation. Micro cause advocacy can ordinarily be carried out by one person. The case of the closed pharmacy on page 277 is an example of micro cause advocacy.

Another example of micro cause advocacy is the case of the overweight teenagers.

> *Susan Gordon, a social worker in the adolescent unit of the Midstate Psychiatric Hospital, noted that most of the female patients on her ward had gained more weight than is ordinarily expectable for users of antipsychotic medications. Upon checking into this matter, Gordon discovered that the hospital cafeteria was serving high-caloric foods to all patients and omitting from its menus low-calorie foods such as fresh salads, yogurt, and fresh fruit. When Gordon brought this to the attention of the hospital dietician, she met with a deaf ear.*
>
> *Gordon prepared a thorough statement, in which she documented the cafeteria's high-caloric diet for the past few months. She marshaled evidence from the psychiatric and medical literature to the effect that the taking of antipsychotic medications was associated with weight gain, particularly in the presence of a high-caloric diet. Gordon then presented her statement to the Chief Medical Officer, who ordered the cafeteria to add fresh fruits, vegetables, and low-caloric foods to its daily menu selections.*

Large-scale, or **macro**, advocacy, involves larger groups, such as all the homeless persons in a city or all patients in state hospitals who receive antipsychotic medications. This type of advocacy requires considerable financial and staff resources and is ordinarily handled by lawyers. But mental health workers can be, and have been, instrumental in identifying problems and in providing useful ammunition for the argumentation of appropriate solutions. For example, it was a social worker and a patient advocate who first identified serious problems in the administration of antipsychotic medications in New Jersey mental hospitals, which ultimately led to major federal litigation of national significance (Rennie v. Klein 1978, 1982, 1983).

> *John Rennie, a patient at a public mental hospital, complained to the social worker and to a patient advocate of overmedication and physical abuse by aides on the night shift. He felt that he was being made into a "zombie" and resisted the administration of antipsychotic medication. Rennie, who was in his early 30s, had been diagnosed as paranoid schizophrenic. The doctors and nurses tended to interpret his complaints as symptoms of his mental illness. For Rennie's "own good," his medication dosages were actually increased. The so-*

cial worker and patient advocate took Rennie's complaints seriously but were unable to prevail with medical and administrative staff.

Having exhausted all internal avenues of appeal, they called Rennie's situation to the attention of the Division of Mental Health Advocacy of the State Office of the Public Advocate. The latter organization then began an investigation that ultimately uncovered widespread medication abuses. As a result, the Public Advocate brought a lawsuit in the federal district court, arguing that patients should have a federal constitutional right to refuse antipsychotic medication. The federal court declared that there was such a right, which was upheld by the federal Circuit Court of Appeals. Today a right to refuse antipsychotic medications, subject to reasonable restrictions, prevails in New Jersey.

Effective macro advocates recruit and involve influential allies, such as directors of large welfare organizations, civic groups, and elected officials. Allies can be most effective by putting pressure on legislators through lobbying, letter-writing campaigns, and media publicity, and on courts by filing *amicus curiae* (friend of the court) briefs.

Case Advocacy

Case advocacy is the representation of an individual, a family, or a small, cohesive group. Case advocacy usually involves unique situations pertaining to the case, such as special ward and grounds privileges, adjusting medication to suit an individual patient, and the like. In performing case-advocacy functions, workers present written and oral demands and arguments in cases where their clients' access to benefits and privileges is blocked. They appeal when their clients are denied Social Security and other entitlements. They persuade reluctant landlords to accept mentally ill tenants and bring unsafe and unsanitary housing conditions to the attention of law-enforcement agencies. They present claims in situations when their clients are too uncomfortable with their medications or when harmful medication side effects appear. The following case illustrates case advocacy on behalf of an individual.

Mark Williams, a rehabilitation counselor at the Inland Community Psychiatric Rehabilitation Center, noticed that Ms. Himmelstein, a middle-aged member of a sheltered workshop group, seemed unusually depressed. Ms. Himmelstein had made excellent progress in skill training in her workshop and was about to "graduate" to a more stimulating and demanding unit of the center. Ms. Himmelstein confided that she did not want to leave the friends she had made in the workshop, especially in view of the fact that she had no family or friends "on the outside."

Williams took Ms. Himmelstein's case to the center's director, asking him to bend the rules and permit the member to remain among her friends, at least until such time as she could develop new friends in the "higher functioning" unit. The director at first refused, but finally William's persistent requests and arguments persuaded the former that friendship bonds were more impor-

281

*tant at this time for Ms. Himmelstein than the more challenging skill train-
ing.*

The next vignette illustrates case advocacy on behalf of a family.

*The Young family consists of Albert, a truck driver in his early 50s, his wife
Mary, a full-time homemaker, and their 25-year-old schizophrenic son Joe,
whose illness prevents him from working and requires frequent hospitalizations. At one time, the family wanted to move to a better apartment. The
owner of the building to which they wanted to move learned of Joe's illness and
refused to rent to the Youngs. When Joe's case manager learned of this, she in-
tervened with the owner on behalf of the Youngs.*

*The case manager explained to the owner that Joe was a client of the Inland
Community Mental Health Center, which provided 24-hour emergency service, as well as sheltered workshops and other services for Joe. When the owner
expressed fears that Joe might become violent or act inappropriately, the case
manager explained that even though Joe was mentally ill he had never be-
haved violently or inappropriately. The owner changed his mind, and the
Young family moved into the new apartment.*

The following Case of the Restrictive Boarding Home illustrates case advocacy on behalf of a small group, a case that presented a difficult choice for
the worker–advocate:

*Harry King, a case manager for the Midstate Psychiatric Rehabilitation
Center, has been assigned to visit Mrs. Strick's boarding house, where five
chronically ill Center members are boarded. King soon realizes that all the
boarders are unduly confined by Mrs. Strick. The boarders, on returning
"home" after a day at the daycare center, must remain in the kitchen. They
are not allowed to go to their bedrooms. The kitchen contains no television set
and there are no books, magazines, or games. After dinner is served, the
boarders are then required to go to their bedrooms, where they are compelled to
remain until morning.*

*When King suggests to Mrs. Strick that the boarders should have access to
the living room and should in general have more freedom of movement, the
landlady responds that she doesn't care to make any changes. Rather than
change the routine of her house, she will evict the boarders. King knows that
housing, and especially boarding homes for mentally ill persons, is very difficult
to come by in the town and county served by Midstate Center. If Mrs. Strick
evicts her boarders, no other housing would be available for them. (See the end-
of-chapter questions for some of the issues raised by this case.)*

Expanding Case into Cause Advocacy

It is rare that a problem calling for case advocacy does not also affect others.
Almost all macro or micro cause advocacy actions have their roots in case advocacy.

There are problems that, by reason of their constant recurrence, should no longer be handled on an individual case-by-case basis, as illustrated by the case of the Slow Social Security Office:

> *In Seaboard County Social Security disability claims were being processed at an extremely slow rate. Claims in other counties in the same state were being processed within a period of three months, but in Seaboard County the processing often took more than seven months to complete. Social workers, who were handling complaints on a case-by-case basis, spent an inordinate amount of time and effort in demanding quicker service for each individual client. When it became obvious that the snail's pace processing occurred only at the Seaboard County Social Security office, a formal complaint was filed to the district office, which in turn ordered the local office to speed up its operations.*

Identifying Appropriate Decision Makers

Initial advocacy requests always have to be presented to first-line decision makers whose authority bears directly on the problem of an individual client or groups of clients. A landlord is the primary decision maker when a client's apartment is found to be structurally unsafe; a doctor when medication needs to be changed; an activity director when a client complains of cigarette smoke in the activity room; and so forth.

In micro cause advocacy the first-line decision makers are hospital and agency administrators, as the administrator was in the case of the closed pharmacy. In macro advocacy, first-line decision makers are judicial authorities (as in the case of Rennie *v.* Klein), administrators of large organizations such as the Veteran's Administration, and elected officials. In large agencies, tables of organization are necessary tools in identifying various levels of decision makers.

It is a poor, self-defeating strategy to bypass first-line decision makers in favor of someone higher up. Requesting medication changes from the director of medical services without first discussing the matter with the prescribing physician may not change anything for the patient but result in enmity between doctor and advocate. Only after the primary decision maker has rejected the advocate's request, and the advocate considers an appeal, should the next level of authority be approached.

The Presentation of the Claim or Demand

The effectiveness of the presentation of a claim depends on how thoroughly the claim has been prepared and the manner, or posture, in which it is presented.

Preparation

Pertinent data and evidence bearing on the claim must be carefully gathered. In the case of the slow Social Security office, it was necessary to find out what the claims processing time of Social Security offices in general was. In the case of the closed pharmacy, the social worker had to devote some time to identifying other patients who were adversely affected by the absence of weekend hours.

Thorough preparation also includes the anticipation of objections that decision makers are likely to make. For example, in the case of the closed pharmacy, the worker believed that the hospital administrator would be concerned about the additional costs entailed in keeping the pharmacy open on weekends. The worker also was aware, however, that the administrator took pride in providing quality care for patients in "his" hospital. In preparing his case, the worker highlighted the "inadequate care" issue and advanced suggestions for minimizing the cost of weekend openings.

The Advocate's Posture

The advocate's posture in presenting claims is a significant factor not only in winning cases but also in maintaining credibility. Whether advocacy takes place within an alliance or in the context of an adversarial confrontation, advocates must always remain polite and calm. They should come across as acting from a position of strength and conviction. Raising one's voice, appearing unduly nervous or agitated, or threatening dire actions ("You will not get away with this!" "I'll see to it that justice gets done!" or "If need be, I'll take this case all the way to the Supreme Court!") only makes an advocate look foolish and does not further clients' claims.

Comportment is a frequently overlooked factor in achieving advocacy objections. Assertiveness and firmness, accompanied by an unfailingly polite and nonabrasive manner, have probably helped to win as many cases as did carefully thought-out strategies. The mark of a professional who acts from a position of strength and conviction is a courteous, assured, and nonthreatening manner. It is only when advocates act out of frustration and a sense of inadequacy that they become unnecessarily provocative, thus raising hackles and creating opposition to their requests.

The first approach to the primary decision maker should always be a polite request, rather than a demand. For example, the advocate may phrase a patient's complaint to the effect that the doctor would not sign a weekend pass as follows: "Doctor, Miss Smith would like a weekend pass to see her mother. I think she has improved and it would do both her and her mother good if she were to visit. Would you please sign the pass?"

Only if the request has been rejected should it be turned into a polite demand. Should the advocate decide to "appeal" the case to the next level of authority, the courteous as well as strategically correct thing to do is to inform the decision maker accordingly. "But doctor, it is important for Miss Smith to see her mother. If you won't grant the pass, I'll have to ask the medical director to do it."

Identifying and Minimizing the Risks

Sometimes it becomes necessary to disagree with or oppose the actions of one's own colleagues, other professionals, or one's own supervisors and agency administrators. This is an unpleasant prospect. Just about every worker tends to place uncomplicated collegial relationships above the interest of clients. Because mental health professionals, unlike lawyers, have not been trained to assume adversarial positions, they exaggerate the risks involved in questioning or opposing those who have more status and power, or in challenging the rules of one's agency.

Yet these risks exist, be they as trifling as bruised egos or as considerable as the loss of one's job, not getting a promotion, or being ostracized by one's coworkers (Mailick and Ashley 1981; Richan 1973; Patti 1974). What protections do workers have and what can they do to minimize risks?

Most risk-takers and "whistle-blowers" can find some protection in their own professional organization. For example, the National Association of Social Workers, in urging its members to assume an advocacy role, also proclaimed its commitment to protect both NASW members and nonmembers who suffer reprisals from their own or from other agencies. This commitment has been operationalized in the form of "Committees on Inquiry," which are part of each NASW state chapter, and which have the authority to investigate and censure agencies that have taken reprisals against challengers, whistle-blowers, risk-takers, and change agents.

To minimize risks, advocates need a power base. They need allies. Allies can be colleagues from one's own agency, especially other social workers, one's supervisors, and other professionals who are committed to the importance of advocacy. Allies serve three important functions. First, they can be consulted about the merits of projected undertakings and can be helpful in mapping strategies. Second, they can provide moral support in times of stress. Third, the backing of two or more agency staff reduces the risk of reprisals.

SUMMARY

This chapter has had three major objectives. The first is to define the advocacy function in such a way as to meaningfully distinguish it from other typical social work functions and to highlight its contribution to social work practice. The second is to analyze the evolution of social work advocacy as we know it today, so that we can understand the need for it. The third is to discuss the knowledge and skills that are needed for effective advocacy on behalf of the chronic mentally ill. The three-pronged definition of advocacy advanced here emphasizes the particular constituency served, their rights and entitlements, and modes of representation.

Advocacy should be differentiated from other helping roles such as those of the broker, teacher, mediator, and enabler. Advocacy, as conceptualized here, does involve service to underserved, disadvantaged, and previously neglected clients. It entails the identification of their needs, rights, and entitlements. Finally, it reflects a basic attitude of asserting and expanding these rights and entitlements in the face of an unwillingness to grant them. This new attitude is a repudiation of such previously held views as "the doctor knows best," or "the supervisor knows best," and the like. It exemplifes greater assertiveness, a refusal to be subservient, and a preparedness to challenge authority.

Successful advocacy for the chronic mentally ill requires knowledge of mental illness, a reasonable familiarity with antipsychotic medication and mental health law, and skills in implementing advocacy strategies. Finally, advocates must be prepared to solve the ethical dilemmas that will inevitably confront them.

FOR DISCUSSION AND THOUGHT

1. Have you engaged in any advocacy activity on behalf of a chronic mentally ill client or group of clients? If yes, discuss the circumstances of your case, the problems you encountered, and how you dealt with them.

2. Which clients ("clients" can be individuals, families, or formed groups) in your caseload are most in need of advocacy at this time? On what basis did you identify these clients as "most in need of advocacy"?

3. Are all advocates change agents? Are all change agents advocates? Discuss the reasons for your answers.

4. The legal model of advocacy, as defined here, is based on argumentation; the union model extends to activism. Provide examples from recent local or national events in which either the legal model or the union model was deployed as a means to an end.

5. Would you prefer to deploy the union or the legal model of advocacy in advocating for your cases or causes? Discuss whether temperament and personality characteristics or reasoned choice dictates the use of one model over another.

6. Explain the difference, if any, between being assertive and adversarial. Provide examples from your practice in having taken either an assertive or adversarial stance on behalf of clients.

During her regular rounds in a ward of the Mainland Hospital, social worker Helen Johnson is approached by Mr. Doyle, an elderly patient diagnosed as paranoid schizophrenic. Mr. Doyle's illness is resistant to treatment. In the past six years he has had to be hospitalized eight times. Doyle is a "good patient"—he complies with his treatment plan and is friendly and cooperative with staff.

Doyle tells Ms. Johnson that he wants to be transferred to another ward, and the sooner the better. When the social worker inquires the reason for this request, Doyle at first demurs, but then, in the "strictest confidence," he tells Ms. Johnson that an aide on the night shift "slaps people around" when they don't give him cigarettes or when they want to go too often to the toilets. Doyle becomes very agitated when he asks his social worker not to tell on the aide, fearing the latter would get even with Doyle and other patients for "snitching on him."

Under the hospital's regulations, no action can be taken against employees unless some evidence is provided, either by a statement from the social worker or, better yet, direct testimony from Doyle. This is the first time Ms. Johnson has heard a complaint about the aide, who otherwise appears to be a friendly man, concerned with the well-being of patients in his ward.

7. How should Ms. Johnson establish the validity of Mr. Doyle's complaint?

8. If, in fact, Doyle's complaint is valid, would you choose case or cause advocacy? Discuss the reasons for your choice.

9. Identify the primary decision maker in either advocacy action you choose.

10. Does Doyle have a right to have his communication to the social worker kept confidential?

11. Discuss Doyle's right to self-determination ("Don't tell anyone what I have told you" and "Just get me out of this ward") as against the alleged abuse by the aide.

12. What would be the effect on the worker–client relationship should the social worker reveal, for Doyle's own good, what she had been told in confidence?

13. What risks would Ms. Johnson face should she testify against the aide?

14. Role-play the best manner in which the social worker can present her claim to decision makers.

Review the Case of the Restrictive Boarding Home on page 282.

15. Discuss the ethical dilemmas involved in this case.

16. If you were the social worker in this case, what would you do now?

17. What are the costs and benefits of your contemplated actions to you, personally?

18. What are the costs and benefits of your contemplated actions to your clients?

19. What are the costs and benefits of your contemplated actions to your agency?

GLOSSARY

Advocacy: the pleading of a client's cause, or case, to a resistant decision-making individual or group.

Ambivalent: having contradictory feelings.

Anticholinergic side effects: side effects resulting from antipsychotic medications that are related to functions of the autonomic nervous system, over which we have no conscious control, such as breathing, digestion, and perspiration.

Antipsychotic medications: drugs that help to control the symptoms of major mental illnesses.

Apathy: a seeming lack of caring about what is happening to one or going on around oneself; the absence of an emotional response.

Ataxia: an inability to coordinate and control muscles that are ordinarily under one's control.

Atrophy: the wearing away of functional capacities or body tissue.

Attentional deficit: the inability to concentrate on and therefore to understand an external situation.

Autonomous: under one's own control; relatively independent.

Cardiovascular: pertaining to the heart and blood vessel system.

Case management: an approach to planned service delivery in which the primary aim is to provide for clients with chronic, serious, and complex problems appropriate services for as long as they need them.

Casework: a social work practice method in which the primary focus is on the individual, the family, or a small group.

Client: a specific person, family, group, or organization that is being helped through social work services and with whom an agreement has been reached about the nature and delivery of these services.

Coma: a stupor; loss of consciousness.

Community organization: a social work practice method in which the primary focus is on working with groups who are representative of relatively large populations who share similar problems.

Decompensation: regression from a state of remission; the flaring up of the signs and symptoms of mental illness.

Deinstitutionalization: a large-scale release of patients from institutions, such as mental hospitals.

Delirium: an acute and severe loss of the ability to attend to the immediate environment that is often marked by agitation and hallucinations.

Delusions: illusory beliefs that are only minimally related to reality.

Deterioration: a progressive impairment of a mental or physical condition as well as of functional capacities.

Diagnosis: the identification of an illness or a disorder.

Direct practice: practice in which the social worker is directly and immediately involved in service delivery: "hands-on" service delivery that involves casework, groupwork, and community organization.

Dysfunction: functioning that is not within a normal range.

Dysphoria: a mood disorder characterized by a general loss of interest in life, sadness, anxiety, and depression.

ECT: electroconvulsive therapy.

Electroconvulsive therapy: the treatment of a mood disorder by an electric shock to the brain.

Euphoria: an exaggerated feeling of well-being and elation.

Extrapyramidal side effects: side effects resulting from psychotropic medications that are related to that part of the central nervous system that is responsible for motor behavior and over which some control can be exercised, such as walking, talking, writing, and the like.

Florid: the full and acute manifestation of symptoms of mental illness.

Focal: localized.

Groupwork: a social work practice method in which the primary focus is on working with specific groups.

Habilitation: treatment that is primarily aimed at helping clients to attain necessary skills that enable them to function adequately in a given setting.

Hallucinations: distorted or totally unreal sensations that are experienced as if real.

Homeostasis: the maintenance of a balance, or equilibrium, in one's health, relationships, or functional capacities.

Intervention: a planned and deliberate activity that is undertaken in order to help a client.

Latent: inactive, dormant.

LSD: lysergic acid diethylamide—a hallucinogenic drug.

Maintenance treatment: treatment that is primarily aimed at the prevention of relapse and enabling a client to function at a current level.

Mania: a pronounced mood of elation, expansiveness, or irritability.

Mood disorder: a marked and long-term disturbance of the mood that may involve extreme swings between elation and depression, or long-lasting depressions or manias.

Paranoid ideation: in the absence of delusions or hallucinations, the abnormal suspicion that one is being persecuted, singled out for unfair treatment, ignored, or belittled.

Patient: a person whose primary care is provided by a physician, such as a psychiatrist or an internist.

Prognosis: the prediction of the course of an illness or social functioning, based on state-of-the-art knowledge, from currently available data about a client and the client's circumstances and environment.

Psyche: the human mind.

Psychiatry: a medical specialty dealing with the identification and treatment of mental and emotional disorders.

Psychic: pertaining to the mind.

Psychoactive medications: drugs that directly affect an individual's emotional or psychological state.

Psychogenic: having an origin in the mind.

Psychosocial assessment: the identification of a person's strengths, deficits, and weaknesses in the context of his or her social situation.

Psychotherapy: the treatment of mental, emotional, or behavioral disorders primarily by verbal means, such as education, re-education, suggestions, psychoanalysis, family therapy, and the like.

Regression: return to a mental state or to behaviors that were used during an earlier state of life.

Remission: a period of improvement during the course of a mental illness, notable for the abatement and easing of its symptoms.

Restoration: treatment aimed at recovery to a pre-illness condition or level of functioning.

Schizophrenia: a mental illness that is characterized during its active phase by such psychotic symptoms as agitation, delusions, and hallucinations. Persons afflicted with this illness suffer from attentional deficits that cause problems with functional capacities.

Schizophrenogenic: giving rise to schizophrenia through an influence in the environment.

Social situation: a person's immediate environment, especially as it relates to and is experienced by the person.

Social work roles: typical roles carried out by a social worker in the course of helping a client, such as those of enabler, broker, advocate, teacher, mediator, and therapist.

Sociogenic: having an origin in the environment.

Somatic: pertaining to the body.

Somatic treatment: treatment of a physical or mental condition with primarily physical means, such as medications, electroconvulsive therapy, and operations.

Vertigo: dizziness.

BIBLIOGRAPHY

Abramson, M. 1981. "Ethical Dilemmas for Social Workers in Discharge Planning." *Social Work in Health Care* 6: 33–42.

Allen, J. C., and Barton, G. 1976. "Patient Comments about Hospitalization: Implications for Change." *Comprehensive Psychiatry* 17: 631–40.

Ames, D. 1983. "The Limits of General Hospital Care: A Continuing Role for State Hospitals." *Hospital and Community Psychiatry* 34: 145–49.

Anderson, C. M. 1983. "A Psychoeducational Program for Families of Patients with Schizophrenia," pp. 99–116 in W. R. McFarlane, ed. *Family Therapy in Schizophrenia.* New York: Guilford.

———; Hogarty, G. E.; and Reiss, D. J. 1980. "Family Treatment of Adult Schizophrenic Patients: A Psychoeducational Approach." *Schizophrenia Bulletin* 6: 490–505.

———; Reiss, D. J.; and Hogarty, G. E. 1986. *Schizophrenia and the Family: A Practitioner's Guide to Psychoeducation and Management.* New York: Guilford.

Andreasen, N. C. 1986. *Can Schizophrenia Be Localized in the Brain?* Washington, D.C.: American Psychiatric Press.

———. 1987. "The Diagnosis of Schizophrenia." *Schizophrenia Bulletin* 13: 9–21.

Anthony, W. A. 1979. "The Rehabilitation Approach to Diagnosis." *Community Support Systems for the Long-Term Patient.* New Directions for Mental Health Services No. 2: San Francisco: Jossey-Bass.

———. 1980. *Principles of Psychiatric Rehabilitation.* Baltimore, Md.: University Park Press.

———. 1984. "The One-Two-Three of Client Evaluation in Psychiatric Rehabilitation." *Psychosocial Rehabilitation Journal* 8: 85–87.

———; Cohen, A.; and Vitalo, R. 1978. "The Measurement of Rehabilitation Outcome." *Schizophrenia Bulletin* 4: 365–83.

A.P.A. Task Force on Community Residential Services. 1982. *A Typology of Community Residential Services*. Washington, D.C.: American Psychiatric Association.

Applebaum, A. 1987. "Crazy in the Streets." *Commentary* 83: 34–39.

Arce, A. A., and Vergare, M. J. 1987. "Identifying and Characterizing the Mentally Ill among the Homeless," pp. 75–89 in H. R. Lamb, ed. *The Homeless Mentally Ill*. Washington, D.C.: American Psychiatric Association.

Bachrach, L. L. 1978. "A Conceptual Approach to Deinsitutionalization." *Hospital and Community Psychiatry* 29: 573–83.

———. 1982. "Young Adult Chronic Patients: An Analytical Review of the Literature." *Hospital and Community Psychiatry* 33: 189–97.

———. 1984. "Interpreting Research on the Homeless Mentally Ill: Some Caveats." *Hospital and Community Psychiatry* 35: 914–17.

———. 1987. "The Context of Care for the Chronic Mental Patient with Substance Abuse Problems." *Psychiatric Quarterly* 58: 3–14.

Baldessarini, R. J. 1985. *Chemotherapy in Psychiatry: Principles and Practice*. Cambridge, Mass.: Harvard University Press.

———. 1988. "Antipsychotic Agents." *The Psychiatric Times* 5: 1–42.

Barnes, D. M. 1987. "Biological Issues in Schizophrenia." *Science* 235: 430–33.

Bassuk, E. L., and Birk, A. W. 1984. *Emergency Psychiatry: Concepts, Methods, and Practices*. New York: Plenum.

Bassuk, E. L.; Schoonover, S.; and Gelenberg, A., eds. 1983. *The Practitioner's Guide to Psychoactive Drugs*. New York: Plenum.

Bateson, G. 1978. "The Birth of a Matrix of Double-Bind and Epistemology," in M. M. Berger, ed. *Beyond the Double Bind*. New York: Brunner/Mazel.

Baxter, E., and Hopper, K. 1982. "The New Mendicancy: Homeless in New York City." *American Journal of Orthopsychiatry* 52: 393–408.

Beaty, L. S., and Seeley, M. 1980. "Characteristics of Operators of Adult Foster Homes." *Hospital and Community Psychiatry* 31: 774–80.

Beels, C. C. 1976. "Family and Social Management of Schizophrenia," pp. 249–83 in F. Guerin, ed. *Family Therapy: Theory and Practice*. New York: Gardner Press.

———. 1981. "Social Support and Schizophrenia." *Schizophrenia Bulletin* 7: 58–72.

Bender, M. G. 1986. "Young Adult Chronic Patients: Visibility and Style of Interaction in Treatment." *Hospital and Community Psychiatry* 37: 265–68.

Bergman, H., and Harris, M. 1985. "Substance Abuse among Young Adult Chronic Patients." *Psychosocial Rehabilitation Journal* 9: 545–47.

Berkowitz, R.; Kuipers, L.; Eberlin-Fries, R.; and Leff, J. P. 1981. "Lowering Expressed Emotion in Relatives of Schizophrenics," in M. J. Goldstein, ed. *New Development in Interventions with Families of Schizophrenics*. New Directions for Mental Health Services No. 12. San Francisco: Jossey-Bass.

Bernheim, K. F., and Lehman, A. F. 1985. *Working with Families of the Mentally Ill*. New York: W. W. Norton.

Bernheim, K. F., and Lewine, R. J. 1979. *Schizophrenia: Symptoms, Causes, Treatments*. New York: W. W. Norton.

Beveridge, A. W., and Renvoize, E. B. 1988. "Electricity: A History of Its Use in the Treatment of Mental Illness in Britain during the Second Half of the 19th Century." *British Journal of Psychiatry* 153: 157–62.

Biestek, F. P. 1957. *The Casework Relationship*. Chicago: Loyola University Press.

Bland, R. C., and Orn, H. 1981. "Schizophrenia: Sociocultural Factors." *Canadian Journal of Psychiatry* 26: 186–88.

Blaustein, M., and Viek, C. 1987. "Problems and Needs of Operators of Board-and-Care Homes: A Survey." *Hospital and Community Psychiatry* 38: 750–54.

Blazyk, S., and Canavan, M. M. 1985. "Therapeutic Aspects of Discharge Planning." *Social Work* 30: 489–96.

Bleuler, E. 1950. *Dementia Praecox or the Group of Schizophrenias*. Translated by J. Zinkin. New York: International University.

Blum, J. D. 1978. "On Changes in Psychiatric Diagnosis over Time." *American Psychologist* 33: 1017–31.

—— and Redlich, F. 1980. "Mental Health Practitioners: Old Stereotypes and New Realities." *Archives of General Psychiatry* 37: 1247–53.

Bowen, M. 1960. "A Family Concept of Schizophrenia," pp. 346–88 in D. Jackson, ed. *The Etiology of Schizophrenia*. New York: Basic Books.

Brager, G. A. 1968. "Advocacy and Political Behavior." *Social Work* 13: 5–15.

Breggin, P. R. 1979. *Electro-Shock: Its Brain-Disabling Effects*. New York: Springer.

Briar, S. 1967. "The Current Crisis in Social Casework," pp. 19–33 in *Social Work Practice, 1967*. Selected papers from the 94th Annual Forum National Conference on Social Welfare. New York: Columbia University Press.

Broekma, M. C.; Danz, K. H.; and Schloemer, C. U. 1975. "Occupational Therapy in a Community Aftercare Program." *American Journal of Occupational Therapy* 29: 22–27.

Brooks, A. D. 1974. With 1980 supplement. *Law, Psychiatry and the Mental Health System*. Boston: Little, Brown.

Brown, G. W., and Birley, J. L. T. 1968. "Crisis and Life Changes and the Onset of Schizophrenia." *Journal of Health and Social Behavior* 9: 203–14.

Brown, G. W.; Birley, J. L. T.; and Wing, J. K. 1972. "Influence of Family Life on the Course of Schizophrenic Disorders: A Replication." *British Journal of Psychiatry* 121: 241–58.

Brown, G.; Carstairs, G. M.; and Topping, G. G. 1958. "The Post-Hospital Adjustment of Chronic Mental Patients." *Lancet* 2: 685–89.

Brown, G.; Monck, E. M.; and Carstairs, G. M. 1962. "Influence of Family Life on the Course of Schizophrenic Illness." *British Journal of Preventive and Social Medicine*. 16: 55–68.

Burger, A.; Kimmelman, L.; Lurie, A.; and Rabiner, C. J. 1978. "Congregate Living for the Mentally Ill: Patients as Tenants." *Hospital and Community Psychiatry* 29: 590–93.

Cade, J. F. J. 1949. "Lithium Salts in the Treatment of Psychotic Excitement." *Medical Journal of Australia* 2: 349–52.

Cannon, M. 1977. "The Halfway House as an Alternative to Hospitalization," pp. 199–220 in J. Zusman and E. F. Bertsch, eds. *The Future Role of the State Hospital*. Lexington, Mass.: Lexington Books.

Caplan, G. 1964. *Principles of Preventive Psychiatry*. New York: Basic Books.

——. 1974. *Support Systems and Community Mental Health*. New York: Behavioral Publications.

Carpenter, W. T. 1987. "Approaches to Knowledge and Understanding of Schizophrenia." *Schizophrenia Bulletin* 13: 1–8.

Carroll, J. A.; Jefferson, J. W.; and Gresit, J. H. 1987. "Treating Tremor Induced by Lithium." *Hospital and Community Psychiatry* 38: 1280–88.

Carty, R. R., and Breault, G. C. 1967. "Gheel: A Comprehensive Community Mental Health Program." *Perspectives in Psychiatric Care* 5: 281–85.

Cason, C. L., and Beck, C. M. 1982. "Clinical Nurse Specialist Role Development." *Nursing and Health Care* 3: 25–39.

Cassel, J. C. 1974. "Psychosocial Processes and 'Stress': Theoretical Formulation." *International Journal of Health Services* 4: 471–82.

Caton, C. L. M. 1981. "The New Chronic Patient and the System of Community Care." *Hospital and Community Psychiatry* 32: 475–78.

———; Goldstein, J. M.; Serrano, O.; and Bender, R. 1984. "The Impact of Discharge Planning on Chronic Schizophrenic Patients." *Hospital and Community Psychiatry* 35: 255–62.

Chamberlin, J. 1978. *On Our Own: Patient-Controlled Alternatives to the Mental Health System.* New York: Hawthorne.

Chernis, C., and Egnatios, E. 1978. "Is There Job Satisfaction in Community Mental Health?" *Community Mental Health Journal* 14: 309–18.

Christ, W. 1984. "Factors Delaying Discharge of Psychiatric Patients." *Health and Social Work* 9: 178–87.

Christenfeld, R.; Toro, P. A.; Brey, M.; and Haveliwala, Y. A. 1985. "Effects of Community Placement on Chronic Mental Patients." *American Journal of Community Psychology* 13: 125–37.

Churgin, M. J. 1985. "An Essay on Commitment and the Emergency Room: Implication for the Delivery of Mental Health Services." *Law, Medicine and Health Care* 13: 297–303.

City of Cleburne *v.* Cleburne Living Center, 105 S. Ct. 3249, 1985.

Clausen, J. A., and Kohn, M. L. 1954. "The Ecological Approach in Social Psychiatry." *American Journal of Sociology* 60: 140–51.

Cohen, C. I., and Berks, L. A. 1985. "Personal Coping Styles of Schizophrenic Outpatients." *Hospital and Community Psychiatry* 36: 407–10.

Cohen, C. I., and Sokolovsky, J. 1978. "Schizophrenia and Social Networks: Ex-Patients in the Inner City." *Schizophrenia Bulletin* 4: 546–60.

———. 1979. "Clinical Use of Network Analysis for Psychiatric and Aged Populations." *Community Mental Health Journal* 15: 203–13.

Collins, A. H. 1973. "Natural Delivery Systems: Accessible Source of Power for Mental Health." *American Journal of Orthopsychiatry* 43: 46–52.

———; Emlen, A.; and Watson, E. 1969. "The Day Care Neighbor Service: An Interventive Experiment." *Community Mental Health Journal* 5: 219–24.

Craig, T., and Shang, P. L. 1981. "Death and Deinstitutionalization." *American Journal of Psychiatry* 138: 224–27.

Crow, T. J. 1986. "A Re-evaluation of the Viral Hypothesis: Is Psychosis the Result of Retroviral Integration at a Site Close to the Cerebral Dominance Gene?" pp. 241–57 in A. Kerr and P. Snaith, eds. *Contemporary Issues in Schizophrenia.* London: Gaskell.

Cumming, J., and Cumming, E. 1962. *Ego and Milieu.* New York: Atherton.

Deitchman, W. S. 1980. "How Many Case Managers Does It Take to Screw In a Light Bulb?" *Hospital and Community Psychiatry* 31: 788–89.

Demone, H. W., and Schulberg, H. C. 1975. "Has the State Mental Hospital a Future as a Human Service Resource?" pp. 9–29 in J. Zusman and F. Bertsch, eds. *The Future Role of the State Hospital.* Lexington, Mass.: Lexington Books.

Depp, F. C.; Scarpelli, A. E.; and Apostoles, F. E. 1983. "Making Cooperative Living Work for Psychiatric Outpatients." *Health and Social Work* 8: 271–87.

D'Ercole, A.; Peters, E. A.; and Robinson, C. 1988. "The Effectiveness of Case Management: A Controlled Clinical Trial Study. Progress Report 1988." Unpublished mimeographed report. Bronx, N.Y.: The Rehabilitation, Research and Training Center for Psychiatrically Disabled Individuals of the Albert Einstein College of Medicine.

DeRisi, W., and Vega, W. A. 1983. "The Impact of Deinstitutionalization on California's State Hospital Population." *Hospital and Community Psychiatry* 34: 140–44.

Diagnostic and Statistical Manual of Mental Disorders. 1987. Third edition—revised. Washington, D.C.: American Psychiatric Association.

Diamond, R. 1985. "Drugs and the Quality of Life: The Patient's Point of View." *Journal of Clinical Psychiatry* 46: 29–35.

Dickey, B.; Gudeman, J. E.; Hellman, S.; Donatelle, A.; and Grinspoon, L. 1981. "A Follow-up of Deinstitutionalized Chronic Patients Four Years after Discharge." *Hospital and Community Psychiatry* 32: 326–30.

Dill, A. E. P. 1987. "Issues in Case Management for the Chronically Mentally Ill," pp. 61–70 in D. Mechanic, ed. *Improving Mental Health Services: What the Social Sciences Can Tell Us.* New Directions for Mental Health Services No. 36. San Francisco: Jossey-Bass.

Dittmar, N. D., and Franklin, J. L. 1980a. "State Hospital Patients Discharged to Nursing Homes: Are Hospitals Dumping Their More Difficult Patients?" *Hospital and Community Psychiatry* 31: 251–54.

———. 1980b. "State Hospital Patients Discharged to Nursing Homes: How Are They Doing?" *Hospital and Community Psychiatry* 31: 255–58.

Dohrenwend, B. P., and Dohrenwend, B. S. 1976. "Sex Differences in Psychiatric Disorders." *American Journal of Sociology* 81: 447–54.

Donaldson, S.; Gelenberg, A. J.; and Baldessarini, R. J. 1983. "The Pharmacological Treatment of Schizophrenia: A Progress Report." *Schizophrenia Bulletin* 9: 504–23.

Durham, M., and La Fond, J. 1985. "The Empirical Consequences and Policy Implications of Broadening the Statutory Criteria for Civil Commitment." *Yale Law and Policy Review* 3: 395–446.

———. 1988. "'Thank You Dr. Stone': A Response to Dr. Alan Stone and Some Further Thoughts on the Wisdom of Broadening the Criteria for Involuntary Therapeutic Commitment of the Mentally Ill." *Rutgers Law Review* 40: 865–88.

Eaton, W. W. 1980. "A Formal Theory of Selection for Schizophrenia." *American Journal of Sociology* 86: 149–58.

Eckert, J. C. 1980. *The Unseen Elderly: A Study of Marginally Subsistent Hotel Dwellers.* San Diego, Calif.: Campanile Press.

Egeland, J. A., and Hostetler, A. M. 1983. "Amish Study I: Affective Disorders among the Amish, 1976–1980." *American Journal of Psychiatry* 140: 56–76.

Ell, K. 1984. "Social Networks, Social Support, and Health Status: A Review." *Social Service Review* 58: 133–49.

Ellison, J. M., and Wharff, E. 1985. "More Than a Gateway: The Role of the Emergency Psychiatry Service in the Community Mental Health Network." *Hospital and Community Psychiatry* 36: 180–85.

Ely, A. R. 1985. "Long-Term Group Treatment for Young Male 'Schizopaths.'" *Social Work* 20: 5–10.

Erickson, G. 1984. "A Framework and Themes for Social Network Intervention." *Family Process* 23: 187–98.

Estroff, S. 1981. *Making It Crazy: An Ethnography of Psychiatric Clients in an American Community.* Berkeley, Calif.: University of California Press.

Ewalt, P. L., and Honeyfield, R. M. 1981. "Needs of Persons in Long-Term Care." *Social Work* 26: 223–31.

Fairweather, G. W. 1969. *Community Life for the Mentally Ill: An Alternative to Institutional Care.* Chicago: Aldine.

———, ed. 1980. *The Fairweather Lodge: A Twenty-Five Year Retrospective.* New Directions for Mental Health Services No. 7. San Francisco: Jossey-Bass.

Falloon, I. R. H. 1984. "Relapse: A Reappraisal of Assessment of Outcome in Schizophrenia." *Schizophrenia Bulletin* 10: 293–99.

——— and Liberman, R. P. 1983. "Interactions between Drug and Psychosocial Therapy in Schizophrenia." *Schizophrenia Bulletin* 9: 543–54.

———; Liberman, R. P.; Lillie, I.; and Vaughn, F. J. 1981. "Family Therapy of Schizophrenia with High Risk of Relapse." *Family Process* 20: 211–21.

———; Boyd, J. L.; McGill, C. W.; Razani, J.; Moss, H. B.; and Gilderman, A. M. 1982. "Family Management in the Prevention of Exacerbations of Schizophrenia: A Controlled Study." *New England Journal of Medicine* 306: 1437–40.

———; Boyd, J. L.; and McGill, C. W. 1984. *Family Care of Schizophrenia.* New York: Guilford.

———; Boyd, J. L. McGill, C. W.; Williamson, M.; Razani, J.; Moss, H. B.; Gilderman, A. M.; and Simpson, G. M. 1985. "Family Management in the Prevention of Morbidity of Schizophrenia: Clinical Outcome of a Two-Year Longitudinal Study." *Archives of General Psychiatry* 42: 887–96.

Faulkner, L. R.; Bloom, J. D.; Bray, J. D.; and Maricle, R. 1987. "Psychiatric Manpower and Services in a Community Mental Health System." *Hospital and Community Psychiatry* 38: 287–91.

Fenton, W. S., and McGlashan, T. H. 1987. "Sustained Remission in Drug-free Schizophrenic Patients." *American Journal of Psychiatry* 144: 1306–9.

Ferris, P. A., and Marshall, C. A. 1987. "A Model Project for Families of the Chronically Mentally Ill." *Social Work* 32: 110–14.

Fink, M. 1979. *Convulsive Therapy: Theory and Practice.* New York: Raven Press.

Flaherty, J. A.; Gaviria, F.; Black, M.; Elizabeth, M.; Altman, E.; and Mitchell, T. 1983. "The Role of Social Support in the Functioning of Patients with Unipolar Depression." *American Journal of Psychiatry* 140: 473–76.

Flomenhaft, E.; Kaplan, D.; and Langsley, D. G. 1969. "Avoiding Psychiatric Hospitalization." *Social Work* 4: 38–45.

Folkins, C.; Wieslberg, N.; and Spansley, J. 1981. "Discipline Stereotyping and Evaluative Attitudes among Community Mental Health Center Staff." *American Journal of Orthopsychiatry* 51: 140–48.

Fontana, A. F., and Dowd, B. 1975. "Assessing Treatment Outcome, II: The Prediction of Rehospitalization." *Journal of Nervous and Mental Disorders* 161: 231–38.

Freud, S. 1974. "Analysis of a Phobia in a Five-Year-Old Boy," pp. 1–147 in J. Strachey, ed. *The Standard Edition of the Complete Works of Sigmund Freud.* Vol. 10. London: Hogarth.

Friedberg, J. 1977. "Shock Treatment, Brain Damage, and Memory Loss: Neurological Perspective." *American Journal of Psychiatry* 134: 1010–14.

Froland, C.; Brodsky, G.; Olson, M.; and Stewart, L. 1979. "Social Support and Social Adjustment: Implications for Mental Health Professionals." *Community Mental Health Journal* 15: 82–93.

Fromm-Reichman, F. 1948. "Notes on the Development of Treatment of Schizophrenia by Psychoanalytic Psychotherapy." *Psychiatry* 11: 263-73.

Garrison, V., and Podell, J. 1981. "Community Support Systems Assessment." *Schizophrenia Bulletin* 7: 101-8.

Gelberg, L., and Linn, L. S. 1988. "Social and Physical Health of Homeless Adults Previously Treated for Mental Health Problems." *Hospital and Community Psychiatry* 39: 510-16.

Geller, J. L. 1986. "In Again, Out Again: Preliminary Evaluation of a State Hospital's Worst Recidivists." *Hospital and Community Psychiatry* 37: 386-90.

Gerhardt, S. 1968. "The Evolution of Patient Government." *Hospital and Community Psychiatry* 19: 329-30.

Gerhart, U. C., and Brooks, A. D. 1983. "The Social Work Practitioner and Antipsychotic Medications." *Social Work* 28: 454-60.

———. 1985. "Social Workers and Malpractice: Law, Attitudes and Knowledge." *Social Casework* 66: 411-16.

Glick, I. D.; Klar, H. M.; and Braff, D. L. 1984. "Guidelines for Hospitalization of Chronic Psychiatric Patients." *Hospital and Community Psychiatry* 35: 934-36.

Goering, P. N., and Stylianos, S. K. 1988. "Exploring the Helping Relationship between the Schizophrenic Client and Rehabilitation Therapist." *American Journal of Orthopsychiatry* 58: 271-80.

Goering, P. N.; Wasylenki, D. A.; Frakas, M.; Lancee, W. J.; and Ballantyne, R. 1988. "What Difference Does Case Management Make?" *Hospital and Community Psychiatry* 39: 272-76.

Goffman, E. 1961. *Asylums: Essays on the Social Situation of Mental Patients and Other Inmates.* Chicago: Aldine.

Goldman, H. H.; Adams, N. H.; and Taube, C. A. 1983. "Deinstitutionalization: The Data Demythologized." *Hospital and Community Psychiatry* 34: 129-34.

Goldmeier, J.; Shore, M.; and Fortune, M. 1977. "Cooperative Apartments: New Programs in Community Mental Health." *Health and Social Work* 2: 120-40.

Goldstein, M. J.; and Kopelkin, H. S. 1981. "Short and Long Term Effects of Combining Drug and Family Therapy," pp. 5-26 in M. J. Goldstein, ed. *New Developments in Interventions with Families of Schizophrenics.* New Directions for Mental Health Services No. 12. San Francisco: Jossey-Bass.

Goldstein, M. J.; Hand, I.; and Hahlweg, K., eds. 1986. *Treatment of Schizophrenia: Family Assessment and Intervention.* New York: Springer-Verlag.

Goldstrom, I., and Manderscheid, R. W. 1982. "The Chronically Mentally Ill: A Descriptive Analysis from the Uniform Client Data Instrument." *Community Support Services Journal* 20: 7-14.

Gopelrud, E. N. 1979. "Unexpected Consequences of Deinstitutionalization of the Mentally Disabled Elderly." *American Journal of Community Psychology* 7: 315-28.

Gore, S. 1978. "The Effect of Social Support in Moderating the Health Consequences of Unemployment." *Journal of Health and Social Behavior* 19: 157-65.

Gorton, J. G., and Partridge, R. 1982. *Practice and Management of Psychiatric Emergency Care.* St. Louis: Mosby.

Gottlieb, B. H., ed. 1981. *Social Networks and Social Support.* Newbury Park, Calif.: Sage Publications.

———. 1983. *Social Support Strategies: Guidelines for Mental Health Practice.* Newbury Park, Calif.: Sage Publications.

———. 1985. "Assessing and Strengthening the Impact of Social Support on Mental Health." *Social Work* 30: 293–300.

——— and Schrotter, C. 1978. "Collaborations and Resource Exchange between Professionals and Natural Support Systems." *Professional Psychology* 9: 614–22.

Gove, W. 1970. "Societal Reaction as an Explanation of Mental Illness: An Evaluation." *American Sociological Review* 35: 873–81.

Greenstone, J. D. 1979. "Dorothea Dix and Jane Addams: From Transcendentalism to Pragmatism in American Social Reform." *Social Service Review* 53: 527–59.

Griffith, J. 1984. "Emotional Support Providers and Psychosocial Distress among Anglo- and Mexican Americans." *Community Mental Health Journal* 20: 182–201.

Grinker, R. R., and Harrow, M. 1987. *Clinical Research in Schizophrenia: A Multidimensional Approach.* Springfield, Ill.: Charles C. Thomas.

Grob, G. N. 1973. *Mental Institutions of America: Social Policy to 1875.* New York: Free Press.

———. 1983. "Historical Origins of Deinstitutionalization," pp. 15–29 in L. L. Bachrach, *Deinstitutionalization.* San Francisco: Jossey-Bass.

Grosser, C. F. 1965. "Community Development Programs Serving the Urban Poor." *Social Work* 10: 15–21.

———. 1967. "Neighborhood Community Development Programs Serving the Urban Poor," pp. 247–48 in G. A. Brager and F. Purcell, eds. *Commuity Action against Poverty: Readings from the Mobilization Experience.* New Haven, Conn.: College and University Press.

Gualtieri, C. T.; Quade, D.; Hicks, R. E.; Mayo, J. P.; and Schroeder, S. S. 1984. "Tardive Dyskinesia and Other Clinical Consequences of Neuroleptic Treatment in Children and Adolescents." *American Journal of Psychiatry* 141: 20–23.

Gunderson, J. G. 1978. "Defining the Psychiatric Process in Psychiatric Milieus." *Psychiatry* 41: 327–35.

Gutheil, T. G. 1982. "The Psychology of Psychopharmacology." *Bulletin of the Menninger Clinic* 40: 321–30.

———. 1985. "The Therapeutic Milieu: Changing Themes and Theories." *Hospital and Community Psychiatry* 36: 1279–85.

Haggerty, J. J.; Evans, D. L.; McCartney, C. F.; and Raft, D. 1986. "Psychotropic Prescribing Patterns of Nonpsychiatric Residents in a General Hospital in 1973 and 1982." *Hospital and Community Psychiatry* 37: 358–61.

Halevy-Martini, J.; Hemley-Van der Velden, E. M.; Ruhf, L. L.; and Schoenfeld, P. 1984. "Process and Strategy in Network Therapy." *Family Process* 23: 521–33.

Haley, J. 1980. *Leaving Home: The Therapy of Disturbed Young People.* New York: McGraw-Hill.

———. 1988. "Family Therapy Forum." *Family Therapy News,* May–June, p. 1.

Haller, R. M., and Deluty, R. H. 1988. "Assaults on Staff by Psychiatric Inpatients: A Critical Review." *British Journal of Psychiatry* 152: 174–79.

Hammer, M.; Makiesky-Barrow, S.; and Gutwirth, L. 1978. "Social Networks and Schizophrenia." *Schizophrenia Bulletin* 4: 522–45.

Hammond, K. R., and Joyce, C. R. B. 1975. *Psychoactive Drugs and Social Judgment: Theory and Research.* New York: Wiley and Sons.

Hansell, N. 1978. "Services for Schizophrenia: A Lifelong Approach to Treatment." *Hospital and Community Psychiatry* 29: 105–9.

Harding, C. M.; Brooks, G. W.; Ashikaga, T.; Strauss, J. S.; and Breier, A. 1987. "The Vermont Longitudinal Study of Persons with Severe Mental Illness, I: Methodology, Study Sample, and Overall Status 32 Years Later." And (in the same issue) "The Vermont Longitudinal Study of Persons with Severe Mental Illness, II: Long-Term Outcome of Subjects Who Retrospectively Met DSM-III Criteria for Schizophrenia." *American Journal of Psychiatry* 144: 718–35.

Harkey, J.; Miles, D. L.; and Rushing, W. A. 1976. "The Relation between Social Class and Functional Status: A New Look at the Drift Hypothesis." *Journal of Health and Social Behavior* 17: 194–204.

Harris, M.; Bergman, H. C.; and Bachrach, L. L. 1986. "Psychiatric and Nonpsychiatric Indicators for Rehospitalization in a Chronic Patient Population." *Hospital and Community Psychiatry* 37: 630–31.

———. 1987. "Individualized Network Planning for Chronic Psychiatry Patients." *Psychiatry Quarterly* 58: 51–56.

Hatfield, A. B. 1983. "What Families Want of Family Therapists," pp. 41–65 in W. R. McFarlane, ed. *Family Therapy in Schizophrenia*. New York: Guilford.

——— and Lefley, H. P., eds. 1987. *Families of Mentally Ill: Coping and Adaptation*. New York: Guilford.

———; Spaniol, L.; and Zipple, A. M. 1987. "Expressed Emotion: A Family Perspective." *Schizophrenia Bulletin* 13: 221–26.

Henderson, A. S. 1984. "Interpreting the Evidence on Social Support." *Social Psychiatry* 19: 49–52.

Henderson, S.; Duncan-Jones, P.; McAuley, H.; and Ritchie, K. 1978. "The Patient's Primary Group." *British Journal of Psychiatry* 132: 74–86.

Hersen, M., and Barlow, D. H. 1977. *Single Case Experimental Designs: Strategies for Studying Behavior Change*. New York: Pergamon.

Hirsch, B. J. 1980. "Natural Support Systems and Coping with Major Life Changes." *American Journal of Community Psychology* 8: 159–72.

Hoch, C., and Hemmens, G. C. 1987. "Linking Informal and Formal Help: Conflict along the Continuum of Care." *Social Service Review* 61: 432–46.

Hogarty, G. E. 1984. "Depot Neuroleptics: The Relevance of Psychosocial Factors—A United States Perspective." *Journal of Clinical Psychiatry* 45: 36–42.

———; Goldberg, S. C.; and the Collaborative Study Group. 1973. "Drug and Sociotherapy in the Aftercare of Schizophrenic Patients: One-Year Relapse Rates." *Archives of General Psychiatry* 28: 54–64.

———; Goldberg, S. C.; Schooler, N. R.; and Ulrich, R. F. 1974. "Drug and Sociotherapy in the Aftercare of Schizophrenic Patients." *Archives of General Psychiatry* 31: 603–8.

———; Ulrich, R. F.; Mussare, F.; and Aristigueta, N. 1976. "Drug Discontinuation among Long-Term Successfully Maintained Schizophrenic Outpatients." *Diseases of the Nervous System* 57: 494–500.

Holden, C. 1985. "A Guarded Endorsement for Shock Therapy." *Science* 228: 1510–11.

Hollingshead, A. B., and Redlich, F. C. 1958. *Social Class and Mental Illness: A Community Study*. New York: Wiley and Sons.

Holohan, C. J., and Moos, R. H. 1981. "Social Support and Psychological Distress: A Longitudinal Study." *Journal of Abnormal Psychology* 19: 365–70.

House, W. C.; Miller, S.; and Schlachter, R. H. 1978. "Role Definitions among Mental Health Professionals." *Comprehensive Psychiatry* 19: 469–76.

Hudson, W. W. 1982. *The Clinical Measurement Package: A Field Manual*. Homewood, Ill.: Dorsey.

Hull, S., and Thompson, G. 1981. "Factors Which Contribute to the Normalization in Residential Facilities for the Mentally Ill." *Community Mental Health Journal* 17: 107–13.

Hyde, R. W., and Solomon, H. C. 1950. "Patient Government: A New Form of Group Therapy." *Digest of Neurology and Psychiatry* 25: 207–18.

Hyman, S. E. 1984. "The Emergency Psychiatric Evaluation, Including the Mental Status Examination," pp. 3–7 in S. E. Hyman, ed. *Manual of Psychiatric Emergencies.* Boston: Little, Brown.

Imber-Mintz, L.; Liberman, R. P.; Miklowitz, D. J.; and Mintz, J. 1987. "Expressed Emotion: A Call for Partnership among Relatives, Patients, and Professionals." *Schizophrenia Bulletin* 13: 227–35.

In Re S.L., 94, N.J. 128, 462 A 2d 1252 (1983).

Intaglia, J., and Baker, F. 1982. "Improving the Quality of Community Care for the Chronically Mentally Disabled: The Role of Case Management." *Schizophrenia Bulletin* 8: 655–74.

Jacobs, J. D. 1964. "Social Action as Therapy in a Mental Hospital." *Social Work* 9: 54–61.

Jarvis, E. 1971. *Insanity and Idiocy in Massachusetts: Report of the Commission on Lunacy.* Cambridge, Mass.: Harvard University Press.

Jayaratne, S., and Levy, R. L. 1979. *Empirical Clinical Practice.* New York: Columbia University Press.

Johnson, D. A.; Pasterski, G.; Ludlow, J. M.; Street, K.; and Taylor, R. D. W. 1983. "The Discontinuance of Maintenance Neuroleptic Therapy in Chronic Schizophrenic Patients: Drug and Social Consequences." *Acta Psychiatrica Scandinavia* 67: 339–52.

Johnson, F. N. 1984. *The History of Lithium Therapy.* London: Macmillan.

Johnson, J. M., and Parker, R. E. 1983. "Some Anti-Therapeutic Effects of a Therapeutic Community." *Hospital and Community Psychiatry* 34: 170–71.

Johnson, P. J., and Rubin, A. 1983. "Case Management in Mental Health: A Social Work Domain?" *Social Work* 28: 49–55.

Joint Commission on Mental Illness and Health. 1961. Final report: "Action for Mental Health." New York: Basic Books.

Jones, M. 1953. *The Therapeutic Community: A New Treatment Method in Psychiatry.* New York: Basic Books.

———. 1959. "Toward a Clarification of the Therapeutic Community Concept." *British Journal of Psychiatry* 106: 200–5.

Kane, J. M. 1987. "Treatment of Schizophrenia," pp. 147–70 in D. Shore, ed. *Schizophrenia 1987.* Rockville, Md.: National Institute of Mental Health.

Kane, R. A. 1975. "The Interprofessional Team as a Small Group." *Social Work in Health Care* 1: 19–32.

Kanfer, F. H., and Goldstein, A. P. 1986. *Helping People Change: A Textbook of Methods.* 3rd ed. New York: Pergamon.

Kanter, J. S., ed. 1985. *Clinical Issues in Treating the Chronic Mentally Ill.* New Directions for Mental Health Services No. 27. San Francisco: Jossey-Bass.

———; Lamb, H. R.; and Loper, C.1987. "Expressed Emotion in Families: A Critical Review." *Hospital and Community Psychiatry* 38: 374–80.

Kaplan, N. K. 1976. *Support Systems and Mutual Help.* New York: Grune and Stratton.

Keefe, S. E. R.; Mohs, R. C.; Losonczy, M. F.; Davidson, M.; Silverman, J. M.;

Kendler, K. S.; Horvath, T. B.; Nora, R.; and Davis, K. L. 1987. "Characteristics of Very Poor Outcome Schizophrenia." *American Journal of Psychiatry* 144: 889–94

Kelly, J. A. 1982. *Social-Skills Training: A Practice Guide for Interventions.* New York: Springer.

Kendler, K. S.; Gruenberg, A. M.; and Tsuang, M. T. 1985. "Psychiatric Illness in First-Degree Relatives of Schizophrenic and Surgical Control Patients: A Family Study Using DSM-III Criteria." *Archives of General Psychiatry* 42: 770–79.

Kerr, A., and Snaith, P., eds. 1986. *Contemporary Issues in Schizophrenia.* London: Gaskell.

Kety, S. S. 1976. "Studies Designed to Disentangle Genetic and Environmental Variables in Schizophrenia: Some Epistemological Questions and Answers." *American Journal of Psychiatry* 133: 1134–37.

Kiesler, C. A., and Sibulkin, A. E. 1987. *Mental Hospitalization: Myths and Facts about a National Crisis.* Newbury Park, Calif.: Sage Publications.

Kiresuk, R., and Sherman, R. 1968. "Goal Attainment Scaling: A General Method of Evaluating Comprehensive Community Health Programs." *Journal of Community Mental Health* 4: 433–53.

Kirk, S. A. 1976. "Effectiveness of Community Services for Discharged Mental Health Patients." *American Journal of Psychiatry* 46: 646–59.

—— and Therrien, M. 1975. "Community Mental Health Myths and the Fate of Former Mental Patients." *Psychiatry* 38: 209–17.

Knecht *v.* Gillman, 488 F. 2d 1136 (8th Cir. 1973).

Koch, H. 1984. "Utilization of Analgesic Drugs in Office-Based Ambulatory Care: National Ambulatory Medical Care Survey, 1980–81." *NCHS Advance Data* 96: 1–9.

Kopolow, L. E. 1981. "Client Participation in Mental Health Service Delivery." *Community Mental Health Journal* 17: 46–53.

Kraepelin, E. 1919. *Dementia Praecox and Paraphrenia.* Translated by R. M. Barclay. Edinburgh: E. & S. Livingstone.

Kriauciunas, R. 1974. "A Case-Management Model to Maximize the Use of Professional Staff Time." *Hospital and Community Psychiatry* 25: 247–48.

Kruzich, J. M. 1986. "The Chronically Mentally Ill in Nursing Homes: Issues in Policy and Practice." *Health and Social Work* 11: 5–14.

—— and Kruzich, S. J. 1985. "Milieu Factors Influencing Patients' Integration into Community Residential Facilities." *Hospital and Community Psychiatry* 36: 378–82.

Kutchins, H., and Kirk, S. A. 1987. "DSM-III and Social Work Malpractice." *Social Work* 21: 205–11.

Kutchins, H., and Kutchins, S. 1978. "Advocacy and Social Work," pp. 13–48 in G. H. Weber and G. J. McCall, eds. *Social Scientists as Advocates: View from the Applied Disciplines.* Newbury Park, Calif.: Sage Publications.

Lake *v.* Cameron, 364 F. 2d 657 (D.C. Cir. 1966).

Lamb, H. R. 1979. "The New Asylums in the Community." *Archives of General Psychiatry* 36: 129–34.

——. 1980 "Therapist–Case Managers: More Than Brokers of Service." *Hospital and Community Psychiatry* 31: 762–65.

——. 1981. "Maximizing the Potential of Board and Care Homes," pp. 19–34 in R. Budson, ed. *Issues in Community Residential Care.* New Directions for Mental Health Services No. 11. San Francisco: Jossey-Bass.

Lamb, S. 1979. "The Role of Nurse-Clinicians in Current Nursing Practice." *Journal of Neurosurgical Nursing* 11: 156–59.

Lawrence, R. F.; Cumella, S.; and Robertson, J. A. 1988. "Patterns of Care in a District General Hospital Psychiatric Department." *British Journal of Psychiatry* 152: 188–95.

Lawson, W. B. 1986. "Racial and Ethnic Factors in Psychiatric Research." *Hospital and Community Psychiatry* 37: 50–54.

Leeman, C. P. 1986. "The Therapeutic Milieu and Its Role in Clinical Management," in L. I. Sederer, ed. *Inpatient Psychiatry: Diagnosis and Treatment*. Baltimore: Williams and Wilkins.

Leff, J. P., and Vaughn, C. 1985. *Expressed Emotion in Families: Its Significance for Mental Illness*. New York: Guilford.

Leff, J. P.; Kuipers, L.; and Berkowitz, R. 1983. "Intervention in Families of Schizophrenics and Its Effect on Relapse Rate," pp. 173–88 in W. R. McFarlane, ed. *Family Therapy in Schizophrenia*. New York: Guilford.

Lentz, W. 1976. "The Informal Caregiver: A Link between the Health Care System and Local Residents." *American Journal of Orthopsychiatry* 46: 678–88.

Levy, C. S. 1972. "Values and Planned Change." *Social Casework* 54: 488–93.

———. 1981. "Labeling: The Social Worker's Responsibility." *Social Casework* 62: 332–42.

Lewis, D., and Hugi, B. 1981. "Therapeutic Stations and the Chronically Treated Mentally Ill." *Social Service Review* 55: 206–20.

Liberman, R. P. 1982. "Assessment of Social Skills." *Schizophrenia Bulletin* 8: 63–83.

Lidz, T. 1972. "The Influence of Family Studies on the Treatment of Schizophrenia," pp. 616–35 in C. J. Sager and H. S. Kaplan, eds. *Progress in Group and Family Therapy*. New York: Brunner/Mazel.

——— and Fleck, S. 1985. *Schizophrenia and the Family*. 2nd ed. New York: International Universities Press.

———; Cornelison, A. R.; Fleck, S.; and Terry, D. 1957. "Schism and Skew in the Families of Schizophrenics." *American Journal of Psychiatry* 114: 241–48.

Link, B., and Milcarek, B. 1980. "Selection Factors in the Dispensation of Therapy: The Matthew Effect in the Allocation of Mental Health Resources." *Journal of Health and Social Behavior* 21: 279–90.

Linn, M. W. 1981. "Can Foster Care Survive?" pp. 35–47 in R. Budson, ed. *Issues in Community Residential Care*. New Directions for Mental Health Services No. 11. San Francisco: Jossey-Bass.

Lipton, A. A., and Simon, F. S. 1985. "Psychiatric Diagnosis in a State Hospital: Manhattan State Revisited." *Hospital and Community Psychiatry* 36: 368–73.

Lipton, F. R.; Cohen C. I.; Fischer, E.; and Katz, S. E. 1981. "Schizophrenia: A Network Crisis." *Schizophrenia Bulletin* 7: 144–51.

Lobel, B., and Hirschfield, R. M. A. 1985. *Depression: What We Know*. Rockville, Md.: U.S. Department of Health and Human Services, NIMH.

Lowe, J. L., and Herranen, M. 1981. "Understanding Teamwork: Another Look at the Concepts." *Social Work in Health Care* 7: 1–11.

Lukton, R. C. 1982. "Myths and Realities of Crisis Intervention." *Social Casework* 63: 276–85.

Lurie, A. 1982. "The Social Work Advocacy Role in Discharge Planning." *Social Work in Health Care* 8: 75–85.

Lyons, R. D. 1984. "How Release of Mental Patients Began." *New York Times*, October 30.

Mackay, A. V. P., and Crow, T. J. 1986. "Positive and Negative Schizophrenic Symptoms and the Role of Dopamine: A Debate," pp. 214–29 in A. Kerr and P. Snaith, eds. *Contemporary Issues in Schizophrenia*. London: Gaskell.

Maddigan, R. F.; Watson, C. G.; and Fulton, J. R. 1976. "Prediction of Posthospital Success for Psychiatry Patients." *Social Work* 11: 322–23.

Mailick, M. D., and Ashley, A. 1981. "Politics of Interprofessional Collaboration: Challenge to Advocacy." *Social Casework* 62: 131–37.

Maluccio, A. N. 1979. "Problems and Issues in Community-Based Residential Services as Alternatives to Institutionalization." *Journal of Sociology and Social Welfare* 6: 198–210.

Marcus, L.; Plasky, P.; and Salzman, C. 1988. "Effects of Psychotropic Drugs on Memory: Part 1." *Hospital and Community Psychiatry* 39: 255–56.

Marder, S. R.; Mebane, A.; Ching-Piao, C.; Winslade, W. J.; Swann, E.; and van Putten, T. 1983. "A Comparison of Patients Who Refuse and Consent to Neuroleptic Treatment." *American Journal of Psychiatry* 140: 470–72.

McCormick, M. J. 1970. "Social Advocacy: A New Dimension in Social Work." *Social Casework* 51: 3–11.

McCreath, J. 1984. "The New Generation of Chronic Psychiatric Patients." *Social Work* 19: 436–41.

McDermott, F. E. 1975. "Against the Persuasive Definition of Self-Determination," pp. 118–37 in F. E. McDermott, ed. *Self-Determination in Social Work: A Collection of Essays on Self-Determination and Related Concepts by Philosophers and Social Work Theorists*. London: Routledge Kegan.

McDonagh, M. J.; Tribes, V.; and Crum Malischewski, A. 1980. "Nurse-Therapists in a State Psychiatry Hospital." *American Journal of Nursing* 80: 102–4.

McLaughlin, P. 1988. "The Fairweather Lodge Society: Community Residence Combining Employment, Housing and a Peer Society." *Tie Lines* 5: 3–5.

Mechanic, D. 1968. *Medical Sociology: A Selective View*. New York: Free Press.

———. 1982. "Nursing and Mental Health Care: Expanding Future Possibilities for Nursing Services," pp. 343–58 in L. Aiken, ed. *Nursing in the 1980's: Crises, Opportunities, Challenges*. Philadelphia: Lippincott.

———. 1989. *Mental Health and Social Policy*. Englewood Cliffs, N.J.: Prentice Hall.

Mendel, W. M. 1974. "Lepers, Madmen: Who's Next?" *Schizophrenia Bulletin* 11: 5–8.

———. 1976. *Schizophrenia: The Experience and Its Treatment*. San Francisco: Jossey-Bass.

Meyers, J. K., and Bean, L. 1968. *A Decade Later: A Follow-up of Social Class and Mental Illness*. New York: Wiley and Sons.

Mian, P.; Tracy, K.; and Tulchin, S. 1981. "Expanded Roles for Mental Health Nurses within an HMO." *Hospital and Community Psychiatry* 32: 727–29.

Miller, M. C. 1977. "A Program for Adult Foster Care." *Social Work* 22: 275–79.

Mintz, L. I.; Liberman, R. P.; Miklowitz, D. J.; and Mintz, J. 1987. "Expressed Emotion: A Call for Partnership among Relatives, Patients, and Professionals." *Schizophrenia Bulletin* 13: 228–35.

Mitchell, R. E., and Trickett, E. J. 1980. "Social Networks as Mediators of Social Support: An Analysis of the Effects of Determinants of Social Networks." *Community Mental Health Journal* 16: 27–44.

Mizrahi, T., and Abramson, J. 1985. "Sources of Strain between Physicians and Social Workers: Implications for Social Workers in Health Care Settings." *Social Work in Health Care* 10: 33–51.

Moffic, H. S.; Patterson, G. R.; Laval, R.; and Adams, G. L. 1984. "Professionals and Psychiatric Teams: An Updated Review." *Hospital and Community Psychiatry* 35: 61–67.

Moline, R. A. 1977. "The Therapeutic Community and Milieu Therapy: A Review and Current Assessment." *Community Mental Health Review* 2: 1–13.

Moller, H. J.; Schmid-Bode, W.; Wittchen, H. U.; and Zerssen, D. V. 1986. "Outcome and Prediction of Outcome in Schizophrenia: Results from the Literature and from Two Personal Studies," pp. 11–24 in M. Goldstein, I. Hand, and K. Hahlweg, eds. *Treatment of Schizophrenia: Family Assessment and Intervention.* New York: Springer-Verlag.

Moltzen, S.; Gurevitz, H.; Rappaport, M.; and Goldman, H. H. 1986. "The Psychiatric Health Facility: An Alternative for Acute Inpatient Treatment in a Nonhospital Setting." *Hospital and Community Psychiatry* 37: 1131–35.

Monahan, J. 1984. "The Prediction of Violent Behavior: Toward a Second Generation of Theory and Policy." *American Journal of Psychiatry* 141: 10–15.

Morin, R. C., and Seidman, E. 1986. "A Social Network Approach and the Revolving Door Patient." *Schizophrenia Bulletin* 12: 262–73.

Moscarelli, M.; Maffei, C.; Cesana, B. M.; Boato, P.; Farma, T.; Grilli, A.; Lingiardi, V.; and Cazzullo, C. L. 1987. "An International Perspective on Assessment of Negative and Positive Symptoms in Schizophrenia." *American Journal of Psychiatry* 144: 1595–98.

Mosher, L. R., and Menn, A. 1979. "Soteria: An Alternative to Hospitaliation for Schizophrenia," pp. 73–84 in H. R. Lamb, ed. *Alternatives to Acute Hospitalization.* New Directions for Mental Health Services No. 1. San Francisco: Jossey-Bass.

Mullaney, J. W.; Fox, R. A.; and Liston, M. F. 1974. "Clinical Nurse Specialist and Social Workers: Clarifying the Roles." *Nursing Outlook* 22: 712–18.

Murphy, J. M. 1976. "Psychiatric Labeling in Cross-Cultural Perspective." *Science* 191: 1019–28.

NASW. 1981. "Working Statement on the Purpose of Social Work." *Social Work* 26: 6.

NASW Ad Hoc Committee on Advocacy. 1969. "The Social Worker as Advocate: Champion of Social Victims." *Social Work* 14: 16–22.

National Institute of Mental Health. 1984. "The Community Support Program of the National Institute of Mental Health." Mimeographed progress report.

Neighbors, H. W. 1984. "The Distribution of Psychiatric Morbidity in Black Americans: A Review and Suggestions for Research." *Community Mental Health Journal* 20: 169–81.

Newman, J. P. 1987. "Gender Differences in Vulnerability to Depression." *Social Service Review* 61: 447–68.

"1981 National Survey of Hospital and Medical School Salaries," The University of Texas Medical Branch, Galveston, Tex.

Northern, H. 1982. *Clinical Social Work.* New York: Columbia University Press.

Nuehring, E. M., and Pascone, A. B. 1986. "Single-Subject Evaluation: A Tool for Quality Assurance." *Social Work* 31: 359–65.

O'Connor, G. O. 1988. "Case Management: System and Practice." *Social Casework* 69: 97–106.

O'Connor *v.* Donaldson, 422 U.S. 563, 45 L.Ed. 2d 396, 95 S.Ct. 2488 (1975).

Olarte, S. W., and Masnik, R. 1981. "Enhancing Medication Compliance in Coffee Groups." *Hospital and Community Psychiatry* 32: 417–19.

Olsen, K., and Olsen, M. E. 1967. "Role Expectations and Perceptions for Social Workers in Medical Settings." *Social Work* 12: 70–78.

Ozarin, L. D. 1973. "Moral Treatment and the Mental Hospital," pp. 29–46 in J. J. Rossi and W. J. Filstead, eds. *The Therapeutic Community.* New York: Behavioral Publications.

———. 1978. "The Pros and Cons of Case Management," in J. A. Talbott, ed. *The Chronic Mental Patient.* Washington, D.C.: American Psychiatric Association.

Pakkenberg, B. 1987. "Post-Mortem Study of Chronic Schizophrenic Brains." *British Journal of Psychiatry* 151: 744–52.

Paradis, B. A. 1987. "An Integrated Team Approach to Community Mental Health." *Social Work* 32: 101–4.

Patti, R. 1974. "Limitations and Prospects of Internal Advocacy." *Social Casework* 55: 537–45.

Pattison, E. M.; Defrancisco, D.; Wood, P.; Frazier, H.; and Crowder, J. A. 1975. "A Psychosocial Kinship Model for Family Therapy." *American Journal of Psychiatry* 132: 1246–51.

Pattison, E. M., and Pattison, M. L. 1981. "Analysis of a Schizophrenic Psychosocial Network." *Schizophrenia Bulletin* 7: 135–42.

Paul, G. L., and Lentz, R. J. 1977. *Psychosocial Treatment of Chronic Mental Patients: Millieu versus Social-Learning Programs.* Cambridge, Mass.: Harvard University Press.

Pepper, B.; Kirschner, M. C.; and Ryglewicz, H. 1981. "The Young Adult Chronic Patient: Overview of a Population." *Hospital and Community Psychiatry* 32: 463–69.

Pepper, B., and Ryglewicz, H., eds. 1984. *Advances in Treating the Young Adult Chronic Patient.* New Directions for Mental Health Services No. 21. San Francisco: Jossey-Bass.

Perlman, B. B.; Melnick, G.; and Kentera, A. 1985. "Assessing the Effectiveness of a Case Management Program." *Hospital and Community Psychiatry* 36: 405–7.

Peterson, C. L. 1985. "Regulation and Consultation in Community Care Facilities." *Hospital and Community Psychiatry* 36: 383–88.

Pilisuk, M., and Parks, S. H. 1988. "Caregiving: Where Families Need Help." *Social Work* 33: 436–40.

Plasky, P.; Marcus, L.; and Salzman, C. 1988. "Effects of Psychotropic Drugs on Memory: Part 2." *Hospital and Community Psychiatry* 39: 501–2.

Pogue-Gelle, F. M., and Harrow, M. 1985. "Negative Symptoms in Schizophrenia: Their Longitudinal Course and Prognostic Importance." *Schizophrenia Bulletin* 11: 427–39.

Polak, P. R.; Kirby, M. W.; and Deitchman, W. S. 1979. "Treating Acutely Psychotic Patients in Private Homes," pp. 49–64 in H. R. Lamb, ed. *Alternatives for Acute Hospitalization.* New Directions for Mental Health Services No. 1. San Francisco: Jossey-Bass.

Polanka, W. 1969. "Using Ward Personnel as Case Managers." *Hospital and Community Psychiatry* 20: 93–95.

Pope, H. G. 1983. "Distinguishing Bipolar Disorder from Schizophrenia in Clinical Practice: Guidelines and Case Reports." *Hospital and Community Psychiatry* 34: 322–28.

Prakash, R. "A Review of the Hematologic Side Effects of Lithium." *Hospital and Community Psychiatry* 36: 127–28.

Rachman, S., and Teasdale, J. 1969. *Aversion Therapy and Behavior Disorders: An Analysis*. Coral Gables, Fla.: University of Miami Press.

Radloff, L. 1975. "Sex Differences in Depression." *Sex Roles* 1: 249–65.

Rapp, C. A. 1985. "Research on the Chronically Mentally Ill: Curriculum Implications," in J. Bowker, ed. *Education for Practice with the Chronically Mentally Ill: What Works?* Washington, D.C.: Council on Social Work Education.

Rappaport, M.; Goldman, H. H.; Thornton, P.; Stegner, B.; Moltzen, S.; Hall, K.; Gurevitz, H.; and Attkisson, C. C. 1987. "A Method for Comparing Acute 24-Hour Psychiatric Care." *Hospital and Community Psychiatry* 38: 1091–95.

Rennie v. Klein, 462 F. Supp. 1131 (DNJ 1978).

Rennie v. Klein, 458 U.S. 1119 (1982).

Rennie v. Klein, 720 F. 2d 266 (3d Cir. 1983). *En banc*.

Richan, W. D. 1973. "Dilemmas of the Social Work Advocate." *Child Welfare* 52: 220–26.

Richmond, M. 1922. *What Is Social Casework?* New York: Russell Sage.

Rioch, D. M., and Stanton, A. R. 1971. "Milieu Therapy." *Journal of Nervous and Mental Diseases* 94: 65–72.

Roberts-DeGennaro, M. 1987. "Developing Case Management as a Practice Model." *Social Casework* 67: 466–70.

Rosenfield, S. 1980. "Sex Differences in Depression: Do Women Always Have Higher Rates?" *Journal of Health and Social Behavior* 21: 33–42.

Rovner, B. W., and Rabins, P. V. 1985. "Mental Illness among Nursing Home Patients." *Hospital and Community Psychiatry* 36: 119–23.

Rueveni, U. 1984. "Network Intervention for Crisis Resolution: An Introduction." *International Journal of Family Therapy* 6: 65–67.

Rusch, L. M. 1985. "Managing Medication Compliance: A Systems Approach." *Carrier Foundation Letter* 107: 1–4.

Salzberger, R. P. 1979. "Casework and a Client's Right to Self-Determination." *Social Casework* 60: 398–400.

Scheff, T. J. 1966. *Being Mentally Ill: A Sociological Theory*. Chicago: Aldine.

Schilling, R. R., II. 1987. "Limitations of Social Support." *Social Service Review* 61: 19–31.

Schneider, L. D., and Streuning, E. L. 1983. "SLOF: A Behavioral Rating Scale for Assessing the Mentally Ill." *Social Work Research and Abstracts* 19: 9–21.

Schoenfeld, P.; Halevy-Martini, J.; Hemley-Van der Velden, E. M.; and Ruhf, L. L. 1985. "Network Therapy: An Outcome Study of Twelve Social Networks." *Journal of Community Psychiatry* 13: 281–87.

———. 1986. "Long-Term Outcome of Network Therapy." *Hospital and Community Psychiatry* 37: 373–76.

Schofield, W. 1964. *Psychotherapy: The Purchase of Friendship*. Englewood Cliffs, N.J.: Prentice Hall.

Schrager, J.; Halman, M.; Myers, D.; Nichols, R.; and Rosenblum, L. 1978. "Impediments to the Course and Effectiveness of Discharge Planning." *Social Work in Health Care* 4: 65–76.

Schreiber, H. 1981. "Discharge-Planning: Key to the Future of Hospital Social Work." *Health Care and Social Work* 7: 48–53.

Schulberg, H. C., and Baker, F. 1975. *The Mental Hospital and Human Services.* New York: Behavioral Publications.

Schumacher, D. N.; Namerow, M. J.; Parker, B.; Fox, P.; and Kofie, V. 1986. "Prospective Payment for Psychiatry, Feasibility and Impact." *New England Journal of Medicine* 315: 1331–36.

Segal, S. P., and Aviram, U. 1978. *The Mentally Ill in Community Based Care.* New York: Wiley and Sons.

Segal, S. P.; Chandler, S.; and Aviram, U. 1980. "Antipsychotic Drugs in Community-Based Sheltered-Care Homes." *Social Science and Medicine* 14: 589–96.

Selvini-Palazzoli, M. 1986. "Towards a General Model of Psychotic Family Games." *Journal of Marital and Family Therapy* 12: 339–49.

Shadish, W. R., and Bootzin, R. R. 1984. "The Social Integration of Psychiatric Patients in Nursing Homes." *American Journal of Psychiatry* 141: 1203–11.

Shadish, W. R.; Straw, R. B.; McSweeney, A. K.; Koller, D. L.; and Bootzin, R. R. 1981. "Nursing Home Care for Mental Patients: Descriptive Data and Some Propositions." *American Journal of Community Psychology* 9: 617–33.

Shaw, E. D.; Stokes, P. E.; Mann, J. J.; and Manevitz, A. Z. A. 1987. "Effects of Lithium Carbonate on the Memory and Motor Speed of Bipolar Outpatients." *Journal of Abnormal Psychology* 96: 64–69.

Sheets, J. L.; Prevost, J. A.; and Reitman, J. 1982. "Young Adult Chronic Patients: Three Hypothesized Subgroups." *Hospital and Community Psychiatry* 33: 197–203.

Sherman, S. R.; Newman, E. S.; and Frenkel, E. R. 1984. "Community Acceptance of the Mentally Ill in Foster Family Care." *Health and Social Work* 9: 188–99.

Simon, R. 1987. "Good-bye Paradox, Hello Invariant Prescription: An Interview with Mara Selvini-Palazzoli." *Family Therapy Networker* 11: 16–25.

Simpson, G. M.; Pi, E. H.; and Sramek, J. J. 1988. "An Update on Tardive Dyskinesia." *Hospital and Community Psychiatry* 37: 362–69.

Siporin, M. *Introduction to Social Work Practice.* New York: Macmillan.

Skinner, B. F. 1971. *Beyond Freedom and Dignity.* New York: Knopf.

Smith, C. A., and Smith, C. J. 1978. "Learned Helplessness and Preparedness in Discharged Mental Patients." *Social Work Research and Abstracts* 1: 21–27.

Sokolovsky, J.; Cohen, C.; Berger, D.; and Geiger, J. 1978. "Personal Networks of Ex-Mental Patients in a Manhattan SRO Hotel." *Human Organization* 37: 5–15.

Solomon, P., and Gordon, B. 1986. "The Psychiatric Emergency Room and Follow-up Services in the Community." *Psychiatric Quarterly* 58: 119–27.

Solomon, P.; Gordon, B.; and Davis, J. M. 1984. "Assessing the Service Needs of the Discharged Psychiatric Patient." *Social Work in Health Care* 10: 61–68.

Sosin, M., and Caulum, S. 1983. "Advocacy: A Conceptualization for Social Work Practice." *Social Work* 28: 12–17.

Speck, R. V. 1967. "Psychotherapy of the Social Network of a Schizophrenic Family." *Family Process* 6: 208–14.

Spivack, G.; Siegel, J.; Sklaver, D.; Deutschle, L.; and Garrett, L. 1982. "The Long-Term Patient in the Community: Life-Style Patterns and Treatment Implications." *Hospital and Community Psychiatry* 33: 291–95.

Stein, L., and Test, M. A. 1979. "From Hospital to the Community: A Shift in the Primary Locus of Care," pp. 15–32 in H. R. Lamb, ed. *Alternatives for Acute Hospitalization.* New Directions for Mental Health Services No. 1. San Francisco: Jossey-Bass.

——. 1980. "Alternative to Mental Hospital Treatment 1: Conceptual Model, Treatment Programs, and Clinical Evaluation." *Archives of General Psychiatry* 37: 392–97.

Steinglass, P.; Weisstub, E.; and Kaplan De-Nour, A. 1988. "Perceived Personal Networks as Mediators of Stress Reactions." *American Journal of Psychiatry* 145: 1259–64.

Stone, A. 1987. "Broadening the Statutory Criteria for Civil Commitment: A Reply to Durham and La Fond." *Yale Law and Policy Review* 5: 412–27.

Stotsky, B. A., and Stotsky, E. S. 1983. "Nursing Homes: Improving a Flawed Community Facility." *Hospital and Community Psychiatry* 34: 238–42.

Strauss, G. 1974. *The Worker and the Job: Coping with Change.* Englewood Cliffs, N.J.: Prentice Hall.

Strauss, J. S., and Carpenter, W. T., Jr. 1977. "Prediction of Outcome in Schizophrenia, I: Characteristics of Outcome." *Archives of General Psychiatry* 34: 159–63.

Strauss, J. S.; Carpenter, W. T., Jr.; and Bartko, J. J. 1974. "An Approach to the Diagnosis and Understanding of Schizophrenia: Speculations on the Processes That Underlie Schizophrenic Symptoms and Signs." *Schizophrenia Bulletin* 1: 61–64.

Stroul, B. A. 1987. *Crisis Residential Services in a Community Support System.* Rockville, Md.: National Institute of Mental Health.

Sullivan, H. S. 1953. *The Interpersonal Theory of Psychiatry.* New York: W. W. Norton.

Swazey, J. P. 1974. *Chlorpromazine in Psychiatry: A Study of Therapeutic Innovation.* Cambridge, Mass.: MIT Press.

Szasz, T. S. 1961. *The Myth of Mental Illness: Foundations of a Theory of Personal Conduct.* New York: Harper & Row.

——. 1963. *Law, Liberty and Psychiatry: An Inquiry into the Social Uses of Psychiatry.* New York: Macmillan.

Talbott, J. A. 1978. *The Death of the Asylum: A Critical Study of State Hospital Management, Services and Care.* New York: Grune and Stratton.

—— and Glick, I. D. 1986. "The Inpatient Care of the Chronically Mentally Ill." *Schizophrenia Bulletin* 12: 129–40.

Tardiff, K. 1984. "Characteristics of Assaultive Patients in Private Hospitals." *American Journal of Psychiatry* 141: 1232–35.

—— and Koenigsberg, H. W. 1985. "Assaultive Behavior among Psychiatric Outpatients." *American Journal of Psychiatry* 142: 960–63.

Tarrier, N.; Barrowclough, C.; Vaughn, C.; Bamrah, J. S.; Porceddu, K.; Watts, S.; and Freeman, H. 1988. "The Community Management of Schizophrenia: A Controlled Trial of a Behavioral Intervention with Families to Reduce Relapse." *British Journal of Psychiatry* 153: 532–42.

Terkelsen, K. G. 1983. "Schizophrenia and the Family: Adverse Effects of Family Therapy." *Family Process* 22: 191–200.

Tessler, R. C.; Bernstein, A. G.; Rosen, B.; and Goldman, H. H. 1982. "The Chronically Mentally Ill in Community Support Systems." *Hospital and Community Psychiatry* 33: 208–11.

Test, M. A. 1979. "Continuity of Care in Community Treatment," pp. 15–23 in L. Stein, ed. *Community Supports for the Long-Term Patient.* San Francisco: Jossey-Bass.

—— and Stein, L. 1976. "Practical Guidelines for the Community Treatment of Markedly Impaired Patients." *Community Mental Health Journal* 12: 72–82.

Thompson, E. H. 1988. "Variations in the Self-Concept of Young Adult Chronic Patients: Chronicity Reconsidered." *Hospital and Community Psychiatry* 39: 771–75.

Thompson, J. W., and Blaine, J. D. 1987. "Use of ECT in the United States in 1975 and 1980." *American Journal of Psychiatry* 144: 557–62.

Thorndike, E. L. 1911. *Animal Intelligence: Experimental Studies.* New York: Macmillan.

Tolsdorf, C. C. 1976. "Social Networks, Support and Coping: An Exploratory Study." *Family Process* 15: 407–17.

Torrey, E. F. 1983. *Surviving Schizophrenia: A Family Manual.* New York: Harper & Row.

Toseland, R. W.; Palmer-Ganeles, J.; and Chapman, D. 1986. "Teamwork in Psychiatric Settings." *Social Work* 31: 46–52.

Truax, C., and Carknuff, R. 1967. *Toward Effective Counseling and Psychotherapy.* Chicago: Aldine-Atherton.

Turner, J. C., and TenHoor, W. J. 1978. "The NIMH Community Support Program: Pilot Approach to a Needed Social Reform." *Schizophrenia Bulletin* 4: 319–48.

Turner, R. J. 1981. "Social Support as a Contingency in Psychological Well-Being." *Journal of Health and Social Behavior* 22: 357–67.

U.S. Congress. House. 1962. "Compilation of Social Security Laws." Washington, D.C.: U.S. Government Printing Office. H.Doc. 616.

U.S. Congress. Senate. 1963. "Mental Retardation Facilities and Community Mental Health Act of 1963." 88th Cong., 1st sess., S. 1576.

U.S. Department of Health, Education, and Welfare. 1974. *PSRO Program Manual.* Rockville, Md.: HEW.

U.S. General Accounting Office. 1977. "Returning the Mentally Disabled to the Community: Government Needs to Do More." Washington, D.C.: General Accounting Office.

U.S. Office of Special Education and Rehabilitation Services. 1984. *Digest of Data on Persons with Disabilities.* Washington, D.C.: U.S. Government Printing Office.

U.S. Senate, 94th Congress, Subcommittee on Long-Term Care. 1975a. *Supporting Paper No. 4: Nurses in Nursing Homes: The Heavy Burden (The Reliance on Untrained and Unlicensed Personnel).* Washington, D.C.: U.S. Government Printing Office.

U.S. Senate, 94th Congress, Subcommittee on Long-Term Care. 1975b. *Supporting Paper No. 5: The Continuing Chronicle of Nursing Home Fires.* Washington, D.C.: U.S. Government Printing Office.

van der Kolk, B.A., and Goldberg, H. L. 1983. "Aftercare of Schizophrenic Patients: Pharmacotherapy and Consistency of Therapists." *Hospital and Community Psychiatry* 34: 343–48.

van Putten, T. 1973. "Milieu Therapy: Contraindications." *Archives of General Psychiatry* 29: 640–43.

Vaughn, C., and Leff, J. P. 1976. "The Measurement of Expressed Emotion in the Families of Psychiatric Patients." *British Journal of Social and Clinical Psychology* 15: 157–65.

Velasquez, J. S., and McCubbin, H. I. 1980. "Towards Establishing Effectivenesas of Community-Based Treatment: Program Evaluation by Experimental Research." *Journal of Social Service Research* 3: 337–59.

Walsh, J. 1988. "Social Workers as Family Educators about Schizophrenia." *Social Work* 23: 138–41.

Warren, D. I. 1981. *Helping Networks: How People Cope with Problems in the Urban Community.* Notre Dame, Ind.: University of Notre Dame Press.

Waxman, H. M.; Klein, M.; and Carner, E. A. 1985. "Drug Misuse in Nursing

Homes: An Institutional Addiction?" *Hospital and Community Psychiatry* 36: 886–87.

Weick, A., and Pope, L. 1988. "Knowing What's Best: A New Look at Self-Determination." *Social Casework* 69: 10–16.

Weiden, P. J.; Mann, J.; Haas, G.; Mattson, M.; and Frances, A. 1987. "Clinical Nonrecognition of Neuroleptic-Induced Movement Disorders: A Cautionary Study." *American Journal of Psychiatry* 144: 1148–53.

Weiner, R. D. 1984. "Does ECT Cause Brain Damage?" *The Behavioral and Brain Sciences* 7: 1–53.

Weinstein, R. M. 1983. "Labeling Theory and the Attitudes of Mental Patients: A Review." *Journal of Health and Social Behavior* 24: 70–84.

Weissman, H. H.; Epstein, I. E.; and Savage, A. 1987. "Expanding the Role Repertoire of Clinicians." *Social Casework* 68: 150–63.

Westermeyer, J. F., and Harrow, M. 1984. "Prognosis and Outcome Using Broad (DSM-II) and Narrow (DSM-III) Concepts of Schizophrenia." *Schizophrenia Bulletin* 10: 624–37.

Whittaker, J. K., and Garbarino, J. *Social Support Networks: Informal Helping in the Human Services*. New York: Aldine.

Willard, C. 1970. "Psychiatric Aides as Case Managers." *Hospital and Community Psychiatry* 21: 93.

Willetts, R. 1980. "Advocacy and the Mentally Ill." *Social Work* 25: 372–77.

Wing, J. K. 1977. "The Management of Schizophrenia in the Community," pp. 427–77 in G. Usdin, ed. *Psychiatric Medicine*. New York: Brunner/Mazel.

—— and Brown, G. W. 1970. *Institutionalism and Schizophrenia*. Cambridge, Eng.: Cambridge University Press.

Winston, A.; Pinsker, H.; and McCullough, L. 1986. "A Review of Supportive Psychotherapy." *Hospital and Community Psychiatry* 37: 1105–14.

Wixted, J. T.; Morrison, R. L.; and Bellack, A. S. 1988. "Social Skills Training in the Treatment of Negative Symptoms." *International Journal of Mental Health* 17: 3–21.

Wood, K. M. 1978. "Casework Effectiveness: A New Look at the Research Evidence." *Social Work* 23: 437–58.

Woodward, C. A.; Santa-Barbara, J.; Levin, S.; and Epstein, N. B. 1978. "The Role of Goal Attainment Scaling in Evaluating Family Therapy Outcome." *American Journal of Orthopsychiatry* 48: 464–76.

Wyatt *v.* Stickney, 344 F. Supp. 373 (M.D. Ala. 1972).

Wynne, L. C.; Ryckoff, I. M.; Day, J.; and Hirsch, S. I. 1958. "Pseudo-Mutuality in the Family Relations of Schizophrenics." *Psychiatry* 21: 205–20.

Zito, J. H.; Darwin, D.; Mitchell, J. E.; and Routt, W. W. 1986. "Drug Treatment Refusal, Diagnosis, and Length of Hospitalization in Involuntary Psychiatric Patients." *Behavioral Science and the Law* 4: 327–37.

INDEX

ABOUT THE AUTHOR

URSULA GERHART has been a professor at the Rutgers University School of Social Work since 1965. She received her Bachelors from Temple University and took her M.S.W. and Doctorate from Rutgers while single-handedly raising two daughters. Before becoming an academic, Professor Gerhart practiced social work in public welfare organizations in Pennsylvania for 12 years. She lectures widely and frequently presents workshops on the role of the social worker as practitioner and advocate for the chronic mentally ill in the mental health system.

THE BOOK'S MANUFACTURE

Caring for the Chronic Mentally Ill
was typeset by
Point West, Inc., Carol Stream, Illinois.
The typeface is Galliard for text and display.
Printing and binding were done by
Braun-Brumfield, Inc., Ann Arbor, Michigan.
Cover photograph by Jerry Uelsmann.
Cover design by Lucy Lesiak Design.
Internal design was done by John B. Goetz,
Design & Production Services, Co., Chicago.